John Paul II on the Vulnerable

Jeffrey Tranzillo

# John Paul II on the Vulnerable

The Catholic University of America Press
Washington, D.C.

The paper used in this publication meets the minimum requirements of American National Standards for Information Science—Permanence of Paper for Printed Library Materials, ANSI Z39.48-1984.
∞

Library of Congress Cataloging-in-Publication Data
Tranzillo, Jeffrey.
John Paul II on the vulnerable / Jeffrey Tranzillo.
pages cm
Includes bibliographical references and index.
ISBN 978-0-8132-2011-6 (pbk. : alk. paper) 1. Christian sociology—Catholic Church. 2. Christian sociology—Catholic Church—Papal documents. 3. Church and social problems—Catholic Church. 4. Theological anthropology—Catholic Church. 5. John Paul, II, Pope, 1920–2005—Political and social views. I. Title.
BX1753.T676 2013
233.092—dc23 2012033240

In memory of my mother, Virginia, and my father, Gerald, who cooperated with God to give me life and to form me in the Catholic faith that I might also have life eternal

A person's a person, no matter how small.

—Dr. Seuss, *Horton Hears a Who!*

Every person—no matter how vulnerable or helpless, no matter how young or how old, no matter how healthy, handicapped or sick, no matter how useful or productive for society—is a being of inestimable worth created in the image and likeness of God. This is the dignity of America, the reason she exists, the condition for her survival—yes, the ultimate test of her greatness: to respect every human person, especially the weakest and most defenseless ones, those as yet unborn.

—Pope John Paul II, Apostolic Journey to U.S.A. and Canada, 1987

# Contents

# Acknowledgments

I would like to express my gratitude to Peter Casarella, both for his role in the genesis of this project and for having read and commented generously on my first manuscript, when it was still in much need of refinement. His unwavering enthusiasm for the project has been a source of great encouragement to me. I am also indebted to John Grabowski of the Catholic University of America's School of Theology and Religious Studies. He, too, read the early manuscript and provided me with further excellent commentary. I benefited considerably from the practical guidance and the theological acumen of both these fine scholars. As for the present form of the book, I must extend my sincere thanks to yet another fine scholar, Reverend Thomas Guarino of the Immaculate Conception Seminary at Seton Hall University in South Orange, New Jersey. Father Guarino read the final manuscript eagerly and recommended that I get it published promptly, when I might have been tempted to fuss with it further (or at least more than I did).

Additional thanks go to Maurizio and Grazia Ragazzi and to Ellen Sarnecky for having given me sources indispensable to this work, along with some excellent insights and suggestions. Perhaps I owe them most for having kept me laughing over the years that I worked on so serious a subject. Other generous friends include Judy Barr and Dick McCarthy, who likewise gave me sources contributing to this work, and Beverly Whelton of Jesuit Wheeling University's Department of Philosophy. I have gained much from Beverly's intelligent conversation, her publications on the beginning of new human life, and her comments on a conference paper that I gave a few years ago related to the main theme of this book. I am grateful to the late Dr. William Toth, who taught at the Immaculate Conception Seminary, and to my friend Frank Fletcher, both of whom alerted me to sources that have enriched my work. And I am indebted to my friend Peter Stacha for having patiently helped me translate selected passages from a Polish edition of one of John Paul II's pre-papal works.

I must thank the members of my family, the friends named above, and other friends too numerous to mention, but among whom are the Poor Clares of Perpetual Adoration in Washington, D.C., the Giampietro and Aguilar families, and Matthew Broderick, for the support of their efficacious prayers as I labored over this project. I am certain that I have benefited greatly from them. Of course, my most profound thanks go to my parents, both of whom have died in recent years. The fruits of their sacrifices, generosity, encouragement, counsel, prayers (which, I have every reason to believe, continue), example, affection, and handing on of the Catholic faith have so much become part of my existence that they are amply reflected in this book and, indeed, made it possible.

# Abbreviations of Frequently Cited Works by Karol Wojtyła/John Paul II

| | |
|---|---|
| *AP* | *The Acting Person* |
| *CA* | *Centesimus Annus* |
| *CL* | *Christifideles Laici* |
| *DetV* | *Dominum et Vivificantem* |
| *DM* | *Dives in Misericordia* |
| *EV* | *Evangelium Vitae* |
| *LE* | *Laborem Exercens* |
| *LF* | *Letter to Families* |
| *LR* | *Love and Responsibility* |
| *MD* | *Mulieris Dignitatem* |
| *PC* | *Person and Community: Selected Essays* |
| *RH* | *Redemptor Hominis* |
| *RMa* | *Redemptoris Mater* |
| *SgC* | *Sign of Contradiction* |
| *SRS* | *Sollicitudo Rei Socialis* |
| *SD* | *Salvifici Doloris* |

# Introduction

## The Origin, Purpose, and Outline of This Study

This book grew out of a series of discussions that I had several years ago with Peter Casarella, who is both a professor of Catholic studies at DePaul University in Chicago and the director of DePaul's Center for World Catholicism and Intercultural Theology. Grieved by the brutal sin of abortion, I wanted to address in some way the unfounded denial, by some, of the unborn child's personhood. That denial has long been and continues to be used to promote and justify abortion's legalization, as well as the act itself. As I discussed the matter with Peter, however, we soon agreed that I could not stop there, for the same destructive disregard for the objective truth about the personhood of the unborn has also been extended to "unwanted" infants and to elderly, dying, or severely disabled persons—in these cases for the purpose of foisting the evil of active or passive euthanasia on them. What is more, another pernicious claim—whether based on a denial of personhood or on a defective understanding of the human person—needed to be addressed, namely, that the weakest and most defenseless human beings serve no useful purpose and so have no place in society or in any community of persons. Having gotten this far in our discussions, Peter pointed out that materially poor and oppressed persons are likewise being viewed and treated as nonpersons and as useless burdens, so that I ought to consider their plight as well.

In one way or another, many of Pope John Paul II's speeches and writings have characterized these and other categories of human persons as *vulnera-*

*ble*, both because their condition makes them radically dependent on others and because that very circumstance places them at a disadvantage relative to those who would harm, exploit, or eliminate them on account of it. John Paul was a great defender of truly vulnerable human beings throughout his life, affirming their personhood consistently and eloquently. As time went on, he became equally eloquent in affirming the distinctively personal character of the kinds of *acts* that such persons perform. The question is, would the philosophical and theological anthropology that he developed with other purposes in mind support his affirmations about the personal agency of the vulnerable? Thanks to my conversations with Peter Casarella, I decided to look into the matter. And that is the subject of this book.

Our study will examine some of Karol Wojtyła/Pope John Paul II's key episcopal and papal writings in order to highlight the dynamic intellectual framework behind his vigorous lifelong defense of the dignity and rights of vulnerable human beings. Having lived under two brutal totalitarian regimes, having served as a spiritual guide and confidant to countless persons with countless problems, and having traveled to some of the most poverty-stricken countries in the world, John Paul knew all about, and was profoundly sensitive to, human vulnerability in every conceivable form. So to a large extent, his intellectual achievement gives formal expression to his own experience of the vulnerable, whose absolutely personal being and nature he affirms unequivocally in his philosophical and theological reflections on the human person. What is more, his philosophical/theological anthropology contains elements that affirm, mostly indirectly, the uniquely personal character of the *actions* performed by even the weakest, most defenseless and dependent human beings. From this he will conclude that every vulnerable person can contribute immeasurably and indispensably to the human community in some way by the actions of which he or she is capable. Accordingly, some of the writings that we will be examining exhibit a profound development relative to the commonly held philosophical view that only deliberate (especially moral) actions, which require a fully developed psychological personality and the conscious use of intellect and will, qualify as personal. While John Paul's philosophical/theological anthropology generally centers around ethical and moral concerns, it is nevertheless also true that in the context of the whole, he has laid the foundation for a genuine anthropology of the vulnerable. This book will explore that foundation and perhaps even succeed in developing it modestly.

In chapter 1 we will review selectively the life, thought, and work of Pope

John Paul II. Among other things, this will help us see clearly how his scholarly interest in the human person as such and as an actor reflects, first of all, his religious convictions, and at the same time, the growth of those convictions when they were sorely tried in the crucible of both personal and national sufferings. It was precisely when he and his compatriots were most vulnerable and seemingly most powerless that the greatness of the human spirit—its power to endure all and to act freely for love of objective truth and goodness—manifested itself to him in all its splendor. John Paul reflected on, wrote about, and proclaimed that experience throughout his life, and it is ultimately that same experience that forms the basis of this book.

In chapters 2 and 3 we will examine Karol Wojtyła's *Person and Act,* in which he avails himself of insights and methods drawn from contemporary phenomenology and grounds them in the traditional metaphysics of St. Thomas Aquinas to give us his most extensive philosophical treatment of the human being as a person and an actor. In the first of these chapters, we will focus on how human acting reveals the inner structure of the actor and identifies him as none other than a person. We will then consider what the author's findings tell us or imply, in general, about vulnerable human beings as persons and as actors. In the second of the two chapters, we will examine Wojtyła's treatment of persons acting in interpersonal or social contexts, supplementing our investigation with relevant texts from his subsequent article, "The Person: Subject and Community." Then, with our knowledge of his study as a whole, we will go on to consider how four broad categories of vulnerable human beings might exercise their agency communally.

Chapter 4 will take up Pope John Paul II's "theology of the body," which in many ways complements his philosophical project biblically and theologically. Here, too, our aim will be to bring out its relevance to the vulnerable as persons and agents. Given John Paul's unassailable conviction that Jesus Christ alone reveals to us the full truth of who we are as human persons, chapter 5 will develop the anthropological import of some of his Christological texts. In particular, we will focus on the Incarnation and the Paschal Mystery, since these represent the periods of greatest vulnerability in the human life of Christ himself. In that light, together with the insights gained from the previous chapters, we will consider again four broad categories of vulnerable human beings to illustrate in further detail how different forms of vulnerability can be the very means by which we express ourselves as personal agents, especially with the help of Christ's sacramental grace or the hidden grace that he offers in the Spirit in virtue of the general union that the eternal Son of God has established with each of us by assuming a human nature and effecting our redemption in time.

Chapters 6 and 7 will examine, respectively, Pope John Paul II's three commemorative social encyclicals and *Evangelium Vitae*. John Paul concerns himself very explicitly with specific types of human vulnerability in the four documents, and we will see how he enriches thereby our understanding of the human person and human action. In chapter 7 especially we will find him making a deliberate effort to do what we will have been doing in the preceding chapters, namely, drawing out of his general anthropology the principles that would have to ground a more specific and truly Christian anthropology of the vulnerable.

In chapter 8, the final chapter, we will revisit briefly the most fundamental themes in John Paul II's philosophical and theological anthropology to show how they support his statements, made in other contexts, about the personal character of the agency exercised by even the most vulnerable of vulnerable human beings, such as newly conceived children. Those statements represent a genuine development in his thought, since he had concluded otherwise in *Person and Act*. Still, they are wholly consistent with his anthropology, which he seems to presuppose in making them, though without ever being wholly explicit about the connection himself. Once we have tried to illuminate that connection for ourselves, we will examine selected writings of Thomistic philosopher W. Norris Clarke, who sought in his more recent work to highlight the personalistic elements implicit in Thomistic metaphysics. For that reason, we will find that the work of the two authors is mutually complementary, allowing us to bring out and to develop those somewhat latent aspects of John Paul's anthropology that would lend themselves to our affirming a dynamic capacity for personal self-communication and relationality—for personal agency and interpersonal communion—in even the most vulnerable human beings. The chapter will conclude by considering how the result of our investigation might find confirmation, as well as ideas for further development, in the early childhood experiences of Helen Keller. Helen's illness at age nineteen months resulted in serious, lifelong disabilities that nevertheless spurred her on both to find creative ways of expressing her person to others in knowledge and love and to receive their reciprocal self-communication to her.

Three observations are in order before we proceed. First, this study aims to articulate philosophically and theologically the principles that allow us to affirm true personhood and personal agency in vulnerable human beings.

Generally, we illustrate how those principles apply to each of several broad categories of vulnerable persons. While in that sense our illustrations might seem somewhat abstract, they are nonetheless very meaningful in the concrete, for they are, in fact, often based on the concrete experiences of certain vulnerable persons. But by prescinding from the more specific details characterizing this or that type of human vulnerability, we hope to speak more universally, giving readers the opportunity to consider how our observations might apply both to the vulnerable persons who are part of their own life and experience and to the relationships that they have with them. On the other hand, our reflections on the case of Helen Keller give at least some indication as to what a more multidisciplinary approach to our topic might look like—an approach that might include, among other things, a closer look at the actual physiological, psychological, spiritual, social, experiential, or practical aspects typifying one or more concrete instances of human vulnerability.

Second, our study of personal agency in vulnerable human beings might seem a bit overly optimistic to some, especially if they are treating or caring for someone whose form of vulnerability presents them with seemingly insurmountable personal or behavioral problems. While we are aware of and occasionally note some such problems, our generally optimistic view reflects John Paul II's conviction that the fundamental dynamism of the human person is, from the very beginning, directed toward full human expression and communion with other persons, notwithstanding conditions that might frustrate or cause someone to resist that natural thrust. It is this aspect of his anthropology that we have chosen to emphasize and develop herein. Accordingly, in cases where persons subject to serious forms of vulnerability are still capable of performing fully mature, or voluntary, human actions, we attend mostly to certain types of *morally good* actions that they might perform, especially in a communal context, as these are the most fully personal exercises of human agency. On the other hand, since the vulnerability of the vulnerable is so often caused or exploited by other human beings, our optimism regarding the agency of the vulnerable is paired almost unavoidably with a certain pessimism regarding that of the others, whether as individuals or groups, or as the ones who establish and perpetuate corrupt and alienating social, economic, legal, political, and other systems and structures. However, our sometimes simplified view of rather complex realities serves, nevertheless, to highlight important truths about those realities, and it is to those truths that this study is devoted and wants to call our attention.

The third and final observation is related to the immediately preceding remarks. Our study of human vulnerability inevitably brings up a number of ethical issues. The beginning of this introduction indicates some of them. However, from the brief description of the study's content given above, it should be clear that our main focus, like that of *Person and Act,* is on anthropology, whereas we will refrain from getting heavily involved in complex ethical analyses and debates. In particular, we will focus on the personal character of the agency expressed in and by vulnerable human beings. Still, we would note the following. Our first chapter includes a fairly detailed summary of Karol Wojtyła's *Love and Responsibility,* which introduces what its author calls "the personalistic norm." This norm serves as his foundation for countering the utilitarian philosophy, attitudes, and actions that he addresses rather thoroughly in that work, given the threat they pose to authentic personal dignity and agency. It would likewise be foundational for addressing many of the ethical issues that are necessarily raised in the present work during the course of our reflections.

As some of our preliminary comments suggest, various disciplines are capable of providing indispensable testimony in support of the objective truth about the personhood, the personal agency, and the intrinsic, personal dignity of even the most vulnerable human beings. I hope that this study on the person-centered life and writings of Pope John Paul II relative to the vulnerable will serve as both an invitation and a contribution to those who are willing and able to explore those capabilities in their respective fields.

# John Paul II on the Vulnerable

# 1

# In the Service of the Human Person

## The Life, Thought, and Work of Karol Wojtyła/ Pope John Paul II

While twelve-year-old Karol Wojtyła was serving Mass one day, Jerzy Kluger, one of his Jewish friends, entered the church to wait for him, eager to tell his classmate that they had both been promoted to high school. A Catholic woman saw him and asked, "Aren't you Dr. Kluger's son? What are you doing in the church?" But Jerzy gave no answer. When young Karol heard of this, he got annoyed and said, "What nonsense! We are all children of the same God!"[1] Even at that early age, Karol Wojtyła was already exhibiting the personal qualities that would distinguish him throughout his life: the indignation over unjust discrimination; the sense of solidarity with vulnerable persons; and the conviction that every human being owes his or her origin

1. Related by Karol's friend Irene (Mrs. Jerzy) Kluger in the documentary, *Witness to Hope: The Life of Karol Wojtyła – Pope John Paul II*, VHS, written and directed by Judith Dwan Hallet, (W/R Productions, 2001), based on the book (documented below) *Witness to Hope*, by George Weigel. In *Stories of Karol*, trans. Peter Heinegg (Liguori, Mo.: Liguori Publications, 2003), 7, Gian Franco Svidercoschi depicts Karol as responding with a laugh rather than with vexation.

directly to God and so possesses the same fundamental dignity as any other, regardless of religion, race, socioeconomic status, education, sex, physical or mental condition, age, and so on.

This chapter offers a selective account of Pope John Paul II's life, thought, and work that will richly enhance our understanding of the material in the chapters that follow. In considering his life, we will highlight some of the experiences that helped form his extraordinary appreciation of the intrinsic dignity of the human person, regardless of his or her condition. We will also see how he enacted that appreciation by tirelessly defending vulnerable human beings and their inherent rights. In considering his thought, we will see how he expressed his lofty regard for the human person in some of his principal writings, giving us the opportunity to introduce, if only briefly, the texts that will figure most prominently in the chapters that follow. Finally, we will see that John Paul II's ability to inspire others to act effectively and constructively in and through their vulnerability stemmed (1) from his own authenticity as one who achieved self-mastery by acting patiently and virtuously under conditions that sometimes placed him among the most vulnerable of persons, and (2) from his transparent admiration for persons who acted with supremely self-sacrificial heroism under similar or even more extreme conditions. He learned that such actions bear tremendously good fruit in the end—above all, when they reflect an indomitable inner freedom born of faith in Christ and, consequently, of the willingness to embrace one's share in the *cross* of Christ for *love* of Christ. He was able to teach the world this key lesson persuasively because he lived it with unflagging conviction himself. We have found George Weigel's two volumes on Pope John Paul II's life and legacy to be indispensable to fulfilling our purpose in this chapter and would strongly encourage anyone who has not yet read those marvelous works to do so.[2]

## The Pre-papal Years: 1920–1978

On May 18, 1920, Karol Józef Wojtyła was born in the town of Wadowice in the Second Polish Republic. Constituted in 1918 after the First World War, the new republic restored to the Polish people national sovereignty, which they had lost to Prussia, Austria-Hungary, and Russia for over 125 years. Dur-

2. George Weigel, *Witness to Hope: The Biography of Pope John Paul II* (New York: Cliff Street Books, 2005); George Weigel, *The End and the Beginning: Pope John Paul II—The Victory of Freedom, the Last Years, the Legacy* (New York: Doubleday, 2010).

ing that time, they managed to preserve their national identity by clinging to their cultural heritage and the intense Roman Catholic faith underlying and unifying it. Karol Wojtyła's formative years were therefore spent in a free and very Catholic Poland.[3]

From his early youth, Karol exhibited the deep piety, the exceptional intelligence, and the penchant for vigorous physical activity that would characterize his life. But his life would also be marked by acute suffering, whether personal or collective. His mother, Emilia, died just five weeks before his ninth birthday. The death of his twenty-six-year-old brother Edmund followed less than four years later. An older sister had died in early infancy. So, when Karol was just twelve years old, his father, also named Karol, was the only surviving member of his immediate family. Under his father's guidance, young Karol learned that while we cannot avoid suffering in this life, we need not fear it. For human suffering has been redeemed in Christ. The cross, borne in faith, is therefore the way of salvation.[4]

In secondary school, Karol's early interest in Polish literature, poetry, and drama intensified, and he expressed it on the stage by taking part in theatrical productions. The view of history and of the human condition that he assimilated through these creative works and through his performances would shape his own outlook for a lifetime.[5] During this period, he came under the tutelage of Mieczysław Kotlarczyk, an expert on early-nineteenth-century theater criticism who was also well versed in Polish poetry. Kotlarczyk believed that the spoken word could communicate objective truths and values by eliciting just the right emotional response in the persons listening, moving them thus to change the world around them for the better. Through his experience with this approach to theater, Karol would learn that emotions, a natural human endowment, are meant to serve the truth of right

3. See Weigel, *Witness to Hope*, 17–23.

4. See ibid., 27–33, 41–43.

5. Major themes included the following: the human spirit is the driving force of history; the loss of national sovereignty is linked to the loss of Christian virtue; national suffering is a redemptive vocation leading to the authentic liberation of the human spirit; Christ's Incarnation is the deepest basis of human fraternity, equality, and freedom; God's Spirit alters the course of human history through the proclamation of the Word; the very purpose of human life is to testify to the truth; human labor has its dignity in the laborer, who can transform work, through love, into an authentic expression of human freedom and thus into a redemptive act. These themes reflect the specifically Catholic interpretation of Polish life and history found in Polish authors such as Henryk Sienkiewicz (1846–1916), Adam Mickiewicz (1789–1855), Juliusz Słowacki (1809–1849), and Cyprian Norwid (1821–1883). For the forty years of his life in Poland under Nazi and then communist oppression, Karol Wojtyła would live by that interpretation. And the day would come when, as Pope John Paul II, he would bring out its universal significance. See ibid., 33–35.

reason and hence the true good of the person. He would also learn that the spoken word has tremendous power to transform persons and so, too, the history of which they are, or certainly should be, the protagonists. Finally, his early theatrical experiences taught him something about the meaning of community, as different individuals, each having a specific role to play, came together and contributed to a goal greater than any of them could have achieved alone.[6]

While Karol was still in high school, the kind of anti-Semitism that Hitler was then stirring up in Germany was gaining ground in Poland as well. Karol was outspoken in defending his Jewish friends against students who were involving themselves with anti-Semitic activities. In the summer of 1938, he and his father moved to Kraków so that in the fall he could pursue graduate studies in Polish philology at the venerable Jagiellonian University. There, too, he would side with his Jewish peers. Karol's philological studies increased his appreciation of language, which, as an expression of the human spirit, shapes human history.[7]

## The War Years: Maturity through Adversity

In September 1939, Hitler's forces invaded Poland and quickly seized control. To avoid being executed or sent to a concentration camp, Karol had to get a work card so that he could remain in Kraków. For a short time, he was able to continue his studies at the university while working as a messenger. But his formal studies came to an abrupt end in November when 184 faculty members were arrested at the school and sent to a concentration camp as part of Hitler's plan to destroy Poland's culture and, thereby, its national identity. Toward that end, the Germans also demolished other witnesses of Polish culture and history. As the foundation, the guardian, and the premier symbol of Poland's cultural and historical life, the Catholic Church would not come through the Occupation unscathed.[8]

During the fall of the following year, Karol began working in a quarry for the Solvay chemical company, pulverizing and shoveling limestone. When later transferred to Solvay's bicarbonate plant, he had more opportunity to read. His coworkers encouraged his study and were willing to cover for him, perhaps seeing in him someone in whom Poland's culture, and hence its future, might be kept alive. For his part, Karol saw in the nobility and the industriousness of manual laborers the transcendent dignity of the person

6. See ibid., 37–38.
7. See ibid., 38–41.
8. See ibid., 50–55.

underlying the very dignity of work itself. At Solvay, this key aspect of the future pope's social thought had taken on flesh.[9]

### Preserving Polish Culture

The kinds of cultural resistance with which Karol Wojtyła got involved during the war were likewise formative of the Christian humanism maturing in his mind. Defying German efforts to destroy Polish culture, he and like-minded friends began reciting classic Polish texts and staging dramas in the home of one of the group's members, Juliusz Kydryński. He also wrote three plays in which he tried to probe the meaning of Poland's suffering in a manner akin to the Polish Romantic tradition. And he translated Sophocles's *Oedipus* from the original Greek into contemporary Polish.[10]

On top of all this activity, his reading, and his work, Karol looked after and provided for his increasingly frail father, who would attend his son's clandestine recitations and performances. When Christmas 1940 came around, the elder Karol became bedridden. On February 18, he died alone at home before his son returned from work with the evening meal. Grief-stricken, Karol ran to summon a priest and then remained kneeling beside his father's body the entire night, praying. Juliusz Kydryński stayed with him, but there was little he could do to dispel his friend's feeling of loneliness. Every member of Karol Wojtyła's immediate family was now gone.[11]

In July, Karol was reunited with Mieczysław Kotlarczyk, who moved to Kraków with his wife. Kotlarczyk explained to Wojtyła and others his idea for an underground "theater of the living word" to protest and resist the Nazi assault against Poland's national culture. Though the Nazis might have considered such activity a capital offense if they discovered it, the group's members understood that any hope of Poland's future political revival depended on whether its people could rescue and build on the nation's cultural past. Out of this little troupe came to be what was later called the Rhapsodic Theater. Both Kotlarczyk and Wojtyła understood that the effective proclamation of the word within—of one's inner grasp of the real truth of things—had the power to draw the listener into the transcendent truth of God's Word, which would ultimately crush the Reich's (and, later, communism's) lies and crimes against the human person.[12]

9. See ibid., 55–58. See also John Paul II, *Gift and Mystery: On the Fiftieth Anniversary of My Priestly Ordination* (New York: Doubleday, 1996), 20–22.

10. See Weigel, *Witness to Hope*, 62–63.

11. See ibid., 68.

12. See ibid., 63–66. According to Mieczysław Maliński, a seminary classmate and lifelong friend of Wojtyła's since the Occupation years, "The performers were like a priesthood, guard-

Wojtyła and Kotlarczyk were also members of another cultural resistance movement called UNIA (or Union), founded in 1940. One of its overarching purposes was to establish the principles, based on Catholic moral and social teaching, according to which a reconstituted Poland would conduct its public life. Among other things, the new Polish state would uphold the true good of the family as the basis of society, and it would recognize the inherent dignity of every human being as someone made in God's image. Throughout his future pastoral life, Karol Wojtyła would develop and proclaim UNIA ideas about the essential elements of a just and balanced society.[13]

Cultural resistance in Poland meant, above all, keeping the Church alive. As elsewhere in Poland during the Nazi occupation, the Germans sent most of the priests of Wojtyła's parish—Salesians—to a concentration camp. In May 1941, only two priests were left. In defiance of a Nazi prohibition, the Salesians had been trying to conduct their youth ministry underground. Given the current gravity of the situation, the two remaining priests sought to keep it going with the help of qualified lay leaders, among whom Jan Tyranowski was, by all accounts, a real mystic. Under Tyranowski's leadership, Karol would become part of the hidden effort to preserve the Church's vitality amid the brutal Nazi effort to destroy it.

Impressed with Karol, Tyranowski introduced him to the works of Teresa of Avila and John of the Cross. The writings of John of the Cross, in particular, would have a lasting impact on Wojtyła's life and work. His exposure to the Carmelite saint helped him understand that abandoning oneself completely to God's will resulted in a liberation of the spirit, a true inner freedom that the arrogance and brutality of Nazi self-assertion could neither take away nor overcome. This was surely the freedom at work in the heroic sacrifices and martyrdoms of so many priests during the Occupation. For Karol Wojtyła, Father Maximillian Kolbe, about whom he would learn shortly after the war, was the quintessential example of this Christ-like heroism among priests. As for his association with Jan Tyranowski, this only confirmed Karol's growing awareness that holiness is not the sole reserve of priests, and that the laity have an indispensable contribution to make to the Church's mission.[14]

---

ing and imparting the deepest truths of life; it was their task and their opportunity to regenerate the world by a display of artistic beauty. Such was the ideology of the 'arch-priest' Kotlarczyk." Mieczysław Maliński, *Pope John Paul II: The Life of Karol Wojtyła*, trans. P. S. Falla (New York: Seabury Press, 1979), 33.

13. See Weigel, *Witness to Hope*, 66–67.

14. See ibid., 58–62; John Paul II, *Gift and Mystery*, 23–24, 36–39. Pope John Paul II considered Tyranowski, who died in 1947 at age forty-six, to be a saint. See John Paul's *Crossing the*

### Bound for the Seminary

From this period of his life until he finally decided to enter the seminary in the autumn of 1942, Karol Wojtyła gradually discerned a call to the priesthood.[15] The willingness of so many priests to suffer and to sacrifice even their lives for the sake of Christ exerted a decisive influence on his discernment process. What is more, he had begun to sense a higher purpose to his life because he had somehow been spared the enormous sacrifices that countless other men and women had to make during the war.[16] The Lord would favor him with an interior illumination of sorts to confirm him in his vocational decision.[17] The fact that Karol was not killed or injured even more seriously than he was after being hit by a truck in February 1944 could only have reinforced his sense of God's providential plan for him.[18]

Being a seminarian during the Nazi occupation was a dangerous enterprise. The Kraków seminary was forced to operate completely underground because of frequent German raids on it, culminating in the arrest of five of its students. Karol Wojtyła became one of ten seminarians who would now pursue the priesthood secretly according to a plan devised by Kraków's metropolitan, Archbishop Adam Stefan Sapieha. The candidates would continue with their jobs while preparing for the priesthood without telling anyone. They would study on their own and then be tested periodically by professors. After successfully completing their studies, they would be ordained. During a Gestapo round-up of young men in Kraków in August 1944, the archbishop summoned his underground seminarians to his residence in the hope of hiding them there for the remainder of the war. Karol escaped detection only because the police searching the house where he lived failed to look behind the closed door in his basement apartment, where he was hiding and praying.[19]

An assigned textbook on Aristotelian-Thomistic metaphysics taught Karol Wojtyła that the things he had hitherto learned experientially and intuitively about the world are grounded firmly in human reason. This meant that the world is essentially intelligible, even amid and despite the manmade

*Threshold of Hope,* trans. Jenny and Martha McPhee (London: Random House, 1994), 142. See also Maliński, *Pope John Paul II,* 98 and 260, where the author recounts two occasions on which Wojtyła acknowledged Tyranowski's role in nurturing his priestly vocation.

15. See John Paul II, *Gift and Mystery,* 19–40; Weigel, *Witness to Hope,* 67–69.

16. "[T]he heroism of my contemporaries helped me to define my personal vocation." John Paul II, *Crossing the Threshold,* 119.

17. See John Paul II, *Gift and Mystery,* 35.

18. See Weigel, *Witness to Hope,* 71.

19. See ibid., 69–72.

chaos of war. Since right reason can discern the truth of things objectively, it can also distinguish objectively between moral good and evil. Radical skepticism and moral relativism are therefore intellectually and existentially bankrupt. Wojtyła would develop this basic understanding both philosophically and theologically over the course of his lifetime.[20]

## Déjà Vu All Over Again: Life under the Communist Curse

In mid-January 1945, the Germans retreated from Kraków as the Russians advanced against them from the east. But in planning Germany's final defeat at the Yalta conference in February 1945, Poland's Western "allies" reneged on the pledges they had made to the nation before and during the war, handing it (and other European nations) over to Stalin. Thus, Poland lost the same war twice. Neither the false humanism by which the communist power operated nor the moral injustice of Yalta's having foisted it on the Polish people was lost on young Karol Wojtyła.[21] Throughout his life, he would develop, proclaim, and live a distinctively Christian brand of humanism, one that promises—and delivers—authentic personal and communal fulfillment through the free and total gift of self, something that all the inhuman "humanisms" advanced to justify the violence, deceptions, greed, egoism, and chaos of totalitarian self-assertion could never do.

### A Priest and Scholar

After Karol had passed his preordination examinations early in the summer of 1946, Adam Sapieha, now a cardinal, moved quickly to ordain him to the priesthood so that the intelligent and devout twenty-six-year-old could begin graduate studies in Rome as soon as possible.[22] Two weeks after his ordination on November 1 (All Saints Day), the new priest was off to the Eternal City, where he would pursue a doctorate at the Angelicum.[23] During this eighteen-month period he would encounter different trends in contemporary

20. See ibid., 70–71.

21. See ibid., 75–76.

22. In *The End and the Beginning* (his complementary sequel to *Witness to Hope*), Weigel tells us that Sapieha's haste in this matter might have stemmed from a concern that the communist secret police were watching Wojtyła because of his involvement in a charitable student organization. See 33–34. Part 1 of the book is replete with newly available information from secret police files about the relentless efforts of Soviet and Soviet bloc intelligence agencies to monitor, hinder, or even discredit Karol Wojtyła throughout his priestly, episcopal, and papal life. Toward that end, they often sought to recruit, deceive, or blackmail his closest personal contacts.

23. See Weigel, *Witness to Hope*, 79–81.

Thomism.[24] But his formal studies would provide him with sound training in traditional Thomism, equipping him to assess critically the newer philosophical and theological methods and systems being developed at other European centers of learning.[25] One day, Wojtyła would try to develop aspects of St. Thomas's teaching in the light of more recent currents of thought. Perhaps he was already seeing the need for such a project, for postwar Europe was rapidly becoming de-Christianized and would therefore have to be evangelized in the most compelling way possible. Faith had to become an attitude that shaped the way one lived. In that way, faith would also shape the culture *in which* one lived.[26]

Father Wojtyła wrote his doctoral dissertation, entitled *The Doctrine of Faith according to St. John of the Cross,* under the supervision of the Dominican luminary Father Reginald Garrigou-Lagrange, universally regarded in his day as the greatest representative of traditional Thomism. A number of Karol Wojtyła/John Paul II's signature themes are already present in that work. In the encounter with God through the life of faith, God gives us his love—his very Self—as our own. In that way, we can reciprocate the Love that we have received with a Love that is commensurate with, and hence appropriate to, the Giver, who *is* that Love. That is, the Love that we give to God and that *is* God really comes from us and includes us. Thus, a real, mutual exchange of persons—an interpersonal encounter—takes place between God and us through faith. In that exchange, we become most ourselves by becoming God, both by participation in the divine Life, which is Love, and by imitation—by giving the gift of self fully and unreservedly to God first of all, and to neighbor. The mutual relationship of self-giving love between God and us, as Wojtyła/John Paul understood it through the writings of St. John of the Cross, reflects the intra-Trinitarian dynamic of love in God himself.[27] In time, the author would stress that it also expresses itself outwardly in every authentic, rightly ordered relationship of love between human beings.

24. Examples include the transcendental Thomism of Joseph Maréchal and the existential Thomism of Etienne Gilson. Wojtyła's encounter with these and other trends, such as France's *Nouvelle Théologie* and perhaps also the existential Thomism of Jacques Maritain, might have taken place mainly at the Belgian College, where he resided. See ibid., 82; George Huntston Williams, *The Mind of John Paul II: Origins of His Thought and Action* (New York: Seabury Press, 1981), 93–103.

25. See Weigel, *Witness to Hope,* 84–85.

26. See Rocco Buttiglione, *Karol Wojtyła: The Thought of the Man Who Became Pope John Paul II* (Grand Rapids, Mich.: William B. Eerdmans, 1997), 35, 186–87.

27. See Karol Wojtyła, *Faith according to St. John of the Cross,* trans. Jordan Aumann, O.P. (San Francisco: Ignatius Press, 1985), 194–95, 212–13, 228–31.

These relationships, too—above all, the mutual self-surrender, in love, of man and woman in marriage through the conjugal act—are created reflections of God's own inner life.[28]

Another important theme in Wojtyła's doctoral dissertation on St. John of the Cross is that God transcends every human attempt to objectify him in knowledge. Though God remains incomprehensible to us even in faith, we can nevertheless come to know God most intimately through our mutually self-giving, interpersonal encounter with him.[29] What is more, the fact that we can enter such a relationship presupposes that we are free. It presupposes that we, like God, are personal. Throughout his academic and pastoral life, Wojtyła/John Paul II would develop the implications of those ideas. Since the mutual relation between God and us is constitutive of who we are, we can no more objectify another human being than we can objectify God. True, we might regard or treat others as objects, but the harm we do thereby to them and to ourselves is incalculable, for each of us is a free (or virtually free), personal being who is called to communion with God. Each of us is therefore a "someone" having sovereign worth. If, in our actions, we were to reduce any human being to the level of an object, we would unjustifiably violate the surpassing dignity of a person, with grave consequences for all. The likelihood of our acting that way increases in proportion to the degree that we presume to interpret the human person and human existence without reference to God (or the true understanding of God). Karol Wojtyła/John Paul II would persistently critique both communistic totalitarianism and the radically individualistic "democracies" of the West on the grounds of their operating according to just such an interpretation.

Though Wojtyła's dissertation got high marks, and though he passed his doctoral examinations and his oral dissertation defense in stellar fashion, the Angelicum did not award him the doctoral degree because he could not afford the cost of having his dissertation published, as required. Therefore, on his return to Poland in the summer of 1948, he resubmitted the dissertation to Jagiellonian University's theology faculty, which reviewed the work and awarded him the doctorate in theology in December.[30]

28. See the introduction in the following volume of discourses by Pope John Paul II: *Man and Woman He Created Them: A Theology of the Body,* translation, introduction, and index by Michael Waldstein (Boston: Pauline Books and Media, 2006), 23–34.

29. Wojtyła emphasizes throughout that the intellect, while incapable of apprehending its "divine object" clearly in this life, is nevertheless united with it through faith informed and enlivened by charity.

30. See Weigel, *Witness to Hope,* 85–87; Buttiglione, *Karol Wojtyła,* 45–53.

### A Pioneering Pastor

By the end of the Second World War, Poland had lost roughly one-third of its priests because of Nazi brutality. The key to Poland's reemergence as an independent nation would be to preserve its historical identity through the revitalization of the Church, which would have to resist communist efforts to suppress it. The new situation highlighted the clergy's need to turn to the laity with pastoral initiatives that would help the people understand and fulfill both their vocation to holiness and their role in the Church's mission. On his return from Rome, Father Wojtyła undertook that responsibility with singular zeal.

Through pastoral initiatives too numerous and varied to mention, Wojtyła accompanied people in their lives, creating an atmosphere of openness, mutual respect, trust, friendship, freedom, and spiritual wholesomeness that stood out in marked contrast to the personal and communal fragmentation taking place under the communist regime's atmosphere of suspicion and its destructive atheistic "humanism." He listened and discussed, and then he urged people to make wise decisions. He helped them experience the Gospel truth that would set them free, while also preparing them to resist, and ultimately challenge and prevail over, the godless, anti-human way of life that the communists were aggressively trying to promote and impose. His efforts were exceedingly effective because of the transparent authenticity of his own life and faith.[31]

By his pastorally driven activities, Karol Wojtyła intended much more than simply helping the Church to survive and revitalize itself under oppressive conditions through a more evangelically attuned laity. What he was doing was protecting and promoting the very dignity of the human person. At stake here was the whole future of Poland and, indeed, of humanity itself. Through her proclamation of the Gospel and her sanctifying sacramental ministry, the Church is first and foremost the guardian of human life, dignity, and freedom—of human transcendence. That is her reason for being. To the extent that she fulfills that mission, she builds herself up. To the extent that she fails for any reason, her very existence is imperiled. For every attack on the human person is, directly or indirectly, an attack on the Church and her mission. The Church's survival is not an end in itself. She must survive to defend the human person in his or her totality, but spiritually above

31. See Weigel, *Witness to Hope*, 91–108.

all.[32] And she *will* survive—indeed, thrive—insofar as she does that. So, too, will society as a whole. Karol Wojtyła understood that. And he lived by it.

### Twice a Doctor

Father Wojtyła's nearly two and a half years of parish work and extra-parochial ministry came suddenly to a halt when Archbishop Eugeniusz Baziak, who succeeded Cardinal Sapieha (d. July 1951), ordered him to take a two-year sabbatical, beginning in September 1951, to complete a second doctorate. In Europe, a second doctoral dissertation, called a habilitation thesis, is necessary to qualify for a university-level faculty appointment, and that is evidently what the archbishop had in mind for the thirty-one-year-old priest-scholar.[33] But what would he write about this time? Wojtyła had been convinced for some time now that the human intellect can arrive at a true knowledge of the world as it really is, and that such knowledge immediately makes objective, subjectively discernible demands on us regarding how we ought to relate to the world and to one another. In other words, objective knowledge places us inescapably in the realm of morality, creating a tension between the person I have become and the person I really ought to be—precisely because *I am* a person. Wojtyła's pastoral practice of accompaniment—to say nothing of his own personal experiences—had taught him that people live very concrete lives in which they wrestle with that tension every day. So, the undeniable human experience whereby people are ever confronted with decisions about how to use their freedom must be the point of departure from which to begin addressing moral questions philosophically.

But what if I interpret my experience in a way that is at odds with how you interpret yours? By beginning with the human subject, do we not fall inevitably into a radical subjectivism that would challenge our ability to know anything objectively, leading just as inevitably to moral relativism? While many would argue along those lines, Wojtyła remained convinced that human knowledge can arrive at truths that are universal and absolute, even when it comes to morality. With that in mind, he undertook the study of Max Scheler's work to see whether the German philosopher could help explain how.[34]

Scheler (1874–1928) was a disciple of Edmund Husserl (1859–1938), whose original purpose was to develop a method of philosophical inquiry that would

32. "[A]ll spiritual authority in the Church must be directed towards developing and making evident the dignity of man, his 'kingliness' which comes to him from Christ the good shepherd." Wojtyła, *Sign of Contradiction* (New York: Seabury Press, 1979), 144.

33. See Weigel, *Witness to Hope*, 125.

34. See ibid., 125–26.

get at the real truth of the things—of the phenomena—that present themselves to our experience. By descriptively analyzing them according to the myriad of ways in which they thus present themselves, we can arrive both at the meaning of each whole—at the proper identity of each being as disclosed in the manifold of its expressions—and at the relationships that exist among beings. At the same time, this gives us a take on human experience itself, and consequently on our *own* identity. For it is precisely *we* to whom the objects of our experience are given, and it is we who go on to describe their self-manifestation and its conditions.[35] Scheler applied the method of "phenomenology," as this philosophical movement is called, in an original way to analyze things human—for example, love, religion, emotions, and the ethical life. Among other things, he considered how the emotional impact of the values that we experience affects us, as well as how the human will itself is affected by emotionally felt values. Could Scheler's work establish the basis for a genuinely Christian ethics?

While Wojtyła would remain indebted to Scheler for the insights and leads that the philosopher's phenomenological descriptions of ethical experience provide, his second doctoral thesis—*An Evaluation of the Possibility of Constructing a Christian Ethics on the Basis of the System of Max Scheler*—concluded that Scheler's work is essentially deficient. For one thing, it cannot account for the inescapably dramatic character of one's moral decisions—that is, for the impact that those decisions have on the person who makes them, determining at the deepest levels what kind of person he or she becomes.[36] This deficiency stems not only from the limitations of the phenomenological method itself but also from the assumptions on which Scheler bases his system. Indeed, Scheler denies that human beings can make moral decisions at all, from which it follows that we cannot be the cause of our own moral actions.[37] He places such weight on how we subjectively "feel" values emotionally that he cannot explain—nor has he any interest in explaining—how it is possible for the person to distinguish, rationally and objectively, between a morally good act and a morally evil one. For him, the subject cannot know

35. For an exceptionally clear presentation of what phenomenology is, see Robert Sokolowski, *Introduction to Phenomenology* (New York: Cambridge University Press, 2000).

36. See Jarosław Kupczak, OP, *Destined for Liberty: The Human Person in the Philosophy of Karol Wojtyła/John Paul II* (Washington, D.C.: The Catholic University of America Press, 2000), 61; Karol Wojtyła, "The Problem of the Will in the Analysis of the Ethical Act," in *Person and Community: Selected Essays*, trans. Theresa Sandok, OSM, Catholic Thought from Lublin 4 (New York: Peter Lang, 1993), 19; Karol Wojtyła, "The Intentional Act and the Human Act, that is, Act and Experience," in *The Crisis of Culture: Steps to Reopen the Phenomenological Investigation of Man*, ed. Anna-Teresa Tymieniecka, Analecta Husserliana 5 (Boston: D. Reidel Publishing, 1976), 275–76.

37. See Kupczak, *Liberty*, 12–23, 144.

ethical values intellectually,[38] objective though they are in themselves as a real dimension of common human experience. We experience them intentionally in their essential quality through our conscious acts of feeling and sometimes only secondarily in relation to the objects, the real beings, with which we associate them. Therefore, a value does not exist in itself but only as "an essence in consciousness distinct and independent from being."[39]

Scheler interprets the human will as an essentially passive faculty that merely submits to a particular value because of its emotional impact on the person. The act of willing provides only the occasion for the *experience* of the value, which is "realized" only in that sense.[40] One experiences the value as "good" or "evil" according to how it compares with one's own ethos—emotionally intuited values arranged into a hierarchy based on the a priori emotional experiences of love and hate.[41] But that says nothing about whether the value is objectively, hence morally, good or evil.[42] It does not even require that the value be realized in the existential order. It might just as well remain wholly ideal.[43]

In fact, Scheler denies that a value, a good, might serve as the end of one's actions. For if he were to admit that a person might purposely seek to realize an experienced value by acting on it, then he would also have to admit that the value has the character of a goal—one that the person might be obliged in conscience to achieve. On the contrary, Scheler wants to construct an ethical system that excludes obligation (or duty), which he considers to

38. See ibid., 12–13, 144; Wojtyła, "On the Metaphysical and Phenomenological Basis of the Moral Norm," in *PC*, 82.

39. Waldstein, "Introduction," in *Man and Woman*, 68.

40. See Kupczak, *Liberty*, 11, 13; Wojtyła, "The Problem of the Will," in *PC*, 11; "The Problem of the Separation of Experience in Ethics," in *PC*, 38–39; "The Intentional Act and the Human Act," 271–72.

41. See Kupczak, *Liberty*, 14; Wojtyła, "The Separation of Experience," in *PC*, 35–37; "Basis of the Moral Norm," in *PC*, 82–83; "The Intentional Act and the Human Act," 272–74.

42. See Kupczak, *Liberty*, 23, 145; Wojtyła, "Basis of the Moral Norm," in *PC*, 84–85. In *Defending Human Dignity: John Paul II and Political Realism* (Grand Rapids, Mich.: Brazos Press, 2004), Derek Jeffreys tells us that Scheler's descriptive account of how we rank values includes objective criteria, such as whether the values in question are essentially enduring or transient, limitlessly communicable and unifying or divisible and divisive. Accordingly, values pertaining to the spiritual order rank highest. Jeffreys argues that Wojtyła/John Paul II generally accepts and utilizes Scheler's descriptive account of our emotional attunement to and consequent ranking of values (particularly as regards the priority of spiritual—hence personal—values over material ones, without undue prejudice to the latter), but not without also faulting Scheler for failing to provide an objective basis for positing the moral norms that must govern our active response to the values that we perceive emotionally and, in Jeffreys's account of Scheler, that we classify and order rationally. See 54–66.

43. See Kupczak, *Liberty*, 17.

be both negative and Kantian.[44] So, for all his attention to human experience, Scheler ends up ignoring our very basic human experience of being the cause of, the ones responsible for, our own moral actions.[45] We are inescapably caught up in the drama of being confronted with choices about which the will must freely and actively decide. And our experience of freedom in human decision-making presupposes our ability to evaluate our possible choices by objective, rational means (hence the experience of obligation), or else everything we do would be reduced to the level of personal preference. In that case, our actions would be arbitrary and instinctual, not morally informed and free.[46]

Ironically, in confining his analyses of the person to the subjective domain of conscious emotional experience, Scheler ends up losing sight of the person as a real, concrete being whose deliberate causality is the source of the individual's moral actions and hence of the experience of their moral value.[47] The person, in Scheler's system, tends to be reduced to no more than the sum of various emotionally felt values experienced subjectively in consciousness—a precarious identity indeed.[48] Given Scheler's limited perspective on human experience and the fact that phenomenology as such is concerned with how things present themselves to that experience, neither Scheler's system nor phenomenological description in general—however indispensable they might be to the analysis of human ethical experience—can tell us ultimately why certain actions are objectively morally good and perfective of the person while others are objectively morally bad and destructive of the person.[49]

Despite these and other problems with Scheler's work and with phenomenology in general, Karol Wojtyła would make it his philosophical project over the years to take useful insights from Scheler and others about subjective human experience and to integrate them into the epistemological and the anthropological realism of Aristotelian-Thomistic metaphysics (that is, Aristotelian metaphysics as appropriated in an original and creative way by St. Thomas Aquinas). According to philosopher Rocco Buttiglione, Wojtyła's point of reference in engaging Scheler would always be Aquinas as under-

44. See ibid., 15–16, 144; Wojtyła, "The Separation of Experience," in *PC*, 34.
45. See Wojtyła, "The Separation of Experience," in *PC*, 39.
46. See Weigel, *Witness to Hope*, 129.
47. See Wojtyła, "The Problem of the Will," in *PC*, 8–9.
48. See Kupczak, *Liberty*, 22; Wojtyła, "In Search of the Basis of Perfectionism in Ethics," in *PC*, 53.
49. See Kupczak, *Liberty*, 23, 61.

stood through St. John of the Cross. "St. Thomas was thus given an experiential and existential dimension which made it easier to link his thought with phenomenology."[50]

By December 1953, Wojtyła had satisfactorily fulfilled all the requirements qualifying him for appointment to Jagiellonian's faculty of theology. However, the university's rector would not confer the degree, citing new regulations by the communist government.[51] In the months that followed, the Department of Education suppressed the university's theology faculty entirely. Even so, Wojtyła had already begun teaching a course on Catholic social ethics within the faculty back in October 1953, and he continued to teach it to seminarians after the faculty was suppressed.[52]

Stefan Swieżawski, one of the evaluators of Wojtyła's habilitation thesis, taught philosophy at the Catholic University of Lublin (KUL). He persuaded Wojtyła to join KUL's philosophy faculty. The new professor taught courses in philosophical ethics. About two years later, in November 1956, he succeeded to the faculty's chair of ethics, retaining that position until elected pope in October 1978.[53]

Father Wojtyła's lectures at KUL developed his pastoral and scholarly interests in the human person. In addition, Wojtyła became part of a bold project that the school's philosophers had initiated prior to his appointment there. The savage madness of the Nazi Occupation, juxtaposed with the most extraordinary acts of heroism and self-sacrifice imaginable, had urged the perennial questions about human beings and their nature, condition, purpose, and destiny with renewed intensity. Perpetuating the need to address those questions in a comprehensive and coherent way was communism's dangerously reductive "humanism" and the crimes against humanity that the communist masters "legitimated" on account of it. The Polish people were forced to live under the real consequences of false understandings of the human person that placed intrinsic human rights and authentic human freedom under siege. The KUL philosophers sought to challenge those understandings by developing a philosophical anthropology grounded in

50. Buttiglione, *Karol Wojtyła*, 48. See also 54–62; and Kenneth L. Schmitz, *At the Center of the Human Drama: The Philosophical Anthropology of Karol Wojtyła/Pope John Paul II* (Washington, D.C.: The Catholic University of America Press, 1993), 42–48.

51. See Kupczak, *Liberty*, 24. According to Weigel's account, the Jagiellonian University Faculty of Theology did award the doctoral degree to Wojtyła in 1954, but the faculty was suppressed before he was formally named a docent. See Weigel, *Witness to Hope*, 130.

52. See Weigel, *Witness to Hope*, 130–31n.

53. See ibid., 130, 135–36.

metaphysical realism and having a persuasive ethical core. The path they would take to a full, a reasonable, and an objective accounting of the human person would be through an analysis of human experience. They would thus complement the modern philosophical focus on human subjectivity with the concrete, ontological approach to the person found in classical ancient and medieval metaphysics, seeking consciously in that way to avoid the extremes of idealism and materialism.[54]

The philosophers met frequently to exchange their ideas and to develop their new philosophical program.[55] Of course, Karol Wojtyła would specialize in its ethical facet.[56] His interest in using phenomenological analyses of human experience as the gateway to metaphysical affirmations about the human person, human knowing, and human acting was well suited to the aims of the project as a whole, though some of his colleagues had reservations about his style of philosophizing.[57] The participants became convinced that the significance of their work extended ultimately to the whole world. And that is precisely the audience that their vision of the human person would one day reach in the person of Pope John Paul II.[58]

### Onward and Upward: The Episcopacy

In August 1958, Poland's primate, Cardinal Stefan Wyszyński, informed Father Wojtyła that Pope Pius XII had named him titular bishop of Ombi and auxiliary to Archbishop Baziak in the archdiocese of Kraków.[59] When

54. See ibid., 130–34; and Stefan Swieżawski's "Introduction" in *PC*, ix–xiii.

55. Through these exchanges, especially with Swieżawski, Wojtyła became more versed than hitherto in the Thomism of Gilson and Maritain. See Weigel, *Witness to Hope*, 139.

56. On some of his important contributions to the project, see Swieżawski's "Introduction" in *PC*, xiii–xiv.

57. See Weigel, *Witness to Hope*, 135. During this period, his friend and fellow priest Mieczyłsaw Maliński asked Wojtyła what he was working on. He replied, "[W]hat seems to me most important at the moment is to reconcile Thomist philosophy with that of Max Scheler. . . . Phenomenology seems to me a fine philosophical instrument, but no more than that. It lacks a general world-view, a metaphysic if you like, and it would be worth while to create one." Maliński, *Pope John Paul II*, 113. As it turns out, both Maliński and KUL philosopher Mieczysław Albert Krąpiec, OP, collaborated with the Polish secret police, who referred to Maliński by the code name DELTA. See Weigel, *The End and the Beginning*, 75.

58. See Swieżawski's "Introduction" in *PC*, xiii, xvi.

59. On hearing the news, Wojtyła responded, "I am too young; I'm only thirty-eight." John Paul II, *Rise, Let Us Be On Our Way*, trans. Walter Ziębma (New York: Warner Books, 2004), 9. This brings to mind the objection of Jeremiah when the LORD appointed him a prophet to the nations (see Jer 1:4–6). When Wyszyński advised Wojtyła not to oppose the will of the Holy Father, he accepted the appointment. (Svidercoschi has Wojtyła receiving the news with alacrity in *Stories of Karol*, 144.) It is somewhat ironic that two days before Wojtyła was elected pope twenty years later, Wyszyński himself responded, "No, he's too young," when Cardinal Franz König of Vienna

Wojtyła informed the archbishop of this, the generally reserved Baziak brought the thirty-eight-year-old priest out to the other priests in his waiting room and announced, "'*Habemus papam*'—'We have a Pope.'"[60] And so, on September 28, 1958, Father Karol Józef Wojtyła was consecrated a bishop, the youngest in Poland. He chose the motto *Totus Tuus,* "Completely Yours," for his episcopal coat of arms, offering himself and his episcopal ministry to Christ by entrusting both completely to the Blessed Virgin Mary, the Mother of God. Recognizing what the responsibilities of his apostolic office entailed, Bishop Wojtyła began to express his pastoral solicitude in a more public way, particularly when it came to defending the religious freedom of his people against communist efforts to suppress it. He was also a tireless preacher and teacher, for he saw that as the defining characteristic of the episcopate.[61]

*Love and Responsibility* In the years immediately preceding Wojtyła's elevation to the episcopacy, the communist authorities in Poland were particularly aggressive in trying to weaken the Church, undermining Catholic life and moral teaching by legalizing abortion and encouraging youth to become sexually active. In that climate, Father Wojtyła, who was then delivering a monographic series of lectures at KUL entitled *Love and Responsibility,* prepared a draft for a book that he planned to publish under the same name. *Love and Responsibility* was first published in 1960, when Wojtyła was already two years a bishop. He intended its resounding affirmation of the human person's surpassing value as an authentic interpretation of the Gospel message that he was bound to proclaim, and he considered it his apostolic duty to uphold and promote that value by defending the intrinsic rights and dignity of the human person publicly. *Love and Responsibility* served therefore as an extension of his episcopal activity.

The book is rather remarkable in its analyses of the physical, emotional, psychological, metaphysical, ethical, and spiritual dimensions of human love.[62] What is more, the basic philosophical, anthropological, theological,

suggested to him that then Cardinal Wojtyła would be a prime candidate for the papacy. See Weigel, *Witness to Hope,* 253.

60. John Paul II, *Rise,* 10.

61. The internal communications of the Polish secret police began to refer to Bishop Wojtyła as PEDAGOG. See Weigel, *The End and the Beginning,* 58; and Weigel, *Witness to Hope,* 146–50.

62. *Love and Responsibility* takes up philosophically the themes that Wojtyła explored dramatically in what is perhaps his best known play, *The Jeweler's Shop,* also published originally in 1960. The plays and poems that he would write during his priesthood often echoed his memory of and reflection on the struggles and the triumphs that marked the lives of people he either knew about or had accompanied pastorally himself. His creative efforts thus attempted to explore the

and ethical themes that the author presents in *Love and Responsibility* anticipate those that he will develop, with notable continuity, in subsequent episcopal and papal writings of his that we will be examining in the forthcoming chapters.[63] It will therefore be worth our taking a fairly detailed, if somewhat synthetic, look at the book's overall content, where we will find, in its essential features, the scholarly elaboration of the author's pastoral concern for the human person.[64]

While helping young adults and married couples through the concrete problems they faced each day in the area of sexuality, Karol Wojtyła realized, even as a young priest, that the Catholic Church's biblically based teaching on sexual morality, for all its truth, had still to be presented in a more compelling way. Its rules of conduct had to be interpreted and explained, not just given as a series of commandments and prohibitions. This pastoral concern, along with the lessons he learned as a spiritual guide to those who sought his counsel on matters of love and marriage, led to his writing *Love and Responsibility*.[65]

Underlying Wojtyła's whole approach was his acute awareness that sexual matters pertain not just to the human body itself, as "biologically" male or female, but to a masculine or a feminine *person*, and to the manner in which such persons interrelate. Because man and woman are persons, their nature transcends that of any worldly creature, while their intrinsic worth transcends any worldly value or even the sum of such values. Accordingly, human beings are the subjects of the commandment to love. The content of that commandment is essentially personal, requiring, as it does, a right relation between persons: oneself and God, on the one hand, and oneself and one's neighbor, on the other. For that reason, sexual "love" falls within the

---

drama of human experience and to invite moral decisions in ways that his audience might apprehend more directly or intuitively than it might by reading an extended philosophical or theological treatise about human nature and activity. They were a complementary way of probing truth. See Weigel, *Witness to Hope*, 112–19.

63. It is not our purpose to draw specific connections between *Love and Responsibility* and these other works but rather to present, more or less in the book's own terms, those aspects that will help elucidate our study as a whole.

64. For Weigel's treatment of the work, see *Witness to Hope*, 140–44.

65. See *Love and Responsibility*, trans. H. T. Willetts (New York: Farrar, Straus, Giroux, 1981), 15–18 (author's introduction to the first Polish edition); John Paul II, *Crossing the Threshold*, 200. Wojtyła's conviction that the norms of Catholic morality must be justified so as to assist conscience in choosing the moral good by providing it with suitable premises grounded in reason and revelation also underlies his 1965 article, "The Problem of Catholic Sexual Ethics: Reflections and Postulates," in *PC*, 279–99. The article summarizes much of the content of *Love and Responsibility*.

realm of morality, obliging us to incorporate it into *personal* love, rightly understood. Nor can we, as self-determining creatures, evade our responsibility for doing so. Love and responsibility are therefore the two integral themes that Wojtyła seeks to address in the book to which he gave that title.

In *Love and Responsibility,* Wojtyła measures everything according to what he calls the "personalistic norm," which demands that we affirm a person *as* a person in any action that we direct toward him or her, whether that action is internal, as in our thoughts, or external, as in our words and deeds. Concretely, this says that we must never use another person (nor allow ourselves to be used) as merely a means to the end for which we (or others) act, since a means is always subordinate both to the end itself and to the person who employs it.[66] The inalienable dignity of every human person morally excludes our subordinating him or her to any end that violates that dignity. For the "object" of our actions is, like us, a *subject*—a bodily "someone" who has a spiritual inner life that is intrinsically related to objective truth and goodness, and who can freely decide on that basis about his or her own actions and course of life, at least potentially. We are therefore faced with an ontological equal who is an end in him- or herself.[67]

Stated in its positive form, the personalistic norm says that a person is a love-worthy good of the highest order.[68] In the meeting of rightly ordered personal freedoms, love, or at least trust, becomes a possibility. Love and trust grow from the bond that forms between persons who recognize inwardly, and who strive together to achieve, a true common good. In that kind of mutual striving, a person can freely assume the role of being a means to a morally licit end, as long as that role does not somehow compromise the person's intrinsic value, which must always be regarded as the *primary* value. It is possible, then, for a person to subordinate him- or herself willingly, and in a morally licit way, to a true good for the sake of others, or to others for the

66. Consequently, we must never even use ourselves so.

67. See *LR*, 21–28, 40–41.

68. See ibid., 41–42, 213, 245–46. The personalistic principle "is an attempt to translate the commandment of love into the language of philosophical ethics." John Paul II, *Crossing the Threshold*, 200–201. In that way, it goes beyond Kant's second categorical imperative, according to which we must always act so as to treat our own person or that of another as the end of our action and never merely as a means to the end. In *Memory and Identity: Conversations at the Dawn of a Millennium* (New York: Rizzoli International Publications, 2005), John Paul II elaborates as follows: "When I was writing the essay *Love and Responsibility,* the greatest commandment of the Gospel presented itself to me as a personalist norm. Precisely because man is a personal being, it is not possible to fulfill our duty toward him except by loving him. Just as love is the supreme commandment with regard to the personal God, so too only love can be our fundamental obligation toward the human person, created in God's image and likeness" (133–34).

sake of a true good.[69] On the human plane, the premier example of such a relational dynamic between persons, and between those persons and the true common good, is the mutual subordination of a man and a woman united in marriage, where the spouses freely aspire together toward the objective goods of matrimony—procreation and growth in mutual love—in a way that excludes either person's treating the other as a mere "object" in the intimacy of their sexual life.[70]

Marriage and family life are the natural outcome of the "sexual urge" that arises spontaneously in human beings as they grow and mature. Wojtyła affirms that the human sexual urge, with all its sensorial and emotional effects, is a natural human drive that is good in itself. It is not the source of love, but it provides the raw materials of love, to which it lends an unmistakable vividness. The person does not cause the sexual urge as such and so is not responsible for it. But the person *is* responsible for what he or she wills to do with it. According to the natural order of development, the sexual urge tends to express itself outwardly as a sensual attraction to, and an emotional longing for, someone of the opposite sex, the physiological and psychological attributes of one sex having a sexual value for the other. By thus conditioning the possibility of a relationship of love between persons based on the complementarity of the sexes, the sexual urge establishes the trajectory along whose path free human actions will be decided. Since those actions will determine how the two sexes relate to each other, they *must* incorporate the spontaneous psycho-physical attraction of each person to the other in a way that is consonant with the true, objective good of the person who is their "object." That is, they *must* properly express love, lest the sensual and emotional materials of love become the raw material of *sin* through willful actions that do not conform to the personalistic norm.[71]

Love is always an interior matter of the spirit.[72] It requires the exercise of reason and will, which means that we are responsible for our love. We are therefore also responsible both *for* and *to* the person we love, as someone who has placed special trust in our love.[73] A love that does not personally integrate our spontaneous sensual and emotional reactions to sexual values into actions that seek the other person's true good (as well as our own) is not

69. For example, it is morally permissible for a construction worker to exert himself physically, under the direction of his supervisors, to help build a bridge, if reasonable precautions are taken to ensure his safety, if he is adequately compensated for his work, if he is given time to rest adequately, and so on.

70. See *LR*, 28–30.

71. See ibid., 45–51, 159–61.

72. See ibid., 117.

73. See ibid., 130.

love at all. For as a natural phenomenon, sexual excitability is singly preoccupied with the possibility of using another person's body (or perhaps even one's own) to satisfy itself. And while we might emotionally perceive, in a person of the opposite sex, worthy values that elicit a natural longing for an intimate and exclusive relationship with that person in his or her totality, some or all of those values might be ideal rather than real: we might have projected them onto someone whom we really want to possess them but who really does not. Human sentiments are not equipped to assess whether the values that they lead us to perceive in another person are truly present. In a word, our experience of the sexual urge's natural stirrings is wholly subjective. The "truth" of that experience resides solely in the subject in whom the sexual reactions are taking place, though they are indeed reactions to real, if only falsely perceived or partial, values. The sexual urge as such, then, is not love, though it can lead and contribute to love by turning one's attention away from oneself and toward a person of the opposite sex.[74]

On the other hand, the sexual urge can powerfully resist the realization of authentic love. As experienced spontaneously, it is natural and therefore not sinful in itself. But it does have a certain self-centered tendency to want to satisfy itself physically and emotionally without due regard for the true good of either the person who is its "object" or the person experiencing it. When the human will consents to that tendency by passively acquiescing to it or by actively adopting it as its own, sexual desire becomes sinful. The will is naturally ordered toward the good, but it must turn to reason for knowledge of the *true* good that it is obliged to seek for the good of the *person*—both one's own person and that of anyone to whom one wills to relate. However, the will might content itself instead with pursuing, relative to another (whether just internally in thought or also externally in deed), only the partial goods represented by the other person's sexual values, intending thereby to satisfy immediately the subjective stirrings of the sexual urge. In that case, the will devalues the person by reducing him or her to, or by divorcing him or her from, the value of the body and of sex.

In opposing itself thus to love, the will becomes evil. For love is the very reason for human freedom; it is the highest good that the will can seek. Only by choosing love—only by affirming in action the true value of the whole person—does the will become good, since it then aspires freely to its proper end. Love is based on a true, rational knowledge of another person. Such

74. See ibid., 104–14.

knowledge makes it possible for freedom to commit itself to that person. This commitment places certain restrictions on freedom, especially as to how, and how widely, one's natural experience of sexual values will be allowed to express itself. At the same time, however, freedom exists for love, and so it willingly excludes anything that would essentially limit, damage, or destroy love. Placed in the service of love, then, freedom is truly free.[75]

In its own way, the human experience of shame in connection with sexual values serves the cause of love, as conscience reacts against our tendency to reduce others, and the tendency of others to reduce us, to the level of a mere "thing"—a sexual object that one can use for one's own pleasure and perhaps even dispose of *at* one's own pleasure. Shame thus reveals, indirectly, the value of the person. In doing so, it likewise reveals, indirectly, that the subjective experience of sexual love is properly completed only when integrated within the person and between persons by the will's rational commitment to affirming the sovereign value of the person. We must control and direct our sexual desires so that our relationship with the opposite sex does not so disintegrate as to become utilitarian in attitude or in action, which would reflect our own interior disintegration.[76]

Chastity is the specific virtue by which we achieve wholeness interiorly and relationally in the sexual sphere. When linked, as it must be, to the virtue of love, chastity sublimates, without suppressing, the sexual urge. It issues a resounding spiritual "yes" to the value of the person, so as to expose, from within us, any subjective attitudes and feelings that might try to pass themselves off as love when, in fact, they preclude love. In that way, chastity takes our spontaneous reactions to the value of the body and of sex and raises them to the personal level, where, having apprehended their true purpose, we can incorporate them into acts of real loving kindness toward persons of the opposite sex. Though concupiscence makes chastity difficult by inclining us to satisfy the sexual urge in ways that compromise the value of another person (as well as our own), the grace of God assists us in keeping our sexual desires in check through chastity's habitual regard for the true good of the person and of love.[77]

For Bishop Wojtyła, betrothed love, in particular, is the reciprocal self-surrender of a male and a female *I* to each other, such that they become a *we*. (Analogously, there is a sort of betrothed love that can take place between a

75. See ibid., 107, 135–36, 159–66.

76. See ibid., 174–81.

77. See ibid., 169–72, 194–200.

human being and God, expressed most intensely in spiritual virginity—exclusive, personal consecration to God—symbolized and fostered by physical virginity.)[78] Though a man and a woman are each ontologically and personally inalienable, each of them can freely give the gift of self to the chosen other so fully that they become each other's "property," forming a moral union in the order of love. That kind of mutual "ownership" is completely personalistic, excluding the exploitation of one party by the other, whether in the physical sense or otherwise. For each of the two persons wills for the other the good that they each desire naturally for their own self, namely, unlimited happiness. And since, in that case, the human will seeks to bestow on the beloved a good that is beyond merely human power to supply, what the man and the woman are really willing for each other—at least implicitly—is God, the objective fullness of the good.[79]

Since God has supreme proprietorial rights over all creatures, which depend on him for their existence and its preservation, he has an "interest" in protecting the true value and integrity of man and woman by determining the conditions under which their mutual self-giving, which tends naturally toward physical expression in sexual intercourse, can take place without violating the inherent dignity of either person. And so he has instituted marriage—monogamous and indissoluble in essence—as the place where betrothed love grows in the context of the sexual union, while the latter, having been taken up into betrothed love, expresses a fully personal reality, transcending the merely physical level. Reciprocally, the sexual union of the spouses fosters the exclusivity of betrothed love. As a natural sacrament instituted by God "in the beginning," marriage thus justifies the sexual relationship by establishing the objective framework within which the permanent union of a man and a woman can flourish. As a *supernatural* sacrament in Christ, moreover, marriage justifies that relationship in the order of grace, satisfying completely God's rights relative to the man and the woman undertaking it. This suggests that marriage has its own, distinct institutional and interpersonal structure, though its expansion, where possible, into a family helps ripen marital love.[80]

Indeed, the order of love demands that the objective, procreative purpose of the natural order—informing, as it does, the relationship that develops between a man and a woman—be consciously integrated into the inter-

78. See ibid., 249–55.

79. See ibid., 125–26, 136–39.

80. See ibid., 216–24.

personal, marital relation. Wojtyła observes further that the natural sexual urge belongs not just to the biological order but to the order of existence itself—the existence of the human species. For human procreation, toward which the sexual urge tends intrinsically as the final end of the attraction/longing that it creates between male and female persons, results in the existence of an essentially *spiritual* being—a *person*—and not just a biological entity. Therefore, the couple must never let the sexual urge express itself in actions that violate either the good of human existence, which is the first and most fundamental human good, or the good of their interpersonal love, which is intrinsically ordered toward the creation of a new human existence as an affirmation and extension of that love. The natural order of human existence and the personal order of human love are so integrally related that the human failure to freely assume the former into the latter will inevitably cause harm to both.[81]

It follows that the only way each act of sexual intercourse in marriage can be internally justified is if the spouses leave open, and are consciously prepared to accept, the possibility of procreation—even when they join sexually during the woman's infertile period. When spouses deny themselves and each other the potential for parenthood by resorting to artificial means like contraception and sterilization, they reject their obligation toward the order of existence, in which human society itself has a crucial interest. They also reject a natural perfection to which their state entitles them. Their injustice against both the natural and the personal order changes the character of the spousal relationship objectively and immediately, robbing it of its interpersonal character and so reducing each spouse to the level of an object, intentions to the contrary notwithstanding.[82] For a sexual union that transgresses the objective demands of love, which are rooted in the natural order, is not a true, *personal* union. It therefore falls short of fulfilling the personalistic norm.[83]

Periodic abstinence from sexual intercourse during the woman's fertile period is the only just way for spouses to avoid the possibility of procreation and parenthood when, for serious reasons, that is necessary. While recourse to infertile periods for sexual intercourse and to abstinence during fertile

81. See ibid., 51–55.

82. Any children that the couple might unintentionally conceive under these circumstances will also have been reduced to the level of an object, for the manner in which they came into existence was shorn of its properly interpersonal context.

83. See *LR*, 224–31, 234–36.

periods is a cooperative spousal effort to adapt to the laws of nature and so to protect the integrity of the sexual union, even here the couple's actions must be exercised virtuously rather than as a way of concealing immaturity or selfishness, to the detriment of love. By satisfying the objective requirements of both the natural and the personal order in their marital life, a man and a woman fulfill justice not only toward each other but also toward God, in whom those orders have their origin.[84]

Given the time and place in which it appeared, *Love and Responsibility* is a remarkable achievement. Anticipating and addressing the challenges posed by the sexual revolution that was about to break throughout the Western world, the book was certainly prophetic (and still is). In treating the topic of human sexual love within marriage so forthrightly and putting it in such a positive light, the book was also rather groundbreaking. It even covered certain physiological and medical aspects of the topic—that is, sexology.[85] This was all rather surprising, coming as it did from the pen of a bishop. Nevertheless, *Love and Responsibility* sets forth a philosophical vision of the human person and of human love that is essentially Christian. As such, it is accessible to all men and women of good will in virtue of its inherent intelligibility and universality.

The Second Vatican Council Archbishop Baziak died in mid-June 1962. One month later, the Metropolitan Chapter, composed of senior priests, elected Bishop Wojtyła, the youngest of Kraków's auxiliary bishops, to act as temporary administrator, or vicar capitular, of the archdiocese until a successor to the deceased archbishop was appointed and installed. Three months after that, Wojtyła was in Rome for the opening of the Second Vatican Council, which Pope John XXIII had announced in January 1959.[86]

Wojtyła's initial influence on the council's proceedings arrived sometime ahead of him. For when the Ante-Preparatory Commission had written to the world's Catholic bishops (among others) in June 1959 to invite their

84. See ibid., 240–49.

85. In the English edition, the supplementary final chapter, whose content appeared in the notes of the first Polish edition, is entitled "Sexology and Ethics." It offers a survey of findings from the field of clinical sexology. The author makes it clear that such findings can, at best, only support objective ethical judgments about the love between persons, but they cannot supply them. For the various branches of sexology have no metaphysical basis for understanding the deepest reality either of man and woman as persons or, consequently, of love as a mutual relationship between them. Sexology is therefore subordinate to the personalistic norm.

86. See Weigel, *Witness to Hope*, 152–53.

suggestions for the council's agenda, the then thirty-nine-year-old bishop responded with an essay proposing that the world would like to hear what the Church has to say about the human person, the human condition, human freedom, human dignity, and human destiny in the face of all the modern "humanisms" that degrade and dehumanize persons, leading them to the brink of despair despite promises of "fulfillment," or "self-realization." The effective proclamation of a distinctively Christian humanism would require the Church's clergy and laity to be better informed so that they could better fulfill the witness to which their respective states in life call them in today's world.[87] Since the council, as envisioned by Pope John XXIII, sought to speak universally by engaging the world in dialogue, it would ultimately heed Wojtyła's recommendations, while he, in turn, would be so energized by the council that it would indelibly mark his apostolic activity for the rest of his life.

The council met each fall from 1962 to 1965 for a total of four sessions.[88] Karol Wojtyła attended them all, making oral and written interventions each time.[89] In September 1964, he returned to Rome for the third session of the council as archbishop of Kraków, having been appointed such by Pope Paul VI, who succeeded John XXIII in June 1963. The archbishop's interventions on the subject of religious freedom were particularly forceful, eloquent, and influential. Religious freedom must not be considered apart from the Church's understanding of the human person. Human freedom exists for the sake of truth, according to which every person must live in order truly to be free. That includes religious truth, concerning which state authorities have no competence. Therefore, any state that presumes to authorize or to proscribe religious institutions, or to judge that religion is inimical to human fulfillment, has overstepped its legitimate bounds. The very existence and activity of the Church depend on the principle that no one be denied the intrinsic human right to exercise his or her religion. From this it follows that Catholic parents have a right to teach Christian truth to their children. What

87. See ibid., 158–60.

88. Throughout the council, the Polish secret police tried to advance the communist cause by exploiting ideological tensions in the Church and even by discrediting Cardinal Wyszyński, utilizing clerical recruits and other well-placed collaborators and agents to achieve their purpose. See Weigel, *The End and the Beginning*, 65–68.

89. As Pope John Paul II, Wojtyła would later say that he regarded his attendance at all the council sessions as "a *special gift from God*," since the communist authorities in Poland might just as easily have kept him from leaving the country. See John Paul II, *Crossing the Threshold*, 157–58.

is more, since every person has an intrinsic right to the truth, the Church has a right to hand it on.[90]

At the beginning of the council's fourth session in September 1965, the matter of religious freedom, which had not yet been settled, was taken up again. Archbishop Wojtyła made it clear that religious freedom does not mean religious relativism. Human freedom has a moral obligation to seek (and to abide by) the truth, especially religious truth, for only in relation to objective truth can it be exercised responsibly. And in a written intervention, the archbishop urged that the council's *Declaration on Religious Freedom,* or *Dignitatis Humanae,* affirm that the right to religious freedom not only is consonant with sound reason but also is confirmed by divine revelation, grounded as it is in what God has revealed to us about human persons and their relation to him.[91]

From the third through the fourth sessions of the council, Wojtyła championed the cause of *Schema XIII,* contributing appreciably to the final form it would take under the title *Pastoral Constitution on the Church in the Modern World,* or *Gaudium et Spes.* The Church has something to say to the plurality of worlds that make up the modern world, he told the Council Fathers, and she could neither disappoint those who were expecting her to speak nor let go unchallenged those who denied that she had anything at all to say to modernity. However, she should not speak as one soliloquizing but as one dialoguing with the world in which she herself is journeying, so that together they can search for just solutions to exceedingly difficult human problems. By presenting her proposal through lucid argumentation, the Church could help guide the world to the truth.[92]

In early 1965, Wojtyła worked in a subgroup of notable Catholic thinkers assigned to the subcommission that produced the final draft of *Gaudium et Spes.*[93] Soon after the fourth session of the council convened in September, the debates on the newly revised document began. The draft's principal concern, Wojtyła explained, is the human person, considered in himself, in community, and in the context of the conditions most affecting human life. In her dialogue with the world, the Church examines all this from a single point of reference, namely, redemption in Christ. By doing so, she is telling

90. See Weigel, *Witness to Hope,* 164.

91. See ibid., 164–66.

92. See ibid., 166–67.

93. The subgroup included Yves Congar, Henri de Lubac, Jean Daniélou, and Archbishop Gabriel-Marie Garrone. Stefan Swieżawski was one of the *periti* on the subcommission. See ibid., 167.

the world the story of its beginning, its history, and its hidden aspirations. If the world would be converted by taking its story to heart, then the Church will have rendered her greatest possible service to the world.

The archbishop also spoke of the Church's pastoral duty to address atheism and the deep, inner loneliness that results from atheistic unbelief. In her dialogue with atheism, the Church should begin with our interior experience of liberty, showing that closeness to God does not infringe on human freedom but rather releases it by revealing the deepest truth about ourselves and the world. For that reason, Christian faith is not alienating but fully liberating. And that is the very essence of what the Church has to say to the modern world.[94]

The final version of *Gaudium et Spes* contains two complementary passages that seem to express what lies at the foundation of Karol Wojtyła/Pope John Paul II's life and thought. He would quote or refer to them frequently. The first, from paragraph 22, tells us that our own mystery as human beings is revealed to us most fully only in the mystery of Jesus Christ, the Son of God, who, by his Incarnation, has united himself in some way with every human being. The second, from paragraph 24, tells us that while man is the only earthly creature that God has willed as an end in itself, he can nevertheless not find himself fully except by making a sincere gift of himself. Through the mystery of his own life, Christ has confirmed the truth that self-giving is inscribed as a law in human existence, reflecting the inner life of God himself. That we can live it out effectively by the power of God's grace in Christ is the liberating message of *Gaudium et Spes* that Karol Wojtyła/John Paul II would never tire of sharing with the world.[95]

A Fruit of the Council: *Person and Act* Inspired by the personalism underlying the council's effort to address the crisis of humanism in the modern world, Karol Wojtyła began drafting, during the council itself, the work in which he would present his most comprehensive philosophical treatment of the human person. He entitled it *Osoba i czyn*, or *Person and Act*.[96]

94. See ibid., 167–69.

95. See ibid., 169, 846.

96. For Weigel's treatment of the work, see ibid., 172–78. In a note from the first English edition of *Osoba i czyn*, entitled *The Acting Person* (trans. Andrzej Potocki, revised by Anna-Teresa Tymieniecka [Boston: D. Reidel Publishing, 1979], 302n9), Wojtyła acknowledges his debt to the council in general and to *Gaudium et Spes* in particular with respect to his reflections on the human person. Indeed, he quotes a passage from *Gaudium et Spes*, 76, which states that the Church "is at once a sign and a safeguard of the transcendence of the human person." Kupczak observes that all Polish editions of *Osoba i czyn* begin with that quotation (as an epigraph for the book as a whole, signifying the lofty status and calling of the person). See *Liberty*, 90–91.

Considered in itself, *Person and Act* is Wojtyła's most sustained effort to anchor modernity's understanding of the person as pure subjectivity, or self-consciousness, in the Aristotelian-Thomistic understanding of the person as an objective being.[97] By beginning with a phenomenological analysis of human experience, he unfolds the interior basis of the classical metaphysical affirmations about the person's ontological structure and its operations, arriving thereby at a more complete picture of the human being as a dynamic spiritual-corporeal unity. As spirit, the human being is a transcendent subject having the capacity for acts of consciousness, knowledge, and will. As body, the human being is in contact with, and firmly rooted in, the material world—objective reality. Based on this unique, concrete-yet-transcendent structure, the subject can sensibly apprehend every concrete being that presents itself to him and transpose it into the immaterial mode of apprehension that is properly his, simultaneously (if only implicitly) becoming aware of himself as the one who stands "beneath" this operation as its cause. In that way, he can grasp the objective reality of each being, its interrelations with other objects and with himself, and its real meaning and value—its true goodness.

In turn, his objective knowledge of reality and of value allows the subject to decide on a course of action and to experience himself, in consciousness, as the actor who freely brings that action about so as to achieve a certain end. Because he performs deliberate human actions in the world, he is morally responsible for what he does. The human being is therefore a bodily *person*, a corporeal "someone" who subjectively experiences himself as such in the performance of concrete moral actions, since these require him to engage his inner freedom through the medium of his own body in conformity with the subjectively apprehended, objective truth of things. By showing the integral unity of the subjective and the objective dimensions of the human person, Wojtyła hoped to provide a corrective, on the one hand, for Aristotelian-Thomistic philosophy's lack of explicit attention to the subjective, experiential aspect of human existence and, on the other hand, for the views of Scheler and other moderns whose insights into human experience are significant but deficient because of their partial or complete failure to ground the person and his relations with the world in the objective order of being.[98]

Considered also as a fruit of the Second Vatican Council, *Person and Act*

97. See Buttiglione, *Karol Wojtyła*, 178–87.

98. On the original and creative character of Wojtyła's appropriation of both Thomism and phenomenology, see Kupczak, *Liberty*, 56–57, 65–66, 71–76. See also *The Acting Person*, 301nn4–5, 303–4n16, 304–5n19, 305–6n23, 309n41, 315n71.

seeks to show the theoretical basis for and to develop the council's effort "to make faith an experience of life, to bring about its subjective appropriation, thereby creating a Christian mentality and a Christianity which is not abstractly apprehended but existentially lived."[99] Toward that end, the book explores philosophically the council's teaching on the relation of freedom to truth and reflects its emphasis on the value-laden meaning of human actions. The relation of freedom to truth manifests itself inwardly in human conscience and outwardly (with certain qualifications) in human actions: inwardly, insofar as we experience a moral obligation to engage our freedom in *this* way rather than that, and outwardly, insofar as our free actions and their consequences reflect our decision either to accept or to reject the objective moral good that the experience of truth in conscience has made known. Because of this link between the inner and the outer dimensions of the human act, the end of a freely executed action is not just something extrinsic to the person: it is also the innermost core of the person, since *I* am the one who decides either to harmonize my freedom with the objective demands of truth in action or to ignore what truth requires of me and thus violate the good of my own rational nature by doing something that I know to be objectively bad. In other words, human acts are both teleological and autoteleological. In deciding on and doing what I want, I decide on and form myself into *who* I want *to be*: either a good person or a bad one.

As for what happens beyond us, either our actions will help realize the universal justice, freedom, peace, and prosperity for which the human heart naturally longs or they will lead to the very opposite, depending on whether they are properly ordered toward true goods. For we act in a world of persons who are inevitably affected by our actions, for good or for ill, even when we do not intend other persons as the direct "objects" of our actions. Consequently, the actions of each and of all together must be informed by the deliberate intention to realize a true common good, one appropriate to each community of being and acting. Such actions always accord as well with the authentic good of the individual person, who therefore realizes himself in performing them. When human beings are of one mind concerning a true common good and are habitually ready to collaborate so as to achieve it, they exhibit what Wojtyła calls the attitude of solidarity.

Solidarity, as Karol Wojtyła/Pope John Paul II understood and advocated it, would prove to be a world-changing force just two decades after *Person*

99. Buttiglione, *Karol Wojtyła*, 186–87.

*and Act* was first published in 1969. For by his use of that term, he was challenging and correcting the false communist claim that a person fulfills himself by acting for ends that the state determines and imposes on him, without reference to his own conscience and freedom. According to the anthropology laid out in *Person and Act,* a person cannot fulfill himself *as* a person when thus forced to act—not even where the end of the acting is objectively good in itself. Rather, he fulfills himself personally when acting in concert with others only if he is free to fulfill, and does fulfill, the moral obligation to discern for himself, in conscience, that the good already chosen by others as the end of the community is a *true* good that he is right in making his own. That way, in acting to help achieve it, he acts freely, even—and especially—when he is morally bound to do so. True solidarity thus manifests the inherent dignity of the person, and it can arise as a constructive, collaborative response against attacks on that dignity.

In writing about solidarity, the author of *Person and Act* was not simply expressing an idea. To a greater extent, he was describing philosophically the essential features of a dynamic that he saw good people live out in many ways under two brutal regimes, and that he lived out together with them under the same circumstances. He was describing the challenging but sure solution to the problems, addressed by the council, besetting the human person in the world of persons.

### Prelude to the Papacy

On becoming a bishop, Karol Wojtyła began building solidarity among his people in a number of ways, especially in the public acts by which he defended their religious freedom. Perhaps the most high-profile and symbolic battle in that arena was his unrelenting insistence that the government grant permission for the construction of a church in the churchless town of Nowa Huta outside Kraków. Beginning on December 24, 1959, he initiated an annual tradition of celebrating Christmas midnight Mass in an open field located there. Yielding finally in October 1967 to this and his other persistent efforts, the government gave Wojtyła, by then a cardinal, permission to build the now famous "Ark Church" in the communist-built, symbolically atheistic "model workers' town." During the dedication Mass in May 1977, the cardinal proclaimed that the people of Nowa Huta are the children of God and that the new church was a necessary expression of that fact.[100]

100. See John Paul II, *Rise,* 79–83; Weigel, *Witness to Hope,* 151, 190–91.

Wojtyła was equally intent on asserting the Church's right to express itself publicly. After persistent protests from the archdiocese, the government gave permission for the annual Corpus Christi procession to go modestly beyond the boundaries of Wawel Cathedral before having to return. Preaching before tens of thousands of Krakovians on these occasions during the 1970s, the charismatic cardinal affirmed the people's right to worship God in the city and the nation of which they were citizens. They had a place in society precisely as Catholics, he told them, and they were wholly justified in reclaiming their cultural heritage from a regime that claimed to represent them while trying to deny them the deepest truth about themselves.[101]

In defending the people's right to religious freedom, Karol Wojtyła was assuming, in historic continuity with the ancient tradition of Kraków's episcopate, the role of *defensor populi,* defender of the people.[102] Wojtyła took that role most seriously, for he understood that the dignity of the human person is such that God himself, in the Person of the eternal Son, took on human nature to redeem mankind. Human dignity, even more exalted on that account, is therefore at the heart of the Gospel message, and to uphold one is to uphold the other. Consequently, as *defensor populi,* Karol Wojtyła was also *defensor fidei,* defender of the faith. And in virtue of both he was, by definition, a builder of solidarity, uniting his people with one another by *re*uniting them with their religious and cultural heritage. Because of the inherent convergence of these roles, they all factored somehow into everything he did.

It was not just the people close to home who esteemed Karol Wojtyła for his tireless and innovative episcopal activities, his intellectual and cultural refinement, his unassailable integrity, holiness, and humility, and his charismatic personality. During the Second Vatican Council, his incisive contributions and his admirable personal qualities did not go unnoticed by other participants. Paul VI had also been impressed. As a cardinal (since June 1967), moreover, Wojtyła traveled widely abroad, preaching, lecturing, learning, and invariably increasing the circle of his admirers just by being himself.[103] He also traveled frequently to Rome for meetings as a member of the

101. See Weigel, *Witness to Hope,* 191–93. It was precisely because of bold public proclamations such as this that Polish prosecutors seem to have considered arresting Wojtyła for sedition on three occasions in 1973–74, according to Polish secret police reports. See Weigel, *The End and the Beginning,* 88.

102. See Weigel, *Witness to Hope,* 189.

103. Among other things, the cardinal spent six weeks in the United States in 1976. He lectured at Harvard on July 27, after which the university magazine carried his photograph on the cover with the caption, "A probable successor to Paul VI." Maliński, *Pope John Paul II,* 256–57. Two

international Synod of Bishops and of three congregations of the Roman Curia. In those capacities, Wojtyła gained experience in international Catholic affairs. As an unmistakable public sign of his favor toward the Polish cardinal, Paul VI invited him, in February 1976, to give the annual Lenten retreat to the Roman Curia, with Paul himself in attendance.[104] Thus, by the time of Paul's death on August 6, 1978, Karol Wojtyła was very well known and very well respected among his fellow Church leaders.[105]

## Poland's Gift to the World: Pope John Paul II, 1978–2005

On August 26, Cardinal Albino Luciani of Venice was elected to succeed Pope Paul VI. Taking the name John Paul I, the new pope, with his amiable personality, sincere humility, and winning smile, seemed to be just what the Church needed in the contentious atmosphere of the post–Vatican II period. But he died of a massive heart attack just thirty-three days later, on the night of September 28. Earlier that day in Kraków, Cardinal Wojtyła had celebrated the twentieth anniversary of his episcopal consecration. On learning the following morning about the death of John Paul I, he seemed shaken but said that one must accept life's surprises with deep faith.[106]

Ever since Karol Wojtyła was a young priest, his friends would joke about his becoming pope someday. As the years passed, their thoughts and pronouncements on the matter took a more serious turn, even to the point of solemn conviction.[107] Some had a strong sense that he would now be elected. Wojtyła seems to have been one of them. His countryman Cardinal Wyszyński became convinced more gradually as events unfolded. But in the end, he ad-

---

days later, he lectured at the Catholic University of America, leaving Jude Dougherty, then dean of the School of Philosophy and the cardinal's host, convinced that he was in the presence of "a great man." He was so convinced, in fact, that two years later on the morning of October 16 (the day the conclave elected the successor of Pope John Paul I) he told his children, "Our Polish friend Wojtyła will be elected pope." Catherine Lee, "Papal Anniversary: CUA Celebrates Special Bond with John Paul II," *Inside CUA Online* (April 6, 2004).

104. The Lenten series of talks was published the same year in book form, eventually appearing in English as *Sign of Contradiction* in 1979.

105. See Weigel, *Witness to Hope*, 219–26. Weigel relates the following intriguing detail: "At the moment of his death, the inexpensive alarm clock young Father Montini [later Paul VI] had brought back from Poland in 1923 and had used ever since rang spontaneously." Ibid., 242. Also intriguing is that John Paul II would see special significance in the fact that his immediate predecessor, John Paul I, was elected on the feast of Our Lady of Częstochowa, Poland's special patroness. See ibid., 269–70.

106. See ibid., 246–48.

107. E.g., see ibid., 236–37; Maliński, *Pope John Paul II*, 262–63.

vised the younger prelate ahead of time to "accept it."[108] He did, knowing that Poland's primate was urging him to accept not just his imminent election to the papacy, but, above all, the will of God expressed therein.

Karol Józef Wojtyła became the 264th bishop of Rome—the 263rd successor of St. Peter, and the visible head of the universal Church—on October 16, 1978. He was the first non-Italian pope in 455 years and the first Polish pope ever. Heeding Cardinal Wyszyński's earlier advice, and out of affection for his immediate two predecessors, Wojtyła took the name John Paul II.[109] Time would seem to confirm that he fulfilled the expectation expressed over a century earlier by his compatriot, dramatist/poet Juliusz Słowacki, that "a Slav will be Pope, a brother of the peoples."[110] John Paul II would refer to himself as the "Slav Pope" for the first time during his first papal pilgrimage to Poland, just eight months after his election.[111]

During his solemn inauguration Mass on October 22, Pope John Paul II exhorted his listeners to do exactly as he had done in consenting to be their servant: "Be not afraid." For in welcoming Christ and accepting his power, every human being finds the fulfillment to which the intellect, heart, and will aspire, and which expresses itself readily in service to the person and to all humanity. In that way, every social, cultural, economic, and political institution will likewise become informed by Christ's power. John Paul sought the prayers not only of Catholics but of all Christians and peoples, for he was there to serve all. After the Mass, he moved forward to welcome and bless a group of handicapped people in wheelchairs.[112] In that way, and by the very fact that it was he who had asked that front-row space be reserved for them,[113] John Paul expressed from the outset of his pontificate his special

108. Weigel, *Witness to Hope,* 254.

109. See Stanislaw Dziwisz and Gian Franco Svidercoschi, *A Life with Karol: My Forty-Year Friendship with the Man Who Became Pope,* trans. Adrian J. Walker (New York: Doubleday, 2008), 61; Weigel, *Witness to Hope,* 254.

110. As quoted by Dziwisz in *A life with Karol,* 62. Maliński quotes the following lines from the poem: "He has made ready the throne for a Slav Pope/ He will sweep out the churches and make them clean within/ God shall be revealed, clear as day, in the creative world." Maliński then recalls that Irena Szkocka (d. 1971), whom he and Wojtyła regarded as almost a grandmother, had written opposite those lines in her copy of the poem, "This Pope will be Karol." *Pope John Paul II,* 116.

111. John Paul related the following humorous tale to his friend, French author André Frossard: "The Pope was praying, and he asked God: 'Lord, will Poland regain her freedom and independence some day?' 'Yes,' said God, 'but not in your lifetime.' Then the Pope asked: 'Lord, after I'm gone, will there be another Polish pope?' 'Not in my lifetime,' said God." Frossard, *Portrait of John Paul II,* trans. Mary Emily Hamilton (San Francisco: Ignatius Press, 1990), 46.

112. See Weigel, *Witness to Hope,* 262–63.

113. See Dziwisz and Svidercoschi, *A Life with Karol,* 249.

sensitivity toward, and solidarity with, those whose lives bear the sign of the cross in a particularly acute way.

As shepherd of the universal Church, Pope John Paul II would lead the Church according to the true spirit of the Second Vatican Council's teachings and thus prepare her for her mission in the new millennium. He would typically develop the personalistic content of the council's documents in his writings and addresses, and he would also witness to it by his own pastoral example, making it unequivocally clear that proclaiming, defending, and fostering the authentic dignity and rights of the human person is absolutely central to the Church's mission. It follows that the Church is committed to entering solidarity with any and all human beings whose intrinsic dignity in Christ is somehow being threatened or violated. She is equally committed, moreover, to identifying and denouncing injustices, as well as the immorality that leads to them, working peacefully, but also persistently and courageously, to secure for all people the rights and the dignity that are theirs. If the Church is to accomplish that mission, then she must also tend to the sanctification and the evangelical education of her own members, who must understand and live out their Christian dignity. In what follows, we can do no more than to indicate some of the ways in which John Paul II sought to lead the Church toward fulfilling these aspects of her mission.

## Human Dignity in Christ

Whatever form they took, the prolific activities of Pope John Paul II were invariably directed toward helping others to recognize and to realize, as fully as possible, the astonishing greatness of their dignity and vocation as human persons redeemed in Christ. That, after all, is the mission of the Church. Just five months after becoming pope, he promulgated his first encyclical, *Redemptor Hominis (The Redeemer of Man),* evidently eager to develop and disseminate the basic themes of the Christian humanism that would be the hallmark of his pontificate.[114] We discover the inexhaustible love of God the Father for us, as well as our own transcendent dignity, in the Person of Jesus Christ, the eternal Son of God whom the Father sent into the world as man to redeem us. Because the Son took on human nature in the Incarnation and opened the way to the Father for us through his Paschal Mystery, every human being has been raised to a new dignity and is included within the scope of Christ's redemptive act. The Church continues Christ's mission by bring-

114. John Paul introduced many of those same themes in *Sign of Contradiction.*

ing each person closer to him. She does that, above all, by safeguarding human transcendence through her proclamation of the truth that sets freedom free—that is, the truth of God's unfathomable love for us in Christ. That truth reveals the greatness of the person and gives meaning to the whole of human existence—an existence that is transformed in Christ by the grace of the Holy Spirit and called to share definitively in Christ's resurrection in the everlasting life to come.[115]

## Marriage and the Family

Every attack on human dignity is characterized by the dehumanizing "use" of the person as a means to selfish or other unacceptable ends; however, some such attacks are more subtle than others, and many people view them, rather, as furthering the cause of authentic human liberation. The use of contraception to separate the unitive and the procreative dimensions of the conjugal act represents one of the subtler ways in which human dignity is under attack, while the attempt to rationalize the behavior takes the form of a false humanism resulting from a defective anthropology or, ironically, from the absence of any real anthropology at all. In one of the most significant legacies of a pontificate abounding in significant achievements, John Paul would apply his Christian humanism to the topic of human sexuality in a thoroughly biblical and theological way.

### The "Theology of the Body"

Over the period extending from September 5, 1979, through November 28, 1984, Pope John Paul II devoted roughly two-thirds of his Wednesday general audiences to an elaborate series of discourses on Christian anthropology that would become known collectively as his "theology of the body."[116] In those discourses, 129 in all, John Paul explained that a man and a woman

115. When he first accepted his election to the papacy, John Paul reaffirmed his trust in the Mother of God and expressed it symbolically by keeping the coat of arms he had chosen at the beginning of his episcopal ministry twenty years earlier: *Totus Tuus*. In this we find the special source of his boundless regard for human dignity and of his lifelong commitment to proclaiming, promoting, and defending it. "Mary ... wishes to act upon all those who entrust themselves to her as her children. And it is well known that the more her children persevere and progress in this attitude, the nearer Mary leads them to the 'unsearchable riches of Christ' (Eph. 3:8). And to the same degree they recognize more and more clearly the dignity of man in all its fullness and the definitive meaning of his vocation, for 'Christ ... fully reveals man to man himself.'" John Paul II, *Redemptoris Mater* (March 25, 1987), 46, Vatican translation (Boston: Daughters of St. Paul, 1987). In English, the encyclical's title is *Mother of the Redeemer*.

116. For Weigel's treatment of the topic, see *Witness to Hope*, 333–43.

express themselves as persons through the body, and they do so most fully by reciprocally making a gift of themselves to each other so as to form a genuine communion of persons. While the law of self-giving is inscribed in, and must be appropriately expressed by, every human person *as* a person, it is expressed most intensely and intimately in the sexual union of a man and a woman in marriage, by which the spouses give their whole self, including their fertility, to each other. In thus becoming "one flesh," they open themselves completely both to each other and to the possibility—to the gift—of procreation. Through their interpersonal, bodily union and its procreative fruitfulness, they reflect analogously, on the level of the visible world, the inner life of the Holy Trinity—three divine Persons united substantially as one God in an eternal communion of infinite life and love.

In fine detail, John Paul II's discourses on the body examined the marital relation from the personalistic perspective in the light of the biblical understanding of creation, sin, and redemption. Once he had developed those aspects of his rich, Christian anthropology, the last cycle of discourses allowed him to show in a more persuasive way than the Church had done previously how fidelity to Paul VI's authoritative teaching in *Humanae Vitae* (July 1968) on the natural inseparability of the unitive and the procreative dimensions of the conjugal act, and on the natural regulation of conception, is the only way for spouses to uphold crucial personalistic values. The theological and anthropological import of John Paul's theology of the body as a whole is enormous and extensive. But it will undoubtedly always be ranked, above all, as one of his greatest contributions to, and as one of his greatest expressions of love and concern for, the good of marriage and the family.

### *Familiaris Consortio, Letter to Families,* and *Evangelium Vitae*

That having been said, some of John Paul II's other efforts to strengthen, to defend, and to elucidate the true meaning of marriage and the family are nothing short of extraordinary. For example, to complete the 1980 Synod of Bishops on "The Role of the Christian Family in the Modern World," he issued the apostolic exhortation *Familiaris Consortio (The Community of the Family)* in November 1981, a Gospel-based proclamation of God's plan for marriage and the family that he addressed not only to the Church but to all people. Aware of the circumstances, the concerns, the questions, and the hopes of people today relative to that sphere of human existence, the Church speaks the truth to human freedom with the hope of protecting the dignity of every man and woman, especially as freedom and objective judgment are being threatened by widely disseminated and appealing, but ultimately destructive, ideas about marriage and the family, and about how to solve the kinds of problems that arise therein. The family's mission is to become ever more what the family essentially is: a community of life and love that flourishes by adhering to the law of self-giving. In that way, the family guards, reveals, and communicates love in accordance with God's plan, reflecting and sharing in Christ's love for his Church and God's love for all humanity.[117] The Church and society depend on and so must foster the well-being of the family, which contributes indispensably to their own structure and renewal.

Seizing on the United Nations initiative to observe 1994 as the Year of the Family, John Paul announced that the Church would take part, in her own way, in that initiative. So, on February 2 of that year, he issued his *Letter to Families* as a means of knocking at the door of every family "to greet you with deep affection and to spend time with you."[118] Here, he would not be speaking about the family in the abstract, as in *Familiaris Consortio,* but would personally accompany every family throughout the world in its struggles, while inviting Christ to abide with the whole family of nations in and through each individual family.[119] As a communion of persons reflecting God's love, the family is fundamental to, and reciprocally depends on, a true civilization (or culture) of love, whose source is the love of God.[120] Conversely, broken families foster, and are fostered by, an anti-civilization of selfishness, of freedom without responsibilities. That is what happens when modern cultural agendas, reflecting the loss or the rejection of the truth about the human person, play on human weakness in the sphere of human sexuality, giving rise to the utilitarian assertion of freedom over and against others.[121] At that point, people are willing to kill love by killing the *fruit* of love conceived in the womb,[122] having forgotten that each person's genealogy is linked with the eternity of God, who, before we are even conceived, wills eternally that we should each come to exist in his image and come to share eternal life with him.[123] Only when parents and children fulfill the reciprocal duties implied by the fourth commandment does the family become a fully humanizing reality and a counter-witness to the civilization of death.[124] The

117. E.g., see *Familiaris Consortio,* (November 22, 1981), 17, 43. Vatican website.
118. *Letter to Families from Pope John Paul II* (February 2, 1994), 1. Vatican website.
119. See ibid., 4.
120. See ibid., 6–8.
121. See ibid., 13–14.
122. See ibid., 21.
123. See ibid., 9.
124. See ibid., 15.

true community of persons in the family leads to the kingdom of heaven; it is a preparation for the communion of saints.[125]

In response to a request by the College of Cardinals that he reaffirm authoritatively the value and the inviolability of human life in view of contemporary threats against it, John Paul II issued *Evangelium Vitae (The Gospel of Life)* on March 25, 1995—the Feast of the Annunciation. The encyclical, which deals with attacks on human life mainly in its earliest and its final stages, included input from John Paul's brother bishops throughout the world. With their cooperation, the Church would fulfill its sense of duty at this crucial time in history to speak out for those who have no voice, and thus to defend those who have no means of self-defense. The attacks on human life (for example, abortion, infanticide, and euthanasia), along with the contraceptive mentality and the trivialization of human sexuality, strike at the very foundation of society and of the whole human family, precisely by striking at the heart of the individual human family, whose complicity with these evils threatens its very existence. For God created the family to be the sanctuary of life—the "place" that affirms the intrinsic dignity of the human person as made in God's image, redeemed by Christ, and called to eternal life. While the document covers a broad range of issues, the consistent attention that it gives both directly and indirectly to parenthood and the family makes it fitting to consider *Evangelium Vitae* together with the discourses on the body, *Familiaris Consortio,* and the *Letter to Families* as one of John Paul II's truly inspired efforts to uphold and protect authentic marital and family life.

## Solidarity and Religious Freedom

Pope John Paul II never tired of trying to alert the world to the threats posed to human dignity when, in the name of "progress" identified with "liberation," human sexuality is treated nonpersonally as a kind of "raw material" for human ingenuity to manipulate, exploit, and dominate without any moral restrictions whatsoever. Early on in his pontificate, John Paul had argued similarly on another front when, in *Redemptor Hominis,* he spoke for the whole Church to all people about the threat that their "progress" poses to them because of the destructive, fearsome potential of certain products of their own creativity—modern weaponry, to name but one. When progress in the industrial, technological, and economic spheres of human activity is not governed by sound moral principles, it becomes dehumanizing instead

125. See ibid., 14.

of leading, as it should, to greater spiritual maturity, to a greater appreciation for true human dignity, to greater responsibility for promoting that dignity, and to greater concern and care for the weakest and neediest human beings.[126]

True progress is truly humanistic; it ensures the primacy of persons over things. When that order is reversed, genuine human progress is impeded or even rendered impossible, for the violation of inalienable human rights will inevitably follow on the social, cultural, economic, and political levels, leading to the violation of national rights as well. Material and technological dominance will then become the means by which some people come to manipulate or to dominate others. Moreover, as they carelessly exploit the natural environment in seeking to *have* more rather than to *be* more, human beings will become subject to the world itself, which God has called them, on the contrary, to dominate intelligently as guardians. As long as such conditions prevail, real peace and human development are out of the question. That is as true for consumer societies as it is for totalitarian ones.[127]

At the root of all this is the lack of human solidarity that results from the abuse of human freedom, which always means, for some, that the legitimate exercise of their conscience and freedom is going to be denied by others. Totalitarian regimes are especially notorious for either partially or wholly depriving religious believers, in particular, of their right to participate freely in public and social life. This attack on the right to religious freedom is also an attack on human dignity itself. Therefore, in virtue of his office and on behalf of all believers, John Paul asks those responsible for organizing public and social life to respect the rights of religion in general and of the Church in particular. That is the fundamental measure of real human progress in any regime, society, or system.[128]

Speaking in Rome in December 1978 on the thirtieth anniversary of the UN's Universal Declaration of Human Rights, John Paul II had urged that everyone everywhere respect the intrinsic human right of each and all to religious freedom.[129] And as he personally addressed the Thirty-Fourth General Assembly of the United Nations in New York City the following year on October 2, 1979, he gave powerful testimony, as he had done in his first encyclical, to the crucial importance to human development and world peace of recognizing universal human rights, including the right to freedom of con-

126. See *RH*, 15.

127. See ibid., 15–16.

128. See ibid., 16–17.

129. See Weigel, *Witness to Hope*, 272.

science, of religion, and of public and private religious expression.[130] Rights like these—rights of the spirit—have priority over material goods and values, though modern civilization is becoming less sensitive to that fact. Yet, it is the human spirit that contributes to and that can properly direct all genuine moral, material, technological, civil, and cultural development.[131] To suppress, threaten, or violate the human need for goods of the spiritual order is "a form of warfare against humanity,"[132] reducing the meaning of human life to the material level and causing divisions that lead inevitably to war. Quoting from *Dignitatis Humanae,* John Paul emphasized that respect for the dignity of the human person requires, above all, that human beings be free to seek and to adhere to the truth—especially religious truth—and that they likewise be free to express that truth to, and together with, others.[133]

### June 1979: The First Trip Home

Pope John Paul II had literally brought that message "home" even more forcefully, passionately, and effectively during his nine-day pilgrimage to his homeland the previous June. In doing so, he helped his people recover their history in an unprecedented way. He affirmed the right of the Polish people to participate in the cultural and civil life and formation of their nation. He affirmed their right to autonomy as a nation. He affirmed the right of each person to pursue the truth according to the light of conscience. And he affirmed the Church's right to carry out her evangelical, moral, and charitable missions freely in their nation. These were not separate issues, for Poland's birth, culture, and history were inextricably intertwined with the Catholic faith, and so, too, would be the nation's *rebirth* culturally and historically. John Paul told the people that Poland's spiritual unity, which is reflected in the unity of its episcopate and embodied in the primate, would be the key to that rebirth. It would also serve the cause of Europe's spiritual rebirth, and hence its unity, from east to west. In effect, he was saying not only that the Yalta division of Europe was unacceptable but that its days were numbered.

John Paul declared that to deny Christ his place in human history is to act against the human person, whom Christ has redeemed.[134] The history

130. See *Address of His Holiness John Paul II to the 34th General Assembly of the United Nations* (October 2, 1979), 13. Vatican website.

131. See ibid., 14–15.

132. See ibid., 16.

133. See ibid., 19–20. See also Weigel, *Witness to Hope,* 346–50, and *Message of John Paul II on the Value and Content of Freedom of Conscience and of Religion* (September 1, 1980). Vatican website.

134. "When Christ is denied all rights of citizenship, those same rights are denied to men;

of Catholic Poland and especially of its people, past and present, would not even make sense apart from Christ. That is why attempts to expunge Christ from Polish history have damaged the nation.[135] On another occasion, John Paul, quoting Mickiewicz, declared to the young people of Gniezno that "a civilization truly worthy of man must be a Christian civilization."[136] He also reminded workers that only God, not the products of their labor, can satisfy the human heart, and that Christ will never approve of the view that human beings are nothing more than a means of production or that they are to be valued only as such. On the final day of his pilgrimage, he offered Mass before two to three million people, reiterating the theme of human dignity and destiny in God. He also exhorted the people to be strong in faith, hope and love, so as to overcome all fear. He begged them not to be defeated or discouraged, but rather to trust, and to seek from God the same spiritual power that had sustained the generations of Poles that had gone before them. And he urged them never to lose their spiritual freedom and to exercise it in charity, which is proved through the cross—that is, through sacrifice.[137]

By the end of John Paul's pilgrimage, over one-third of Poland's population—about thirteen million Poles—had seen him in person, while television and radio brought him to virtually all the rest. Suddenly, the people knew they were not alone. John Paul had affirmed for them the things they believed, and he had said for them the things they wanted to say. He rerooted them in their history and their culture, restoring to them both their individual and their collective sense of identity. His words, his presence as an eminent son of Poland, and the opportunity he provided to the Polish people for a massive experience of freedom and solidarity reminded them of their extraordinary personal dignity, while also lifting the cloud of fear that had darkened their existence for so many years. Millions of people began to sense that the key to overcoming the forces that dominated their country and their daily existence lay in their overcoming their own moral and spiritual inertia. That would free them to work together toward a common goal, name-

and when the 'death of God' is proclaimed, the 'death of man' is being planned as well." *SgC*, 133.

135. John Paul was appealing to the vision of man that permeates Polish consciousness. According to Rocco Buttiglione, that vision consists in the "cultural and existential attitude that Christ is the keystone for the understanding of man and of his history." Buttiglione, *Karol Wojtyła*, 6.

136. From *The Books of the Polish Nation and Pilgrimage*. See *Address of His Holiness John Paul II to the Young People of Gniezno* (June 3, 1979). Vatican website.

137. See Weigel, *Witness to Hope*, 291–95, 304–20.

ly, that of reclaiming what is rightfully theirs. True, it would require them to make sacrifices. But was that not precisely what it meant to be a Pole? And so the fear began to dissipate. John Paul showed them the way out of a situation that till then had seemed hopeless. All they had to do was to be their authentic selves.[138]

### The Birth of Solidarity

The first of John Paul II's papal pilgrimages to Poland ended on June 10, 1979. In July of the following year, strikes began to spread spontaneously throughout Poland as workers protested massive food price increases imposed by the Polish leadership. At first, striking workers confined their demands to higher wages and a rolling back of the price increases, but soon they began to include political kinds of demands such as government recognition of the right of workers to strike, legal immunity for striking workers, and direct talks with the government. In effect, the workers were beginning to demand the right to participate in the affairs of their own country. They were reclaiming the right of citizenship that was theirs.

On August 14 in the Baltic port city of Gdańsk, where massive demonstrations against steep food price increases in 1970 had led to the massacre of dozens of Polish workers by Polish security forces, seventeen thousand striking workers at the Lenin Shipyard were protesting the politically motivated firing of a veteran crane operator/free trade union activist. An unemployed electrician and free labor union activist named Lech Wałęsa joined them and became their leader. As the workers remained locked behind the shipyard gates, their strike committee formulated a series of demands, including the right of workers to form an independent, self-governing trade union, the right to free speech and a free press, and the right to erect a memorial to the shipyard workers massacred in 1970. To keep matters from getting out of hand, the authorities allowed the workers to receive pastoral care. A priest celebrated an open-air Mass each day at the shipyard and heard confessions. Pictures of John Paul II and of Our Lady adorned the shipyard gates.

In the days that followed, a group of intellectuals arrived in Gdańsk at the request of the strikers to serve as their advisors. What is more, Pope John Paul II and the Polish episcopate aligned themselves publicly with the strikers' cause. With that, the striking workers stood their ground, and the government delegation with which they had been negotiating capitulated. Hold-

138. See ibid., 320–23.

ing a huge souvenir pen commemorating the papal pilgrimage to Poland the previous year, Lech Wałęsa signed an accord on August 31 in which Poland's communist government officially recognized the legality of autonomous, independent trade unions.

Both before and after the signing of the Gdańsk accord, workers representing other industries in Poland expressed their solidarity with the Lenin Shipyard workers, and so the movement quickly became a national phenomenon having enormous social and political significance. It officially adopted the name Solidarność, or Solidarity. However, it was not immediately clear that this new beginning would not soon come to an end. For example, when Wałęsa tried to register the union legally, the court went into a stalling mode. As it turned out, that was the least of Solidarity's problems.[139]

### Challenges from Without and Within

The Soviet leadership understood well both the threat that Solidarity posed to a totalitarian state and the incongruity of its existence therein. KGB agents posing as friendly foreigners were quickly dispatched to penetrate the organization.[140] Even more serious, Soviet and Warsaw Pact troops were evidently preparing to invade Poland and crush Solidarity, though some have suggested that Soviet leader Leonid Brezhnev was staging an elaborate bluff.[141] Whatever the case, the troops were positioned outside Poland's borders and seemed fully ready for a massive invasion by December 4. United States national security adviser Zbigniew Brzeziński informed Pope John Paul II about the unfolding events.[142]

As a result, John Paul sent a personal letter to Brezhnev on December 16. The letter, while diplomatic in form, was remarkably direct by way of intimation. In recalling the Second World War, the enormous number of Polish casualties suffered during the Occupation, and the fact that the Poles had fought on all fronts with their allies throughout the war, John Paul seemed to be suggesting that he would view a Soviet invasion of Poland as the moral equivalent of the 1939 Nazi invasion, and that casualties would inevitably be high on *both* sides, given the patriotic Poles' demonstrated history of fighting back. He also suggested to Brezhnev that the only way for the Soviet leader to remove the causes of the international tension brought on by recent "internal

139. See ibid., 399–403.
140. See Weigel, *The End and the Beginning*, 120.
141. See ibid., 123.
142. See Weigel, *Witness to Hope*, 405.

events" in Poland would be for him to abide by the 1975 Helsinki Final Act, whose principles include respect for the sovereignty of participating states and noninterference in their internal affairs. Since Poland signed the act as an ostensibly independent nation, John Paul was saying that the Soviet Union had no moral ground for meddling in its affairs and that world opinion would surely condemn an invasion. Finally, he noted that Poland's economic reconstruction had to take place together with a moral one, and that required the "solidarity" of all the forces of society. Here, he was clearly indicating to Brezhnev that Poland's overall recovery could not be achieved without Solidarity.[143]

Warsaw Pact troops had ceased to advance toward Poland on the evening of December 5. The reason, as it turns out, was that the Soviet government called a halt to their movement. Why? John Paul II's December 16 letter to Brezhnev indicates some of the reasons. First, the Soviets had reason to believe that the Poles would not give in to Soviet aggression without a fierce fight. Second, the Soviets had reason to be concerned about the international reaction to an invasion, as John Paul's letter reminded them. Beyond those and other considerations, the Soviets could also see that NATO had gone into a higher state of alert.[144]

In mid-January 1981, after the threat of a Soviet invasion into Poland had receded somewhat, a delegation of Solidarity leaders, including Lech Wałęsa, met with John Paul II at the Vatican. In his public remarks, John Paul made clear his reasons for supporting Solidarity. The movement was committed to working toward the moral good of society, and that is the indispensable condition for achieving real progress in the effort to renew the nation. It ensures that such an effort is not directed against anyone but only *for* the true common good of national reform. In the homily of the Mass that he celebrated for the delegation, John Paul urged the Polish people to let God work through *their* work, so that it would serve the cause of human dignity, of the family, and of the nation. He seemed to be anticipating, by those remarks, his September 1981 encyclical *Laborem Exercens* (*On Human Work*—literally, "Through Work"), where, in the spirit of his nineteenth-century compatriot, poet Cyprian Norwid, John Paul II extols the dignity of work as an expression of the dignity of the worker and as a participation in Christ's work of redemption. In its upholding the right of workers to form free associ-

143. For the full text of John Paul II's letter to Brezhnev, along with Weigel's commentary, see ibid., 406–8.

144. See ibid., 405–6. See also Weigel, *The End and the Beginning*, 122–24.

ations, the document was widely viewed as a papal endorsement of Poland's Solidarity movement, and rightly so.

The Poles would surely need both the tacit encouragement they would find in *Laborem Exercens* and the many explicit expressions of support they would soon be receiving from John Paul II. For it was not long after the Solidarity delegation had returned from Rome that new crises began to unfold. To name a few, the February 9 appointment of defense minister General Wojciech Jaruzelski to head the government did not bode well, nor did the fact that both he and the first secretary of Poland's communist party were summoned almost immediately to meet with the Soviet Politburo on March 4. Solidarity leaders were severely beaten in Bydgoszcz, leading to a paralyzing four-hour national strike on March 27 in which tens of millions of Poles took part. A general strike was set for March 31 but averted. In the meantime, Warsaw Pact military maneuvers resumed outside Poland's borders, presumably a Soviet effort to pressure the Polish government to impose martial law.[145]

### Soviet Retribution?

It might well be that the Soviet plan to get Poland back under communism's iron fist included more than just pressuring subordinates to resort to the use of raw physical force. The Poles had become more restive than ever lately, thanks in large part to a certain Polish pope. So the use of force might not have been enough to subdue them. Did the Soviet leaders decide, then, that it would also be necessary to strike at their heart—to demoralize them in the most radical way possible? Did they wager that the body would fall if they cut off the head? So far, it is only certain that on May 13, 1981, a trained assassin—a young Turk standing amid the crowd in St. Peter's Square—fired twice at Pope John Paul II at point-blank range, using a Browning 9 mm semiautomatic pistol he claimed to have picked up in Bulgaria. One of the two bullets pierced John Paul's abdomen, perforating his colon and tearing parts of his small intestine before exiting the other side. His condition was grave. Intense suffering was once again part of God's plan for him. But imminent death, which initially seemed certain even to his surgeons, was not. John Paul II was shot on the sixty-fourth anniversary of the first apparition of Our Lady of Fatima in Portugal. Fully convinced that hers was the "hand that guided the bullet's path" so that "in his throes the Pope halted at the

145. See Weigel, *Witness to Hope*, 409–10.

threshold of death,"[146] he would travel to the Marian shrine at Fatima exactly one year later to thank Our Lady publicly for protecting his life.[147]

As chief shepherd of the Church, Pope John Paul II felt a paternal responsibility from the beginning of his pontificate to address and to defend every human being. The Church, after all, has a mission to the world. He would fulfill that responsibility mainly through his Gospel proclamation of the human person's intrinsic dignity in Christ, for that is the truth that sets people free. By helping to form consciences thus, he could effectively promote solidarity and the conversion of culture by inviting the cooperation of all people of good will. That alone was enough to put the "Slav Pope" at cross-purposes with totalitarianism in general and with Soviet totalitarianism in particular. But there was more. That each person might have the opportunity to hear, to consider, to accept, and to live that Gospel message, John Paul would always insist that everyone everywhere respect the intrinsic human right to religious freedom. From the moment that Cardinal Karol Wojtyła's election to the papacy was publicly announced, Soviet leaders were concerned about the likelihood of his doing just that, for he would then pose a direct challenge to their claim to power, which depended on communism's atheistic ideology. One of its key doctrines is that God is neither the true liberator of humanity nor the last word on human affairs: the communist leadership is. Individual conscience and freedom—indeed, one's very identity as a person—must be subordinated to the ends, and even to the atheistic doctrine, of the state.

Because the vigorous, charismatic new pope was giving a voice to those who have no voice; because he was affirming their dignity as children of God and demanding that every state recognize, respect, and promote the rights

146. John Paul II, "Meditation from the *Policlinico Gemelli* to the Italian Bishops," *Insegnamenti*, XVII, 1 (1994), 1061, as cited in *The Message of Fatima* (June 26, 2000), issued by the Congregation for the Doctrine of the Faith (hereafter CDF). Vatican website.

147. See Weigel, *Witness to Hope*, 440. While hospitalized a second time in July 1981 because of complications arising from his ordeal in May, John Paul asked to see the Third Secret of Fatima, which the only living Fatima visionary, Sr. Lucia, had written down under obedience in January 1944, and which has been kept in the archives of the CDF since April 1957. On reading it there in the hospital, he became immediately convinced that the 1917 vision of the three children of Fatima concerning the "Bishop dressed in White," who is attacked and killed, pertained directly to him. John Paul had been given back his life, as it were, leading to his conclusion that "One hand shot, and another guided the bullet." Sr. Lucia agreed fully with his interpretation. When the bishop of Leiria-Fatima was visiting Rome, John Paul gave him the spent bullet (till then lodged in the jeep in which he was shot) to keep at the shrine. The bishop decided to set it in the crown adorning the statue of Our Lady of Fatima. See Dziwisz and Svidercoschi, *A Life with Karol*, 130–36; CDF, *The Message of Fatima*. On May 13, 2000, Pope John Paul II beatified Jacinta and Francisco Marto—Sr. Lucia's cousins and co-visionaries—at Fatima.

that accord with that dignity; because he was declaring that political power exists to serve the people and not the other way around; and because he was insisting on the right to national sovereignty, the men in Moscow perceived him, rightly, as a serious threat to the Soviet empire, which relied on coercion, violence, manipulation, and humiliation to perpetuate its existence and to extend its boundaries. The rise of Solidarity in Poland little more than a year after John Paul's first pilgrimage there was proof of his effectiveness. Poland's counterrevolution of truth over lies would prove lethal to Soviet dominance in central and eastern Europe unless thoroughly quelled. So, the Soviet leadership had everything to gain from extinguishing the spark that first ignited it—and this at the same time that Primate Wyszyński, Poland's other great spiritual leader and icon of righteous resistance, was dying of cancer. It seems, then, that the smoking Bulgarian gun of the well-financed, would-be Turkish assassin points toward Moscow and the KGB.[148]

### Trying to Smother Solidarity

While John Paul was still convalescing from the assassination attempt, Solidarity held its first congress in Gdańsk on September 5, 1981. The delegates called for free elections to the Polish parliament and to other decision-making bodies, for the opening of government posts to non–party members, and for self-management in industry. That did not sit well with the Central Committee of the Soviet Communist Party. In mid-October, General Jaruzelski, who already headed the military and the government, was made first secretary—head of the Polish communist party—as well. As the economic situation continued to decline, wildcat strikes began to spread in November, at which time Brezhnev wrote to Jaruzelski urging decisive military intervention. When the Solidarity leaders met in Gdańsk on December 11 and 12, Jaruzelski took the opportunity to arrest them, some four thousand men and women in all. He had already cut off telephone communications to millions of people, sealed the borders, and sent the army in to occupy the country it was supposed to protect. John Paul continued to encourage his countrymen via Vatican radio, and he appealed to Jaruzelski by letter not to shed any more Polish blood, as confrontations in various places had already cost lives. Despite all that was happening, John Paul, though clearly concerned, remained convinced that communist repression in Poland was itself in the throes of death.[149]

148. See Weigel, *Witness to Hope*, 279–81, 361–62, 411–13, 422–25.
149. See ibid., 430–34.

On the other hand, the demoralized Polish people seemed to be losing their sense of solidarity. By going to Poland in June 1983 for his second pastoral pilgrimage there, John Paul II wanted to stand beneath the cross of Christ with his countrymen. He wanted to express his solidarity with them. He also wanted to teach them once again about the inner dynamics of solidarity. It begins with Christ's love, which one can live in freedom regardless of the prevailing political situation. Distinguishing clearly between good and evil and reforming one's life accordingly is the precondition for establishing with others *that* solidarity on which society is founded and which serves as the principle of its moral and social renewal. It is the means by which truth will triumph over lies. John Paul continued to insist on Solidarity's right to exist, at one point showing the people that he sported a Solidarity T-shirt under his tunic.[150]

In speaking publicly to the other side, John Paul would try to persuade Jaruzelski and the rest of Poland's rulers that there would be no social renewal without their honoring the 1980 accords. And that called for dialogue between the governors and the governed. Privately, he tried to persuade Jaruzelski to dialogue with the Solidarity leaders themselves, whom Jaruzelski had imprisoned a year and a half before, for independent workers' associations were essential to real social renewal. John Paul prevailed on the regime to let him see Lech Wałęsa, whose public statements thereafter emphasized the need for dialogue. The very fact of the meeting showed Poland, communism, and the world that Solidarity still existed despite its official nonexistence. Just one month after John Paul's visit, General Jaruzelski ended martial law in Poland, perhaps in an effort to strengthen the regime's credibility both at home and abroad.[151]

During his second visit to Poland, Pope John Paul II had reminded his people of the need to forgive, for the fetters of hatred, not of political oppression, were the real obstacle to freedom. Six months later, he showed the world how important it is to forgive when he visited his would-be assassin in prison. And in December 1984, John Paul issued his post-synodal apostolic exhortation *Reconciliatio et Paenitentia (Reconciliation and Penance),* a reminder that the members of the Church must reconcile themselves to God and to one another, so that the Church might be a sign and a means of reconciliation for all people, whose basic longing for reconciliation, despite the divisions caused by sin, is reflected in the irrepressible desire for peace.[152]

150. See Dziwisz and Svidercoschi, *A Life with Karol,* 153.
151. See Weigel, *Witness to Hope,* 459–64.
152. See ibid., 473–74.

### A New Beginning

In January 1987, General Jaruzelski met with John Paul II at the Vatican and acknowledged that the social and economic reconstruction of Poland would not be possible without involving the leaders of Solidarity, for the people trusted them. What the general was suggesting here might have been unthinkable apart from the policies of greater "openness" *(glasnost)* and of economic "restructuring" *(perestroika)* introduced by Soviet leader Mikhail Gorbachev, who had been elected as general secretary in March 1985.[153] The stage was thus set for John Paul's third visit to Poland in June. On this pilgrimage, he would reaffirm the people's right to participate in public affairs and prepare them to exercise it properly after the triumph of their moral revolution. And he would remind the Polish authorities that they would have to recognize that right if they were serious about national renewal in the social and economic spheres.

Taking part in their National Eucharistic Congress, John Paul told the people that the Eucharist reveals and communicates the salvific power of love, helping to cleanse consciences of hatred and egoism, and thus clearing the path to national renewal. True freedom meant dispensing with the communist lie that God is fictional and that love is weakness.[154]

A few days later, John Paul made his way north to Gdańsk and to the other Baltic coast cities where Solidarity had begun seven years earlier. He reaffirmed the necessity of solidarity between people and among nations. A solidarity without adversaries. A solidarity that struggles for the sake of persons, for their legitimate rights, and for true human progress, but not against anyone. In other words, building a truly democratic society over communism's corpse would require spiritual maturity. Workers have a right to participate freely in that process because their work contributes to the common good of society. That kind of freedom is one not of individualistic autonomy but of solidarity, of sharing burdens as a community. John Paul II was proposing to undo the ideology of class struggle by its polar opposite. And as if to alert a group of young Poles to the dangers they would soon face from another seriously flawed ideology—namely, that of western secularism packaged as "democracy"—he warned them that *having more* must never be allowed to triumph over *being more*. "If it did, we would lose the most precious gift of all: our humanity, our conscience, our dignity."[155] For that reason, they must

153. See ibid., 528–30.

154. See ibid., 545.

155. Recounted by John Paul II in *Rise*, 191.

be prepared to make sacrifices for the sake of defending truth and goodness, as Polish soldiers did during the Second World War.[156]

In April 1988, workers' strikes flared up again in Poland in response to the ever-deteriorating conditions there. Strikers demanded that Solidarity's legal status be restored, while demonstrators in major Polish cities echoed that demand. A mid-August coal miners' strike in Upper Silesia was followed by a flurry of sympathy strikes throughout Poland. Having no other alternative, the government turned to Lech Wałęsa for help, and most strikers heeded his call to resume work. In January 1989, General Jaruzelski announced that the government would recognize Solidarity's legal status as an independent, self-governing trade union. This led to the formation of the Polish Roundtable, which began to negotiate in February. On April 5, a signed agreement provided for semi-free elections on June 4, according to which 35 percent of the parliamentary seats would be openly contested, along with all one hundred seats of a newly created body, the Senate. Solidarity nominated 261 candidates. Of all the contested seats, Solidarity won them all, less one in the Senate (secured by an independent candidate). As for the presidency, the negotiators had agreed at the Roundtable that General Jaruzelski would be elected, though Solidarity's parliamentarians saw to it that he won by only one vote when the election took place in July. Two months later, Tadeusz Mazowiecki, a Catholic, became prime minister, the first noncommunist in forty years to occupy that office in an east central European country. Poland had wrested itself free from Soviet domination.[157]

What happened in Poland was wholly unprecedented among the Soviet Union's European satellites. And the manner in which it happened was wholly unprecedented in nearly two centuries of bloody European politics. Conscious of their dignity and armed only with the truth that their cause was just, Polish workers were willing to stand up to the powers that be. They exhibited remarkable patience and self-discipline. Their commitment to nonviolence gave weight to their call for national moral renewal. And so the general population was supportive. This was solidarity both in name and in fact. The people shared a common vision about the true common good, and they were willing to make the individual and collective sacrifices necessary to realize that good. The Solidarity movement was the fruit of the moral revolution—the revolution of conscience—that Pope John Paul II had "fomented"

156. See Weigel, *Witness to Hope*, 543–48.

157. See ibid., 585–87.

among his people during his pilgrimages by giving them some lessons in Polish history. He taught them that their history belongs to the history of salvation in Christ, and that by placing themselves in the hands of Jesus and Mary, they could become its protagonists.

### The *Domini* Effect

For the remainder of 1989 and into the following year, the irrepressible human desire for freedom and the growing consciousness of basic human rights would find further expression in east central Europe and elsewhere. In keeping with Poland's example, that would happen nonviolently in most cases. Popular demonstrations and changes in the entrenched communist leadership in Hungary, Czechoslovakia, and Bulgaria led to free elections and to the end of communist repression in those countries. For East Germany, it led to official reunification with West Germany on October 3, 1990, less than a year after the Berlin Wall was opened on November 9, 1989. The "fall" of the wall was perhaps the foremost symbol of the Yalta division's demise. Prior to the complete dissolution of the Soviet Union itself in December 1991, the Baltic republics of Lithuania, Latvia, and Estonia, which had been annexed in 1940, reclaimed their independence, as did Ukraine.[158] Romania was the one eastern European country in which the end of a dictatorship was marked by significant violence, mainly because of infighting among communist factions.

John Paul II had no doubt that the largely nonviolent revolution that toppled communism so quickly and unexpectedly in east central Europe was miraculous—the result of a divine intervention, a *gratia domini.* At Fatima in 1917, Our Lady told three young visionaries that she would come and ask for the consecration of Russia to her Immaculate Heart. She said that if her requests were heeded, Russia would be converted and there would be peace. If not, there would be another war during the pontificate of Pius XI (World War II) and Russia would spread her errors throughout the world, causing wars and persecutions of the Church. What is more, the Holy Father would have much to suffer. On June 13, 1929, Our Lady visited Sr. Lucia, the only one of the visionaries still living at that time, in her convent, saying that the time had come for Pius XI to offer the consecration in union with all the world's bishops. But her request was not heeded.

On March 25, 1984, Pope John Paul II—who, perhaps more than any of

158. See ibid., 585–88, 598–600, 605–7.

his predecessors, did indeed suffer much because of communism's errors—would fulfill Our Lady's request by offering the consecration, spiritually united with the college of bishops, in St. Peter's Square before a statue of Our Lady sent from Fatima for the occasion. From then on, events in east central Europe would unfold with breathtaking speed, culminating in "the year of miracles" at the end of the decade. And on May 13, 1991, John Paul would again be in Fatima to thank Our Lady both for delivering east central Europe from the yoke of communism and for saving his life exactly ten years earlier.[159]

Perhaps John Paul II's fulfillment of Our Lady's request also precipitated the collapse of dictatorships and Marxist regimes in Central and South America during the same decade and beyond, bringing to fruition his proclamation of the Gospel there. He affirmed that human beings are the subjects of inalienable rights that the Church must defend, coupling that message with an emphasis on the people's need for reconciliation with God and with one another. Reconciliation precluded violence and fostered the renewal of civil society, thus preparing the way for democratic forms of government. True Christian maturity, which implies interior moral renewal, would therefore bring true liberation, both spiritually and temporally.[160] We might also note the hasty departure into exile of Ferdinand and Imelda Marcos from the Philippines in February 1986. Under the spiritual leadership of Cardinal Jaime Sin (archbishop of Manila) and his fellow pro-democracy bishops, who were inspired by John Paul's visit five years earlier, the People Power movement toppled the corrupt, repressive, and violent Marcos regime by nonviolent, prayerful means. Here, too, we see the triumph of truth, moral rectitude, forgiveness, and Christian charity serving the cause of authentic human rights and religious freedom.[161]

159. See Dziwisz and Svidercoschi, *A Life with Karol,* 179–80; Weigel, *The End and the Beginning,* 235; CDF, *The Message of Fatima*; and Lucia Santos, *Fatima in Lucia's Own Words: Sister Lucia's Memoirs,* trans. Dominican Nuns of the Perpetual Rosary (Cambridge, Mass.: Ravengate Press, 1976), 104–5 (third memoir), 162 (fourth memoir), and 199–200. In a letter dated November 8, 1989, Sr. Lucia confirmed that the solemn act of consecration accorded with what Our Lady had asked for. (See *The Message of Fatima,* Introduction.) In *Crossing the Threshold,* John Paul cautions us about understanding God's action in the fall of communism too simplistically, since, on the one hand, God in Christ is always at work in the Church and in human history, while, on the other hand, God's "work" demands a favorable human response, lest the work of our own hands collapse under the weight of its own weakness—namely, the folly of our trying to live according to a strictly intra-worldly perspective, which necessarily entails the effort to stifle God's voice. See 130–34.

160. E.g., see Weigel, *Witness to Hope,* 451–57, 531–36, 560–62, 773.

161. See ibid., 391–93, 507–11.

## A Rising Threat to Freedom and Solidarity

In his December 1987 social encyclical, *Sollicitudo Rei Socialis (On Social Concern),* John Paul II applies his understanding of the dynamics of human history to the question of social development. Poverty and underdevelopment among individuals and nations are due not just to economic problems. They also signify problems in the social, political, cultural, and spiritual spheres of human life. And all these problems are rooted in moral failures such as unbridled greed, the systematic violation of human and national rights, and the general social apathy and resentment that such abuses can generate. Poverty and underdevelopment, then, reflect an all-around lack of true solidarity.

John Paul's May 1991 social encyclical, *Centesimus Annus (The Hundredth Year),* like his previous one, analyzes economic problems in a wider context. This time, however, his distinctive personalism comes more fully to the fore as he interprets the events surrounding the collapse of communism in east central Europe. Economic failure there stemmed from the disintegration of culture. In turn, the disintegration of culture stemmed from violations of basic human rights. Among those violations, John Paul mentions the state's systematic effort to break down familial and social solidarity, to stifle creative initiative, to pervert and suppress the truth, to exclude the masses from public office and economic planning, and to banish God both from public life and from the human heart itself. In a word, the organization of human society around Marxist principles was doomed from the start because they presuppose a radically flawed anthropology.

But John Paul's incisive analysis goes further. Democratic societies succumbing to a secular ideology having no objective moral foundation are as much a threat to human freedom as the totalitarian systems that had so recently failed. In fact, that threat is even more insidious because "democratic" secularism, precisely in the name of freedom, ends up setting authentic human rights and freedom on the chopping block of ethical relativism, leading to massive human rights violations and, consequently, to social tensions that society will not be able to resolve by legalizing its egregious transgressions of the moral law or by trying to justify them with lies. For society will be equally unable to numb every conscience with the opium of materialism that it incessantly prescribes with the help of the mass media. And so the very survival of the society as a democracy hangs in the balance. Indeed, the so-called democracy stands on the threshold of becoming a fully totalitarian state through the dissolution of culture taking place, as it always does, from society's forgetfulness of and disregard for both human transcendence and God himself.

Both *Evangelium Vitae* and John Paul's August 1993 encyclical *Veritatis Splendor* (*The Splendor of Truth*, which explores the foundations of the Church's moral teachings and exposes certain problems in contemporary moral theology) gave him further occasion to warn about the danger of allying democracy and ethical relativism. In those two documents, together with *Centesimus Annus*, John Paul makes it clear that by severing the essential relation between freedom and truth, individuals and even whole societies lose their moral bearings and, at the same time, their sense of God and of human dignity. Consequently, they become capable of committing the most heinous crimes against the human person and against humanity itself. The freedom of the individual and of society must be governed by the objective moral law, by truth, if it is to be a freedom worthy of persons.

John Paul's September 1998 encyclical, *Fides et Ratio*, on the relationship between faith and reason (or philosophy), explains that the contemporary crisis of truth is rooted in modern philosophy's skepticism regarding human reason's capacity to know, with certainty, anything about the ultimate meaning of reality. That leads to agnosticism and relativism. In thus losing their incentive for inquiring into the truth of existence, human beings likewise begin to lose their sense of the wonder of being, with the result that life becomes increasingly mundane and decreasingly personal. Without truth, the person is at the mercy of human caprice—so much so that his very status *as* a person might be called into question based on arbitrary, purely pragmatic standards of judgment. During his fourth pilgrimage to Poland, in 1991, after the collapse of communism, John Paul had tried to advise his fellow Poles of the need to undergird their new personal and societal freedom with the moral truth expressed in the Ten Commandments and the commandment to love, knowing that totalitarianism could easily resurface on any lesser foundation. The popular mood was such that the wisdom and foresight of his counsel was not really appreciated until his fifth trip to Poland, in June 1997, after the people had struggled for several years with the challenges of free citizenship.[162]

162. See ibid., 641–44, 798–803. Of his 1991 pilgrimage, John Paul would say, "When … I chose the Decalogue and the commandment of love as a theme for the homilies, all the Polish followers of the 'enlightened agenda' were upset. For such people, the Pope becomes *persona non grata*." *Crossing the Threshold*, 57.

## Bearing with Fruit-Bearing Suffering

Throughout his life, Pope John Paul II poured himself out into everything he did, but without, for all that, ever spending himself. The secret to his seemingly boundless energy and astonishing productivity was that he immersed himself with equal or perhaps even greater intensity in prayer. And because he lived consciously in God's presence while here on earth, he also lived by the conviction that nothing happens outside of God's providence. That is why his initiatives and actions, while always prudent, could also be remarkably bold and fearless. He was not afraid to move forward because his decision to follow this or that course was typically made either on his knees or prostrate before the Blessed Sacrament.[163] And out of his conviction that even seemingly accidental occurrences are part of God's saving design, he came to understand, during his pontificate, that relentlessly pushing himself forward was not always enough. To fulfill God's purposes, he had sometimes to suffer too.

In some cases, his suffering was not prolonged. For example, in July 1992 at age seventy-two, he recovered rather quickly from surgery to remove both a large, benign intestinal tumor and some stones from his gall bladder.[164] On the other hand, he experienced pain and disability for the rest of his life when the artificial hip replacement surgery that he had after falling and breaking his femur in April 1994 was only partially successful. His take on his condition is telling. The providential accident, so to speak, occurred during preparations for the September 1994 World Conference on Population and Development in Cairo, whose draft document included provisions that were inherently inimical to marriage and the family. In a public address given after his stay at the hospital, John Paul remarked that his efforts to lead the Church into the third millennium of Christianity by prayer and by various programs were not enough. He had come to understand that he must also lead by suffering. That was likewise the meaning of the attempt on his life thirteen years earlier, he explained. The fact that his latest suffering occurred during the Year of the Family, when certain nations (including the U.S.) were mounting an attack on the family through attempts to control the Cairo Conference, made clear to him the specific reason why he, the head of the universal Church, had to be attacked and to suffer: it was because the

163. See Weigel, *Witness to Hope*, 276.
164. See ibid., 659.

family itself was under attack. The family and the world must therefore see in him the Gospel of suffering, which prepares for the future of every family and of all families in the new millennium. He wanted especially to bear witness to that before the power players of the world.[165]

Interestingly enough, on May 13, 1981, John Paul II had lunch with the world-renowned French geneticist Jerome Lejeune, who also happened to be a leader in the international pro-life movement.[166] Just a few hours later, the Holy Father was shot while on his way to the general audience at which he had planned to announce the creation of the John Paul II Pontifical Institute for Studies on Marriage and Family at the Pontifical Lateran University.[167] Four days earlier, he had established the Pontifical Council for the Family as a permanent office of the Roman Curia.[168] And four days after he was shot, Italy voted to expand legalized abortion, though John Paul had worked hard to prevent that. In a tape-recorded message played for the pilgrims in St. Peter's Square that day, he announced that he was offering his sufferings for the Church and for the world.[169] To be sure, it seems that his hard work and prayers were not always enough. He had sometimes to suffer too—especially for the sake of the family.

In his 1984 Apostolic Letter *Salvifici Doloris (Salvific Suffering),* John Paul II had written eloquently and profoundly about the salvific possibilities of human suffering. Having effected human redemption through his own suffering, death, and resurrection, Christ makes the redemptive power of his self-sacrificing act of love available to human suffering here and now. We need only to accept in love, if only implicitly, Christ's readiness to act in and through our sufferings, so that he can draw us, as well as others, to himself in that way. And Christians who suffer willingly for the sake of Christ can help build up his Body, the Church.

After his hip surgery in 1994, John Paul would always walk with a cane—and even then, only with difficulty. By limiting his physical activity, his condition caused him gradually to gain weight. Rumors about his precipitous decline abounded, abating somewhat in October of the same year with the release of his international bestseller, *Crossing the Threshold of*

165. See ibid., 715–27, esp. 721–22. See also 695.

166. See ibid., 412.

167. See *Address of His Holiness Benedict XVI to Members of the Pontifical John Paul II Institute for Studies on Marriage and Family on the XXVth Anniversary of Its Foundation* (May 11, 2006). Vatican website.

168. See Weigel, *Witness to Hope,* 411.

169. See ibid., 414.

*Hope*.[170] Also in 1994, John Paul was diagnosed as having a form of Parkinson's disease, which was causing his left arm and hand to tremble. Though still mentally alert, his speech would become slurred over time. Regardless of these limitations, he retained good humor and a relentless, if somewhat curtailed, pace.[171] After an ankle operation, he had to be transported temporarily in a wheelchair; however, as arthritis and Parkinson's disease continued to ravage his body, the wheelchair eventually became a fact of life for him.[172] His Parkinson's disease would also cause his once powerful voice to become weak and his once expressive face to become frozen. But through it all, John Paul would witness faithfully both to what he had always taught about suffering and to what he had experienced personally whenever he was in contact with human suffering of any kind. He would show the world that persons retain their full dignity *as* persons even when infirm, and that a person's determination, contributions, meaningfulness, and spiritual greatness can shine forth even more intensely through, despite, and sometimes even because of, infirmity.

## On to His Father's House

In late January 2005, John Paul II seemed to have developed a bad flu. On the evening of February 1, he was having trouble breathing and was therefore taken to the hospital. His larynx and trachea had become acutely inflamed, and the condition was aggravated by a larygnospasm. He seemed to improve and was released from the hospital on February 10, only to be readmitted again two weeks later because of severe respiratory distress. A tracheotomy was necessary to prevent suffocation, but it also deprived him of speech. He was allowed to return home, where he made some modest but fleeting progress in his ability to speak and overall. Then on March 31, he suffered a severe septic shock and a cardiovascular collapse due to a urinary tract infection. The condition resulted in a fever of nearly 104 degrees and very low blood pressure. John Paul had already made it clear that he wanted to suffer and die in his private residence (and near St. Peter's tomb), where he could still be adequately monitored and cared for. For the next two days, tens of thousands of people gathered in and around St. Peter's Square to hold vigil for the dying pope. On Saturday, April 2, he recited his daily prayers, assisted by those standing by. He prayed the Sunday Office of Readings and

170. See ibid., 735–37.
171. See ibid., 781–83.
172. Dziwisz and Svidercoschi, *A Life with Karol*, 252.

meditated during exposition of the Blessed Sacrament. He bid farewell to his closest collaborators and asked to have the Gospel of John read aloud to him. To one of the Polish sisters in attendance, he whispered his last words, "Let me go to the Father's house."[173]

Around 7 P.M., John Paul II fell into a coma. Almost two hours later, his friend and secretary of forty years, Stanislaw Dziwisz, whom he had ordained to the priesthood in 1963 and to the episcopate in 1998, felt a strong, interior command to celebrate Mass right there at John Paul's bedside. He concelebrated with the other two bishops and the two priests who were present. It was the vigil Mass of the Second Sunday of Easter. Just five years earlier on April 30, 2000, John Paul had designated that day as Divine Mercy Sunday during the canonization of a Polish mystic, Sr. Maria Faustina Kowalska (1905–1938), in accordance with the request that Jesus made of her in the 1930s. During Holy Communion, Bishop Dziwisz was able to give the Holy Father a few drops of Christ's precious blood as viaticum. And at 9:37 P.M., Pope John Paul II departed from this life. He would have celebrated his eighty-fifth birthday in a little over six weeks.[174] As George Weigel put it so well, the heroic, saintly way in which John Paul II bore his final sufferings and crossed the threshold of death constituted what was perhaps his most powerful lesson—"his last encyclical."[175]

Cardinal Joseph Ratzinger, who would himself be elected pope on April 19, presided over the Requiem Mass for Pope John Paul II on Friday, April 8. By that time, roughly four million pilgrims had come to Rome to pay their last respects. About eighty heads of state gathered to attend John Paul's funeral—the largest gathering of such dignitaries in history. Fourteen non-Catholic and non-Christian religious leaders were also in attendance. The sight of so many kings and peoples of the earth gathered before the mortal remains of the Vicar of Christ seemed, in a way, like a preview of the Last Day, when all the nations will be gathered before the Lord himself.[176] Shortly after the distribution of Holy Communion to the faithful in St. Peter's Square, the crowds in and around Vatican City began spontaneously expressing their belief that John Paul II ought to be declared a saint at once, chanting, "*Santo Subito!*" that is, "A Saint Immediately!" and "*Giovanni Paolo Santo*," or "Saint John

173. Weigel, *The End and the Beginning*, 385. Cf. Dziwisz and Svidercoschi, *A Life with Karol*, 257.

174. See Weigel, *The End and the Begining*, 378–87; Dziwisz and Svidercoschi, *A Life with Karol*, 253–60.

175. Weigel, *The End and the Beginning*, 371, 514.

176. My thanks to Dr. Ellen Sarnecky for sharing that thought-provoking analogy with me.

Paul." Some even chanted "*Il Grande*" and "*Magnus*," thus conferring on John Paul the title "the Great." After the Requiem Mass, John Paul II's body was interred in a grotto beneath St. Peter's Basilica.[177]

Given the extraordinary outpouring of public acclaim that Pope John Paul II received after his death, Cardinal Camillo Ruini—who, as vicar general of the Diocese of Rome, would be responsible for promoting his cause for beatification and canonization—had no difficulty convincing Pope Benedict XVI, during a private audience on April 28, to waive the usual five-year postmortem waiting period. The new pontiff announced the waiver on May 13, exactly twenty-four years after the attempt on John Paul's life. Less than a year after his death, the Vatican was already investigating a possible miracle attributed to his intercession. Forty-six-year-old French Sister Marie-Simon-Pierre, a member of the Congregation of Little Sisters of Catholic Maternity Wards, was completely and permanently cured of an incapacitating form of Parkinson's disease after members of her community invoked the late John Paul's intercession. And a mere six years after his death, Pope John Paul II was beatified in Rome by his immediate successor on May 1, 2011—Divine Mercy Sunday.

## A Brother and a Father to All

Juliusz Słowacki's "Slav Pope," the brother to humanity, seems truly to have materialized in the person of Pope John Paul II. He encouraged dialogue, reconciliation, solidarity, and peace among all people. He stood spiritually, and often physically, in solidarity with those who were oppressed or suffering in any way, at times providing them with their only voice. He offered his own sufferings for the sake of individual families and the whole human family. He affirmed and defended the rights that flow from the very dignity of the person, and he never ceased to promote that dignity. John Paul II was a man in awe of the human person, each of whose singular personal history unfolds dramatically with the unfolding of his mind, heart, will, and conscience in the history that he shares and helps shape with the rest of the human family. Above all, John Paul II was a man in awe of the human person as created in God's image and redeemed in Christ. And so, the profound reverence of the Slav Pope, of humanity's brother, for every human person was ultimately rooted in his surpassing reverence for God himself.

In wholly giving himself fraternally to the Church and to the human fam-

177. See Weigel, *The End and the Beginning*, 390–97, for additional details.

ily, Pope John Paul II modeled himself closely on Christ. At the same time, he was a spiritual father to all, reflecting the very Fatherhood of God, whose mercy and solicitude have been revealed in the Son of God incarnate. His paternal instinct was nurtured by the reflection of God's Fatherhood in the paternal figures most important in his own life: Karol senior, Cardinal Sapieha, and St. Joseph.[178] Since God's Fatherhood radiated so clearly in the person of Pope John Paul II, we can understand his papacy—indeed, the whole of his priesthood—as a mission of mercy.

It is interesting to note that John Paul II has acknowledged a certain spiritual kinship with his compatriot, Sr. Maria Faustina Kowalska, whose mystical experiences centered on the mercy of God in Jesus Christ, and who has consequently become known as the Secretary or the Apostle of the Divine Mercy.[179] John Paul, who, during his tenure as archbishop of Kraków, was involved in the diocesan investigation into the virtues and writings of Sr. Faustina as the first step toward her beatification,[180] had been thinking of her at length when he undertook to write his encyclical on God the Father, *Dives in Misericordia*, or *Rich in Mercy* (1980).[181] And it might well be that Sr. Faustina had, in a way, been thinking of him, too, when she heard Jesus speak these words to her in 1938, the year of her death: "I bear a special love for Poland, and if she will be obedient to My will, I will exalt her in might and holiness. From her will come forth the spark that will prepare the world for My final coming."[182]

178. On the role of St. Joseph as a paternal model for his episcopacy, see John Paul II, *Rise*, 137–42.

179. During the Second World War, young Karol Wojtyła would often visit Sr. Faustina's grave, which was not far from the Solvay chemical factory where he worked at the time. See ibid., 194. On his sixth and final trip to Poland in August 2002, he returned to the site to dedicate the Shrine of Divine Mercy erected there. See Weigel, *The End and the Beginning*, 306–7.

180. Pope John Paul II beatified Sr. Faustina on April 18, 1993—the Second Sunday of Easter. As mentioned above, he canonized her seven years later—also on the Second Sunday of Easter.

181. See Weigel, *Witness to Hope*, 387.

182. Maria Faustina Kowalska, *Diary: Divine Mercy in My Soul*, 3rd ed. (Stockbridge, Mass.: Marians of the Immaculate Conception, 2000), par. 1732. Again, I must thank Dr. Ellen Sarnecky, who called my attention to this entry in Sr. Faustina's diary.

# 2

# Person and Act

Having selectively reviewed the life, thought, and work of Pope John Paul II, we can appreciate more fully why the human person, and the true good of the person, was always the center of his concern. And because he dedicated his life to defending and fostering the personal dignity and rights of vulnerable human beings, we can expect that his person-centered writings will somehow embrace the theme of human vulnerability, even when that is not mainly or explicitly his focus. His philosophical anthropology is most fully expressed in his 1969 work *Osoba i czyn*, or *Person and Act*. The English translation of the work appeared in 1979 under the title *The Acting Person*.[1]

1. Basing itself on the Polish original, the first English edition of *Osoba i czyn* is highly problematic because of editorial liberties taken by Anna-Teresa Tymieniecka, who collaborated with the author on the text. At this point, we would note that the translation of the title itself as *The Acting Person* is somewhat problematic. Translated literally, *Osoba i czyn* means *Person and Act* (or *The Person and the Act*). In that way, the title captures accurately the whole thrust of Wojtyła's argument: it indicates the primacy of the (human) person, as subject, in relation to the concrete moral act, while the dependence of the latter on the former indicates the unity of the two, so that the act itself reveals the concrete reality and inner structure of the personal subject who performs it. The title thus serves as a shorthand expression of the author's thesis and of the philosophical principle underlying it: *operari sequitur esse*, action follows on being. On the other hand, when "acting" becomes descriptive of "person" in the loose translation *The Acting Person*, the expression lends itself to the modern misconception that only deliberate action—whether of the moral,

In this chapter, we will highlight some of the main themes of *Person and Act* to the extent that they bear on the topic of vulnerable human beings as persons and as agents. Once we have treated those themes, we will show their significance with respect to the vulnerable.

## The Revelation of the Human Person through Human Action

In *Person and Act*, Cardinal Wojtyła is mainly concerned with disclosing the interior conditions by which a human being performs, through the body, the most distinctively human kind of act, namely, the *moral* act. This means that he is going to focus on actors whose level of physical, psychological, and moral development is sufficiently mature to allow for the performance of such an act. Because he is occupied with the operations taking place within the person who performs the moral act rather than with specific moral values as such, Wojtyła prescinds largely from detailed ethical considerations in favor of a more general analysis of the fully actualized personal structure that comes to light through the deliberate moral actions by which we determine the world around us. For actions of that kind presuppose that we have also determined *ourselves* deliberately and morally as the condition of performing them. To that extent, we can say that moral values begin with and end in the one who is the self-conscious, voluntary cause of his own acts, the one who grasps values and makes decisions about his own person based on the values he wills to realize. Wojtyła therefore reflects on mature human action as a self-revelatory expression of the human *person*, whose being and nature we come to understand most fully by examining the highest form of activity of which that person, *as* a person, is capable. Accordingly, he stresses anthropology over ethics, while recognizing the inseparability of the two, giving due attention to the most fundamental—and dramatic—consequences

---

merely productive, or otherwise manifestly purposeful kind—constitutes and signifies the person *as such*, so that the "non-acting" person, the one incapable of acting deliberately, is no person at all. And that, for Wojtyła, is an ontological impossibility, since he views *every* form of human acting—even biological or instinctual—as a dynamic reality whose dynamic source is ultimately the original act of human *being* itself, which is always *personal* being. The English rendering of the title also lends itself to subjectivistic misinterpretations that disregard the objectivity of human actions and their consequences in relation both to the concrete, personal subject who authors the acts and to the world beyond that subject. For these reasons, we will refer to *Osoba i czyn* according to its literal translation, *Person and Act*, throughout this work. At the same time, we will use the abbreviation *AP* for *The Acting Person* in the notes whenever quotations or page references have been drawn from the English translation.

of one's deliberate moral actions for one's own person: either personal fulfillment or nonfulfillment.[2]

### The Experience of Personal Subjectivity through Human Action

Wojtyła begins his analysis of human action by reflecting on something so natural to us that we are each likely to overlook it. Whenever I consciously experience anything in life external to me, I become conscious of *myself* simultaneously, if only implicitly, as the one who is having the experience. No matter how many and varied my experiences of the outer world might be, I still experience myself in them consistently as both their nearest object and their selfsame subject, for they all bear a direct relation precisely to the concrete *me*. In that way, my every experience contributes to my self-understanding, while my self-understanding accompanies my every experience.[3]

Wojtyła is referring, above all, to the inner experience that I have of myself as I experience the world through my own conscious, voluntary activity therein. Such activity issues from, shapes, and so relates directly to my own person. Because my "outer" experience of myself as a concrete being who performs actions in the world originates from within me, my primary experience of what it means to be a human person comes also from me. The experience that I have of other persons originates from the outside only, when they become an object of my experience (or when I learn about their self-experiences as a means of supplementing, in a way, my own). For that reason, I can experience the interiority of another person only indirectly by recognizing that "he" is another like "me"—especially insofar as I also see him performing voluntary actions.[4] Anyone capable, as I am, of performing such actions would have to possess the same kind of interior structure by which I perform them. Since action serves thus as a special moment in experiencing (or apprehending) a person *as* a person, Cardinal Wojtyła does not presuppose the person

2. See *AP*, 11–14.

3. See ibid., 3–4.

4. See ibid., 4–10. I can observe, speak with, and even live with others, but all this contact "from the outside" must ultimately be referred back to my interior for interpretation, which will be colored to a greater or lesser extent by my own self-understanding, even if my experience of others also contributes to it. While the effort to understand someone else from the inside can never be wholly successful, neither is it wholly impossible: "When based on a definite relationship [my knowledge of another person] may occasionally develop into something similar to an experience of somebody else's interior" (ibid., 7). That is why he who finds a friend—a kindred spirit—finds a treasure (see Sir 6:14). We will see in subsequent chapters that despite the interior access he has to himself, man cannot understand even his own self fully, and so he remains always something of a mystery to himself.

in order to explain the special character of human action. Rather, he argues that "action constitutes the specific moment whereby the person is revealed. Action gives us the best insight into the inherent essence of the person and allows us to understand the person most fully. We experience man as a person, and we are convinced of it because he performs actions."[5] In particular, Wojtyła has in mind here actions of moral consequence.

By seeking to understand the human person through an analysis of distinctly human activity, Wojtyła points from the outset to the basic principle on which his philosophical anthropology rests, namely, *operari sequitur esse*: action follows on being. Very simply, a being must exist before it can act, while its way of acting will normally correspond to the nature of the being from which it issues.[6] Therefore, by looking at the proper activity of any given being, we arrive at a retrospective understanding of the kind of being it essentially *is* from the first moment of its coming into existence. Any attempt to comprehend a being before it is fully capable of exercising its proper operations would be limited at best, if not thoroughly flawed. Relative to Wojtyła's study, this means that distinctly human action is the key to disclosing and understanding the human person, its author.[7]

Human self-experience tells us that regardless of the variety of activities that flow from each of us as their dynamic source, every such activity is characterized by either dynamic activeness or dynamic passiveness. The difference depends, respectively, on whether or not I am the act's direct, conscious cause and experience myself as such.[8] In either case, however, the act is rooted in me as its dynamic subject. To each of the two kinds of activity, active or passive, there corresponds an objective structure, namely "a man acts" or "something-happens-in-man." Alternatively, Wojtyła employs the terms "human acts" and "activations."[9] We will explain each one in turn.

### Human Acts/"A Man Acts"

The human act, strictly speaking, corresponds to our experience of freedom. As a human being, I am aware that I *could* take this or that course of action—I *could* seek to realize this or that value—but I am not inwardly

5. *AP*, 11.

6. See ibid., 72–73, 82–83. Note that the first English edition of *Osoba i czyn* has deleted references to the scholastic formulation *operari sequitur esse* that appear in the Polish editions.

7. See Wojtyła, "The Person: Subject and Community," in *PC*, 223–25, 260n6.

8. Wojtyła refers to one's experience of being the author, the efficient cause, of one's action as "the moment of efficacy." *AP*, 66.

9. See ibid., 60–69.

compelled to do so. This fundamental human experience implies that there is in each of us a faculty of choosing, namely, the human will.[10] Since the will's freedom, precisely *as* freedom, cannot be predetermined to choose a particular value,[11] the person must possess along with it an internal principle for deciding on one value over another. That principle is truth: what is the *true* good for which I ought to act? Our ordination toward truth is deeply inscribed in our being. It is the ground of our rational potentiality—our capacity to know reality, to understand it as it really is, and to act according to the meaning and requirements of its objective structure. Given our inherent relation to truth, when we perform actions deliberately—that is, knowingly and willingly—we are simultaneously aware that we are personally responsible for them and for their effects. We consequently experience ourselves as moral subjects.[12]

It is *human consciousness* that forms in us the unique experience that we each have of our concrete, personal being in action. In Wojtyła's view, consciousness is the deepest aspect of our cognitive capacity. It relates our deliberately performed actions back to us as their author, so that we each experience both our concrete being as our own "I" (or "self") and our actions as owing to that "I": "*I* am *doing this.*"[13] Because it discloses our objective being

10. See ibid., 100–101, 115, 120–22, 175, 309n38. According to the translation in *AP*, freedom is manifested in the experience, "I may but I need not." Unlike the past indicative *might*, the present indicative *may* expresses not only a present uncertainty about whether I will perform a given action: it can also express the *permissibility* of my carrying it out. In the present context, the moral connotation is misleading. What is more, neither form of the verb places the accent on my ability—my power—to perform the action if I want to, though it is precisely this potential that gives rise to my experience of freedom. For that reason, the present conditional *could*—"I could but I need not"—conveys more accurately the author's meaning. Kenneth L. Schmitz notes the problem and resolves it accordingly in *At the Center*, 83.

11. See *AP*, 132.

12. See ibid., 136–39; *LR*, 115.

13. While for our purposes we need not labor over it, Wojtyła's discussion of human consciousness is fairly extensive. To avoid the excesses of subjectivism and idealism, which view consciousness as the self-subsisting source and unifying ground of its own content and of our subjectivity itself, Wojtyła sees consciousness as but a potentiality of our concrete, personal being, rooted specifically in our cognitive potentiality and without any intentional capacity of its own. (In denying that consciousness and its "acts" have an intentional character, Wojtyła acknowledges his departure from the classic phenomenological view of the matter. See *AP*, 32, 303n16). It is not consciousness but cognition that "goes out" to meet the world of objects, penetrating and comprehending each object by constituting it for itself *as* an object according to its own mode of operation, thus introducing some extrapersonal reality into the subject. Similarly, based on our concrete, personal being, cognition makes each person, together with each one's actions, an object to one's own self, thus providing the basis for objective self-knowledge. These acts of cognition take place *in* consciousness, but they are not proper to consciousness itself. In one, unified process, cognition takes its objective comprehension of oneself and one's actions—as

to us interiorly as a really existing "I" that performs actions, consciousness constitutes us in what Wojtyła calls our *personal subjectivity:* it establishes each of us as a psychological and moral subject in the concreteness of our objective, personal being.[14] As a personal subject, I am actively both *self-possessing,* the owner of myself, and *self-governing,* the director of myself. This inner structure enables me also to be *self-determining,* the "creator" (or shaper) of myself.[15] Implicit, therefore, in the essentially moral question that we each pose to ourselves before taking some course of action, "For what good ought I to act?" (since I *could* but *need not* act thus rather than so), is the question, "Will I *fulfill* myself *as a person* in choosing and actualizing this action rather than that one?" The answer to those questions resides in the rationally apprehended, objective truth about the moral goodness or badness of each possible course of action, while the actual determination of my personal subjectivity for better or worse depends on whether my "I will" freely subordinates itself in action *to* that truth so that I do good and avoid evil.[16] By enacting my objective decision, I will experience, in consciousness, its real effects on my person.[17]

From what we have just said, it should be clear that while consciousness enables us to experience our objective existence subjectively in the act of self-dynamization so as to disclose us to ourselves "from the inside," we are not for that reason turned in on or trapped within ourselves as in the post-Cartesian view, which creates an artificial split between the inner consciousness of self, on the one hand, and any reality outside that experience—including

---

well as of external realities, their interrelations, and their meanings—and passes it on to what Wojtyła calls the *reflective* function of consciousness. Objective reality is then reflected in consciousness as in a mirror and understood by it objectively but also at the deeper, more interior level proper to it. This immanent perception, in consciousness, of oneself, one's actions, and the external world provides the "material" that consciousness needs to perform its second function, which Wojtyła terms *reflexive.* It is the reflexive function of consciousness that turns the objective image provided by its reflective function back upon the concrete subject, constituting an inner, *subjective* awareness of oneself and one's actions, and of the relation of oneself and one's actions to other people and to the world. We use the term "experience" (in a restricted sense), or "self-consciousness," to describe this ability to witness ourselves and what we do (and also what happens to and in us) from the inside. The objective, comprehending *experience* of one's own subjectivity in consciousness co-constitutes the ontologically constituted (the really existing, concrete) subject precisely as a *moral* subject. This is an essential condition of conscience, about which we will say more later. See ibid., 28–50.

14. To avoid the needless multiplication of philosophical jargon, we will borrow the expression "personal subjectivity" from "The Person: Subject and Community," where Wojtyła employed it consistently.

15. See *AP,* 69–71, 106–8.

16. See ibid., 158–59.

17. See ibid., 112–13.

our whole bodily organism—on the other.[18] On the contrary, it is precisely *because* of the unique interiority that human consciousness, together with rationality, affords us that we are open to, have the widest possible contacts with, and can act freely and integrally in the world of objects beyond us. Our experiential quest for truth and goodness and hence for self-fulfillment, along with the experience of morality connected with that quest, makes our contact with, our involvement in, and our transcendence over the outer world an undeniable fact.[19]

### Activations/Something-Happens-in-Man

We are sometimes aware and perhaps more frequently *unaware* of the spontaneous activity in us of which we are not personally the cause, not the "I will." Psychical activities such as sensations, feelings, and emotions express themselves in consciousness, and so we can experience them. But in those activities, we each experience our own self simultaneously as only their passive subject, in contrast to our experience of self as the *active* subject of the acts that we perform voluntarily. On the other hand, we are generally unaware of somatic activities such as heartbeat, blood pressure, or digestion; however, these, too, can enter consciousness when coupled with sensations of psychical origin, as when problems such as cardiac arrhythmia, dizziness, or heartburn develop in relation to them. Wojtyła uses the term "activations" for all the activities that happen in us spontaneously through our psychosomatic structure, whether we are aware of them or not.[20]

Of themselves, activations do not result in our psychological and moral growth. Taken together, however, they do contribute to such growth, for they constitute the indispensable foundation of our voluntary acts. We must consciously incorporate certain activations into the acts that we perform deliberately as the very condition of their execution. Wojtyła refers to this process of incorporation as *personal integration*.[21] The fact of personal integration is

18. See Wojtyła, "Thomistic Personalism," in *PC*, 169.

19. On this point, see Wojtyła, "The Person: Subject and Community," in *PC*, 233; *LR*, 22–23; and *AP*, 158.

20. See *AP*, 88–90, 93–94, 97–98, 210–12, 228–29. Wojtyła uses terms such as "psychical" and "psycho-emotive" to denote interior realities, immaterial in themselves, that are nevertheless conditioned by, or that condition, the "somatic"—the body as a dynamic, physical organism. For that reason, any of the multifarious psychical dynamisms might also be termed "psychosomatic," though Wojtyła seems to use the latter term more commonly to signify the psyche-soma structure in its integral totality.

21. In this case, the expression or its equivalent appears in chapter 6 of *Person and Act*, though it does not appear at all in "The Person: Subject and Community," which does not treat the topic of integration explicitly.

especially evident to us when our acts call for bodily movement such as running or jumping, which requires that we appropriate our natural somatic motility to accomplish our purpose. Similarly, we must personally integrate our spontaneous emotions, such as joy or anger, and our drives, such as those toward self-preservation and sex, into our voluntary acts in such a way that they foster, rather than detract from, our perfection as persons.[22] We can do that only insofar as our psychosomatic energies are accessible to consciousness (hence to our experience), in which case they represent a rich complex of human potentialities that can, through action, be actualized according to the pattern of subjectivity proper to each of us as a person. Even as stored in the subconscious and ordered toward consciousness, however, our somato-vegetative and our psycho-emotive energies contribute to our internal history and, consequently, to the development of our personality.[23]

Before proceeding, we should take note of Wojtyła's conviction that the metaphysical categories of *potency* and *act* are indispensable to our understanding of how *either* the active or the passive dynamism characteristic of human beings is realized through its respective structure of "a man acts" or "something-happens-in-man." "Potency" means that a given being is inherently ready for a specific kind of fulfillment. "Act" means that the proper fulfillment of a potency has been accomplished, contributing in some way to the fulfillment—that is, to the proper perfection—of the being itself. The correlation of the terms "potency" and "act" implies the transition from one state of existence to another—the *actualization,* or coming-to-be, in an already existing being of what had resided in its inner structure only potentially as a real possibility.

Even though the structures "a man acts" and "something-happens-in-man" differentiate the human dynamism into the opposing lines of activeness and passiveness respectively, each one entails a process of actualization in which the dynamic unity of potency and act is realized. The term "act" can therefore be applied in the broadest sense to either our dynamic activeness or our dynamic passiveness, to actions or to activations. The "fulfillment" of either dynamism fulfills *us* in some way, insofar as it is consonant with the objective requirements of our nature. Nevertheless, though

22. Wojtyła distinguishes between spontaneous "instinctive reactions," which represent a dynamization proper to nature itself, and "drives," which represent "nature's dynamic orientation in a definite direction." *AP,* 215. Following the very place where he makes that distinction, the English text repeatedly uses the term "instinct" (translated "urge" in *LR*) where the author means "drive." See *AP,* 216–19, 238, 251. Schmitz alerts us to this problem in *At the Center,* 80n40.

23. See *AP,* 46–47, 95, 217–19.

each type of "act" brings something to perfection in us, the term is usually reserved for the *human* act in the strict sense.[24]

## Metaphysical Subjectivity

We have seen above that according to Wojtyła's understanding, our personal subjectivity is formed by our self-experience in consciousness as we relate freely to the world of persons and to the world as such. But Wojtyła is clearly no idealist. He does not equate "person" with "consciousness" or with the sum of one's successive self-experiences therein. Rather, he points to our conscious self-experience as the immanent means by which we become aware that human acts and activations, the two basic categories into which all our activity falls, issue from each of us as from one and the same subject. That is why the most fundamental personal experience that we each have of our concrete subjectivity is that of its dynamic unity. Since action follows on being, the modes of activity proper to us flow from the kind of concrete, unified being that each of us is, while at the same time actualizing its potentialities so as to perfect it. It follows, therefore, that if, after a suitable period of development, we are capable of performing and perfecting ourselves through distinctly *personal* actions, then our concrete existence, from which those actions issue, must likewise be personal from the start.

### The *Suppositum*

The nature of any species is defined by the modes of operation or activity common to each member of that species. But that which is common to all does not subsist in itself. Rather, it is *this* being that possesses the nature, *this* being that exhibits the activity characteristic of that nature, and *this* being to which we ascribe the nature and its activity. Every creaturely nature is therefore individualized in a concrete, unified subject, a *suppositum*—the owner and bearer of *this* particular instance of real existence in which the nature inheres.[25] Wojtyła uses the terms "metaphysical subjectivity" and

24. See *AP*, 60–65.

25. As noted already, the first English edition of *Osoba i czyn* was heavily edited and revised. Among other things, the term "*suppositum*" was replaced in each instance by a circumlocution of some kind, and so we lose the continuity between the author's thought and that of the medieval scholastic traditions (see Schmitz, *At the Center*, 59–60). George McLean notes that in summarizing much of *Person and Act*, the first part of Wojtyła's essay, "The Person: Subject and Community," employs the technical Scholastic terms "substance" and "*suppositum*" some thirty-eight times, showing the author's intent to emphasize their importance at the very time they were being removed from the first English edition, then being prepared. See George McLean, "Karol Wojtyla's Mutual Enrichment of the Philosophies of Being and Consciousness," in Nancy Mardas Billias,

"*suppositum*" interchangeably to denote this substantial being in its concrete individuality.[26] The original act of every such being, the act of its coming into existence, is the ground of all its subsequent activity, the activity proper to its nature. In turn, the being's natural activity enacts its dynamic existence in some respect.[27]

In human beings, the metaphysical subject is a really existing *somebody* who individualizes a human nature and thus grounds its existence, along with the somatic, psychical, and rational potentialities and activities that characterize it. That same subject, subsisting by the dynamic act of existence by which he first came to be, is therefore the personal, substantial source of all the subsequent, accidental (or derivative) dynamizations of human nature, whether acts or activations. This means that *what is specifically human* (deriving as it does from human nature) *can subsist in no other way than personally: where there is a human being, there is a person.* At the same time, the dynamizations of human nature constitute the actualization, the "coming-to-be," of perfections in the already existing, personal being that had resided in his inner structure only potentially. This means that *the activities of human nature enact and thus perfect the person's existence in a distinctly human way, so that we are dealing with none other than a human person.*

We have implied above that metaphysical subjectivity necessarily entails *metaphysical* (or *ontic*) *integration,* wherein a specific nature and its corresponding dynamisms are given with, hence individualized in, the subject of existence and activity, so as to constitute a particular being in its concrete unity. In our case, the metaphysical integration of human nature and its dynamisms in our person constitutes our metaphysical subjectivity, our ontic unity as a personal being having a concrete, psychosomatic nature. Conversely, since human nature and its dynamisms reciprocally enact our personal existence, it integrates us as persons. That is why all human dynamizations cohere with the person.[28]

---

Agnes B. Curry, and George F. McLean, eds., *Karol Wojtyła's Philosophical Legacy* (Washington, D.C.: Council for Research in Values and Philosophy, 2008), 22–25. See also the detailed footnote in Weigel's *Witness to Hope*, 174–75.

26. Wojtyła used the expression "metaphysical subjectivity" consistently in "The Person: Subject and Community" as the correlative of "personal subjectivity." We will do likewise. In *AP,* we find the synonymous expressions "ontic subjectiveness" (45) and "ontic subjectivity" (211), which translate suitably the expression used in *Osoba i czyn.* See *Persona e atto: Testo polacco a fronte* (Santarcangelo di Romagna: Rusconi Libri, 1999), 130 and 498 respectively.

27. See *AP,* 72–73, 96–97. In this context, Wojtyła refers us to the Thomism of Josef de Finance. See ibid., 307n30.

28. See ibid., 76–78, 80–85. While I know of no place where Wojtyła uses the expression

### The Relation between Metaphysical and Personal Subjectivity

Our metaphysical constitution as personal beings with an inherent psychosomatic structure serves as the *objective foundation* for the emergence of consciousness and for the emergence *in* consciousness of the *subjective, self-experiencing, psycho-moral personality* in virtue of which we each refer to our concrete, personal being as "I." Here we are at the heart of Wojtyła's philosophical project, his effort to integrate the phenomenological analysis of subjectivity as the lived experience of self in consciousness into the anthropological realism of Aristotle *(homo est animal rationale),* Boethius *(persona est rationalis naturae individua substantia),* and St. Thomas (for whom the *suppositum naturae rationalis* is the concrete locus of the person's conscious existence and activity).[29] According to Wojtyła's understanding, then, the "I" formed in consciousness does not subsist in itself but only in my objective, concrete existence, with which it subjectively, or experientially, identifies. Metaphysical (ontic) and personal (self-experiencing) subjectivity coalesce, as it were, so that my self-reference using the personal pronoun "I" designates the real being that is, at the same time, the personal self of my experience.[30]

Corresponding to the dependence of personal subjectivity on metaphysical subjectivity is the dependence of *personal integration* on *metaphysical integration.* Because I am subjectively conscious of my own concrete "I," of the fact that I am objectively a person, I can freely—that is, *personally*—integrate into deliberate, self-fulfilling actions the appropriate activations of the metaphysically integrated psychosomatic structure given with my existence. In that way, I consciously enact, and so actualize more fully, the person I am, raising the otherwise spontaneous, natural activations that happen in me to an incomparably higher level and unity: to the level of my person in dynamic unity with the actions I perform. Personal integration thus presupposes the metaphysical integration of the somatic and the psychical dynamisms in the person, in whom they form a complex unity on the basis of which we can

---

"metaphysical integration" himself, it does reflect accurately what he says in other terms (along the lines indicated in the text above), while serving also as an apt analogate of "personal integration," an expression that he *does* use.

29. In *PC*, see Wojtyła, "Subjectivity and the Irreducible in the Human Being," 209–17; "Thomistic Personalism," 169–71. See also Aquinas, *Summa Theologica* (hereafter *ST*) I, 29, 2; III, 2, 2–3.

30. See *AP*, 43–45, 112–13.

incorporate them into our actions to establish the *superior* dynamic unity of the person in action.[31]

By grounding personal subjectivity and personal integration in their concrete, metaphysical antecedents, Wojtyła rejects any dichotomy—phenomenological or otherwise—between *person* (more or less identified with consciousness, regarded as the independent subject of self-conscious, autonomous activity) and *nature* (more or less identified with the psychosomatic structure—or even with the bodily organism alone—regarded as the independent subject of activations, of instinctive actualizations), which would posit two separate subjects of activity.[32] Those who subscribe to that view tend to degrade human nature into something unessential to, or even unworthy of, who we "really" are, while improperly exalting the person, who, as the independent, exclusive source of autonomous activity, is granted the "right" to manipulate or to dispose of "nature" as he or she will. Moreover, the tendency, in this perspective, to identify personhood with self-conscious, free activity can lead its adherents to place more value on what one *does* (a functional view of the person) than on who and what one *is* (where personal worth is viewed according to the superior ontological status of the person as such). But this dichotomous understanding of the human person has no basis in actual human experience, which supports instead the metaphysical position that the underlying source of all human activity, both activations and autonomous human actions, is the concrete, unified person-subject.

So, Wojtyła makes it clear that human beings possess an integrated, personal existence from the first moment of their coming to be. Their personal existence sustains the human nature that inheres in it, permeating all the natural dynamisms. Consequently, personhood is not something that accrues to human nature after a lengthy period of normal development. Rather, the personal subjectivity by which one is aware of *being a person* is simply the lived experience of one's *personal being*, one's metaphysical subjectivity.[33]

31. See ibid., 196–99.

32. See ibid., 78–82, 210–11. See also Wojtyła, "The Human Person and Natural Law," in *PC*, 181–85.

33. Wojtyła criticizes Max Scheler for regarding the person not as an objective being, but as a construct of consciousness, whereby consciousness gives a unifying meaning to multiple experiences stemming from one's emotional responses to value. See "Perfectionism in Ethics," in *PC*, 53. Accordingly, Robert F. Harvanek, SJ, writes that, for Scheler, person is "the act which unifies all the functions of the moral act. Person is not an ontological concept but a dynamic one. As a result, the person is not present until all the conditions for a fully functioning person are present. Thus, a fetus is not a person, nor even is a young child until he or she has become a moral adult." From "The Philosophical Foundations of the Thought of John Paul II," in *The Thought of Pope*

It is the actualization of the self-experiencing "I" contained virtually in the concrete, personal existent, which is thereby revealed to itself precisely *as* personal.[34]

We can approach this from another angle by observing that the personal integration of somatic and/or psychical activations in the voluntary performance of self-determining actions signifies the actualization of the *I*'s capacity for self-possession and self-governance. To be actualized at all, that capacity, the personal structure of self-determination, must always already be contained in the concrete, metaphysical subject. For Wojtyła, it is fundamentally identical with the person, whose personal status is thus assured, regardless of whether the personal structure is ever really actualized. Consider the following key text:

> In virtue of his self-governance and self-possession man deserves the designation of "somebody" regardless of whether he has this distinctive structure actually or only potentially. Thus man is somebody from the very moment of his conception even when and if something intervenes and prevents his fulfillment of himself in actions, that is to say, if his mature actualization of self-governance and self-possession were to be prevented.[35]

While the actualization of the personal structure in the self-determining act is still the foremost means of expression, and hence the fullest revelation, of the person, Wojtyła considers the formation and the manifestation of the

---

*John Paul II: A Collection of Essays and Studies,* ed. John M. McDermott, SJ (Rome: Editrice Pontificia Universitá Gregoriana, 1993), 9. Peter J. Colosi takes a different view. While granting that certain passages in Scheler's work sound like ontological statements denying full personhood to young children, he suggests that in those instances, Scheler might not actually be speaking thus but only of our own inability *to perceive* signs of their personhood. Colosi concedes that the verdict is not yet in on this matter, but he argues that Scheler's notion of the divinely determined "individual value essence" of the person (which ontologically establishes one's personal uniqueness) seems to militate against the view that he denies real personhood to the embryo or to other young children. See Peter J. Colosi, "The Uniqueness of Persons in the Life and Thought of Karol Wojtyła/Pope John Paul II, with Emphasis on His Indebtedness to Max Scheler," in Billias et al., *Legacy,* 61–99 (particularly 92–93n57).

34. See "The Person: Subject and Community," in *PC,* 232.

35. *AP,* 180 emended/*Osoba,* 223. In *PC,* see Wojtyła, "Subjectivity and the Irreducible," 214; and "The Person: Subject and Community," 225. With the generous help of Peter Stacha, the passage from *AP* quoted above has been emended to reflect more accurately the actual language used in the third Polish edition of *Osoba i czyn* (Lublin: Scientific Society of the Catholic University of Lublin, 1994). For that reason, I have cited the page number of the passage in both texts and notified the reader of the emendation. The same method of citation will be used wherever such emendations occur. I have also checked selected passages in *AP* using the reliable Italian translation of the third Polish edition (which appears together with the translation). See *Persona e atto,* cited earlier.

psycho-moral personality (the "I," or "self") in the act to be something secondary or derivative, since it presupposes the being of the person as already constituted by the personal structure.[36]

## Human Actions and Activations

We would do well now to draw together and elaborate on what we have said about Cardinal Wojtyła's understanding of human actions and activations in relation to the person, since the manner in which he treats that topic will prove essential to how we, in turn, come to understand the personhood and agency of developing, weak, disabled, poor, suffering, elderly, and dying human beings. It might also underlie the development that seems to take place in Wojtyła/Pope John Paul II's own thought on the matter in the years following the original publication of *Osoba i czyn* in 1969.

### The *Specifically* Personal Character of Human Actions versus Activations

When Wojtyła considers human actions and activations in terms of the level at which each is dynamized, he says that only actions are personal in the strict sense, for in them we have the experience of ourselves as the free and deliberate source of their actualization. From that perspective, activations are in a sense nonpersonal because we do not in their case experience the moment of our personal causality. Instead, it seems to us as though human nature is their exclusive cause. Something merely happens in us.[37]

### The *Fundamentally* Personal Character of Human Actions *and* Activations

From the more remote perspective of their fundamental source, both the human acts that we perform deliberately and the activations that happen in us are the actualizations of natural potencies deriving ultimately from the original act of existence by which our personal being first came to be. Therefore, human actions and activations are *both* personal in the sense that each of those activities is grounded in our dynamic being as persons, in our uniquely personal metaphysical subjectivity with its integral, psychosomatic nature.[38]

36. See *AP*, 193; Wojtyła, "The Personal Structure of Self-Determination," in *PC*, 192.
37. See *AP*, 80–82.
38. See ibid., 72–74, 82–84.

### The Specifically *Human* Character of Human Actions and Activations

Both actions and activations are formed by drawing on the potentialities of human nature, from which they receive their distinctly human quality. It is only the mode of causality that differs. When the person initiates and sustains the operation of a natural dynamism or integrates spontaneous and instinctual activity or natural drives into an act, the act is at once personal and human. That is the meaning of the term "human act," properly speaking. Otherwise, the dynamism issues from human nature, without the direct causal involvement of the person as a free agent. In that case, we are dealing with an activation, but one that is nevertheless distinctly human as well.[39]

### Activations as Passively Revelatory of the Human Person

Because our spontaneous activations are specifically human, they are in themselves revelatory and expressive of the kind of being from which they issue, namely, a person; for human nature does not exist but for the personal being in which it inheres. Conversely, human nature with its particular dynamisms (somatic, psychical, and rational) is specially suited to enact the existence of a person in a way *proper* to a person, whether that enactment is realized through an act or an activation.[40] So from that standpoint, too, human activations reveal the fact that a person, and only a person, is present or given. As compared with human actions, however, they do so in only an objective and passive—a "nonpersonal"—way. Actions, on the other hand, are *subjective*—personal—expressions and revelations of the fact that the person who is presented or given objectively but passively through activations is the same one who acts freely to present or to give *himself,* precisely *as* a person, through the *active* appropriation and integration of nature's otherwise personally passive actualizations.

### Human Activations as Ordered toward Human Actions

Wojtyła's concept of personal integration makes it clear that activations are the building blocks, the "raw material," on the basis of which we form the actions that express and determine us most fully as persons. While our being *as* personal is given with our first coming into existence from nonexistence, we are nevertheless perfected by the actualization of the potencies corresponding

39. See ibid., 84–85.
40. See ibid., 82–85.

to the nature of our being. Therefore, both human activations and human actions are accidental forms of becoming belonging to our perfection as persons, though in qualitatively different ways.[41] Because our being is essentially personal from the start, human nature is intrinsically directed toward that perfection whereby we can direct *ourselves* toward our properly personal perfection in the moral good, as we come actively to possess and to govern our own nature and its dynamisms. Consequently, the activations of human nature, though "nonpersonal" in themselves, are necessary perfections of the person because they constitute the foundation for our uniquely personal perfection in integrative, self-determining acts, which, when fully mature, terminate in our true moral good. The former are ordered toward the latter.

### The Moral and Ontological Effects of the Self-Determining Act in the Person

In and through the "fulfillment" (the performance) of voluntary acts that are, objectively, morally good, we achieve our proper subjective fulfillment: we become good persons, and our psycho-moral personality develops. That alone accords with our rational nature. By forsaking truth and goodness, we act contrary to nature and so become bad persons, to the detriment of our psychological and moral development. In that case, we are the cause of our own nonfulfillment as persons.[42] As we saw above, human activations are naturally ordered toward human action, into which we personally integrate them as the condition of the act's execution. Since that is so, we can also say that our passive, or involuntary, "becoming" on the psychosomatic plane—

41. See ibid., 96–99; "Perfectionism in Ethics," in *PC*, 48–49.

42. For that reason, the "fulfillment," or *performance*, of the act does not guarantee, in and of itself, the fulfillment, or *perfection*, of the person. See "The Person: Subject and Community," in *PC*, 232–36, 260n11. Certain passages in *Person and Act* help us to see that in "fulfilling" (performing) an action, the person also "fulfills" the dynamism proper to him: he actualizes the personal structure of self-determination as the condition of performing the action (e.g., *AP*, 112, 149–53, 177). Thus understood, the person would "fulfill"—that is, *actualize*—himself in performing *either* a morally good or a morally bad act. But in "fulfilling" (or actualizing) himself so, he would also "fulfill" (actualize) himself accordingly as a "somebody" who is either good or bad, such that he might or might *not* fulfill (here meaning *perfect*) himself in the psycho-moral and ontological orders (see ibid., 152–53). The equivocal meanings of the term "fulfill" that arise as a byproduct of the English translation must therefore be kept in mind when Wojtyła expresses himself in this manner. He is trying to capture thereby the unity of the person and the action, both of which are "fulfilled" together because of the dependence of the latter on the former. *Actus personae* is the consequence and the reflection of *persona in actu*. Likewise, see the distinction Wojtyła makes between the *personalistic* value that inheres in the self-actualizing performance of an action and, on the other hand, the action's *ethical* value, which is rooted in and conditioned by it (see ibid., 320–22; "The Problem of the Theory of Morality," in *PC*, 146–50).

the level of activations—is ordered toward our active, or voluntary, "becoming" on the psycho-moral plane, where we either achieve or forfeit our proper perfection as persons, even ontologically, according to how we freely determine ourselves.

By considering the process of personal integration in more detail, particularly in conjunction with the role of consciousness in the experience and the interiorization of values, we can arrive at a better understanding of how the objective goodness or badness of an act can impress itself right into the ontological fabric of the person who performs it. The process begins with the emergence, in consciousness, of our spontaneous psychical reactions to certain objects that affect our senses as the world unfolds before us. Through consciousness, therefore, the psycho-emotive dynamism supplies the will with its "raw material," with its possible objects of choice. But the values that those objects represent must be rationally evaluated according to their true worth—that is, according to their proper place in the objective order of values. For only then does the will have an objective basis for choosing and deciding among them.[43] At the same time, consciousness interiorizes the objectivity of the intellect's judgment about our values of choice so that, in deciding on any one of them, we make it personally our own. In that way, we experience subjectively the moral significance of our prospective actions, along with the sense of obligation to do the good that moral truthfulness demands and to refrain from doing anything opposed to it. At that point, we have entered the realm of conscience.

Since our spontaneous, psycho-sensory perception of and reaction to values mediates our rational apprehension of them and conditions our decision for one of them as our good, both the "raw" experience of value and the rational appetite's—the will's—acceptance or rejection of a given value (whether rightly or wrongly) take place always in and through the body. In some cases, we enact our decision for a particular value by initiating and governing the body's natural reactive motility, so as to obtain through the medium of our physical structure the good that we have chosen inwardly. But even when the element of bodily movement is or appears to be lacking, it remains true that, given the dependence of the self-determining act on the actualization of the psychosomatic dynamisms mediating our contact with both ourselves and the world outside us, we cannot assert our ascendancy over the dynamism by which we act, nor therefore can we manifest our personal transcendence,

43. See *AP*, 225–26, 231–35.

without simultaneously immersing ourselves *in* the act by personally integrating into it the natural activations that contribute to its possibility and its accomplishment. That is why I am at once the subject-person who possesses and governs himself and the object-person possessed and governed *by* himself: I am both the subject who wills to determine and the object determined by the willing.[44]

It follows that if I want to determine the world "out there" based on my personal experience of the values that its objects present to me, I must first determine *myself* by conforming my will and my action to one of those values, which I must inwardly choose to realize in the light of the rational truth about it.[45] Of course, this is not to say that reason necessarily favors my realization of that particular value, hence the experience of guilt or moral evil when I choose something contrary to what I have judged to be truly good.[46] In one sense, the effects of my external action, relative to the world and to me, last only as long as the duration of the act by which I concretize the value willed. Wojtyła calls these the *transitive* effects of the act. But in the most dramatic sense, the effects of my action far exceed the duration of the act itself, taking lasting root in *me*. These are the act's *intransitive* effects.[47] By engaging my intrinsic, personal structure of self-possession and self-governance so as to decide on and perform the act, I have necessarily to make *myself*, and not just something outside of me, the object, the "raw material," that I determine in the act. And I determine myself precisely in accordance with the moral goodness or badness of the values that I have subjectively chosen to objectify by acting in the world. It is consequently the moral character of those values that objectifies itself *in me*.[48]

44. See ibid., 68–69, 108–9, 173, 183, 189–92. See also *LR*, 101–18, "Psychological Analysis of Love," which addresses concretely the topic of personal integration in the context of sexual love between a man and a woman.

45. In other words, the intentional aspect of my action, the "I will *something*," presupposes the self-determining aspect of that same action, the "I will."

46. See *AP*, 139.

47. In this context, Wojtyła does not seem to take note of the fact that one's external actions can, in their "transitive" aspect, have a relatively lasting impact—whether tangible or intangible, good or evil—on the persons or other created realities directly or even indirectly affected by them. He seems to reserve the concept of "intransitive effects" for the relatively lasting personal impact that one's voluntary activity has on *oneself* as an actor. However, see Wojtyła, "The Problem of the Constitution of Culture through Human Praxis," in *PC*, 263–75; John Paul II, *Reconciliatio et Paenitentia*, 16; *Sollicitudo Rei Socialis*, 36. In Chapter 3, we will see that Wojtyła's understanding of "participation" and "alienation" imply the relatively lasting social effects, for good or for ill respectively, of one's "transitive" acting in the community of persons.

48. See *AP*, 69–71, 109–10, 149–52. In *PC*, see "Self-Determination," 190–93; and "The Person: Subject and Community," 229–30. To put it another way, the proper end or limit—the *telos*—

Because consciousness forms in me the interior experience of myself as the object of my own acting, it discloses to me exactly what kind of person I have decided, based on my choice of values, objectively to be: a good person or a bad one. Wojtyła means this in both the psycho-moral and the ontological sense. Depending on the moral quality of the values that I will to crystallize in action, I become either enriched or diminished both in my personality and in its very foundation, my personal being. Through my free and deliberate activity, I become either more or less the person I ought to be and essentially am.[49]

It is ultimately conscience that conditions my self-fulfillment in freedom and manifests my transcendence by transposing reason's judgment concerning the objective truth about a given value into an experience of my obligation, hence also of my responsibility, either to realize or to avoid realizing that value in action. But as we have seen, I am not inwardly compelled to subordinate my freedom to the imperatives of conscience that insert me into the drama of values enacted on my inner stage and, from there, on the outer stage of the world existing beyond me. Because I perceive a certain concrete value as somehow good, I might seek to actualize it by willfully "fulfilling" (performing) an action that is contrary to the moral truth that I experience as a duty in conscience; however, I could not fulfill (perfect) myself as a person by doing so, for I would then be actively undermining the structural condition of my ability to perform actions freely. In the case of an objectively good act, the reverse would be true: to the extent that my action subordinates freedom to truth in response to the obligation imposed on me by conscience, the "fulfillment" of the act would accord with the exigencies of my personal structure, and so I would fulfill my psycho-moral and my ontological constitution.[50] It is conscience, therefore, that ultimately explains and conditions

of human action is not the "something" willed but the "someone" who willed it; that is, the teleology of the will's intentional movement toward values ends in the self-teleology of the person. See Wojtyła, "The Transcendence of the Person in Action and Man's Self-Teleology," in *The Teleologies in Husserlian Phenomenology*, ed. Anna-Teresa Tymieniecka, Analecta Husserliana 9 (Boston: D. Reidel Publishing, 1979), 203–12. See also "Theory of Morality," in *PC*, 146–50; and John Paul II, *Veritatis Splendor*, 71. (Nos. 72–73 of this encyclical explain that the very actions by which we determine ourselves interiorly also express and determine whether we are ordering our lives toward our Ultimate End. Self-teleology is inescapably connected with our decision for or against our supreme *telos*.)

49. Thus, when we determine ourselves either according to or in opposition to the truthful judgments of conscience, something "happens" in us: we become either good or bad, both morally and as persons. In that case, however, we have *willed* this "something" for ourselves. We are personally responsible for this "happening."

50. Our consciousness of the moral obligation to realize the true good in action shows that

the coherence of the action's intransitive effect with the person.[51] The manner in which I respond to the moral urgings of conscience will cause me, inescapably and commensurately, to become what I do, inclining me, in turn, to do what I have become, what I have made myself to be in and through my self-determining acts.

### Activations as an Asset or as a Detriment to Human Actions

Given the interrelation of—even the continuum existing between—activations and actions, it is not always clear which of these two forms of the human dynamism predominates when it appears that someone has performed an action. For example, sometimes the emotions generated by the psychical dynamism flood consciousness to such a degree that they diminish or overcome one's ability to determine oneself according to the objective demands of the true moral good. Wojtyła calls this *the emotionalization of consciousness*.[52] Insofar as I am personally compliant in allowing my emotions to govern me, I am proportionally responsible for what I do while under their influence. But whether or not I bear any personal responsibility for complying with the urgings of emotion, the emotionalization of consciousness results in my personal disintegration as an actor because it causes me to evaluate

we, as human beings, "experience the unconditionality of the good, and in this way we encounter the element of the absolute within ourselves, yet we ourselves are not the absolute, for we are constantly oscillating between the possibility of good and evil." This experience "evokes in us a relation to the Absolute in both the ontic and the ethical sense. Religion and morality are mutually related to one another by a very deep bond." From "Theory of Morality," in *PC*, 157.

51. See *AP*, 152–71. Given Wojtyła's clear position on the crucial role of conscience in forming one's experience of moral duty as an expression of the rational truth about the goodness or badness of realizing a certain value in action, it is hard to understand Williams's conclusion that Wojtyła "leaves much room for personal dissent" from normative ethics because the true value of ethical norms "lies in their essential truth, if they are true, not in the duties they generate, since for the author all action is free and not bound by duty." *The Mind of John Paul II*, 209. Action is truly free only insofar as conscience forms in us a subjective sense of our objective moral obligation relative to a perceived good, for only then do we each have a basis for deciding whether we ought to realize the value connected with that good. We posit moral norms on that same basis, so that they, in turn, can serve as an objective basis for human behavior. Though the individual conscience might blamelessly err in fulfilling its task, one cannot fulfill *oneself* either morally or personally by performing an act that is objectively bad. Williams's remark stems perhaps from his claim that in rejecting Kantian formalism, Wojtyła opts instead for Scheler's understanding of "the *experience of truth* and the direction of personal action toward it" (ibid.). Williams seems to overlook the fact that Wojtyła, though critical of Kant's work, finds it praiseworthy in several respects—especially in the importance that it attaches to duty. And while Wojtyła favors Scheler's work in general, he criticizes it precisely for substituting Kant's rational *a prioris* (which Scheler rightly rejects) with emotional ones, and for failing to account for the ethical component of human experience, which has a normative element that entails duty.

52. See *AP*, 53–56, 246–48.

my prospective acts not according to the objective criterion of rational truth, but according to subjectivistic "truth" of my own emotion. Consequently, I do not so much *act* for the sake of a value because it *is* true as *react* to the value because it *feels* true.[53] If my emotional feeling does not simply pass away but becomes instead a fixed, psychical state, my will might adopt it passively and uncritically, leading to an emotional (or affective) attitude in which the immanence of psychical emotivity dominates my transcendence as a person.[54]

Wojtyła makes the important point that emotional experiences—especially those radiating from a deep emotional stirring and having, in consequence, a more purely spiritual, less somatically based quality—are not opposed in themselves to a person's integration in action. On the contrary, they can lend a certain vividness to the conscious experience of values and inspire the performance of spontaneous yet truly free human actions based on that experience and on the energy it generates. Attention to the proper integration of the emotions can therefore lead to growth in virtue and hence to one's growth as a person.[55] At the same time, the self-transcending act of integration, which always means integration according to truthfulness, frees us from depending solely on our feelings in responding to values. We can therefore act for the sake of the true good and thus fulfill ourselves personally even when a feeling contradicts the objective truth about the value, or when the authentic decision for a truly good value is not reinforced by any feeling at all.[56]

53. See *LR*, 154.

54. See *AP*, 239–40, 244–45. In some cases, external conditions exceeding our conscious control spontaneously effect in us the transition from genuine human acting to that which happens to us. We might then *seem* to be acting, though we are really only operating under the sheer force of powerful factors impinging on us from without, as in cases of "mass psychology," or "going along with the crowd." Here, we accommodate our behavior unreflectively to the equally unreflective behavior of a large group of people reacting spontaneously and uniformly to a given situation. We would not be responsible for such "actions" because they "happen" without our being aware of it. Lacking the elements of personal transcendence and integration, they are not self-determining. See ibid., 326; see also 246–47, 321–22.

55. See ibid., 238–40, 243–48, 253. Wojtyła agrees with Scheler that feelings manifested in consciousness contribute to the experience of value, but he also insists that the experience will be complete and authentic only if we integrate our psychical sensitivity to values with the intellectually apprehended truth about them in the act of self-determination. See ibid., 232–34. For Scheler, human willing intentionally directs one toward an emotionally "felt" value as a condition of our experiencing it as either good or bad. But the will merely acquiesces passively to such values according to their emotional impact, and so it has no real ability to choose and decide among them. Despite this and other deficiencies in Scheler's work, Wojtyła acknowledges the influence that it has had on his own philosophical project. See "The Intentional Act," 269–80.

56. See *AP*, 232–34.

But to the extent that I willingly forsake my responsibility for undertaking the self-creative task of personal integration and seek rather to satisfy myself by following the lead of the emotional events happening in me, I experience disintegration in action and tend toward egoism. To settle for the merely transitory emotional and psychical fulfillment that my emotion generates spontaneously in me would be to forfeit the genuinely *personal* fulfillment that I would otherwise experience in dutifully and responsibly subordinating my freedom of action to the true good.[57] As a result, I would be "acting" contrary to my rational nature, "dehumanizing" and "depersonalizing" myself by impeding or perhaps even reversing my personal, psychomoral growth. Outwardly, I might appear to be acting personally when allowing my passions to govern me, but in fact I am undergoing a reversion from free human actions to subservience to activations, which are no longer ordered in and by an integrated personality but are rather like haphazard, isolated episodes having no meaningful inner connection.

We see, then, that human nature and its dynamisms, which are metaphysically integrated *in* the person, must also be integrated *by* the person in human action. Because of the close relationship between natural and personal causality, transitions can occur in either direction from one kind of activity to the other. The transition from activation to action is effected by, and thus manifests, our personal, self-transcending causality. Conversely, human actions regress either partially or fully into activations when our personal engagement in the acting becomes somehow inhibited, prevented, or even willfully withdrawn, such that the causations of nature hold sway and something merely happens in us. A regression of that kind, however, would be contrary to the dynamic trajectory of our whole development, which clearly tends toward and fulfills itself in the personal.[58]

## The Interior Act

As we have just seen, the fact that someone appears to be acting does not guarantee that we are actually witnessing the performance of a truly personal action. On the other hand, the outward characteristics of the act might accurately convey to us that the act we are witnessing is truly personal, but they might not accurately tell us whether the person's inner determination of himself truly corresponds to what we see him doing (as when the outwardly

57. See ibid., 244–45, 249–50; *LR*, 158.

58. See "The Person: Subject and Community," in *PC*, 225.

discernible features of one's actions belie one's real motives). While the visible component of the act contributes materially to the act's accomplishment and produces effects in the world of objects and persons beyond the actor himself, the really formal, or essential, element of the act is deeply interior to the person. Out of that interiority we decide freely on a course of action and what we mean to accomplish by it. And it is from deep within us that consciousness makes us subjectively aware of our decision as being the product of our own agency, so that the very act of decision by which we settle on a given action determines us according to the value or anti-value that we freely intend to realize in that action—even if circumstances were to intervene and prevent our carrying it out, or even if the action performed were to produce wholly unanticipated effects for good or for ill. Because the interior act constitutes the core of every act of self-determination, it precedes and is distinct from the somatic activity that might be necessary to put the act externally into effect, though the interior and exterior acts seem sometimes to coincide (and, considered morally, do coincide).[59]

In view of what we have just said, it seems that the following possibilities exist relative to the internal and external dimensions of human acting.

1. The interior act is accurately reflected in the exterior act: both are either morally good or morally bad.
2. The interior act is morally good while the exterior act appears to be morally bad.
3. The interior act is morally bad while the exterior act appears to be morally good.
4. The interior act is not executed at all, though outwardly it appears that the person is acting.
5. The interior act, whether morally good or morally bad, is executed without any outward indication whatsoever.

Though external indications that a human action has been performed might be lacking or might belie the manner in which we have actually determined ourselves (assuming that we have determined ourselves at all), Wojtyła contends, nevertheless, that the interior act always entails the external revelation of the person.

> Every action is an external manifestation of the person, even when it is performed wholly internally and thus deserves the name *actus internus*. [The name] is given in

59. See Aquinas, *ST* I-II, 20, 1–5.

the manuals to actions that do not involve anything of what in man makes his acting outwardly discernible. An act that bears the trait of outward discernibility has traditionally been called *actus externus*. But external discernibility is not the only, and even less the best, test of that outwardness with regard to the person that we assert in the action.[60]

How, in Wojtyła's view, can an outwardly imperceptible act be construed as an external manifestation of the person? Is that not self-contradictory?

### The Externalization of the Personal Actor through the Body

Cardinal Wojtyła tells us that the personal structure of self-determination (the capacity for self-possession and self-governance) "traverses" the body, as it were, employing the psychosomatic dynamism as a "compliant tool" in every act of self-determination. In that way, the body becomes the territory and the medium of our personal self-expression and so, too, of our external manifestation *as* persons.[61] Our ability to express ourselves through the body is founded on the habitual "self-feeling" with which our psychically mediated experience of the body in consciousness endows us. That is to say, in virtue of our psychosomatic constitution, we have a fundamental experience of the body as our own, of being in our own possession, while that same experience, in turn, is the prerequisite of self-governance. The experience of our bodiliness founds also the experience that we have of our own objectivity, our own externality, in action. And through sensation and feeling, it founds our experience of the world by disclosing our relation to, and our distinction from, the other beings that fall within the range of our sense experience.[62]

Through the body, then, we are externalized in, and hence in contact with, the world around us. That is why the psychical dynamism is spontaneously attracted to or repelled by the values that we sensibly apprehend from the surrounding world. These values present the will with its possible ends, which the will, in turn, moves reason to judge in the light of truth. Sensory cognition thus establishes a direct link between intellectual cognition and objective reality, furnishing the mind with the "raw material" of its proper acts.[63] Likewise, regardless of whether the will accedes to or opposes rea-

60. *AP*, 114–15 emended/*Osoba*, 160. Note that the English edition replaces *actus internus* with "immanent act" and *actus externus* with "transcendent [act]," despite the fact that the Polish edition employs, in Latin, the familiar scholastic terms.

61. See *AP*, 204–6.

62. See ibid., 228–32.

63. See ibid., 225–26, 234–35, 250–52. See "Self-Determination," in *PC*, 188.

son's judgment, the act by which it arrives at its decision, as also the act by which it puts that decision into effect, requires a certain personal integration of the psychosomatic structure.

We see, then, that in the very act of possessing and governing our body when we rationally evaluate the data received from the outside world and subsequently enact a voluntary response (at least inwardly, if not also outwardly), we become, by means of the body, the object, the "raw material," of our own acting. When the body has been thus objectified in the human act, the personal subject who "has" the body and who integrates it into the action is objectified with it and so "externalized." Thus understood, the externalization of the person in action occurs even in the case of the wholly interior act, when it is not apparent to others that the person is acting at all.

Our externalization through the body in action is also the self-manifestation of our person as a "somebody" who is objectively either good or bad, depending on whether we realize a truly good value or an anti-value in the act. As explained earlier, at the same time that we become our own object in acting, consciousness interiorizes, or subjectifies, our objectiveness so that each of us experiences himself not only as an actor, but also as the one who is determined by himself in the act of acting. By consciously and freely possessing and governing our body to perform an act, we simultaneously experience ourselves in consciousness as *self*-possessing and *self*-governing, and hence as the personal source of the act. As a result, the action issuing from our interior remains always somewhat interior to us, even when it also expresses itself outwardly in a transitory way visible to all. This inner, relatively lasting (or intransitive) effect either perfects or deforms our psycho-moral personality and, indeed, our very being, depending on whether or not we have willed to realize a truly good value in the act. The objectively good or bad "somebody" that we each become and subjectively experience ourselves to be through the act of self-determination accomplished in and through the body thus constitutes our external self-manifestation in action.[64]

To sum up, then, our outwardly discernible activity might or might not reflect the true nature of the interior act that motivates it, or it might even issue from an activation, while appearing to be deliberate. In other cases, our interior acting might not be bodily manifested at all as an outwardly discernible act. That is why Wojtyła does not ground the authentic, external self-manifestation of the personal actor in mere appearances. He prefers instead

64. "In the action the person achieves his own accomplishment by becoming 'somebody' and the being 'somebody' is his manifestation of himself." *AP*, 157.

to ground it in the objectivity that our bodily existence in the world affords us. He can then maintain that the manner in which we manifest ourselves externally as a person in action is fundamentally the same for the wholly interior act as it is for the act having outwardly visible features, irrespective of how those features might be interpreted or how they might belie the true nature of the interior act. The realization of *every* action is "visible" in the sense that the person must in some way consciously integrate the concrete body and its spontaneous psychosomatic dynamisms, through which we are in contact with the visible world, into the action by means of, and as the condition for actualizing, the personal structure of self-determination. By the experience that we have of ourselves in consciousness, the manner in which we have thus objectified, or externalized, our person in the body becomes immanently, if not also outwardly, perceptible: we see that we have objectively determined ourselves in the action to be either a good "somebody" or a bad one. Thus, we "outwardly"—that is, bodily—manifest ourselves as persons in and through our every self-determining act, even when it is wholly interior and, to all appearances, no act at all.

### The Self-Determination of the Bodily Disintegrated Person through the Interior Act

Since the somatic element of our being is essential to the self-actualization by which we express ourselves "visibly" (that is, in a concretely perceptible, though not necessarily an outwardly discernible, way) as a unique and unrepeatable "somebody," human actions, even when wholly interior, imply a certain bodily integrity. To the extent that we must utilize the reactive dynamism of the body in the performance of a self-determining action (as when we must run to someone's aid), the body's integrity cannot be significantly compromised in that respect (for example, by a missing limb or organ, or by independent reactive movements that escape our conscious control). On the other hand, purely physical forms of disintegration, while perhaps limiting somatic mobility or the development of certain somatic skills, do not on that account deprive us of the essential means of determining ourselves. The reason is that somatic disintegration alone does not necessarily distort our consciousness, nor therefore does it necessarily impair our ability to perform morally significant, self-determining actions.[65]

In consequence, when we actualize our personal structure through the

65. See ibid., 212–15.

self-transcending integration of psychical dynamisms (which are always somatically conditioned) into our actions, we can develop a personality of surpassing value, even if our actions are largely or completely confined to the internal sphere because of serious physical disintegration. Examples of extraordinary personal development among persons who are subject to that kind of disintegration illustrate that when someone does not appear to be acting or appears incapable of acting at all, he might still be performing, through the medium of the body, wholly interior acts that are supremely personal, even heroic, because supremely conscious and free. And in that way, the body manifests him precisely as a person.[66]

## The Source of Our Personal Transcendence

We saw above that wholly interior acts having no outward signs of their execution still require, like any human act, the personal integration of psychosomatic dynamisms essential to the self-manifestation of the actor as a good or a bad "somebody." When we personally integrate the appropriate somatic and psychical dynamisms of our concrete being in freely performed actions, we have the simultaneous experience of our self-transcendence and of our personal, integral unity. On the other hand, the achievement of that unity reveals an interesting paradox: to transcend ourselves in the self-determining act, we must subordinate ourselves *to* ourselves. We are at once the subject who acts and the "object" we act upon. We transcend ourselves in personal acts precisely by immersing ourselves in them. Despite this complexity, our experience of personal unity in action is primary: it is always one and the same person who is the determining subject and the object determined in the self-transcending, self-integrating act.[67]

### The Spiritual Source of Personal Unity

The transcendence by which somatic and psychical dynamisms are integrated into self-determining acts expressing the unity of the person in action cannot be explained by the dynamisms themselves, whether singly or in their totality. The modes of transcendence involved in those acts (for

66. For example, a person suffering from amyotrophic lateral sclerosis (Lou Gehrig's disease) in its most advanced stages might be completely unable to move or to communicate verbally, but he might still be able to manifest his inner disposition with a serene expression that communicates both his gratitude toward those caring for him and his inner peacefulness, which consoles them.

67. See *AP*, 183–84, 189–92, 196–99.

example, self-consciousness, personal freedom, and the subordination of freedom to truth in conscience) are immaterial and hence irreducible to a material source, whereas somatic reactivity is wholly material and psychical emotivity is always somatically linked. While in itself nonsensible, human transcendence is intuitively perceived in the experience of our personal integration in action. For in expressing ourselves through the various natural dynamisms, we simultaneously assert our ascendancy over them, which gives rise to the experience of human transcendence in all its constituent modes. Transcendence thus reveals itself in action as the dynamism proper to the person as such. The phenomenological analysis of human action therefore leads directly to the insight that the source of our personal unity is ultimately spiritual.[68]

Were we to posit a material cause for our transcendence, we would violate the principle of noncontradiction because the corporeal dimension of our being does not exhaust the reality of either our substantial existence or our distinctively human activity.[69] Rather, the transcendent, or spiritual, acts on the basis of which we live our life and manifest ourselves through the body as persons require a suitable ontic basis as their structural precondition: they presuppose that we are spiritual beings. Only if we are spiritual beings from the start do the manifestations of human transcendence in our lived experience as personal actors have a sufficient cause. This follows from the principle *operari sequitur esse*. Our experience of ourselves in action confirms for us that we are persons, and the existence proper to a person can be none other than spiritual. Intraworldly nature alone is incapable of generating spiritual modes of activity, and so human beings cannot be understood solely on analogy with the natural world.[70]

Earlier in *Person and Act*, Wojtyła showed us that from the first moment of our coming to be, the metaphysical integration of human nature in the person constitutes us and all our dynamisms as an ontic unity. He is now in a position to show us that our substantial spiritual existence as persons is itself the source of that unity. Moreover, it determines not only our ontic unity but also the personal unity, founded on the former, that is actualized and revealed in the self-transcending integration of the person in action.[71]

68. See ibid., 181, 257–58.
69. See ibid., 181–82.
70. On this point, see "Subjectivity and the Irreducible," in *PC*, 209–17.
71. See *AP*, 183–85.

### Our Ontic Composition: A Unity of Soul and Body

Because the experience of acting reveals to us that we are each a corporeal "someone"—a bodily person—the phenomenological insight about the spiritual foundation of both our ontic and our personal unity implies also our ontic complexity, the fact that we are composed of soul and body. While we have no direct experience of the spiritual soul or of the soul-body relation, the reality of both the soul and its relation to the body can be inferred from our experiences of transcendence and integration respectively. As stated above, the dynamism of human transcendence as such is inaccessible to sense and hence immaterial. Yet, our self-experience as persons in action manifests it as that which is innermost expressing itself through the medium of the body. The effects of human transcendence intuited in this experience demand the spiritual soul as a commensurate cause. That same experience yields the intuition of the soul's abiding relation to the body, since the spiritual effects of which we are the efficient cause include, require, and are revealed in the integration of somatic and psychical dynamisms into the person-action unity.[72]

### The Independent and the Somatically Dependent Powers of the Human Soul

Since our experience of active self-transcendence leads us to infer that our personal dynamism issues from the dynamic spiritual element constitutive of our being, the potentialities correlative to human transcendence in action, namely, the spiritual powers of intellect and will, must be grounded in our spiritual soul and properly dynamized by it. These powers correspond, respectively, to cognition's dynamic reference to truth and to self-determination's freedom (which presupposes freedom's dynamic dependence on truth). Together they establish the means by which human tran-

72. See ibid., 185–86, 204–5, 256–58. Just as classical epistemology asserts the identity of the knowing subject and the object known in the act of self-knowledge, Wojtyła seems, in his dynamic philosophy of human action, to assert the identity of the *willing* subject and the object willed in the self-transcending act of personal integration. In each case, the absolute identity of subject and object points to an immaterial principle, the spiritual soul, which alone can explain why the two, subject and object, are not spatially dispersed but one and the same. Wojtyła's whole argument suggests that the union of the immaterial soul with the material body stands out more clearly when we analyze the human act in terms of self-determination and personal integration than when we restrict ourselves to analyzing only the act of conscious self-knowledge, which can easily distort our understanding of the person in the direction of idealism.

scendence manifests itself in the dynamic person-action unity. From that perspective, they have a personal character.[73]

It is not just the powers of intellect and will—the powers of self-transcendence—that share in our ontic spiritual ground. The somatically conditioned psychical dynamisms that "happen" in us and that need to be integrated into the unity of the person in action have also a basis therein. Eyesight, feelings, and emotions are examples of human activations that are in themselves psychical, or immaterial, while yet being manifestly dependent on the somatic dynamism. The term "psyche" applies to the soul in this phenomenal sense.[74] Our aesthetic, religious, and moral feelings are also somatically conditioned, though generated essentially by the psycho-emotive dynamism. As Wojtyła observes, sensitivities like these correspond clearly to what is spiritual in us, but they still fall short of achieving the level of human transcendence. They will reach that level only insofar as we integrate them into our personal actions.[75]

The phenomenological description of the human psyche both implies and depends on the fact that the psychical operations of the soul are integrated with the soma. Being immaterial in itself, the psychical dynamism belongs to our inner life, and there it would remain inaccessible to phenomenological analysis were it not indirectly exteriorized and expressed through the body. Only thus does it become an "object" of experience for us, at least as an experiential intuition. Because the psycho-emotive dynamism does not function in a purely spiritual way but rather conditions, and is conditioned by, the reactive and vegetative dynamisms of the soma, it mediates between and unites our corporeal and spiritual elements.

In a strictly phenomenological account, one cannot identify the source of psychical activity with the soul outright, as this falls properly within the domain of metaphysics rather than phenomenology. But assuming the traditional philosophical concept of the soul, Wojtyła concludes on the basis of his phenomenological analysis of the person in action that the psyche implies the soul as the principle determining our psychosomatic integration—our ontic integrity—as a spiritual-corporeal composite.[76]

73. See ibid., 184–85.

74. See ibid., 201, 222–23.

75. See ibid., 231–33.

76. See ibid., 185–86, 221–22, 226–27. Recognizing that the phenomenological method, with its appeal to human experience, is generally more accessible to modern understanding than metaphysics, Wojtyła uses it to bring us to the *threshold* of metaphysics. While phenomenology is not itself equipped to cross that threshold, it provides Wojtyła with a reasonable basis for introducing metaphysical affirmations that at one time could have been taken for granted (e.g.,

### The Abiding Transcendence of the Human Person amid Disintegrating Factors

The conclusion that the spiritual soul is the ultimate source of our ontic unity and not just of our personal unity in action explains why, in Wojtyła's view, we do not and *can*not lose our fundamental dignity and transcendence as persons when we fail personally (whether partially or totally) to act consciously and responsibly or when we have a structural inability to act so. True, there is a disintegration of the person in action when the dynamisms that happen in us are not, or because of some defect *can*not be, subordinated to our personal transcendence. We do not achieve our proper unity and fulfillment as personal actors when we willfully refuse to subject our self-determining freedom in action to the rationally apprehended truth about some value, or when a defect on the psychosomatic plane impedes the actualization of our intrinsic structure of self-possession and self-governance in personally fulfilling, self-determining acts. Such conditions might result in the formation of a distorted or an underdeveloped psycho-moral personality. In extreme cases, certain psychosomatic defects might render impossible any psycho-moral formation at all. Yet under any of the conditions just mentioned, we still remain essentially spiritual (hence rational) beings, persons who are ontologically constituted as such by the union of the human soul and body.[77]

So, even when self-possession and self-governance seem absent because never actualized, the spiritual soul still abides permanently as the transcendent basis of that essentially personal structure. From the first moment of our existence, each of us is a transcendent "somebody" because we have the personal structure virtually, regardless of whether we ever actualize it. For that reason, even the most serious forms of disintegration do not directly affect the fundamental transcendence of the human person, though the actualization and manifestation of human transcendence cannot be accomplished except through the integration, by the personal structure, of the dynamic psychosomatic totality into the dynamic person-action unity. But

---

concerning the existence of the human soul). See John Paul II's encyclical *Fides et Ratio*, 83, which seems to endorse, in a solemn papal teaching, the principle to which Wojtyła adhered as a philosopher, namely, the necessity of moving from the human *experience* of transcendence to the metaphysical *ground* of transcendence. The reason he gives for crossing over thus into metaphysics is telling: it allows us to secure our dignity as persons by grounding it in our substantial, spiritual existence.

77. See *AP*, 180, 192–95.

as we proceed now to our reflections on the implications of *Person and Act* for our understanding of vulnerable human beings, we will want to keep in mind that our transcendence as persons is never definitively compromised or destroyed by any disintegration of the personal structure for which we might or might not be personally responsible.

## Vulnerable Persons and Their Agency in the Light of *Person and Act*

The themes from Karol Wojtyła's philosophical anthropology that we have considered so far seem to undergird his understanding of developing, weak, disabled, suffering, and dying human beings as persons and as actors. While in *Person and Act* he conveys that understanding in a somewhat brief and restricted way in the course of examining the personal self-revelation of psychosomatically-psychologically-rationally mature human beings in and through their deliberate actions, it seems that Wojtyła/John Paul II draws from the principles that he laid down in his 1969 study as he addresses specifically, in subsequent written and verbal discourses, the question of the personhood and agency of vulnerable human beings. So let us now highlight the relevant principles, which we will see at work repeatedly, if sometimes only implicitly, in the forthcoming chapters on the work of Karol Wojtyła/Pope John Paul II.

### The Unconditionally Personal Existence of Vulnerable Human Beings

Wojtyła's integral treatment of metaphysical and personal subjectivity stands opposed to post-Cartesian views that would reduce the human person to merely a center of consciousness and autonomy, or to a unity formed in consciousness out of disparate subjective experiences. Reductionistic, disincarnate views like these, foreign to actual reality and experience, would deny personhood and even humanity to anyone who has not yet a fully developed capacity for self-consciousness and rationality, or to anyone in whom that capacity has diminished or seemingly been lost through accident, old age, or infirmity, in each case rendering the person radically dependent on others. Take, for example, the following statement by animal rights activist Peter Singer and his co-author, Helga Kuhse: "The morally relevant differences [between humans and animals] are those based on our superior mental powers—our self-awareness, our rationality, our moral sense, our autonomy, or some combination of these. They are the kinds of thing, we are inclined to say, which make us 'uniquely human.' To be more precise, they are the kinds of thing which make us persons."[78]

Now consider just one example of where that premise leads: "Let us say ... that we decide that what is characteristic or distinctive of men and women is a [functional] capacity of self-awareness or self-consciousness. Then we will not count severely retarded infants as human beings even though they are clearly members of *Homo sapiens*."[79] Of course, ideas have consequences. Singer, among others, uses groundless presuppositions like this to support his advocacy of infanticide—of active euthanasia for disabled infants. Singer's "rationale" is as follows:

> [I]t is not easy to see on what grounds mere potential could give rise to a right to life, unless we valued what it was that the being had the potential to become—in this case a rational, self-conscious being.... But most of us think that there are enough rational, self-conscious beings around already—in which case I find it hard to see why we should place great moral weight on every potentially rational, self-conscious being realizing its potential.[80]

Singer's position would justify not only infanticide but also abortion and euthanasia in general. It would even justify genocide—of which "population control" is perhaps the most insidious form—should "most of us think" that there are *too many* rational, self-conscious beings around already. In the end, Singer undermines completely his unqualified exaltation of "our superior mental powers" with his suggestion that "most of us" do not really value what it is that disabled infants supposedly have only the potential to become, namely, "rational, self-conscious beings." But he does succeed in showing thereby that his radically flawed premises lead inevitably to the absolute devaluation of *all* human life.

In response to Singer's position, Wojtyła would affirm that one has the

78. Helga Kuhse and Peter Singer, "Individuals, Humans, and Persons," in *Unsanctifying Human Life: Essays on Ethics* (Malden, Mass.: Blackwell Publishers, 2002), 193.

79. Peter Singer, "Unsanctifying Human Life," in *Unsanctifying Human Life,* 222. Singer continues: "[A]t the same time we might decide, after examining the abilities displayed by apes, dolphins, and perhaps some other mammals, to count these beings as human beings." Note the incongruity of Singer's position. "We" (probably the members of the "Self-Conscious and Rational Club," though it is chilling to consider what "elite" subset of that group the "we" might become) can decide that severely retarded human infants *are not* human beings because they presumably lack the capacity for self-awareness by which to decide for themselves that they *are,* while "we" can also decide that certain mammals *are* human beings even though they, like retarded infants (again, presumably), lack the same capacity.

80. Ibid.

potential for rationality and for experiencing oneself as a person in consciousness only because one is *already* a concrete person—a metaphysical subject constituted of the integral unity of soul and body—from the first moment of one's existence. While consciousness is the condition for the subjective experience, the self-awareness, of the fact that one is objectively—that is, essentially—a person from the beginning, it does not establish one's existence as personal. On the contrary, consciousness is somehow constituted by that existence during the normal course of development. But regardless of whether the inherent capacity for rationality and self-conscious experience is ever fully realized, if realized at all, the uniquely personal and transcendent character of human existence abides, thanks to the presence of the spiritual soul as the substantial principle of that existence.

In his 1976 article entitled "The Person: Subject and Community," Cardinal Wojtyła revisits the main themes of *Person and Act* and has this to say: "The fact that the human *suppositum*, or metaphysical subjectivity, does not display the traits of personal subjectivity in certain cases (i.e., in cases of psychosomatic or purely psychological immaturity, in which either the normal human self has not developed or the self has developed in a distorted way) does not allow us to question the very foundations of this subjectivity, for they reside within the essentially human *suppositum*."[81] Wojtyła is reaffirming here that the consciousness of oneself as a personal subject is but an aspect, not the definition, of a person. In his view, consciousness is rooted in the rational potentiality of human nature, and human nature exists only in the concrete, personal being whose nature it is. Therefore, human beings do not really have any "potential" to be persons: they *are* persons, regardless of whether or to what degree they are conscious of that fact.

## Activations as Constitutive and Revelatory of the Person

Activations and actions are personal in the *foundational* sense that they both derive ultimately from the original act by which our personal being first came to exist. In turn, those same two dynamisms enact our personal being, in different ways, according to its properly human potentialities. More specifically, the originating and unifying principle of both human activations and human actions is the spiritual soul—the principle of one's dynamic sub-

81. In *PC*, 225. Writing in a similar vein, Wojtyła gave a specific example years earlier in *LR*: "[A] child, even an unborn child, cannot be denied personality in its most objective ontological sense, although it is true that it has yet to acquire, step by step, many of the traits which will make it psychologically and ethically a distinct personality" (26).

stantial existence as a person—while the principles governing each of those two kinds of activity are the particular powers of the soul in its union with the body (in the case of human actions, as exercised freely by the person). In their own way, then, human activations always express the presence and the inestimable dignity of a person, the subsistent subject of the natural psychosomatic potentialities from which the activations issue so as to actualize that subject more fully.

In that light, we can conclude that vulnerable human beings for whom personally integrative, autonomous action is not possible either because of the early stage of development or because of some kind of psychosomatic disintegration can nevertheless disclose themselves as persons, albeit only *passively*, in the concrete *activity* by which the spiritual (or personal) soul and its somatically dependent powers constitute and enact the essential soul-body unity of the metaphysical subject. In other words, the human activations by which the soul, united to and operating through the body, constitutes and perfects the basic psychosomatic structure bear witness to the person whose structure it is. What is more, they play an indispensable role in the emergence and formation of the personal subjectivity—the concrete, psycho-moral "I"—of the human being. Taken together, the two texts below from Wojtyła's writings contain the essential elements of this position.

> The human soul is the principle of the life and activity of the human being; it operates, in turn, through the mediation of faculties. The faculties that express and actualize the soul's spirituality, and thus the human being's spirituality, are reason and free will. They are also the principal means, so to speak, whereby the human person is actualized; based on their activity, the whole psychological and moral personality takes shape.... As the substantial form of the body, the soul also has ... faculties that are intrinsically dependent on matter. These are primarily sensory faculties, both cognitive and appetitive. These faculties, as belonging to the concrete human being, are likewise found in the person and contribute in their own way to the shaping of the psychological and moral personality.... [The spiritual aspect of the human being] is eminently suited to unite into a substantial whole with the corporeal, and thus also with the sensory. This union must, therefore, also play a special role in shaping the human personality. According to St. Thomas, all the faculties of the human soul work to perfect the human being, and so they all contribute to the development of the person.[82]

In the preceding text, Wojtyła probably does not envision the cognitive and appetitive senses as contributing to personality formation apart from their

82. "Thomistic Personalism" (1961), in *PC*, 168–69.

conditioning reason and will, nor should he. However, in the next text, written fifteen years later, we gain a broader perspective.

> The self constitutes itself through action, through the *operari* proper to the human being as a person. It also constitutes itself through its entire psychosomatic dynamism, through the whole sphere of *operari* that simply happens in the subject but that nevertheless somehow shapes the subjectivity of the individual. Of course, the human self is able to constitute itself in this manner only because it already is and has been constituted in an essential and fundamental way as a *suppositum*.[83]

While by the author's design, the second text, like the article from which it comes, does not mention or allude to the underlying role of the spiritual soul in the process of our dynamic self-constitution, it does bring out more clearly than the first that the whole range of human activations, and not just certain sensory operations, contributes to the self-constitution of the concrete person's psychosomatic structure and to the emergence therein of the psycho-moral personality ("the self"), revealing the person thus. Given that understanding, the first text makes it clear that the substantial, spiritual soul, together with its powers, is the source of all this self-constituting activity and so reveals the person—the spiritual-corporeal subject of the activity—through it. Though the detailed series of phenomenological analyses carried out in *Person and Act* can somewhat obscure the fact that Wojtyła takes the same basic position there, we were still able to uncover it based on the dynamic philosophy of personal being presented in that work and to arrive thereby at an understanding of the "active passivity" of the most vulnerable human beings, about which we will say more later.

## The Absence of Mature Personality and of Personal Agency in *Some* Vulnerable Persons

We recalled above that, in Cardinal Wojtyła's view, both activations and actions are personal relative to the dynamic source from which they ultimately issue, namely, the original, spiritual act of our coming to be. Relative to each other, however, activations seem nonpersonal, since a specific dynamization of human nature is the immediate source of what happens in us, whereas the *self*-dynamization of our person is the immediate source of what we do deliberately. Wojtyła will eventually modify that position by developing, it would seem, the implications of what we said under the previous two subheadings, as we will see further on. But in terms of his philosophical un-

83. "The Person: Subject and Community," in *PC*, 225.

derstanding in *Person and Act,* he would not regard certain vulnerable persons, such as infants and people with advanced Alzheimer's disease, as *actors,* strictly speaking, because they are incapable of expressing themselves with complete *freedom* as persons through actions that issue from their own personal agency—lacking, as they do, an adequately developed or an unimpaired consciousness, rationality, and psycho-moral personality. The formation, expression, growth, and continuation of our psycho-moral personality occur through personal acts of self-determination, while these presuppose, in turn, the proper functioning of consciousness and rationality.

Wojtyła has nevertheless made it clear that self-determining acts, while constitutive of the psycho-moral *personality,* do not constitute us essentially as *persons.* Rather, they reveal the personal ground out of which such acts arise in the first place, namely, our intrinsic structure of self-possession and self-governance, whose abiding basis is the spiritual soul. Each of us must always already *be* a person in order to be able to *act* as one. Personal activity requires a sufficient cause. It cannot issue from what is nonpersonal.

That is why Wojtyła would have unequivocally affirmed, based on his position in *Person and Act,* that the infant, the Alzheimer's patient, and other human beings in analogous states of development or decline are fully *persons,* even though weak, wholly dependent on others, and unable to form or to maintain a mature personality through self-determining acts because lacking full self-awareness and rational functionality. The psycho-moral personality formed through the actualization of the personal structure in action presupposes the being of the person as already essentially constituted by that structure; therefore, the self-reflective "I" is not fundamental to the person as such. Rather, the spiritual soul, metaphysically integrated with the body, underlies the personal structure as the permanent core of the person's transcendence, ordering vulnerable human beings (and everyone else) toward their free self-expression as persons in action, even when that level of actualization is not yet or is no longer possible.[84]

84. Given Wojtyła's utter clarity in this matter, one is at a loss to explain how Williams can assert that, even as a Catholic, "Wojtyła is not considering, philosophically, every member of the human family as a full person. The person, for Wojtyła, is a conscious, rational, and responsible human being." While Williams interprets another aspect of Wojtyła's position correctly as saying that "[y]oung children, senile adults, and the mentally incompetent are not able to act fully as persons," his inexplicable misconstrual of the author's meaning on the most crucial point—that concerning the ontologically personal structure of every human being—leads him to interpret Wojtyła, wrongly, as saying that disintegration, "through which the functioning of the active person is inhibited[,] ... can rob the person of his true personhood, as in the case of the severely mentally handicapped." *The Mind of John Paul II,* 207.

## Personality Development in Somatically Disabled Persons through the Interior Act

In the first part of this chapter, we saw that activations are ordered toward authentic human actions, in which they receive a new, personal meaning and unity that they do not have of themselves as causations of nature. At the same time, human actions are built on the foundation of activations and cannot therefore be executed apart from the natural dynamisms. Given this close relation between the two, we said that transitions can occur in either direction from one form of activity to the other, depending on whether our personal agency is engaged or somehow inhibited, prevented, or even willfully withdrawn. Though a regression from action to activation would frustrate the dynamic course of our whole development toward the emergence and growth of a fully mature psycho-moral personality, it is not always easy to tell when that particular form of personal disintegration has taken place, for the outward appearance of human acting might mask the fact that it has.

When human acting regresses, despite appearances, more or less to the level of activations, we might or we might not be personally responsible, in some measure, for the degree to which we are being governed not by ourselves, but by something that is "happening" in us. We are certainly blameworthy when we disregard our duty to integrate our feelings, emotions, passions, excitements, instincts, and drives into our person according to the rational order of truth, preferring instead to give ourselves over deliberately to the purely *subjectivistic* "truth" about the values that we experience spontaneously through them. Even if that leads to ways of "acting" that are objectively bad both personally and morally, we might still lose the will to forsake them, leading to our further disintegration as actors. The dehumanizing and depersonalizing distortions that accrue to our psycho-moral personality as a result will distort, in turn, the manner in which we view and treat others—especially the most vulnerable human beings, whose needs confront us with our egoism and whose helplessness subjects them to our abuse should we refuse to renounce it.

Just as there can be "acting" that appears real to others (and to oneself) but is not (at least not completely), there can also be acting that is real but does not appear to others (or, if it does, it does not appear to be real acting). In that case, the person engages his agency through interiorly executed actions, thus determining himself *as* a person, but with little or no external evidence to back it up, as far as many others are concerned. This whole understanding of the interior act is of capital importance to Wojtyła's understanding of agency in certain types of vulnerable human beings. In *Person and Act,* he observes that somatic disintegration might impede the performance of actions requiring bodily movement. It follows that severe physical defects might render certain people exceedingly dependent on others, some of whom might consequently regard them as useless, burdensome, or even less than human and personal. However, since their rationality and self-consciousness are not necessarily impaired or distorted at all by their condition, physically disabled persons are capable of performing self-determining, interior acts of the highest order. As a result, they are also capable of forming themselves into *personalities* of the highest order. Like anyone else, they must undertake that task freely. To forsake it deliberately would run counter to their authentic personal development and so deprive them of their proper perfection as persons, of their subjective fulfillment in the objective good.

Some provocative studies of the phenomenon called "unconscious experience" seem to confirm, paradoxically, that persons can retain their consciousness while in a state of unconsciousness.[85] That is, persons can have an undistorted awareness of their inner self and of the external environment while yet being unable to respond, at the psychomotor level, to what is happening around them.[86] To all outward appearances, such persons are unconscious and consequently unaware. But according to their own testimony on "regaining" consciousness, they *perceived* their "unconsciousness" inwardly, retaining, for example, the ability to hear, to understand, to feel sensibly, to respond emotionally, or to sense movement. Since the continued

85. See Madelaine Lawrence, "The Unconscious Experience," *American Journal of Critical Care* 4 (1995): 227–32. See also her earlier article (under the name Madelaine Podurgiel), "The Unconscious Experience: A Pilot Study," *Journal of Neuroscience Nursing* 22 (February 1990): 52–53.

86. Other states of unconscious experience include: (1) inner consciousness without consciousness of the external environment; (2) distorted consciousness, involving perceptual, memory, or personality distortions; and (3) paranormal (e.g., "out-of-body") experiences. See Lawrence, "The Unconscious Experience," 229–31. For her most comprehensive account of the various states of unconscious experience, see Madelaine Lawrence, *In a World of Their Own: Experiencing Unconsciousness* (Westport, Conn.: Praeger Publishers, 1997). The relative frequency with which people claim to have experienced one or more of these "unconscious" states, the generally similar way in which they tend to describe them, and the knowledge that many of these persons have about what was going on around them when they were apparently unresponsive and unaware all argues in favor of the reality of their experiences. The manner in which such experiences are investigated and interpreted is another question. In her effort to shed light on the matter, Lawrence considers paradigms ranging from medical science and psychology to Eastern pantheism and the occult. Still, her conclusions regarding the care and treatment of unconscious patients are indispensable, especially when she reminds us of the importance of treating such persons *as* persons.

functioning of consciousness in patients like these sometimes leaves their self-awareness fully intact and so also their ability to act in a strictly human and personal way, the studies would suggest that it is possible for a person to perform wholly interior acts even when the somatic disintegration causing "unconsciousness" would seem, by every outer measure, to preclude such a possibility. The phenomenon of unconscious experience thus indicates that Cardinal Wojtyła's integral understanding of the human person, particularly in its application to bodily disintegrated persons, finds support in recent case studies.

# 3

# The Person Acting in Community

In this chapter, we will consider Cardinal Wojtyła's treatment of persons as agents both of and within their interpersonal and social relations with others. We will be examining not only the ideal structure of the communities or societies formed of those relations but also some of the defects that can undermine them. We will see that any such defects can always be traced back to defective relationships among persons. Mindful of what we learned in chapter 2, we will then reflect on how psychosomatically developing, psychorationally disintegrated, and somatically disintegrated persons can exercise their agency in the communal or larger societal setting so as to contribute indispensably to its enrichment, unless alienated from it by self, by others, or by unjust social structures. Our study of both ideal and defective human communities/societies will also provide us with the opportunity to consider yet another category of vulnerable persons: the poor and oppressed.

## Participation and Alienation

Most of *Person and Act* is devoted to Wojtyła's analysis of the common experience that we each have of ourselves as actors. Through that analysis, he is able to specify the conditions in the human person that allow for the performance of the human act as such. He thus arrives at an understanding of the essential constitution of the personal subject. In the book's final chapter, called "Intersubjectivity by Participation," Wojtyła offers a comparatively brief and general analysis of certain types of interpersonal and social relations that form among human persons as they exist and act together.[1] The reason why he proceeds from the personal subject to the community of persons is both logical and metaphysical. Our ability to form and take part in various types of communities with other persons presupposes in us a subjective structure that constitutes each of us, in the first place, as a person. And our ability to *fulfill* ourselves as individuals by acting communally presupposes that we are thereby acting according to our personal nature and, furthermore, that our cooperative actions cohere with, shape, and perfect us, precisely because we act *personally* in and through them. We must therefore understand the person first as a subject revealed through action before we can properly understand him *inter*subjectively—that is, in his relations with others.[2]

It seems certain that Wojtyła has taken a key statement from Vatican II's *Gaudium et Spes* as the inspiration for his approach: man is "the only creature on earth which God willed for itself," but he "cannot fully find himself except through a sincere gift of himself."[3] This means that regardless of what, if any, interpersonal and social relationships we might have with other human beings, each of us exists essentially as a person. Yet, we cannot *fulfill* ourselves as persons *apart from* such relationships. In particular, we cannot fully discover who we really are, nor therefore possess ourselves fully, without giving ourselves away to others—that is, without acting disinterestedly for their sake so as to make a gift of ourselves to them. Still, we must in some sense possess ourselves already if ever we are to give ourselves away to begin with: we must already be constituted essentially as givers, as actors, as *persons,* if ever we are to manifest ourselves as such in any intersubjective context.

## The Concept of Participation

With that in mind, Wojtyła introduces the key concept of *participation.* Participation is a property of the person corresponding to the sociality in-

1. Actually, the first English edition has *two* "final" chapters. One is an edited translation of the Polish text and the other, nearly identical, is an unedited translation included as an appendix. It is to the latter that we will be referring throughout.

2. See *AP,* 316n77.

3. See Walter M. Abbott, SJ, ed. "*Gaudium et Spes*" [hereafter *GS*] in *The Documents of Vatican II* (New York: America Press, 1966), 24.

scribed into human existence itself.[4] It enables us to perform genuinely personal actions precisely by performing them together with other persons (and ultimately *for the sake of* other persons). Because each of our actions is grounded in our own personal structure of self-determination, we can still fulfill ourselves as persons when we coexist and collaborate with others in communal and societal settings, choosing as our own good the good that is common to all. We thus choose to realize with others what others have chosen, and we might even choose it *because* they have chosen it. The true common good never contradicts the inherent requirements of our personal fulfillment, and so our identity does not, in principle, get compromised or lost in the context of communal life with others. On the contrary, the common good provides the occasion for our own fulfillment in self-transcending, personally integrative actions: first, because we are each responsible for verifying the truth of that good through the judicious acts of an upright conscience; second, because we must freely choose as our own a good that was initially chosen by others; and, third, because we engage our personal capacity for participation (toward which the previous acts are ordered) by existing and acting with and for the sake of others in the communal effort to realize the true common good. What is more, because our fulfillment as persons is bound to our actualizing our personal capacity for genuinely participatory actions, we have a natural right to perform them.[5]

The possibility of fulfilling ourselves as persons through the true common good is especially evident when its realization requires great personal sacrifice on our part, for we are then more intensely related to and personally invested in that good; consequently, our efforts to realize it communally redound to our own good as well. And by contributing thus to the true good of a given community by participating freely therein, we simultaneously benefit from its growth and enrichment in that good. This mutually beneficial interplay between the person, the larger community, and the authentic good of both characterizes Wojtyła's general understanding of the term *solidarity*.[6] But for him, the concept has an even deeper basis.

True solidarity exists within a community of persons only when each member regards every other as a neighbor—as having an intrinsic value simply because he or she is a unique and unrepeatable human being. One will

4. See *AP*, 318.

5. See ibid., 327, 329–30, 332, 337–40, 344–45. In *PC*, see "The Person: Subject and Community," 233–38; "Participation or Alienation?" 200.

6. See *AP*, 339–42.

then see that the persons who make up the community also transcend it individually in virtue of their concrete, personal humanity. The concept of neighbor thus refers us beyond every particular community to the community of *all* human beings, who collectively constitute the human "family." It refers us to our solidarity in humanness, which underlies the formation of every authentically human community. It must therefore never become limited or overshadowed in such a way that the person becomes subordinated to, and hence alienated from, a given community. The true measure of any community is whether it facilitates one's ability to participate in the humanity of others—that is, one's ability to view and to relate to every other person as a neighbor, as a unique and unrepeatable "second self," as another like me. Every truly *human* community forms and develops based on this more fundamental sense of participation, while also deriving its personal meaning from it. Wojtyła tells us that the content of this understanding of "neighbor" is contained implicitly in the commandment to love.[7]

The task of building a truly human community is not an easy one, so Wojtyła tells us that genuine solidarity might express itself through a legitimate attitude of *opposition*. Persons who express opposition in a true spirit of solidarity seek, through respectful dialogue, to work constructively within the community to establish both a proper perspective on the common good and a proper place for themselves. To the extent that they succeed, they can participate more fully in communal efforts to achieve the common good, which each person has always to confirm as such through an upright conscience.[8]

While we have the capacity, proper to us as persons, to participate in the humanity of another person, Wojtyła explains that we must *choose* to do so by actualizing that capacity personally. The commandment to love our neighbor, though corresponding to what is most personal in us, cannot move us to act merely by our hearing its summons from the outside. The impulse to act on it must arise from *within* as we make a spontaneous, yet rationally based, choice to accept and affirm the person who makes a claim on us here and now. For that reason, our need to actualize the personal property of participation, and thus to relate to other people as other *I*'s, arises in us as a *task* to be fulfilled, a task that has ethical import and whose measure is the commandment to love.[9] So, we have not only the natural right to perform partici-

7. See ibid., 348–55.

8. See ibid., 340–44, 349–50.

9. See "Participation or Alienation?" in *PC*, 202–4; *AP*, 354–55.

patory actions: we have also the moral obligation to do so. What is more, that same right implies our obligation to establish and uphold the conditions that allow everyone else to perform truly participatory actions along with us.

### The Interpersonal and Social Dimensions of Community

Cardinal Wojtyła's 1976 article, "The Person: Subject and Community," shows at greater length that participation in the community's common good through participation in the humanity of another or others is the natural means by which the person achieves self-fulfillment. The author speaks in general about both the interpersonal, or *I-thou,* community and the social, or *we,* community.[10] The life of each of us begins and develops in interpersonal and social relationships, and they continue to define our existence even before our experience of them reaches the level of conscious reflection. For the purpose of his analyses, however, Wojtyła considers the *I-thou* and the *we* structures only in their fully developed form. For just as we can adequately understand the foundations of human subjectivity only retrospectively after having first analyzed the later stage of development in which we each experience that subjectivity for ourselves in the performance of properly human actions, so, too, we can better understand the earlier stages of the *I-thou* and the *we* structures of human community life only after having first analyzed those structures at the consummate level of development that only mature personal subjects are capable of jointly bringing about.[11]

#### The "I-Thou" Relation

Even as we recall that my *I* is constituted on the foundation of the metaphysical subjectivity that established me as a personal being from the first moment of my existence, and presuming that it has already been so constituted, there is still a sense in which my *I* is also constituted by the communal relationships of which I am a part. That is but another way of saying—and indeed of verifying—that we are inherently social beings. Where interpersonal relations are concerned, I need a *thou*—another *I*—to help bring out more fully the *I* in *me.* For that reason, Wojtyła speaks of the *reflexivity* of the *I-thou* relation. On the one hand, I go out of myself, I transcend myself, to relate to a *thou.* At the same time, I experience that relation in consciousness, through which it returns to me in a way that touches me interiorly as a person. That

10. See "The Person: Subject and Community," in *PC,* 236–52.
11. See ibid., 240–41.

is, I see myself in the light of another *I*, in the light of a *thou*, who contributes thereby to my self-understanding. The *I-thou* relation can thus influence the person I become, hence the importance of good role models. Though Wojtyła does not say it explicitly in this context, we can suppose that if the relation of my *I* to a *thou* were somehow distorted (because of some problem on either or both sides), it could detract from my self-understanding and from the person I consequently become.

While I have a real experience of the interpersonal *relationship* even when the relation of my *I* to a *thou* is unilateral, the formation of a fully interpersonal *community* and, with it, the fullness of the interpersonal experience require that the *I* who is a *thou* for me regard my *I*, in turn, as a *thou*. In other words, my participation in the other person's humanity must be reciprocated such that we both experience the mutuality of our relation. As a prerequisite, we must *reveal* ourselves to each other as persons through self-transcending acts, particularly acts of right conscience, in which our personal transcendence is most decisively realized and manifested. And we accomplish that precisely by directing such acts toward each other. In that way, we also accept and affirm each other mutually as a "second self"—that is, according to the truth of the other person's transcendent value precisely *as* a person. It is through these actions of each toward the other that we establish our interpersonal community. We see, then, that the subject has a metaphysical priority over the community.

At the same time, however, both the *thou* who is the "object" of my actions and the *I-thou* relation formed of our reciprocally directed activity returns to me in consciousness, where I experience myself as newly confirmed in my transcendent subjectivity, precisely because of the affirming welcome I have received as the *thou* of my *thou*. In that sense, the *I* is constituted by the *thou*. Similarly, the *I* for whom I am a *thou* would have a richer self-experience based on the community formed of our interpersonal relationship. As the relationship intensifies, it grows in mutual trust and self-giving, as well as in each *I*'s need to be accepted and affirmed by the counterrelative *thou* in a way that corresponds fully to the depth of subjectivity proper to the person. Of course, this will all be expressed appropriately according to the nature of the relationship—depending, for example, on whether it is the *I-thou* of friends, of a man and a woman in marriage, or of siblings. But in every case, the interpersonal relation will entail each person's responsibility to seek and to act for the true good of the other—a good that each one must discern through an upright conscience. As the highest expression and manifestation of human transcendence, the exercise of conscience is indispensable to personal fulfillment and to the formation of that authentic, mutually enacted interpersonal relationship that Cardinal Wojtyła likes to call the communion of persons *(communio personarum)*.[12]

### The "We" Relation

Whereas the interpersonal community calls attention to the individual persons that constitute it (namely, the *I* and the *thou*), the social community calls attention to the *multiplicity* of persons that constitute it (for example, all the people living in Littletown, U.S.A.). Because many persons can be identified based on something they have in common (like place of residence—"Littletown"), they might regard themselves or appear to others, accordingly, as a *we*.[13] But the mere fact that people exist and act together does not mean, in itself, that they form a community, or "co-unity"—a unity constituted of multiple subjects. It is only when the objective dimension of the community is complemented by a properly subjective dimension that a multiplicity of persons forms the "single subjectivity" of the *we*. The subjective moment occurs when, in accordance with the judgment of right conscience, many individual subjects consciously identify with and freely work together to achieve the same value, namely, the true common good. This is what underlies the authentic social community. The same applies, analogously, to the interpersonal community.

It is often necessary, and even morally obligatory, for certain interpersonal communities ( such as the marital community of a man and a woman) to insert their relationship into the *we* of the social community or to become also a *we* themselves, by accepting and helping to realize the values represented by the true good of the social order as a whole. In turn, the *I-thou* relationship and those who form it will be enriched by and not lost within any social community that strives to realize the true common good. Similarly, the single *I*'s that make up a true *we* community are not lost but constituted, in a way, therein. How? According to Wojtyła, the *we* relates these *I*'s to a good that has greater value than the individual goods that they each pursue singly; therefore, they achieve greater personal fulfillment, fuller self-expression, in existing and acting together with one another to achieve that

12. See ibid., 240–46.

13. And because some people are members of a given *we*, others might consequently transfer the relationally based identity of the collectivity to each person therein: "She is a Littletown resident." See ibid., 238, 246.

greater good, which is the true common good. In Wojtyła's words, the true *we* community "signifies a human multiplicity with the kind of structure in which the person as a subject is maximally actualized."[14] He means here that the community encourages and facilitates the self-fulfilling participation of each member.

Of course, the true common good and its significance vary according to the type of *we* community that is relating itself to such a good as an end. In addition, the common good becomes more difficult to realize as the disproportion between the community and its level of unity increases with its size. The family, the neighborhood, the nation, the state, and the whole human world are all *we*'s having different goods for which their participants act, and it is not always easy to balance them (for example, the good of the family versus the good of the nation in time of war), even if we assume that a sufficient number of *I*'s are willing to try. If the legitimate common goods of the different *we* communities to which I belong conflict because they cannot be simultaneously realized, which of them is the greatest good that I am morally bound to uphold by my actions? It is precisely the personal effort, in good conscience, that each *I*, as a member of those different *we*'s, must invest in the attempt to achieve, here and now, the greatest good amid legitimate common goods that lends itself to personal growth—to genuine self-discovery and fulfillment. At times, that does not happen without heroic personal sacrifices on the part of many of the *I*'s who help form the subjectivity of the *we*'s.

The same type of thing can happen when a tension arises between the particular good that one might want to realize for oneself—however legitimate in itself—and the true common good. But those types of occasions often testify to the superior value of the latter over the former. Legitimate individual goods are sometimes reduced to insignificance when the urgent need to realize the true common good takes priority or when, deprived of that good, persons can no longer realize their own goods in the very context that gave them meaning.[15] On the other hand, the willingness of many subjects to identify with the *we* of a given community because of the authentic good that

14. Ibid., 251.

15. See ibid., 250. It seems that here, as elsewhere, Wojtyła is speaking out of his own life experience. Confronted in his homeland with the grim realities of World War II (and later of communism), he abandoned his earlier ambition of becoming an actor and redirected his talent and energy to the priesthood. With Poland deprived of the possibility of pursuing its own true good, Wojtyła's personal goal of being an actor lost its prior meaning. By becoming a priest, however, he could maximize his contribution to restoring Poland to its true good, which was historically bound to its vibrant practice of the Catholic faith.

defines it leads to the "subjectivity" of the many, to the unity established by and among numerous persons, which basically coincides with the real *communion of persons* underlying any authentic *we* community.[16]

## The Concept of Alienation

Whether we are speaking of an *I-thou* relation or a *we* relation, we imply, as its basis, that the personal property of participation is being actualized by the ones who form it. In virtue of that property, persons open up to one another by existing and acting together with a view toward achieving the true good of all. They fulfill themselves individually by the personal transcendence that they achieve in doing so; they establish a healthy communal life; and they each benefit from the communal good that they have helped foster. *Alienation* threatens or destroys all this by hindering or preventing persons from participating in the humanity of others, whether on the interpersonal or the social level. It is therefore the antithesis of participation.

### Individualism and Totalism

In *Person and Act,* Cardinal Wojtyła outlines two alienating systems that obstruct social participation, namely, *individualism* and *totalism,* which elsewhere he calls *social egoism* and *totalitarianism.*[17] Each of these systems denies that the person has a proper ability to act together with others without compromising, respectively, either personal or communal development. Cutting off participation, as they do, from opposite directions, both systems presuppose anthropologies that are decidedly nonpersonalistic.

In the system of individualism, the person regards the interests of the social community or the larger society as conflicting with his or her own good, to which collective interests must therefore be subordinated. While preferring, perhaps, to alienate themselves entirely from any social groupings, radical individualists might "submit" to some forms of participation because a certain amount of communal acting is necessary, as they see it, to protect their own individual good from "the others." But the idea that participation is a property of the person through which one can find fulfillment as a member of an acting community is foreign to the system of individualism. That kind of system typifies the so-called free societies that have betrayed wor-

16. See ibid., 246–52; *AP,* 333–40.

17. On "individualism" and "totalism," see *AP,* 329–31. Wojtyła uses, in passing, the synonymous terms mentioned above in "The Person: Subject and Community," *PC,* 250.

thy democratic principles aimed at promoting the true common good and the participation of each citizen therein.[18]

On the other hand, Wojtyła describes totalism as "reversed individualism," and so he also calls it "anti-individualism."[19] According to this view, every individual will pursue only his own interests to the detriment of the common good. So it is *society* that must defend itself from the individual, not the reverse. As with individualism, there is a denial here of the person's capacity for participation, for attaining personal fulfillment by acting freely, together with others, for the true good of all. However, since totalism presumes that the good that persons would choose for themselves as individuals is always at odds with the common good, it demands that individuals be restrained from pursuing their own ends and perhaps even coerced into complying with societal objectives. The modes of communal acting established according to the tenets of totalism are therefore inherently inimical to participation, hence alienating.

### Conformism and Avoidance

We saw above that the alienating system of individualism rejects, in principle, the idea that human beings are endowed with a capacity for social participation that leads to personal fulfillment. Wojtyła also describes two alienating *attitudes* relative to the common good that are likewise individualistic—not because of a self-seeking, thoroughgoing denial of the personal capacity for participation, but because of a selfish refusal to exercise it. The two attitudes of which he speaks are *conformism* and *avoidance*, distortions of the authentic attitudes of solidarity and opposition mentioned earlier.

The attitude of conformism, or servile compliance, insinuates itself when community members become apathetic about fostering the conditions needed for real participation. Forsaking their personal responsibility for ascertaining both the true common good and the means by which they can actively participate with others so as best to achieve it, conformists submit passively

18. Wojtyła explains that his overview of this system (and that of totalism) is simplified, necessarily leaving aside the wide range of variations in which it occurs. He seeks only to show the implications of the system, its possible threat to participation (see *AP*, 273). Nevertheless, based on the few examples he gives of communities of being and acting, Williams somehow arrives at the startling conclusion that Wojtyła regards every voluntary association in the individualistic society as selfish. He seems to take an inordinately defensive posture against what he perceives to be an attack on Anglo-American society in particular. See Williams, *The Mind of John Paul II*, 212–13.

19. See *AP*, 331.

to what others have decided and thus become absorbed by the community rather than actively self-realized therein. Somewhat paradoxically, their passive compliance with what happens externally signifies their *withdrawal from* the community, and it might also signify an indifference toward the common good. Conformism is therefore inherently individualistic, even though the nonengagement of persons with the community, perceived as a threat to the individual good, takes place under the guise of cooperation. Such appearances result only in uniformity, not in unity.[20]

Whereas conformism maintains at least a semblance of interest in the common good through passive compliance with the demands of the community, the attitude of avoidance, or noninvolvement, shuns any feigned manifestations of common concern. In that respect, avoidance is somewhat more authentic than conformism and constitutes its rejection, especially when actual withdrawal from the community is undertaken as an active response to objectively unjust conditions. At the most fundamental level, however, both conformism and avoidance reflect the same individualistic attitude: apathy toward participation and the common good. With avoidance, the person protests the community's problems by withdrawing so as not to be associated with them. Though "making a statement" thus, he simultaneously refuses to work constructively for the betterment of the community. Consequently, avoidance merely completes conformism's hidden withdrawal from the community by manifesting it. Solidarity and opposition, on the other hand, are self-transcending attitudes because they require explicit concern for the common good and demand one's participation in the effort to realize that good.[21]

### Interpersonal Egoism

Though Wojtyła does not use the term "interpersonal egoism" himself, it designates appropriately (by analogy with "social egoism") the kind of individualism that he sees as causing alienation in interpersonal relationships. In the final analysis, egoists are not really capable of entering genuinely interpersonal relationships at all, for participation therein is based, more intensely than in the social realm, on the recognition and the experience in consciousness of other *I*'s besides one's own.[22] Participation enables us to enter interpersonal communion with others by seeking and acting for

20. See ibid., 345–47.
21. See ibid., 347–48.
22. See *LR*, 156.

the sake of *their* true good, though certainly in a way complementary to our own. In that way, and through the reciprocal relation of each *thou* to our *I*, we experience ourselves in consciousness in the light of other *I*'s: our own subjectivity is affirmed, confirmed, revealed, and fulfilled—in a word, "constituted"—through those persons with whom we have established a mutually participatory *I-thou* relation. We see, then, that as a personal property, participation must be actualized for the psycho-moral growth and the overall perfection of the person.

Conversely, by being self-enclosed, egoists are never properly self-*dis*closed. They are alienated both from themselves and from every person to whom they might otherwise relate as a *thou*. Because egoists do not regard any potential *thou* in the uniqueness and totality of his or her personal humanity—that is, as a "neighbor"—every *thou* becomes reduced, in their eyes, to a nondescript "other," a stranger, or even an enemy.[23] As with the social egoist, the interpersonal egoist relates to others only for self-serving, utilitarian reasons at best, though he might not be fully aware of this.

### The Source and the Resolution of Alienation

Since every human community has its ground in our personal subjectivity and develops in relation to it, the source of alienation ought not to be sought in the structures of human social existence but in our personal failure or refusal to make participation in the humanity of others the criterion of intracommunal life.[24] That is what prevents us from realizing authentically personal actions. We become separated—estranged—from our own self in becoming estranged from others. The "dehumanizing" effect of alienation takes place, therefore, at the level of our personal subjectivity, whereas our humanity as such—that is, ontologically speaking—cannot be dehumanized.[25] Since alienation is rooted in the person's misuse of the personal structure, the power to reverse it resides also in and with the person.[26] The course of action that we choose will invariably be reflected in the life of the community, for good or for ill.

23. See "The Person: Subject and Community," in *PC*, 256–57.
24. See "Participation or Alienation?" in *PC*, 205–6.
25. See "The Person: Subject and Community," in *PC*, 237–38, 257.
26. See *AP*, 353–54.

## The Intracommunal Agency of Vulnerable Persons in the Light of *Person and Act*

Building on the insights gained from chapter 2, we will now reflect on how Cardinal Wojtyła's analysis of persons acting in community sheds light on the different modes of agency exercised, or in some cases willfully forsaken, by four categories of vulnerable human beings. We will consider first the agency of psychosomatically developing persons (particularly, the human embryo and the infant) in the context of the family, which we will take as the foundational model for every other form of human community. We will then consider the communal agency of persons having severe psychorational disintegration (for example, persons suffering from serious mental retardation or from advanced Alzheimer's disease). Next, we will consider how persons having severe somatic disintegration might act in and for the community. Finally, we will consider some of the ways in which poor and oppressed persons might exercise their agency interpersonally and socially.

As we proceed, we must keep a few things in mind. First, in describing this or that mode of agency in relation to a given category of the vulnerable, we do not necessarily intend to restrict it to that category only. Indeed, it might just as well apply to human beings in general. Second, neither the four categories selected for review nor the modes of agency discussed in each of them are exhaustive or always as clearly delineated as our presentation might suggest. And third, we would do well to recall that when *Person and Act* was first published in 1969, its author neither affirmed explicitly, nor did he even seem inclined to affirm the possibility of, personal agency in vulnerable persons falling into either of our first two categories. Nevertheless, we will try to show how the dynamic ontology that undergirds his understanding of the unity of person and act ultimately supports the view that *uniquely personal* forms of activity remain open even to the most vulnerable of the vulnerable, while granting that they remain incapable of performing actions requiring a fully mature psycho-moral personality. As contradictory as that might sound, Cardinal Wojtyła/Pope John Paul II would later reach a conclusion like that himself in no uncertain terms, as we will see here and in subsequent chapters.

### The Agency of Psychosomatically Developing Persons within the Human Community

With these preliminary considerations in mind, let us now look at the significance of Wojtyła's reflections on intersubjective communion in connection with the vulnerability, the active passivity, of the child (whether unborn, newly born, or very young) within the family. Here, the child's vulnerability is not caused by some form of disintegration but is due rather to the gradualness of the psychosomatic and the psycho-moral development that naturally precedes and establishes the basis for personal acts of self-determination. We know already that at every stage of that development, the substantial principle of the child's personal existence, the spiritual soul, actively determines the integrity and, by its somatically dependent faculties, the continuous unfolding of the psychosomatic dynamisms through which his personal transcendence will eventually manifest itself. Since the end of this rather lengthy period of psychosomatic growth is the emergence of the self in human action, we can regard the process leading up to it as being, from the first, a form of self-determination: "Somehow on the basis of [the] *suppositum,* the human self gradually both discloses itself and constitutes itself—and it discloses itself also by constituting itself."[27]

The preceding passage from "The Person: Subject and Community" expresses clearly and concisely the meaning that Wojtyła manages more gradually and obscurely to convey through the labyrinth of analyses that he undertakes in *Person and Act,* namely, that the human being is in some way the agent of his own self-constitution and self-disclosure through the dynamic unfolding of the activations actualized in the psychosomatic structure of which he is the subject. We can therefore regard the developing child as actively presenting himself through his activations, even if, from the standpoint of human agency understood in the strict sense, we can regard him as only passively expressed by them.

Because he is temporarily subjected to his own dynamisms, the psychosomatically developing child is also temporarily unable to govern himself personally. This renders him radically dependent on others, his parents above all. In that sense, his activations present him as passively active, as vulnerable. That is why people who equate personhood with rationally autonomous self-sufficiency do not recognize him as being a vulnerable *person.* But the dynamic activity of the self-subsisting, personal soul and its powers necessarily underlies the actualization of the psychosomatic dynamisms. In that sense, activations are the very means by which the child actively presents (or expresses) himself as a vulnerable "someone," as a person who is both endowed with and ordered toward actualizing the spiritual potentialities of self-possession and self-governance.

27. "The Person: Subject and Community," in *PC,* 225.

That is how even the newly conceived child initially presents himself to his parents and to any other children they might already have. Indeed, he offers himself thus, in all his helplessness, as a gift to them. The following passage from Wojtyła's 1975 article, "Parenthood as a Community of Persons," seems to mark a notable advance in his understanding of human agency, but one that is utterly consistent with the dynamic philosophy of being he sets forth in *Person and Act* and more concisely in "The Person: Subject and Community."

> It is significant that the child—although deprived for a long time of the personal fullness of activity—nevertheless enters at once into the community as a person, as someone capable not only of receiving but also of giving. From the very beginning, the tiny new member of the family makes a gift of its humanity to its parents, and also, if it is not the first child, to its siblings as well. . . .
>
> [E]ach child from the very beginning—not just from the moment of birth, but right from the moment of conception—presents itself as a person and a gift.[28]

By this incipient form of participation in their lives, the newly conceived or the newly born child effectively invites his parents (and any siblings he might have) to participate, in turn, in *his* life. Because the vulnerability now characterizing that life is part of the gift that the child presents and *is* to his parents, he presents himself as a task for them as well. Precisely because he is *essentially* self-possessing and self-governing—that is, essentially a *person*, even prior to the actualization of the personal structure—the child actively beckons his parents, through his vulnerability, to "possess" and to govern him for a time.[29] Only if they affirm him thus by actions commensurate with his essential identity will his dynamic impulse to realize his personal structure in mature, self-determining acts eventually reach its term. In giving himself to his parents, therefore, the child "entrusts" them with the responsibility of giving him *to himself*, of helping him take up for himself the task that he essentially is for himself, so that he might, in turn, give himself more fully back to them, and later to others as well. To the extent that his parents prove worthy of that trust, the child will gradually succeed (barring some impediment) in transcending his passive (yet essentially personal) activeness through the deliberate self-actualization of his inherent, personal structure, in time assuming for himself the responsibility of determining his own person.

28. "Parenthood as a Community of Persons," in *PC*, 333.

29. In this context, to "possess" means "to take responsibility for," not to appropriate, regard, and treat as an "object."

In accepting their child as a gift, his parents, for their part, discover in him the special task with which they have been entrusted. During each stage of the child's development, they must discover anew the manner in which they are to fulfill that task, which, together with the child, presents itself to their love. To the extent that they receive their child in love and lovingly fulfill their responsibility toward him by giving themselves to him, the parents fulfill *themselves* and *are thus given to* themselves, discovering and living out more fully their parental, and indeed their personal, identity. Through parenthood, therefore, spouses "can and should find themselves in the gift that children are for them."[30]

We see, then, that both the child and his parents find themselves insofar as they give themselves to and receive one another in a way corresponding to each stage of their personal and intracommunal development. Through the passive activeness (hence also the active passiveness) by which he gives himself as a gift to his parents in his *vulnerable* humanity, the child receives from them, through their actively receiving *him,* the gift of their *mature* humanity.[31] And through that dynamic interrelation, the child will also receive, in due time, the gift of his *own* mature humanity, which, in the normal course of things, he will be disposed to give freely to his parents in return. On their side, his parents receive from him the very reality of their motherhood and fatherhood, which begins from the moment their first child is conceived (and which is renewed, in a way, each time they receive and nurture a subsequently conceived child or, analogously, an adopted child). In addition, by actively receiving their child in the vulnerability through which he presents himself to them, his parents also receive from him their conscious *experience* of their parenthood.

It is clear, then, that through the passive activeness by which he unfolds the original givenness of his own person, the child strengthens and deepens the life of the marital community. He introduces himself into, develops within, and enriches the original communion of persons established by the interpersonal life of the spouses. Similarly, each subsequent child enriches, and is enriched by, the wider community of the family. "The whole family community develops as a *communio personarum* as through stages, and this development in each of its stages includes the development of each person who comes into the community. This development, in turn, is simply an in-

30. "Parenthood," in *PC,* 334.

31. See ibid.

creasingly more complete and mature actualization of the human being."[32] It is only when the self-giving, other-receiving structure of the family community begins to break down because of defective relationships for which the spouses bear sole responsibility—at least initially—that parents and children become subject to psychosomatic and/or psycho moral disintegration having no "natural" underlying cause.[33] Alienation in the family is profoundly detrimental to the development and self-discovery of each family member and of the family as such, for it ruptures the uniquely intimate character of the coexistence and cooperation connatural to authentic family life. The true *communio familiaris*, on the other hand, is cohesive. It encourages the full participation of all its members, each of whom accepts and affirms the others in the way and to the degree that he or she can. As a result, the positive potentialities of these persons, especially their capacity for disinterested self-giving, are actualized, or at least, in the case of the psychosomatically developing child, drawn out further toward the fullness of personal expression. In that way, to anticipate our next chapter, the family community develops as a symbol and a revelation of Love.

## The Agency of Psycho-Rationally Disintegrated Persons within the Human Community

We will now turn our attention to psycho-rationally disintegrated—that is, severely mentally disabled—persons and their communal relationships according to the family model. In fact, relationships involving such persons are often at the very center of family life, since the seriously disintegrated human being might be, for example, one's own child, parent, or grandparent. Like psychosomatically developing persons, persons whose psychosomatic integrity is seriously compromised still express themselves actively through their natural dynamisms, precisely as their passive subject—that is, as vulnerable. Their personal passivity relative to the activations that happen in them is at once an active expression of their vulnerability, of the dependence they have on others because of their inability to subject their natural dynamisms personally to their own governance. Their disintegration prevents them from actualizing the inherent, personal structure by which they are virtually self-possessing and self-governing from the first moment of their coming into existence from nonexistence. And so they each present

32. Ibid., 333–34.

33. In a young child especially, alienation might distort his capacity for or his manner of expressing self-giving and other-receiving, as in the different kinds of reactive attachment disorder.

themselves through the actualization of their natural potencies as a dependent "someone," assigning themselves passively thereby to the care of others, while also expressing in that way their inherent potency for and drive toward fully active participation in the humanity of other persons. Those who accept this "assignment" participate actively in the life of the vulnerable "someone," with a view toward drawing out as far as possible his inherent capacity to take charge of himself. In time, he might even develop certain basic somatic and cognitive skills that will enable him to achieve, in proportionate measure, a certain level of "independence" and, with it, a greater realization of his personal capacity for reciprocal participation.

On the other hand, it might be that the severity of his condition will prevent other people from being able to do anything more for him than to affirm his personhood by their actions. His level of disintegration might be so great as to render him incapable of realizing his potentialities as a person in any appreciable way—at least by every outward indication. But that does not mean he is incapable of reciprocating in some way the participatory relations that others direct toward him. According to Cardinal Wojtyła, there is an extent to which the unilateral relation of an *I* to a *thou* reflexively discloses the *I* to himself. The relation returns, as it were, from the *thou* to the consciousness of the *I* from whom it proceeded, thus helping to constitute that *I* through his active participation in the *thou*'s humanity. If we now follow the lead that Wojtyła has given us in the immediately preceding section on psychosomatically developing persons within the family community, we can conclude as follows. Even when a *thou*'s psycho-moral personality, his *I*, has not emerged from the inherent potentialities of his concrete, personal being because of a radical developmental problem, or when the *I* he once had has seemingly been lost through the subsequent onset and progression of a serious mental disorder, the unilaterally reflexive relation by which one or more *I*'s affirm the person of this *thou* through the activity that they direct toward him affords them a deeper understanding of their own identity. In other words, by the personal presence that he constitutes as the active subject of his own existence, the vulnerable *thou* so affirmed is really involved in helping to constitute and confirm others in their own subjectivity, enriching them thus in a way perhaps different from, but not necessarily inferior to, what they might experience through their intersubjective relationships with others.

So, in passively offering himself to one or more *I*'s (or even to a *we*) as an actively self-constituting presence that is at once human and personal, the vulnerable *thou* (though presumably not in this case self-aware or appreciably so) effectively invites—indeed, obliges—them to discover themselves anew in actions that take this *thou* as their "object." The self-discovery attained by these *I*'s through their acceptance of this invitation implies as well a new awareness of how their further participation in his humanity must be carried out to ensure that he is always completely affirmed as a person. Their actualization of those forms of participation of which they have newly become aware effects in them yet another fresh discovery of themselves. The process of self-discovery and self-fulfillment through participation in the humanity of the vulnerable *thou* who offers himself is therefore ongoing. This is perhaps the most fundamental reason why we sometimes hear caregivers express, with gratitude, that they have received from more than they have given to the vulnerable person(s) for whom they are caring. Here we have an implicit acknowledgment that the vulnerable are truly personal givers in their own way, for the level of self-realization and self-discovery that others attain through the agency of these givers is specifically the fruit of the interpersonal relation and possible only therein.

If, instead, the *I*'s choose to alienate a vulnerable *thou* simply because they regard him as inconvenient, embarrassing, burdensome, "threatening," or useless in his weakness and dependency,[34] then the egoism that lies at the bottom of their reaction to him will simultaneously alienate each of them from the deepest truth about his or her own being as a person. Conversely, when the *I*'s accept the implicit but concretely insistent invitation of the vulnerable *thou* to affirm him as a "someone," he contributes not only to their greater self-understanding but also to the formation of an authentic communion of persons. By his reception into that communion, he is reciprocally invited to become, to the extent possible, a more fully participating member.

## The Agency of Somatically Disintegrated Persons within the Human Community

In chapter 2, we saw that severe forms of somatic disintegration do not necessarily deprive a person of the interior conditions for actualizing the personal structure of self-determination or, consequently, for developing a superior psychological and moral personality.[35] While it is true that seri-

34. This kind of alienation might even be a factor that contributes to the psycho-rational disintegration of the vulnerable person.

35. In chapter 5, we will consider the fact that less severe forms of psychical/cognitive disintegration do not necessarily prevent the actualization of the personal structure nor therefore the development of an outstanding psycho-moral personality. Indeed, the condition itself might serve as the very means through which the person develops such a personality.

ous somatic disintegration can prevent people from "doing" anything in the functional sense of physically "pulling their own weight" in a given community, it does not prevent them from *being* good persons through the participatory acts that they *are* capable of performing. That includes, in the first place, their interior acts.

In the two cases that we have already examined, we saw that a new child or a mentally disabled person might be unilaterally alienated, rather than accepted and affirmed, by the people on whom he makes a claim through his vulnerable humanity. The present case is different. The somatically disintegrated person might just as easily be the source as the "object" of alienation because, unlike the persons in the previous two categories, he has command over his personal dynamism. However, serious forms of vulnerability do not exempt mature human actors from the moral obligation to be agents of their own development and mediators of the development of other persons by participating in their humanity and in the true common good. Through the interior act, therefore, persons afflicted with incapacitating somatic disabilities must resist any tendency to alienate themselves or others—a tendency that might become more pronounced, for example, if they feel so useless and burdensome that they want to withdraw psychologically from the world, or if they feel so resentful about their condition that they want to *blame* the world.

If, on the other hand, they succeed in mastering themselves, such persons will be free to express their interior resolve to grow personally by exemplifying, through their condition and their dependency (whether partial or total), the true meaning of courage and forbearance, of inner peace in adversity, of joy amid a sea of long faces. They can become models of pleasantness, propriety, and dignity; witnesses to the virtue of humility; centers of graciousness and wisdom for anyone who takes the time to "bother." As "functional" people scurry about trying to accomplish at least some of the many things they believe they must "do" to ensure their success and their acceptance by others, the "nonfunctional," somatically disintegrated person can give them pause to reconsider what is truly important in life by the sheer warmth of a heartfelt smile radiating from a broken body.

That kind of other-centeredness is constructively self-determining at the same time that it is other-affirming. What is more, persons having incapacitating somatic disabilities can remind others, at least on an intuitive level, that sheer "functionality" is not a value in and of itself. For given the extreme restrictions that their condition might place on what they can physically do, they can nonetheless reveal more clearly through outwardly less grand yet beautifully simple and sincere ways of affirming others that authentic interpersonal and social life begins with *being*-with-and-for-others (first as an ontological disposition and then, consequently, as a psycho-moral one) before it is actually realized in *doing*-with-and-for-others. Perhaps we see in this the deepest intersubjective application of the adage *operari sequitur esse*. In the case of the strictly interior act, the will to *be* with and for others is identical with the act of *doing* with and for them—that is, it is identical with an act of solidarity. In the case of *every* voluntary human act, it is because of this interior way of "being" that any kind of "doing" with and for others redounds also to one's own ontological and personal fulfillment. And so, in a unique and indispensable way, the physically disabled can give people insight into the most fundamental, meaningful, and worthwhile dimensions of interpersonal and social relationships.

Yet, it is sadly true that individuals, communities, and even whole societies often erect or fail to dismantle barriers that keep the person with severe physical disabilities from participating in interpersonal and social life to the extent that he can. In that way, they infringe on his natural right so to act. Like all injustices perpetrated against individual persons, the negative effects of alienating him thus will ultimately rebound on the wider human community, which is deprived of the unique, personal contributions that he might otherwise have made. As for the disabled person himself, he has unfortunately to endure, on top of his physical problems, the indignity of being devalued and rejected by the larger community of persons when such conditions prevail. Even under those circumstances, he is still capable of forming a personality of the highest order by mastering himself interiorly. However, lacking adequate personal and social support, he would certainly not find it easy to bear the burdens that others have placed on him unnecessarily and unjustly.

Because the task of psycho-moral self-formation takes place always through the medium of the body, even the wholly interior acts by which we determine ourselves as persons depend on our bodily externalization in the world, from which we get the "raw material" on the basis of which we act. That is why inhospitable surroundings can negatively affect the kind of person that we choose to become. This threat to the person is especially acute in the case of persons who are physically so deteriorated that they are neither free to move of themselves to a more favorable environment nor capable of expressing outwardly their desire to do so. They might have even reached the point of becoming subject to some form of "unconsciousness" of which they are nevertheless fully conscious.[36] For such as these, the fully personal interior act is their only means of self-expression. It is therefore also their only means of rising above negative external factors beyond their control.

Since the wholly interior act is not accompanied by signs that are readily discernible from the outside, the most radically vulnerable of somatically disintegrated persons, having recourse only to such acts, cannot directly convey to anyone that they are being deprived of the fundamental rights and care to which they are entitled as human beings. Nor can they go out and confront the larger community with their humanity so as to awaken consciences to their plight and thereby elicit an appropriate response. In fact, it seems that they cannot directly do anything to advance their own cause. It would take a sterling personality not to be crushed under such a weight; a personality that would retain its serenity despite such unfavorable circumstances; a personality that would resolutely strive to grow in virtue, if only by not inwardly wishing ill to befall those who have so callously disregarded the welfare of one in such great need. In short, it would take a personality willing to act on the impulse to fulfill the commandment to love, if only inwardly.

Sometimes a personality like that manifests the power to reach those nearby so that they somehow "feel" a personal presence radiating through a seemingly unresponsive body. For there is a bidirectional significance to our externalization in the world through the body. We not only receive bodily *from* the world the "raw material" that conditions, for good or for ill, the personal acts by which we determine ourselves: we also manifest bodily *to* the world the kind of person we have thus chosen to become. We do not necessarily manifest ourselves through an external act, which is neither always telling nor always possible. Rather, we might manifest ourselves only *in* the body, insofar as we integrate its dynamisms personally into a self-determining, interior act. The good or the bad "someone" that a person thus becomes is revealed, first of all, to the person himself in the consciousness that he has of having freely integrated his bodily dynamisms into either a morally good or a morally bad act. But it can also be revealed to others in a subtle but powerful way when the intensity of the person's goodness or badness somehow projects itself through the body even without any outwardly perceptible movement of the body itself.

So, when a person is so somatically disintegrated that he cannot physi-

36. See the last paragraph of chapter 2 on unconscious experience.

cally do anything, the body nevertheless inserts him into the human community both interpersonally and socially, not just because it is, metaphysically speaking, the body of a person, but also because it is the body of the unique "I" that this person has formed therein by voluntarily actualizing his personal structure and by his concomitant consciousness of having thus actualized himself. This "I" can make his presence felt: he can make a positive difference in the communities of which he is a part by the diffusion of his own goodness, not only in the ontological sense, but in the moral sense as well, insofar as he has freely formed his "I" into a center of virtue, of personal goodness, through his interior acts. Unfortunately, many of us have not always the other-centered sensitivity needed to perceive this personal subject in his broken body, and so this "other self" goes frequently unnoticed or ignored. He becomes alienated. And many are likewise apt to be just as insensitive to other types of vulnerable human beings: the poor, the weak, the mentally disabled, the suffering, the elderly, the dying. The interpersonal and the social realms of human existence are inevitably impoverished as a result.

## The Agency of Poor and Oppressed Persons within the Human Community

There are different kinds of agency that persons who are materially poor, through no fault of their own, might exercise, depending both on the condition in which their poverty has left them and on the amount of participation that the various levels of community will allow them. In some cases, communal and societal structures make it possible for the poor to engage in, even to initiate, interpersonal dialogue with members of the larger social structures who are in a position to help them change their lives for the better. Respectful dialogue means an honest, mutual effort to identify communal and societal problems and to find constructive solutions for them. That is not always easy where a web of injustices resulting in gross social and economic inequalities has become woven into the very fabric of societal life. But genuine dialogue does not eschew such difficulties, nor does it exclude a proper spirit of opposition—in this case, on the part of the poor as they challenge any notion of the common good that would deprive them of a proper share in, and of the means to attain, the basic goods to which they are entitled as human beings. On the contrary, by expressing their opposition in that way, the poor are exercising an authentic form of solidarity, one in which they express a genuine concern for the true common good while seeking their rightful place in society as co-participants in the realization and benefits of that good.

Where possible, the poor can also collaborate actively with one another to manifest their personal transcendence before the social and interpersonal egoism, and even before the totalitarianism, that has robbed them of the minimal resources they need so as to live according to their dignity as human beings. If those who can help them have not suppressed or killed their own consciences by the unbridled desire to magnify themselves and their own opulence at the expense of the poor, then their encounter with the humanity of the poor will be an occasion for new forms of collaboration with them in the interest of eradicating all forms of social injustice. Where such possibilities still exist, the poor would be remiss if they did not seek to improve their lot, and the well-to-do would be remiss if unsupportive of their efforts.

It might be, however, that the poor are so impoverished that they can do nothing other than to occupy themselves with the business of surviving. This is still an active, transcendent manifestation of their humanity that would enable others to identify with them unilaterally as other *I*'s who merit incorporation into the larger *we*. As such, it makes an urgent and incessant appeal to those who can help, one that the surrounding community would have no right to ignore. It is an appeal to that community—which in some cases extends as far as the world community itself—to discover or to stop justifying the reasons why it is constituted, not as a *we*, but as an *us and them*, and why the good toward which it strives, if it is truly a *human* good, is not shared by all.

If the larger communities remain egoistically indifferent to, feigned in their concern for, or covertly hostile to the poor by perpetrating and perpetuating injustice under the guise of doing good, the poor can still exercise a powerful form of agency through their will to survive and to affirm thus the goodness of their lives; through their will to reject recourse to injustices and indignities like the ones to which they are being subjected; through their will to be concerned for and generous with one another; through their will to be dignified and virtuous despite adversity—refusing, for example, to be blackmailed into accepting the radically evil ideological agendas that "donors" of "humanitarian" aid seek to impose on them as a condition of their receiving it. By manifesting their transcendence thus, the poor might succeed in shaking those materially better off out of their selfishness and complacency so that they regard and treat the poor as "neighbors." If the actions of the poor fail to elicit a fitting response, then they will serve instead to confirm the more fortunate in their individual or collective egoism, exposing how impoverished is the sort of person or the sort of people they have chosen to become.

That is true, above all, when the poor have no longer the physical strength to do anything other than to await death, and yet, even in the face of it, they maintain their serenity, their courage, and their dignity through interior acts that increase their virtue and thus manifest them as heroic personalities, whether or not anyone else cares to notice. For the body still externalizes them as persons in the interpersonal and social world through the exercise even of wholly interior acts, and also, in a more fundamental way, through the activations that constitute their humanity naturally. So whether by the personally active or just the passively active expression of their person through the body, the poor proclaim to the larger community that its members need to take account of them and to act for their true good, lest those who forsake that charge forsake also their own personal, human, and moral good, as well as the common benefit of having the poor form with them an authentic community of persons.

As human beings, the poor have a natural right to fulfill themselves through voluntary activity that accords with their rational nature, and they have the obligation to exercise that right to whatever extent they can. As *social* beings, moreover, the poor, like their more prosperous neighbors, have a natural right to fulfill themselves through actions performed freely and responsibly in and with the social community for the sake of its true good. The structure of that community is defective when it limits or prevents their participation in the realization and benefits of the common good. It is also defective when the values for which the community exists and acts are not truly good. Such "values," really anti-values, conflict with the true good of each and all, and they provide a telling commentary as to why the community permits the impoverishment and exclusion of at least some persons. In totalitarian systems and, more subtly, in secularized "democracies," the whole society is radically defective on both counts. In practice, this often means that very many persons, if not always a majority, will be materially impoverished, demoralized, and alienated. The poor are not necessarily excluded completely from society, but rather from participating in decisions that affect their life and that determine the ends on which they will collaborate. In social systems like that, expressions of opposition seeking constructive change in a spirit of solidarity are generally quashed in ways ranging from corrupt legislation to outright violence. In the face of this, the inauthentic attitudes of conformism and avoidance might easily come to substitute for the authentic attitudes of solidarity and opposition, so that genuinely self-initiated and creative human activity, and hence truly personal fulfillment, become quite impossible.

When the manner in which human beings exist and act together is forced on them by overtly or covertly oppressive regimes, they are neither truly free in their outward activity nor rationally convinced of the goals toward which their oppressors compel them to work. The subjective conditions for collective unity are essentially lacking because the authorities are violating the fundamental structure and rights of the person by violating legitimate personal freedom, initiative, creativity, and responsibility, and by smothering authentic truth and solidarity. In a word, they are depriving people of the essential conditions for authentic *participation*. What is left is only the mere semblance of a community or society, an empty shell that will not indefinitely be able to support its own weight.

In the meantime, the poor and oppressed who determine to fulfill themselves as persons by promoting and upholding real truth, goodness, justice, and human dignity might well do so at the cost of their own lives, or at least at the cost of further deprivations of basic goods and rights. But the alternative is worse. While, objectively speaking, each of them is and remains essentially a human person regardless of how negatively their life in society affects them, they can still lose their sense of human and personal dignity when they allow the injustices perpetrated against them by their oppressors to go unchallenged. Worse still, they might compromise that dignity themselves by using their situation as an excuse for dispensing with the obligation to conduct themselves in a morally upright way. In either case, they would experience a kind of "dehumanization" and "depersonalization," imposed this time from within.

And what about totalitarian arrogance, which is, in the end, but another form of egoism? The unrelenting heavy-handedness of totalitarian authorities and their "democratic" counterparts in depriving poor and oppressed people of their rightful share in material goods and of their natural right to social participation betrays, in the first place, a profoundly self-centered and self-destructive greed. At a deeper level, perhaps, it betrays a personal insecurity that hides from itself by controlling people and the ends for which they must strive. Were the people allowed to exercise their intelligence, freedom, creativity, initiative, and personal responsibility in a genuine spirit of solidarity, they might challenge the structure, goals, and leadership of a society that has been built at their expense for the benefit of only a few. So in their cowardice, the oppressors strip the oppressed of their intrinsic rights and attack their dignity as a means of both maintaining their grip on power and affirming for themselves their own superiority. For if they were to allow anyone or anything to remind them of their own "vulnerability," the confrontation with the truth would shatter the fragile illusion of greatness that they have contrived for themselves and that they often try to compel everyone else to believe. As egoists, therefore, totalitarian authorities refuse to participate in the humanity of others, while structuring society so as to keep the people from participating in the humanity of one another. The disintegration of so many people as actors leads ineluctably to the disintegration and destruction of the society itself.

As with social and interpersonal egoism, the "totalitarian egoism" of which we speak rejects the humanity of others by rejecting truth and goodness, and it rejects truth and goodness by rejecting the humanity of others. But that is tantamount to rejecting the very conditions of personal fulfillment. Therefore, egoists of every kind "dehumanize" themselves by acting contrary to nature, and they "depersonalize" themselves in the psycho-moral sense by disregarding the conditions necessary for achieving full self-transcendence in action. They thus form themselves into bad persons by the destructive activity that they direct toward others, or by failing to engage in the constructive activity that they can and ought to direct toward them. In a word, they culpably deprive themselves of their ontological and psycho-moral—their personal—perfection: they become "poor." In effect, therefore, egoists inflict on themselves a vulnerability that is different in kind from the others we have discussed, one that we will call analogously, here and elsewhere, *moral vulnerability*. Still, they abide in the fundamental transcendence by which they are persons, and so they retain the capacity to change themselves and the inequities of social life for the better. They can step out of their self-centered isolation in favor of authentic participation, rediscovering themselves in the humanity that they come to see and welcome in others, especially the poor and oppressed.

4

# The Theology of the Body

In this chapter, we will focus on Pope John Paul II's "theology of the body," which he laid out systematically as a series of discourses during his Wednesday general audiences over the five-year period extending from September 1979 to November 1984. Centering on the language—on the personal expressivity—of the human body, John Paul's reflections complement, enrich, and develop the philosophical project that he had undertaken over ten years earlier as cardinal of Kraków.[1] We can therefore expect that they will likewise complement, enrich, and develop our understanding of vulnerable human beings and their agency.

1. In the introduction to his recent re-translation of John Paul II's "theology of the body" (hereafter TOB) from Italian into English, Michael Waldstein shows that Cardinal Wojtyła had already completed the project in Polish before his elevation to the papacy, though it had not yet been published. (According to Weigel, John Paul II recalled working on the draft texts during the conclave that elected his immediate predecessor. See *Witness to Hope*, 336.) The manuscript was originally entitled *Man and Woman He Created Them*. John Paul modified the parts of the text that he planned to present during his weekly audiences, after which they would be translated into Italian. In a letter written on his behalf replying to queries sent by Waldstein in February 2005, he indicated that the Italian version is to be considered the authoritative text. Waldstein also informs us that during the period over which John Paul delivered the series on the body, there were several interruptions, most notably the one resulting from the assassination attempt on May 13, 1981. See Waldstein, "Introduction," in *Man and Woman*, 4–11.

## Theology of the Body and *Person and Act*: A Basic Look at Structure and Content

John Paul II's theological discourses on human self-expression through the body reach a level quite different from that of his earlier work, as a private Catholic philosopher, on the person as revealed in action. For one thing, they are grounded deeply in sacred Scripture, taking into account the Church's authoritative understanding of the sacred texts. In other words, John Paul has based his discourses explicitly on revealed truth. What is more, he referred to these discourses as "catecheses"—instructions—on concluding the long series, making clear his purpose in presenting them during his Wednesday general audiences.[2] Catechesis is an essential activity of the episcopal office. Given the setting and the activity, therefore, John Paul II was exercising his role as pastor and teacher of the universal Church when he presented his catechesis on the body.[3] At the same time, the whole direction of Wojtyła's 1969 philosophical project was clearly informed by insights that only his Catholic faith could have afforded him. Consequently, an admirable continuity exists between Wojtyła/John Paul's philosophical and his theological understanding of the self-expression of the person through the body in action.

*Person and Act* and the catechesis on the body are somewhat similar in their basic structure. Each work concerns itself initially with analyzing the experience and implications of fully mature human acting, so as to arrive at an understanding of the personal attributes and essential constitution of the human subject. This leads in each case to an analysis of certain types of relations that can form among subjects as they exist and act together. Simply stated, Wojtyła/John Paul proceeds from the personal subject to the community of persons. In chapter 3 we explained why in the light of the text quoted from *Gaudium et Spes*, 24, which would remain foundational to the author's anthropology. Though God constitutes us as persons from the start, we achieve our authentic self-fulfillment only in giving ourselves sincerely to and for other persons. The concept of alienation, as the antithesis of participation in the humanity of others, shows philosophically why we cannot

2. See TOB 133:1–2, 4; see also 129:2. Note that we are citing each discourse using the numbering and subdivisions found in Waldstein's critical edition of TOB, which in turn follows the one-volume Italian edition published in 1985. In the citations just given, we see that the number of the discourse is given first, followed by the paragraph number(s). While John Paul actually delivered 129 discourses, the aforementioned editions include a few catecheses that he did not deliver.

3. See Waldstein, "Introduction," in *Man and Woman*, 14–18.

fulfill ourselves humanly and personally apart from sincere self-giving. Pope John Paul II develops that idea *theologically* in terms of the detrimental effects of original and personal sin on the image of God in us. By damaging the integrity of our personal structure, sin threatens our ability to make a sincere gift of ourselves to one another (and to God) through the body, thus threatening also the possibility of our forming together an authentic communion of persons.

Beginning, then, with the experience of distinctly human activity, both *Person and Act* (which examines our own acting experience) and the catechesis on the body (which examines the human experience of acting as typified in the person of Adam in Genesis 2) call our attention to the basic features of human transcendence revealed to us in and through the actions we perform: objective knowledge of ourselves and of the world, self-consciousness, self-determination, personal integration, moral conscience, and, finally, self-fulfillment in actions where freedom serves the objective truth about the good. We refer here, above all, to the good of other persons, whose value in each case transcends completely that of other worldly goods, whether singly or in their totality. Since that is so, both *Person and Act* and the catechesis on the body proceed toward and reach the conclusion that the greatest possible expression, and hence fulfillment, of oneself takes place in actions constitutive of the communion of persons. John Paul II's reflections on chapter two of the book of Genesis show in a particularly concise way that the first man is ontologically and existentially ordered toward communion with another person. Then, John Paul devotes the remainder of his catechesis to examining the communion of persons, whether in its original state, as threatened by sin, as redeemed by Christ, or as an eschatological reality.

John Paul spends comparatively little time in his catechesis analyzing the features of personal subjectivity, dwelling rather on the rich biblical sources concerning the marital community as the fundamental form and model of interpersonal communion. In that respect, the catechesis differs from *Person and Act*, which approaches intersubjective participation in a relatively brief and general way. Another difference, as we have noted already, is that the catechesis on the body is based explicitly on the sources of revelation, whereas Cardinal Wojtyła's philosophical project, while clearly informed and guided by Scripture and the Church's theological tradition, keeps revelation's contribution largely below the surface.

Nevertheless, the passage from *Gaudium et Spes* that we mentioned above, and to which John Paul II refers or alludes so frequently, is the hinge on which both works turn, developed therein in perfect continuity. The catechesis makes it clear that this passage is ultimately a commentary on Genesis 1:27, itself the central affirmation of John Paul's biblical anthropology: man and woman have been made in the image and likeness of God. We can see that even more clearly by considering, as John Paul does, the lines immediately preceding the *Gaudium et Spes* passage: "Indeed, the Lord Jesus, when He prayed to the Father, 'that all may be one ... as we are one' (Jn. 17:21–22) opened up vistas closed to human reason. For He implied a certain likeness between the union of the divine Persons, and in the union of God's sons in truth and charity." Whether implicitly or explicitly, therefore, Genesis 1:27 is the supreme measure of everything that Karol Wojtyła/Pope John Paul II has to say about human beings as persons and about their relations with other persons. "[T]he revealed truth concerning man as 'the image and likeness' of God constitutes the immutable *basis of all Christian anthropology*."[4] That being so, John Paul II's catechesis on the body will prove to be thoroughly Trinitarian and Christological.

## The Divine Image in Man: A Reflection of Intra-Trinitarian Love

Let us take a moment to consider the Trinitarian foundation of Pope John Paul II's theology of the body, keeping in mind the pertinent remarks we made in chapter 1 when discussing his first doctoral dissertation, *The Doctrine of Faith according to St. John of the Cross*. We will base our current reflections mainly on relevant passages from his encyclical *Dominum et Vivificantem* (1986) and his Apostolic Letter *Mulieris Dignitatem* (1988). While each of these documents was published a few years after John Paul had given his last discourse on the body, they reflect his already well established conviction that the intra-Trinitarian communion of the divine Persons is the source and model of every true communion of *human* persons. That applies, above all, to the communion of man and woman in marriage, which, insofar as it corresponds to God's original creative plan, is the premier revelation in the visible world of the invisible Love that it reflects, shares in, and mediates.[5]

Jesus Christ revealed God himself to us definitively as Love (see 1 Jn 4:8, 16). Through that revelation, the Church has come to understand that love in

4. *Mulieris Dignitatem* (August 15, 1988), 6, Vatican translation (Boston: Pauline Books and Media, 1988). See also *MD*, 7. The document's title is given in English as *On the Dignity and Vocation of Women*.

5. See Waldstein, "Introduction," in *Man and Woman*, 23–34.

God consists in an ineffably deep communion of three divine Persons—Father, Son, and Holy Spirit—who, though distinct in their eternal relations, constitute therein the essential unity of the divine nature, of Love itself. Love is therefore an essential attribute of each divine Person. However, the Holy Spirit alone subsists as the Person-Love of the intra-Trinitarian life of God, for he proceeds personally and eternally from the Father and the Son as the mutual Love of each for the other. That is why his procession from the Father and the Son is, at the same time, his bestowal by the Father and the Son on each other as their eternal, uncreated *Gift* of Love.[6]

Because he is the personal Love-Gift of God's inscrutable inner life, the Holy Spirit is "from the beginning" the eternal source of all God's giving to creatures in the order of creation. Fundamentally, this means God's giving the gift of existence to creatures that would otherwise not exist. But in our case, God has also given us the divine image as the defining feature of our existence, as the special gift that constitutes us as persons from the moment we are brought into being. For one thing, this means that God has endowed us essentially with intellect and will, entrusting us, consequently, with governing the earth responsibly. We have therefore received the world, and the world has received us, as a gift.[7] What is more, our unique likeness to God has endowed us with the capacity to receive and to respond personally to God's salvific, covenantal initiatives and, ultimately, to participate in God's own inner life by the gift of the Spirit. In a word, God calls us to intimate friendship with himself.[8] Finally, in virtue of the divine image in us, we can give ourselves to each other as a personal gift. Indeed, we must do so in order to fulfill that image in ourselves.[9] So, through the revelation of God in Jesus Christ, the gift-character that is impressed on the world and its creatures, especially human beings, can be "traced back," as it were, to the very depths of God's own interior life—to the unfathomable, eternal Love that the Father and the Son bestow on each other as their mutual, personal Gift: the Holy Spirit.

In the anthropology of Karol Wojtyła/Pope John Paul II, one cannot give the total gift of self where there is no other person to receive, to reciprocate, and to be received in turn by that gift. So, personal giving and receiving are really two different aspects of the same dynamic reality, forming the basis of true interpersonal communion. On the human level, the authentic recep-

6. See *DetV*, 10.

7. See TOB 13:4.

8. See *DetV*, 34; see also nos. 10, 39, 50, 54.

9. See *MD*, 7.

tion of another person, or even of oneself through others (whether ontologically or by one's self-discovery in the light of another *I*), presupposes, like authentic self-giving, the Trinitarian model, while to some extent clarifying it.[10] In *Dominum et Vivificantem*, John Paul elaborates a Trinitarian theology that highlights the aspect of self-giving, or gift, but he still implies, necessarily, the strictly correlative notion of reception, in a manner appropriate to the relations among the three divine Persons. It would seem that the Trinitarian doctrine of the "processions" (whereby the Son receives his Person by eternal generation from the Father, and the Holy Spirit receives his by eternal procession from the Father and the Son), together with the related doctrine of circuminsession (the mutual indwelling, or co-penetration, of the three divine Persons in the unity of both essence and Love), requires as much.[11] In *Evangelium Vitae*, John Paul does, in fact, state specifically that the new relationships of fraternity and solidarity established between human beings through their charitable communion with one another in the Spirit constitute "a true reflection of the mystery of mutual self-giving *and receiving* proper to the most holy Trinity."[12]

From the world's inception, man and woman, created in the image of God, are called to live in a way that reflects, on the creaturely level, the interpersonal communion of Love within God. They respond to that call, above all, through the interpersonal communion of love that they establish together in marriage.[13] The power of spousal love is manifested in the indissolubil-

10. If man is created in God's image and likeness, then "*God too* is in some measure 'like man,'" and so "he can be humanly known." However, John Paul's immediate qualification makes it clear that this principle has immense limitations: "Biblical Revelation says that, while man's 'likeness' to God is true, the '*non-likeness*' which separates the whole of creation from the Creator is *still more essentially true*." God remains ever "the one 'who dwells in unapproachable light' (1 Tim 6:16)." *MD*, 8. See also John Paul's Wednesday audience of October 2, 1985, in *God, Father and Creator: A Catechesis on the Creed*, vol. 1 (Boston: Pauline Books and Media, 1996), 145.

11. It is perhaps in those doctrines that we find the very ground of God's receptive actions in the economy of salvation—e.g., the Father's receiving, through the Spirit, the self-offering of Christ on the cross (see Heb 9:14; *DetV*, 40), and God's receiving *us* when we receive him in the Eucharist (see Wojtyła, *SgC*, 26).

12. See *Evangelium Vitae* (March 25, 1995), 76 , Vatican translation, *Origins* 24, no. 42 (1995): 689–727. Italics added. The Most Rev. John R. Sheets, SJ, writes that *Dominum et Vivificantem* discloses the profound roots of John Paul's theology and spirituality, for in it, he comes "to a kind of spiritual metaphysics, an absolute basis behind all spirituality: the nature of the person as one who finds himself in making a gift of himself. The theme of the Holy Spirit as uncreated love-gift, the energizing power behind all gift-giving, whether in nature, or in salvation, is the heart of Pope John Paul's spirituality. The giving of gift, and receiving of gift is found primordially in the communion that constitutes the Trinitarian life." From "The Spirituality of Pope John Paul II," in McDermott, *Pope John Paul II*, 112.

13. See *LF*, 6.

ity of the marital bond, fidelity to which reflects God's love for us and Christ's love for his Church, insofar as it shares in that love.[14] It is also manifested in the fruitfulness of the marital bond, in the generation of offspring conceived lovingly through the marital union and nurtured lovingly through selfless parental care. The reciprocal spousal self-giving and other-receiving that results in the gift of new life is a real participation in the creative power of God. In addition, the parenthood of the spouses reflects, analogously, the mystery of eternal generation *within* God.[15] As the original *I-thou* community of the married couple widens with the introduction of each child into the family, the interpersonal dynamic of self-giving and other-receiving enlarges to include the children, who participate increasingly in that dynamic as they mature.[16] Consequently, an authentic love reflecting the mystery of God's inner life, as well as his love for humanity, is communicated to the world through the interpersonal communion of every family sustained by the personal Gift of God's Love—that is, by the Holy Spirit poured out into the "heart" of the family (cf. Rm 5:5).[17]

## The Theology of the Body and Its Relevance to Vulnerable Human Beings

We will now introduce briefly some of the central themes of John Paul II's biblical anthropology in the light of its Trinitarian substructure. We will group those themes under three subheadings pertaining, respectively, to the state of man and woman (1) in God's original creative plan, (2) following the first sin, and (3) within the horizon of redemption in Christ. Immediately following each of the three sections, we will show, in general, how the themes introduced therein apply to vulnerable human beings and their agency.

### God's Original Creative Plan for "the Body"

John Paul informs us that the book of Genesis begins with two distinct creation accounts. The first one, Genesis 1–2:4, was composed in a chronologically later period than the second, Genesis 2:5–3:24.[18] Genesis 1–2:4 has

14. See *MD*, 7; *Familiaris Consortio*, 20.

15. See *MD*, 18.

16. E.g., *Familiaris Consortio*, 21.

17. See ibid., 63.

18. TOB 2:1–2. As part of his analysis of the second creation account prior to the fall (depicted in Genesis 3), John Paul includes the text of Genesis 4:1 (see TOB 2:1), retaining v. 2a as a subsidiary text (e.g., TOB 20:2–5). The verses read as follows: "Adam united himself with [lit. "knew"] Eve his wife, who conceived and gave birth to Cain and said, 'I have acquired [lit. "gained," *qanithi*, related to "Cain"] a man from the LORD.' Then she gave birth also to his brother Abel." Unless

a distinctly objective character. It portrays human beings according to their place in the cosmological scheme of all that God made "in the beginning." By specifying that they were created male and female, the account points to the corporeality that relates them to the material world and to every other creature therein. On the other hand, by revealing that of all worldly creatures, human beings alone have been made according to the divine image, the first creation narrative announces their irreducibility to the world or to any of its creatures (see Gn 1:26–27). That is why God can give man and woman dominion over the earth, which entails, first of all, the divine command to "Be fruitful and multiply," the precondition of their filling the earth and subduing it (Gn 1:28).

In contrast, the chronologically prior, second creation narrative has a decidedly subjective character, attending as it does to the first human experiences of knowledge, self-knowledge, self-consciousness, self-determination, and moral conscience, both in the person as such and in the complementary male-female relationship. It therefore views God's creative activity from the perspective of the human subject, who is its "object" and recipient. For that reason, many of the text's fundamental anthropological insights are psychological in nature. The first creation account in Genesis, which affirms objectively that God created man and woman in the divine image, thus finds its complement in the second account, which develops the subjective implications of that affirmation.[19]

### Original Solitude

Genesis 2 shows that the first man—who, up to the creation of the first woman (vv. 21–22), represents every human being[20]—is "alone" in the world in two respects: essentially and relationally. Through his concrete, bodily activity of tilling the ground and naming the animals (that is, of exercising his dominion over the earth), the man becomes aware that, though he is of the world, he also transcends it. He is a personal subject endowed with knowledge of the world, and also with knowledge of *himself* as different from all other worldly creatures. In addition, he discovers through his activity that the body is the very means by which he expresses himself as a person in the world and before God. The man is thus conscious of his unique structural

otherwise noted, all scriptural quotations in this chapter will be given as translated from the Italian in *Man and Woman*.

19. See TOB 3:1.

20. Ibid., 5:2.

complexity, which was specially created when God breathed the breath of life—the human soul—into the man's earthly body (see Gn 2:7).[21]

Heightening the man's consciousness of his "concrete transcendence" is the fact that God gives him the command not to eat of the tree of the knowledge of good and evil (Gn 2:16–17). By this he knows that he stands in direct relation to God, that he has the power to determine himself through the choices that he makes and carries out in the body, and that the integrity or the dissolution of his relationship with God depends on those choices. The man is thus confirmed in the awareness of his irreducibility to the world, of his ontological superiority over every other worldly creature. Given this experience of his essential solitude, he is disposed to seek another like himself, someone else in the world to whom he can relate; for he has discovered that essential solitude also means, for him, *existential* solitude.[22]

### Original Unity

Seeing that "it is not good that the man should be alone" and that none of the other living creatures satisfied the man's need for companionship (Gn 2:18, 20), God forms a woman from the man's substance, from his "rib" (vv. 21–22).[23] The man rejoices at the sight of her, recognizing in her body, so similar to his own, a personal subject of the same nature: she is bone of his bones and flesh of his flesh (v. 23).[24] She is the helper, the "second self," with whom he can form an interpersonal communion based on the complementarity of the sexes, thus surpassing the limit of his solitude. The bodily sign of their personal unity is expressed when, having established the marital covenant through the reciprocal, self-determining choice of each for the other, the two become "one flesh" (Gn 2:24).[25] In that way, they also coop-

21. Of course, those responsible for the text of Genesis 2:7 as we have it did not distinguish so neatly between the soul and the body as distinct components of our unified existence as human beings (see TOB 9:4n18). But as John Paul points out relative to the first man, "Consciousness of the body seems to be identical in this case with the discovery of the complexity of one's own structure, which in the end, based on a philosophical anthropology, consists in the relation between soul and body." TOB 7:1; see 14:4. Later biblical texts are more clear on the soul-body distinction, e.g., Ws 3:1–3; Mt 10:28.

22. See TOB 5–7:2.

23. In his analysis of the Song of Songs, John Paul suggests that "rib" in this context might also contain an oblique reference to the heart. See ibid., 108:4.

24. See ibid., 8:4; 9:4. Thus, "*love unleashes a special experience of the beautiful,* which focuses on what is visible, although at the same time it involves the entire person. The experience of beauty gives rise to pleasure, which is reciprocal." Ibid., 108:6 (on the Song of Songs).

25. *Communio* is the fundamental reason for the differentiation of the human body into male and female. Still, John Paul states, "*the fact that man is a 'body' belongs more deeply to the*

erate personally with the blessing of procreative fruitfulness.[26] Through the masculinity and the femininity that grounds the sexual differentiation of the man and the woman respectively, each discovers in the other the body's capacity for expressing freely the unreserved giving of their persons to each other. In this mutual self-giving, therefore, the two discover *themselves* more completely: the man co-discovers his masculinity in his discovery of the woman's femininity, while the woman co-discovers her femininity in her discovery of the masculinity of the man. For John Paul II, it is not just in their personal transcendence but in the interpersonal communion formed by their reciprocal, bodily expression of that transcendence that man and woman reflect God's image in the world, the image of three divine Persons united substantially in an ineffable communion of eternal Love.[27]

---

*structure of the personal subject than the fact that in his somatic constitution he is also male or female.* For this reason, the meaning of original solitude, which can be referred simply to 'man,' is substantially prior to the meaning of original unity." Ibid., 8:1. While if overly scrutinized the preceding statement might seem counterintuitive or even problematic, it is really just a restatement of John Paul's basic anthropological principle, itself a restatement of *GS*, 24: "person," then "community"; "actor," then "relational act." Every human being, male and female, is originally constituted as an ontological unity of soul and body, because of which he or she transcends the whole material world and every other kind of creature therein: the human being is the only creature on earth that God willed as an end in itself. The incarnation of their solitude in its masculine and feminine forms disposes man and woman to seek companionship with each other: they cannot find themselves except through the sincere, mutual gift of themselves (see TOB 9:2; *GS*, 12). *Original solitude,* with its objective basis in the human soul-body structure, emphasizes what is common to man and woman as human persons made equally in God's image. On the other hand, *original unity,* with its objective basis in the duality of the masculine and the feminine structure, emphasizes what is different about man and woman. The former pertains to the essential unity of each as bodily persons. The latter pertains to the accidental unity of the two, which aspires, in a way, to be essential (in imitation of its exemplar, the substantial unity of the three divine Persons in God; cf. Gn 2:24; Jn 17:21–22). That original solitude is the more fundamental reality is clear from the fact that the unity of man and woman, even in its original state, can never fully dispel their solitude; for the image of God in each of them can find its full, reciprocal complement, so to speak, only in God himself. Ironically, that very fact might constitute the ultimate condition of the possibility of the fall (see Gn 3:5–6). But it also underlies our hope in the resurrection of our whole person, soul and body, unto everlasting life through God's spousal/quasi-essential union with each of us. And it inspires the choice for continence for the kingdom of heaven (e.g., TOB 77:1–2).

26. See TOB 10:2–3. Significantly, God addresses the command to "be fruitful and multiply" and to "have dominion" directly (i.e., *personally*) to the man and the woman whom he had just created in his image—"and God said *to them* ..." (Gn 1:27–28, RSV, italics added)—entrusting them with the responsibility of carrying it out.

27. See TOB 9:3; 10:1, 3–4. The fact that the personal subjectivity of the woman is revealed to the man through the correspondence of her bones and flesh to his confirms that the body, being constitutive and expressive of the human person, is included in our likeness to God (see ibid., 9:4). In contrast, both Augustine and Aquinas locate God's image in us chiefly in our rationality, which places us above the other creatures of the visible world; for from the intellect proceeds the word and from the rational appetite, or will, proceeds love, reflecting, in a way, the processions

### Original Nakedness

Though naked in each other's presence, the first man and woman are not ashamed (see Gn 2:25). Irradiated by God's grace, they enjoy a purity of intention, a holiness, a fullness of life that John Paul calls *original innocence* (that is, "original justice," according to the traditional formulation).[28] In their innocence, the man and the woman are fully conscious of and conformed to God's original creative plan, for their exterior perception of created reality is informed by an interior vision that corresponds precisely to God's own valuation of creation as "very good" (Gn 1:31). They understand, then, that in its masculine and its feminine "incarnations," the human body reveals a person made in God's image, and that the body is consequently meant to express and to facilitate a totally unreserved communion of persons. In a word, the sexual difference evident in their nakedness leads them, through original innocence, to understand that the meaning of human sexuality is essentially *spousal.*[29]

Through the acuity of their interior vision, the first man and woman also understand that the creation of which they are a part is, at root, a profound gift. Precisely *as* creation, it has been given the gift of existence when once it

---

in God (e.g., *ST* I, 93, 2, 6, 7). Aquinas rejects the idea that the image of God is in human beings communally (or "severally," versus "individually") because he is occupied with refuting the view that the relations between a man, a woman, and their offspring correspond, respectively, to those between the Father, the Holy Spirit, and the Son. For one thing, this view depicts the relations of origin in the Trinity falsely by making the Holy Spirit the principle of the Son, as the woman is the principle of the man's offspring. Aquinas also expresses the opinion that Scripture would not have referred to the divine image in man and woman until *after* the birth of the first offspring if the communal idea of the image were correct (see *ST* I, 93, 6, *ad.* 2). And he wants to equate the divine image with what is highest and most distinctive in human beings, namely, our rationality, whereas we share with the animals the same basic male-female-offspring structure. Aside from us, every visible creature bears the likeness of God only as a "trace," i.e., only insofar as the effect points to the cause. In the rational creature, however, one finds the likeness of *image* according to the intelligence, endowing human beings with a quasi-specific likeness to God (see *ST* I, 93, 2, 6). Nevertheless, John Paul insists that "*man became the image of God not only through his own humanity, but also through the communion of persons,* which man and woman form from the very beginning." TOB 9:3. See also TOB 28:1; Wojtyła, "The Family as a Community of Persons," in *PC,* 318. John Paul's personalism helps resolve the matter. Because the "unity of the two" established in the beginning is not merely the result of an impulse of nature but is rather a personal act by which each wills to exist for the other, the interpersonal communion of man and woman (which is a quality of their personal being)—and by extension, any genuine communion of persons—belongs to the divine image, such that human beings reflect, together in their common humanity, both the unity of God and the Trinitarian communion of Persons *in* God. The commandment of love, which confirms our vocation to love, presupposes this foundation. See *MD,* 7.

28. See TOB 16.

29. See ibid., 12–13:1.

did not exist. Since they alone among the creatures of the world can comprehend the meaning of creation, the man and the woman recognize that they have received the world, that the world has received *them*, and, above all, that they have received *each other* from the Creator as a gift. The fact that God creates what is good and is pleased with it implies that the divine motive for the gift of creation in all its goodness is Love. The language of gift, then, is ultimately inscribed in the Creator himself, whose Love has created the body and endowed it, in both its masculine and feminine forms, with its spousal meaning—that is, with its power to express personal love and to establish a communion of persons through the sincere gift of self.[30]

It follows that by expressing themselves as subjects of truth and love (of holiness) through the body in its sexual duality, man and woman proclaim visibly in the world the invisible mystery of the unqualified Truth and Love (of the Holiness) that lies at the heart of creation itself. To the extent that they participate in that mystery, they also communicate it to the world. As lived according to God's original creative plan, therefore, the body is a sacrament. It signifies the divine image in man and woman, who express themselves as persons and, in their spousal communion, as mutual gifts through it. In its spousal meaning, the body also signifies the gift-character of all creation, whose own sacramentality is thus revealed.[31] And so the body signifies, above all, the divine Source of every created gift.

When the first man and woman offer themselves as gifts to each other through the body in the grace of original innocence, they are not merely following the lead of sexual instinct, for each of them enjoys a perfect interior freedom born of the perfect mastery of the spirit over the body. It is this freedom—the *freedom of the gift*—that inwardly disposes and enables man and woman to give themselves to each other spousally in the totality of their personal being as soul-body creatures; that is, according to their full truth and value as person-gifts. However, the possibility of their giving themselves so to each other implies also that each will receive the other in a way that is commensurate with the gift that the other *is*, the gift of a masculine or a fem-

30. See ibid., 13:2–5; 14:2–5.

31. See ibid., 19:3–6. Note that when John Paul speaks of the body, of creation, and, later, of redemption, of the Church, and of marriage in the beginning (precisely in virtue of the body's spousal meaning) as sacraments, he is using the term "sacrament" in the broad sense as that which signifies visibly and in some way realizes historically, in human life, an invisible, divine reality. Ultimately, he has in mind the mystery of the Father's calling us eternally in Christ to be "holy and immaculate in his sight" (Eph 1:4), which, as a work of grace, implies also the call to be his adopted children in Christ (see Eph 1:5). See TOB 87:5; 93:5; 98:7–8.

inine "someone" willed into existence by God in the divine image for his or her own sake, and recognized as such through original nakedness. Man and woman form a true communion of persons when each one welcomes fully, and thus affirms, the sincere gift of self offered by the other.[32]

In giving themselves fully to each other, the man discovers the gift that he is in the depth of his humanity and masculinity, and the woman likewise discovers the gift that she is in the depth of her humanity and femininity—but only because each gift has been affirmed according to its true value by the other's having received it in its totality. In that way, the man and the woman achieve greater self-possession through a greater consciousness of the meaning of their own self as gift, leading them to offer themselves anew to each other in proportion to their new depth of self-understanding. Not only is each person enriched in the very act of giving the gift of self to, and of being received by, the other, but so, too, is each one enriched for having received the gift of the other.[33] In the reciprocity of this exchange, "giving and accepting the gift interpenetrate in such a way that the very act of giving becomes acceptance, and acceptance transforms itself into giving."[34]

The discovery of self and of the other that man and woman experience in the reciprocal exchange of their persons reaches its height when the bodily expression of their spousal unity in the conjugal act results in the conception of new life, for the mystery of fatherhood in the man and of motherhood in the woman reveals itself therein. Their original consciousness of the procreative end of human sexuality thus comes to term in the reality and the experience of parenthood. Through their child's somatic likeness to them, the new parents see in him both *their* living image and the image *of God*. God's creative participation in the conjugal communion of persons—"I have acquired a man from the LORD" (Gn 4:1)—enables man and woman to transmit the divine image so as to "create" a new human being. Thus, the couple's bodily union and its procreative fruitfulness constitute, in a way, a renewal of the original creation, for, like it, they are gifts of creative Love and reflect that Love.[35]

32. See TOB, 14:6; 15:1–4; 17:1.

33. See ibid., 17:4–6.

34. Ibid., 17:4. See *LR*, 129. The giving of myself to another "self" implies not only my being accepted *by* that other, but also my prior acceptance *of* that other. Consequently, the offer of myself to another as a gift contains already my pledge to receive that other as a gift (and it presupposes the prior self-manifestation of the person through the body precisely as a gift, at least in essence). For that reason, self-giving and other-receiving are really just two sides of the same coin, such that the receiving is as much a wholly personal act as the giving.

35. See TOB, 10:4; 14:6; 21:2, 4–6.

## The Vulnerable in the Light of God's Original Creative Plan for "the Body"

Because man and woman have each been created in the image of God, who is Love (see 1 Jn 4:8, 16), they find their deepest personal fulfillment in the vocation to love and in the experience of *being* loved.[36] The marital relationship between man and woman "produces the primary form of interpersonal communion,"[37] achieving its fullness in family life, of which it is the foundation. The vocation to love is therefore revealed preeminently in and through the family as constituted according to God's creative plan "in the beginning." So, to the extent that the reciprocal love of spouses and their children for each other participates in and reflects the Trinitarian communion of love within God, it contains and reveals what is essential to every authentic form of interpersonal and social relation.[38]

That is why the loving relation of spouse-parents to their infants and young children—who, in their psychosomatic immaturity, their defenselessness, and their dependency, typify the meaning of human vulnerability—says much about the fundamental principles that ought to govern how individuals and societies view and treat vulnerable human beings of any kind. In turn, just as from the beginning of their existence children are, objectively, gifts "from the LORD" that enrich and share in the lives of their parents and other family members (leaving aside the irreplaceably enriching effects of those gifts on the human race and the created order as a whole), so, too, are vulnerable persons of every kind, precisely *as* persons, divine gifts that contribute inestimably to the formation and enrichment of genuinely personal relationships and societies. With that in mind, let us consider further what John Paul II's analysis of God's original creative plan as revealed in Genesis 1 and 2 tells us about the person, the agency, and the vocation of vulnerable human beings.

Every human being is a bodily person created in God's image. That decisive fact of human existence is the true measure according to which we must understand both ourselves in general and the meaning of human vulnerability in particular.[39] Like everyone else, vulnerable human beings transcend

36. Cf. *Familiaris Consortio*, 11.

37. *GS*, 12. "Love between man and woman is one particular form of love, in which elements common to all of its forms are embodied in a specific way." *LR*, 73.

38. See *Familiaris Consortio*, 43.

39. To the extent that our understanding of the divine image in us does not properly corre-

the whole material order of created being—they are ends in themselves—from the first moment of their existence. That is true regardless of whether the nature of their vulnerability allows them self-consciously to reflect on and to assert that truth for themselves. Their very existence is still defined by that "solitude" that places them on a level ontologically superior to the world and to every other kind of creature therein, for God "breathed the breath of life," the human soul, into them when they first came to be. However weak, undeveloped, unaware, poor, disabled, deformed, or dependent some vulnerable persons might be, their somatic homogeneity with us (which we can now recognize even at the strictly genetic level) signals to us, objectively, the real presence of a person, just as the somatic homogeneity of the first woman with the first man enabled him to see in her a "someone" like himself in and through the sexual difference. When our rational consciousness of reality corresponds to God's creative vision, the eyes of physical sight see things as they really are; therefore, to see a real person, made in God's image, manifested in the body behind the many forms of vulnerability that might otherwise deceive our sensory vision, we must be inwardly "innocent," that is, imbued with and favorably responsive to God's grace. In a word, we must be *holy.*

So, the living body of every human being expresses the presence of a person made in God's image. That is why as male or female, the human body is inscribed with the exclusively personal capacity for self-giving and other-receiving, providing the subject with the means of expressing him- or herself objectively and concretely *as* a subject, a person. That same capacity can therefore be exercised in an incipient but real way "from the beginning" of one's life, in the always active exercise of one's own personal being in its male or female form. It follows that even the most vulnerable persons can and do establish bonds of mutual self-giving and other-receiving with other human beings directly and concretely through the body. Indeed, their bodily manifested vulnerability is often the main or the only means by which they express themselves as person-gifts and thus invite others—with the force of a moral imperative—to welcome that gift freely by the reciprocal gift of themselves, which the vulnerable are naturally disposed and able to receive in turn. Like every other human being, then, vulnerable persons communicate one way or another by means of the same Gift-Language spoken by the three divine Persons in the intra-Trinitarian communion of Love.

---

spond to God's self-revelation in Christ as interpreted in the authentic tradition and magisterial teaching of the Catholic Church, our self-understanding will invariably be deficient or distorted.

Since that is the case, it follows that from the moment we come into existence as exceedingly vulnerable persons, we are equipped for and entrusted with the mission to love and to be loved, to give the personal gift of self and to welcome the personal gift of other selves. Requiring, as it does, self-transcending beings to fulfill it, that mission accounts ultimately for the essential solitude of both the vulnerable and the not-so-vulnerable with respect to the world, and consequently for our inherent ordination toward interpersonal relationships with one another. According to God's creative plan, moreover, the mission to love must inform the way in which human beings fulfill the commandment to be fruitful. In that way, we proclaim that the commandment itself issues from Love as a *decree* of Love.

On the one hand, John Paul II makes it clear that the creation accounts in the book of Genesis set forth the essential structure, conditions, and purpose of marriage as willed by God. Thus, the commandment to be fruitful refers, first of all, to procreation within the marital covenant formed between a man and a woman united in love. We see in this that authentic love-giving is inherently *life*-giving, reflecting the Creator, who is Love and Life itself, and who, motivated by Love, bestows existence on the world and its creatures freely and generously.[40] Procreation is, in turn, the means by which man and woman populate the earth so as to transform it according to their lawful needs, thereby exercising their dominion to the glory of God. And in this we see an indispensable social end of marriage—a life-sustaining and life-enriching one. By fulfilling God's original commandment thus, man and woman cooperate with his act of creation, guiding and bringing to term the fruitfulness with which God has endowed both them and the earth itself. Again, obedience to God's commandment is a truly life-giving love.

On the other hand, while some forms of vulnerability do not prevent personally mature human beings from validly marrying and freely fulfilling God's original commandment to fruitfulness as it applies concretely to marriage, that is not always the case. Like anyone else, however, vulnerable persons at any stage of development or in any condition can still fulfill the underlying love/life dynamic of the commandment in ways that are appropriately analogous to its fulfillment in marriage, the commandment's primary object. They thus manifest God's image in themselves.

40. John Paul is keenly aware of the inextricable relation between life and love in the personal order, hence his unequivocal warning: "when the conjugal act is *deprived of its inner truth* because it is deprived artificially of its procreative capacity, it also *ceases to be an act of love.*" TOB 123:6. See *LR*, 228, 230–31, 235–36, 249.

For instance, the vulnerable might reinvigorate our life by any of the endless variety of ways in which they might express love: by sharing their knowledge or the wisdom of their experience with us; by touching us with the humbling example of their self-forgetfulness, for our sake, in the face of their own adversity—even when our problems are comparatively small; by helping us see that, despite difficulties and seemingly impossible odds, our life, like theirs, is a gift to be lived courageously, generously, and selflessly. The vulnerable affirm our life even when they can do no more in their weakness or frailty than to express their love for us as a heartfelt wish that they could do something beyond their power in order to help ease whatever load we carry. And should even that exceed their power of self-expression, the vulnerable can infuse our lives with meaning and happiness just by being there as person-gifts who entrust themselves to our care and invite our love through the offer of themselves in the body and its vulnerability. By drawing us thus into communion with themselves as personal gifts of love, vulnerable persons enrich our lives, and we theirs, through the mutual self-giving that occurs in the very act of mutual acceptance according to each one's capability. Together with us, therefore, the vulnerable help perfect the divine image in the humanity that we share.

The more vulnerable some people are, the more "naked" they stand before us. In its original sense, nakedness refers to the personal transparency of the woman to the man and of the man to the woman. They were "not ashamed" because their mutual transparency was a function of the complete openness of each to the other—of the mutual willingness to give oneself to the other in the full truth and value of one's own person, and hence with the freedom of the gift, while receiving the other as someone possessing that same truth, value, and freedom. In the grace of original innocence, neither the man nor the woman was "vulnerable" to being used—degraded—by the other.

Still, vulnerability did exist in their original state. But like everything in God's "very good" creation, it was ordered toward a good end. The man and the woman were vulnerable to the existential "loneliness"—to the need to love and to be loved—that brought them together so as to advance, in a sense, their humanity and the divine image in them. And we can suppose that, had the first woman conceived and given birth to offspring prior to the fall, the young would still have been subject to the vulnerability characteristic of infants and children, requiring the love, care, and nurturing of their parents. Yet, partly because of that vulnerability and the parental response that it calls forth, the family united in love reflects most fully God's image in the world.

Similarly, while some forms of vulnerability—for example, physical and mental disorders, terminal illness, and material poverty resulting from injustice—did not exist in the original human state but rather followed as consequences of original sin (as we will see), God can draw from them, even still, the good that he intended "original vulnerability" to serve. The creation accounts in Genesis reveal that human vulnerability was found originally in that solitude that disposed the first man and woman to open themselves to communion with each other in a completely transparent and authentic way. It is in that light that we must view conditions of vulnerability like those just mentioned.

Because vulnerable persons are subject to conditions that are often difficult to hide and that might make them radically dependent on others, they appear "naked"—transparent—before us. But the vulnerable do not on that account have reason to be "ashamed" (to the extent that they are aware of their "nakedness" at all). The fact that human vulnerability lays bare some real facet of their life serves to provide an opening for us to establish communion with them, unless either or both sides are unwilling. It serves, in a way, as the basis for that initial "mutual attraction" by which persons possessing equally the very same nature are invited to surpass the current limit of their existential loneliness through the reciprocal exchange of their persons in truth and love. The experience, to which all are vulnerable, of being imprisoned in a vast sphere of inner solitude, and which reflects the limitless capacity for intersubjective relations that *original* solitude—our deep awareness of being irreducible to the material world—opens in us, always allows for the possibility of welcoming yet another person into one's life through the sincere gift of self. On the one hand, somatic, psychical, psycho-rational, or material vulnerability sometimes intensifies a person's fundamental experience of loneliness, or existential solitude, by becoming an occasion for his withdrawing or being forced by rejection back into it. But that same vulnerability can signify and thus become the means by which both he and others can transcend that kind of solitude, that sense of isolation or alienation. In and through the window of human vulnerability, especially in cases of acute human need, we ought to see the truth, the value, and the beauty of a *person* who, though beset by certain limitations, is dynamically ordered toward full, personal self-expression, within the human community, as a gift of love that offers itself "packaged" in vulnerability to be *received* in love, according to God's creative plan.

The offer of self that vulnerable human beings extend to others in and through their dynamic, existential act of *being* vulnerable is therefore not mainly a plea for help but an expression of their inherent drive toward fulfilling the image of God in themselves through interpersonal and social communion with others. By receiving their self-gift in the very act by which we reciprocally give ourselves as a gift to them, we affirm the vulnerable as subjects of truth and love whose value and dignity transcend their vulnerability and shine forth through it. And in receiving us in the love and care that we extend to them, the vulnerable help us likewise to discover our own identity as subjects of truth and love: they affirm us as person-gifts. The dynamic communion of persons thus established encourages both them and us to come out of ourselves even more, to give ourselves reciprocally in greater measure as we come to discover, to the extent possible, the power for life-giving and love-giving that the fully personalized body contains and that we actualize according to its spousal meaning whenever we express ourselves through its masculinity or its femininity in harmony with God's creative plan, under God's grace.

### Original Sin as a Threat to "the Body"

Prompted by the serpent (the "tempter"), man and woman called into question the very Love that had motivated the gift of the world and of the original covenant. With God now under suspicion, they willfully disobeyed the divine command not to eat of the tree of the knowledge of good and evil (see Gn 3:1–7).[41] By this original sin, man and woman alienated themselves from God, with disastrous results. Their act of rebellion shattered the perfect integration of spirit and body with which they were endowed when God first created them,[42] depriving them of the ability to recognize and to live out the gift-character of existence fully and innocently through the body and its sexual differentiation into male and female. Instead, man and woman became ashamed of their nakedness and covered themselves (see Gn 3:7).

Their act of covering themselves suggests that man and woman no longer participated inwardly in God's vision of creation through the grace of original innocence. But it also suggests that original sin did not wholly destroy the divine image in which they had first been created, for they each apparently sought to protect the personal value that they somehow still sensed in themselves and perceived now as threatened. Suddenly, they each

41. See TOB 26:4; *DetV*, 37–38; *SgC*, 28–31.
42. See TOB 28:2–3.

felt inwardly compelled to hide the bodily signs of their sexuality from the other. Above all, they felt compelled to hide their "nakedness" from God (see Gn 3:8–10). Love and trust had given way to guilt and fear in their relation to both God and each other. Their fall from the grace in which they had originally been constituted obscured their understanding of the body's significance (1) as the expression of a human person; (2) as the means by which to build a true *communion* of persons; (3) as the means by which to exercise dominion over the world; and, consequently, (4) as the visible image of God in the world.[43]

Together with this loss in their consciousness of the full meaning of the body, man and woman experienced a new kind of vulnerability: a deep sense of insecurity stemming from their inability, in their fallen state, to dominate their own self and, by extension, the world that God had charged them with the task of subduing (see Gn 3:17–19). The aftermath of their rebellion against God, therefore, was the rebellion of their own body and of creation itself against *them*. Once alienated from God, man and woman were confronted with their own helplessness—their "nakedness"—before the powers of the body and of the world. Their practical experience of their personal disintegration, of their failure to master themselves and the world completely, dramatically underscored their contingency, thus anticipating the death to which they would be subject as the ultimate consequence of their disobedience to God's command.[44]

The shame that man and woman experienced immanently as a reflection of the ontological consequences of original sin in each of them expressed itself especially in their relations with each other. According to John Paul II, shame is the response of conscience to concupiscence, which John the Evangelist tells us manifests itself in three ways: "the concupiscence of the flesh, the concupiscence of the eyes, and the pride of life" (1 Jn 2:16).[45] As an immanent reality, shame manifests one's uneasiness with original sin's rupture of the original integration of spirit and body, for on account of that breach, the body asserts itself over and against the spirit. Out of that opposition arises the power of concupiscence, the incessant inclination toward sin—especially sexual sin—that threatens the structure of self-possession and self-governance by which man and woman can express themselves authentically as persons through the body. In a way, then, the sense of uneasiness, the

43. See ibid., 26:4–5; 27–28:1.

44. See ibid., 27:4.

45. See ibid., 26:1–2; 30:6.

guilt, generated by shame bespeaks a certain perception of, and a desire to preserve, the inherent value and dignity of the bodily person, for it somehow echoes the original meaning of the body against the urgings of concupiscence. Since that meaning includes man and woman's call to communion through the body's male-female duality, immanent shame refers always in some way to another human being, particularly one of the opposite sex.[46]

When man and woman actually yield to concupiscence, it becomes an act of inordinate desire, of lust, which destroys the possibility of true interpersonal communion. That seems to be the ever-present danger to which Genesis 3:16 refers: the "desire" of the woman for the man, in this case her own husband, will be met by his "desire" to dominate her. Once the first couple turned away from the Father and toward the world on breaking the first covenant (see 1 Jn 2:15), concupiscence inclined the two to view the sexually differentiated body reductively, as merely an *object*. Concupiscence thus obscured the body's meaning as that which manifests an inestimably valuable *subject*, an utterly unique and unrepeatable person-gift to be offered and received in love and in its totality through the body's masculinity and femininity. Ironically, while "the eyes of both were opened" as a consequence of original sin (Gn 3:7), man and woman saw not more but less, hence the experience of shame at their nakedness.

Once sexual concupiscence crosses over from a spontaneous inclination to a willful act of reductive desire, the body constrains the spirit so that man and woman lose the freedom of the gift. As a result, each approaches the other's body as an object from which to extract sexual pleasure by appropriating it unilaterally for his or her own "use."[47] That amounts to their *taking from* the other what each of them lustfully desires rather than their *being for* each other, and their *welcoming* each other as a freely given gift in the totality of who he or she really *is*. While the body never loses its objective meaning as the "substratum" through which man and woman express and realize their mutual love in the communion of persons, it cannot serve that purpose

46. See ibid., 28; 31:1. For an extended treatment of sexual shame, see *LR*, 174–193, "The Metaphysics of Shame."

47. In doing so, one necessarily allows one's own body to be approached in the same way (see *LR*, 37, 39). Leaving aside the spontaneous manifestations of concupiscence in young children (who are not yet morally responsible for their behavior), we can add that one might also view reductively and consequently use one's own body as an object from which to extract sexual pleasure. While other complex factors might be at work, this seems to be what lies at the root of autoeroticism. In the final analysis, the latter seems, for the same reason, to factor into morally illicit and aberrant forms of sexual behavior between persons, where it is enacted by reducing others to the rank of mere accessories to narcissistic sexual indulgence.

when they subjectively (that is, inwardly) violate that meaning by allowing lust to dominate the "heart." To the extent that man and woman live under the cloud of concupiscence, the body will always be a possible source of confrontation and mutual exploitation between the sexes, whereas God created it to be the means by which they would entrust themselves freely and unreservedly to each other in the full depth of their personal truth and beauty—that is, as gifts.[48]

We see, then, that by willfully reducing the full value of a person to merely a sexual value, man and woman undergo a radical change not only in their way of cognitively perceiving each other, but also, and for that reason, in their way of existing in relation to each other: they live according to the dictates of concupiscence in its three forms, especially the first. Even when it does not express itself outwardly, as in a lascivious leer or in the act of adultery, sexual lust determines the person's very existence from within through the interior act, hence the words of Jesus: "Whoever looks [whether just cognitively or also by physical sight and facial expression] at a woman to desire her [as no more than a sexual object] has already committed adultery with her in his heart" (Mt 5:28).[49] It also determines who the other person "becomes" *for me*, as we see more clearly in the alternative translation of the text: he "has already made her an adulteress in his heart."[50]

The text of Matthew 5:28 suggests that even if the will to exist lustfully relative to another is coming from one side only, in this case the man's, it still destroys, unilaterally, the possibility of either the man or the woman's giving the gift of self and receiving the gift of the other in a full and proper way. The lustful man has neither the interior freedom to give himself unreservedly as a gift nor the disposition to receive the woman as a gift, should she want to offer herself freely and fully as such. He has already cognitively

48. See TOB 29–33. "If the only value involved in the attitude of a man and a woman to each other is pleasure there can be no question of reciprocity or of the union of persons. The fixation on pleasure as their purpose restricts each of them to the confines of his or her 'I'.... Egoism excludes love, but permits calculation and compromise ... there can be a bilateral accommodation between egoisms. In these circumstances there cannot, however[,] be any question of a 'common I' of the sort which comes into being when one of the persons desires the good of the other as his own and finds his own good in that of the other person." *LR*, 156–57. In short, the utilitarian attempt to harmonize different egoisms by mutual recourse to the pleasure principle "can never deliver us from egoism." *LR*, 39.

49. John Paul notes that the expression *ho blépōn*, "one who looks," encompasses both the external look manifest to all and the strictly internal, or perceptual, look in which it has its origin. See TOB 39:4.

50. John Paul informs us that this rendering, from ancient translations of the text, seems more precise. See ibid., 24:4.

reduced her to the level of an object having only a sexual value, blinded as he is to the whole range and proper order of sexual and spiritual values that her body and femininity represent. As far as he is concerned, she exists only to satisfy his sexual urge. Because the lustful heart deceives itself about the human vocation to interpersonal communion and its realization through the body's spousal meaning (whether within marriage or, in a morally appropriate way, outside of it), men and women who have given themselves over to lust set themselves in conflict with their own conscience and so with their own personal dignity. By thus "depersonalizing" themselves, they end up "depersonalizing" each other.[51]

Christ's reference to the "heart" in Matthew 5:28 is ultimately an appeal to human conscience.[52] He invites man and woman to examine themselves, to recognize their need to overcome personally, from within, the movement of concupiscence "in the flesh," and thereby to recapture and to live out, in the power of the Redemption, the original meaning of the body in its masculine and feminine forms. To the extent that they allow his words to penetrate the heart and make them aware of their own sinfulness, Christ can summon them back to the vocation to *love*, for which they were created and for which they must be "pure of heart" (Mt 5:8). Purity of heart—sanctification—is a consequence and a manifestation of life in the Spirit, of the restoration to grace by which man and woman can put to death a life lived according to the flesh (where interior subjection to concupiscence yields the bitter fruit of sin and guilt) and replace it with a life of faith that bears good fruit by working through love (cf. Gal 5:6, 16). In the gift of the Spirit—the fruit of his redemptive act of love—Christ has set man and woman free with the freedom by which they can exchange, once more, the gift of self through the body as a sign and a realization of God's image in them. By doing so, they glorify God in the body, which has become a temple of Holy Spirit (see 1 Cor 6:19–20).[53]

## Original Sin as a Threat to "the Body" of the Vulnerable

Let us now consider how John Paul II's biblical reflections on original sin and its consequences pertain to vulnerable human beings as regards both their condition and the way that others relate to them on account of it. In that context, we will also see how the consequences of original sin pose a threat to the agency of the vulnerable.

51. See ibid., 25; 39–43:4.

52. See ibid., 35:5 for the stark appeal that Christ makes to conscience in John 8:7.

53. See ibid., 45–46; 49–54; 56–57:1–2.

### The Ontological Effects of Original Sin on Some Types of Vulnerable Persons

The condition of many vulnerable persons *as* vulnerable can be traced back, at least indirectly, to original sin and its consequences, which continue to unfold in the lives and history of human beings. Somatic, psychical, and psycho-rational defects, disabilities, and related sufferings are rooted in and manifest the loss of that perfect integration of spirit and body that the first man and woman enjoyed before their sinful transgression of God's original covenant with them. A passage from Pope John Paul II's apostolic letter *Salvifici Doloris* is particularly germane: "[S]uffering cannot be divorced from the sin of the beginnings, ... *from the sinful background* of the personal actions and social processes in human history. Though it is not licit to apply here the narrow criterion of direct dependence ... , it is equally true that one cannot reject the criterion that, at the basis of human suffering, there is a complex involvement with sin."[54] John Paul has in mind here every type of evil and suffering that human beings experience in the temporal and historical realm, including moral evil and moral suffering. These latter imply the involvement of intellect and will, the higher powers of the soul. However, at this point we will restrict our considerations to conditions and sufferings caused by forms of soul-body disintegration involving only the lower, somatically dependent powers of the soul. Blindness would be an example. This type of disintegration might or might not affect the development or the operation of the higher powers themselves; however, in cases where those powers are operative, the condition would affect the kind or the degree of integration that the person could achieve through them. We will prescind, for the moment, from any consideration of personal sin (whether that of the person afflicted or of others) as a proximate cause of this type of disintegration and the vulnerability that might result from it.

Despite the imbalance in the relation between soul and body that resulted from original sin, the soul still informs the body as its substantial principle. The human body as such could no more develop out of genetically human matter without the spiritual soul than the already developed human

54. *Salvifici Doloris* (February 11, 1984), 15, Vatican translation (Boston: Pauline Books and Media, 1984). "By virtue of a human solidarity which is as mysterious and intangible as it is real and concrete, each individual's sin in some way affects others.... Consequently, one can speak of a *communion of sin*." From *Reconciliatio et Paenitentia* (December 2, 1984), 16, Vatican translation (Boston: St. Paul Editions, 1985).

body could sustain its existence after the soul leaves it at death. The spiritual soul is the central organizing and governing principle of the body as a biological organism. It sustains and guides the complex vegetative processes that characterize the bodily component of human existence.

Since the time that our first parents fell from grace, however, the body has rebelled, in various ways and degrees, against the power of the spiritual soul and its faculties over it. To the extent that it succeeds in asserting its "independence" from the soul (possibly with the "help" of some foreign agent, such as a pathogen, toxin, or chemical), the body can limit or prevent the effective use of the soul's faculties in and through it. The body's "success" in that regard might explain the degeneration or aberrational development of some of its parts, for it has been "liberated," at least partially, from the soul's integrative guidance. Insofar as the soul's faculties are dependent on the structural integrity of those parts (for example, the eyes, the limbs, or the brain), they might not be able to operate, or to operate fully, through them. The body, or some part of it, is no longer "well-disposed" toward the soul.[55]

If the condition of vulnerable persons subject to that type of disintegration is particularly severe (as in the wake of a devastating stroke), they might not be able to express themselves through the body in a fully, or at least a manifestly, personal way. Their state might become akin to that of someone who is still at an early stage of development. Nevertheless, they remain, like everyone else, ineluctably ordered toward perfect human self-expression. "From the very moment of conception, and then of birth, the new being is meant *to express fully his humanity,* to 'find himself' as a person. This is true for absolutely everyone, including the chronically ill and the disabled. 'To be human' is his fundamental vocation."[56] The dynamic inner thrust of developing, weak, sick, or seriously disabled persons toward their full self-expression as human beings is the defining feature of their existence—not only because the image of God abides in them, as in every human being, despite its diminution by sin and its consequences, but, above all, because each of them, as much as anyone, is heir to the hope of redemption, body and soul, in Christ. We will take up that point later.

55. This idea is conveyed in *AP*, 212.
56. *Letter to Families from Pope John Paul II,* 11.

### The Effects of Original Sin on Human Relations Involving Vulnerable Persons

Because original sin has damaged us interiorly by initiating the body's resistance to the spirit, our intersubjective relationships have also become damaged, basically in two different ways. We just saw that some forms of psychosomatic disintegration stemming from the disharmony of spirit and body can significantly hinder the persons subject to them from expressing themselves fully through the body as persons, which means that their interpersonal relations with others will be affected accordingly. Presuming for the moment that those disintegrative conditions are strictly "accidents of nature," we can say that vulnerability of this kind is only remotely connected with sin, in that it is ultimately an effect of original sin.

On another level, however, the opposition between spirit and body that is rooted in original sin and that sometimes causes forms of somatic and psychical disintegration for which neither the subject nor other human beings are personally responsible (in any proximate sense) can cause in us the inclination toward personal sin, depending on the impact that it has on our consciousness, emotions, reason, and will. By our deliberately submitting to that inclination, our personal sins will invariably distort the way in which we relate to other persons. We will become "vulnerable" to moral and spiritual ruin in proportion to the degree of that distortion. This is the second, more pernicious way in which original sin and its consequences affect us both personally and interpersonally. It might lead us to inflict harm on others simply because they are already weak and vulnerable, or to become the proximate cause of their vulnerable condition ourselves. In doing so, we inflict the most devastating harm on ourselves, though we tend to overlook that fact.

The intersubjective dimension of personal sin always manifests itself in characteristic ways, for we have all inherited the same concupiscent disposition from the damage that original sin caused to our fundamental structural integrity. In other words, we all tend to act according to the dictates of lust.[57] Because the disorderliness of human relationships weighed down by sin is marked in each instance by the same essential features, Pope John Paul II's careful analyses of the effects of original sin on the relationship of the first couple provide an indispensable basis for analyzing, in turn, the attitudes

57. Of course, Jesus and Mary are the preeminent exceptions, though it would seem safe to include as well St. Joseph, the "just man" (Mt 1:19), whom God specially sanctified to fulfill a crucial mission in the history of human salvation.

and behaviors underlying any human relationship that is marred or threatened by sin. In particular, it will be possible for us to understand, in terms of John Paul's analyses, why human beings who are subject to somatic, psychical, psycho-rational, material, or externally imposed constraints are especially vulnerable to being viewed and treated in depersonalizing ways by others.

The Twofold Vulnerability of the Vulnerable Because original sin had the immediate effect of obscuring our view of the body as a visible sign of the personal subject and as the means of facilitating full interpersonal communion with other bodily persons, vulnerable human beings stand particularly in danger of not being affirmed as persons by others, whether in principle or in action. If their condition makes it impossible or seemingly impossible for them to perform manifestly personal actions through the body, some people might not recognize their inherent personal dignity, even to the point of denying that the vulnerable are, or are still, members of the human community. Sometimes certain external conditions over which their victims have no control and that might even be imposed deliberately (examples include abject poverty, lack of educational opportunities, and political imprisonment) reduce persons to a vulnerable status by placing limitations on their personal growth and freedom of self-expression. Such conditions make it easier for other people to view those subject (or subjected) to them as nonpersons. Some might even use the misfortune of these vulnerable persons to justify a preexisting or a tendentious, prejudicial opinion about them. The vulnerability of the vulnerable has therefore two dimensions. They are subject not only to the structural (somatic, psychical, or psycho-rational) or the external conditions (and in some cases, both) that restrict their modes of self-expression and their self-sufficiency; they are also subject to the consequent "condition" of having others disregard them as persons, or at least as worthwhile persons. From there, it is only a small step for those others to begin actively treating the vulnerable according to a subpersonal standard.

Behind the Depersonalization of the Vulnerable: Lust in the Heart Persons who are not presently vulnerable in terms of their self-awareness, rationality, physical integrity, or material or other circumstances—let us call them the "strong," insofar as their favorable state of life, precarious though it always is, puts them at an advantage relative to the vulnerable, who are comparatively "weak"—will view or treat a vulnerable person as a mere object, as a some*thing* rather than a some*one*, to the same extent that they fail to see in his or her distinctly human somatic structure a transcendent subject of incalculable worth. If the "strong" overcome (through God's grace in Christ) the three forms of concupiscence that original sin introduced into the human heart, they will see in the bodily self-presentation of each vulnerable human being *as* vulnerable, a vulnerable *person*, and thus recognize the call to extend themselves to that person in self-giving love. Otherwise, concupiscent desire will desensitize them to the authentic identity of the vulnerable as persons and as gifts. If that happens, the "strong" will inevitably come to view and to treat vulnerable human beings in one way or another as objects—perhaps as *dispensable* objects.

In some cases, vulnerable persons such as young children, the physically or mentally weak or disabled, and even the poor are exploited as sexual objects by individuals who seek to satisfy their own carnal desires. Ironically, we are referring to these self-absorbed individuals, enslaved though they are to lust, as the "strong" (hence the use of quotation marks). Having first "depersonalized" the vulnerable in their heart, the "strong" proceed to "depersonalize" them *in fact* by appropriating them unilaterally for "use" in a way that grossly caricatures, so as to mock and profane, the sacred activity that is meant to signify and to effect true interpersonal communion between a man and a woman in marriage according to God's creative plan. While sexual exploitation is perhaps associated most often with the concupiscence of the flesh, it can also issue from the other two forms of concupiscence mentioned in 1 John 2:16, namely, the concupiscence of the eyes and the pride of life. In the latter case, it seems more a question of using sexual means to subjugate, humiliate, and thus exert control over those who are weaker. It is a raw assertion of one's "power," "dominance," and "superiority."[58]

The concupiscence of the eyes, which so often arouses that of the flesh, also arouses tendencies toward greed that go beyond the "greed" for carnal satisfaction. Included among these is the tendency to appropriate the vulnerable as instruments of personal gain. Human trafficking and the exploitive use of migrant labor are concrete realizations of inordinate human desires seeking to achieve their avaricious ends by "objectifying" weak and disadvantaged human beings. The same goes for "caregiving" services that exist solely or to any degree as a pretext for robbing and defrauding persons

58. In TOB 30:6, John Paul's passing comment on "the pride of life" in connection with Genesis 3:16 seems to contain this idea.

needing care—and through them, their families, the insurance industry, public and charitable assistance, and so on—of money and property for services that were never rendered or that were rendered unnecessarily and even incompetently, perhaps compromising the personal well-being of the very ones requiring real care. In these and similar cases, vulnerable persons are treated as commodities so that others can satisfy their lust for money, possessions, status, power, or the like.

Of course, some people profit off vulnerable persons in ways that also involve and capitalize on the concupiscence of the flesh, as when the vulnerable are forced into prostitution or used in pornography distributed for sale. Even images produced or evoked by the immoral use of the communications media, the arts, or computer technology so as to depict vulnerable persons (especially women and children) pornographically will fan the flames of sexual lust in those who make use of them, increasing the likelihood that the evil desires thus aroused in the "heart" will translate into action against those depicted so. At the same time, the victimizers, having typically become addicted to pornography, will increase the demand for it, leading inevitably to the further victimization of the vulnerable by both the producers and the consumers of pornographic material. Its producers, who have given their heart over to lustful greed, profit thus at the expense of the weak and defenseless, many of whose psycho-physical problems are exacerbated or caused directly by the shattering personal abuse to which they are subjected as a result.

In each of the examples given so far, we can see that the "strong" base their relation to the vulnerable solely on their greed for sexual gratification, profit, or both. Such relations are wholly selfish and utilitarian, depersonalizing both victim and victimizer. As long as the "strong" persist in relating to others thus, they exclude outright any possibility of or interest in their ever forming authentic interpersonal relationships with the persons whom they would rather exploit to satisfy their own lusts.

Returning for a moment to the third form of concupiscence, we would add that the expression "pride of life" has reference not only to sexual exploitation as an assertion of power, but also to the inordinate trust that the "strong" place in material possessions, and to the boasting that they do because of the lifestyle and social status that those possessions afford them.[59]

59. The interpretation of the expression depends on whether "the pride of life" is regarded as signifying an objective or a subjective genitive. Whereas the preceding two expressions, "the concupiscence of the flesh" and "the concupiscence of the eyes," are generally taken to be subjec-

Thus understood, the pride of life can elicit in the "strong" and materially well-to-do a certain fear of vulnerable human beings, whether at the conscious level or not. For one thing, they might see the vulnerable as an obstacle to the pursuit and realization of personal goals or other forms of fulfillment connected with their accustomed or desired way of life. Or perhaps the vulnerable person is a family member whom the others regard as a drain on their wealth or as an embarrassing contradiction to the image that they want to project, thus depriving them of their grounds for boasting. But it seems that beneath all this, those who are not currently subject to somatic, psychical, psycho-rational, material, or imposed forms of vulnerability see, at some level, their *own* vulnerability in the vulnerable, or at least the potential for it. Their fear of vulnerable persons arises, therefore, from a self-centered fear for themselves and for the lifestyle in which they take pride. For that reason, their "pride of life" may well lead the "strong" to arrogate to themselves the power *over* life, so that, in seeking to eliminate the perceived threat posed by the vulnerable, they eliminate the vulnerable themselves. Abortion and euthanasia are prime examples of just where the pride of life can lead. They are manifestations of the cowardly spirit of this world, the spirit of lust that invariably overtakes us when we turn away from the Father and his gift of Love in the Spirit, through which alone we attain real power, love, and self-control (cf. 2 Tm 1:7; Rom 8:2–6, 15).

Shame in the "Strong" as Revelatory of the Personhood of the Vulnerable The fact that the "strong" see and fear their own vulnerability reflected in vulnerable human beings reveals that on some level they do, after all, perceive them as persons like themselves. That is why they sometimes experience

tive genitives, the last of the triplet seems to include as well the meaning given by the objective genitive. On the three forms of concupiscence (often translated as "lust") mentioned in John's First Letter, see Raymond E. Brown, *The Epistles of John*, Anchor Bible, vol. 30 (Garden City, N. Y.: Doubleday, 1982), 307–312, 325–327. Brown does not exclude the meanings given in the text above regarding the three forms of concupiscence, or lust, but in considering the overall context of the Johannine writings, he concludes as follows: "Not the sinful but an absence of the otherworldly is what characterizes the three factors.... They belong to what is below, not to what is above" (326). Brown seems to overlook the fact that the "absence of the otherworldly" in human life is itself the direct result of the first sin and the reason for sin's continuation in human life, as the three forms of concupiscence take root in the will deprived of or resistant to sanctifying grace. This "absence" indicates a turning away from what is "of the Father" (i.e., from the everlasting Love that leads to Life) to what is "of the world" (i.e., to what is passing and leads to death). See 1 John 2:15–17. Cf. Pheme Perkins, "The Johannine Epistles" in *The New Jerome Biblical Commentary*, ed. Raymond E. Brown, Joseph A. Fitzmyer, and Roland E. Murphy (Englewood Cliffs, N.J.: Prentice Hall, 1990), 990.

shame for their exploitation of the vulnerable. In the experience of shame, their conscience reacts against the destructive actions that issue from their abandonment to lust. Such actions depersonalize not only their victims but also, and above all, their perpetrators. Consequently, in failing to affirm the vulnerable as persons by the deeds that they direct toward them, the "strong" simultaneously fail to affirm and fulfill *themselves* as persons.

In order for human beings to achieve self-fulfillment, each of their actions must correspond appropriately to the true value of its "object." Therefore, if the "strong" experience shame rather than fulfillment in their actions toward the vulnerable, then: (1) they must be inwardly aware of their *own* rightful value as persons, which their actions did not uphold; and (2) they must likewise be aware that the true value of the vulnerable corresponds precisely to their own, since in treating them according to the standard of any lesser value, the "strong" experience only nonfulfillment accompanied by shameful guilt (unless they have already deadened their conscience by allowing prideful arrogance to hold sway). It follows that the objective order of reason, which corresponds to the objective order of truth, is gravely violated any time the "strong" use vulnerable human beings as merely the means to an end (even if good in itself) presumed to have greater value than the vulnerable themselves. And because the human vocation to love God and neighbor goes thus unfulfilled, the objective order of the world is likewise violated, as with the first sin.

The Human "Heart" as Source of the Interior Act We see, then, that as the objective order of values is overturned in the lustful heart, a person will begin to view the vulnerable reductively or even as a counter-value rather than according to the totality of values that they represent as persons. The lustful person will consequently fail to see in human vulnerability an invitation—indeed, a *personal* invitation—to aspire to a greater love by reaching out to vulnerable human beings and establishing a true communion of persons with them. On the contrary, the degradation of the vulnerable in the interior act of the lustful heart tends invariably toward some form of alienating exterior expression, such as the dehumanizing way in which one looks at or away from them.

In some instances, however, the interior and exterior acts of the "strong" might not correspond. For example, some people try to disguise their negative attitude toward the vulnerable by projecting an air of respectability or benevolence toward them. A pretense like that might be wholly self-serving but, as we saw above, it might also be motivated by a certain sense of shame, revealing to the "strong" the attitude that they *should* have toward the vulnerable but do not. Since in that case they really do have a fundamental grasp of the personal value of vulnerable human beings, their effort to deceive others on the exterior plane serves, in the end, to expose the interior deceit that lust has effected in *themselves*. Having interiorly denied the truth about the personal dignity and worth of the vulnerable, they end up contradicting the truth of their own conscience and degrading themselves thus as persons. They allow lust to determine how they view the vulnerable, even if, for various reasons, they exist in relation to them in less noxious ways.

In a manner consistent with and complementary to his approach in *Person and Act*, Pope John Paul II explains the distinction and the possible disparity between the interior and the exterior act by referring, in his theology of the body, to Matthew 5:27–28. His reflections promote a deeper and more complete understanding not only of the "strong" who, in their self-determining actions, have given themselves over to lust, but also of certain vulnerable human beings as actors. As we have seen, John Paul's analysis of Jesus' words on the "heart" direct our attention to the interiority of the person, to the "place" from which every human action issues. To be sure, human actions have often an external component visible to all; however, to the extent that the exterior act corresponds to the interior act, it simply reflects, while reinforcing, the manner in which we have inwardly chosen to determine ourselves as persons. And it sometimes does so in a relatively subtle way—by means of a "look," for example. On the other hand, John Paul indicates that we are capable of largely suppressing any outwardly discernable expression of our interior acts, noting that the "look" by which we express them might refer solely to our own way of inwardly perceiving—of cognitively knowing, or "looking at"—someone or something. This is the "look" that reveals us interiorly to ourselves, particularly insofar as conscience reacts to it in one way or another. Based on Genesis 3, John Paul has also indicated that we are capable of performing exterior acts by which we deliberately intend to deceive onlookers (and perhaps even ourselves) about how we are actually determining ourselves inwardly: we thus "cover" ourselves to hide the inner secrets of our heart, lest we stand "naked" before others. Self-determination is therefore grounded in the interior act, which might or might not be expressed, or expressed accurately, in an outwardly discernable way (cf. 1 Sm 16:7).

John Paul II's analysis of the human "heart" serves to confirm that there must indeed be vulnerable persons who determine themselves freely through the interior act, outward appearances to the contrary notwithstanding. For if someone can purposely confine his self-determining act to his "heart," as when he wills to regard another person interiorly in a certain way, then we have to hold that a vulnerable person subject to serious somatic disintegration, to lesser degrees of psychical or psycho-rational disintegration, or to externally imposed limitations can still determine himself interiorly, even if his condition or situation compromises in some way his ability to express the act outwardly. In each case, the body mediates the exercise of the interior act of self-determination so that it is simultaneously an "external" expression of the "someone" who, in performing the act, is newly self-aware and newly "self-created" (for better or worse) through it.

Moral and Spiritual Vulnerability The fact that many vulnerable persons qualify fully as actors does not necessarily mean that others will recognize, acknowledge, or value the self-determining actions they perform, especially wholly interior ones. The "strong" might count any dependency or limitation on the part of the vulnerable as evidence against their personal status, equating freedom of self-determination with self-sufficiency, and self-sufficiency with personhood. Yet, to the extent that vulnerable persons capable of performing voluntary actions determine themselves in a morally good way even in the face of depersonalizing attitudes and treatment by others, they will perfect themselves as persons, whereas those who depersonalize them will not. Though it might not always seem so, it is really the vulnerable who are in such cases the ones most fully integrated: they transcend themselves by allowing no one to discourage or prevent them from attaining, by their actions, their personal perfection as subjects of truth and love in God's image.

On the other hand, those whom we might by every worldly measure consider "strong" *make themselves vulnerable* to moral and spiritual ruin by willfully violating the whole truth about the personal identity and dignity of undeveloped, physically or mentally disabled, poor and oppressed, or other such vulnerable human beings. By forsaking truth and love in their attitudes and actions, the "strong" are forsaking the ultimate condition for the realization and perfection of their personal structure, thereby depersonalizing and dehumanizing themselves. Since the eternal vocation to love in truth defines the whole meaning of the distinctly personal existence of every human being, those who willfully harm the vulnerable, if only in their own "heart," become subject to psycho-physical and moral states destructive of their own person. These include carnal lust, egoism, fear, disquiet, guilt, and depression—all signs of their personal disintegration for having chosen "life according to the flesh," which is radically opposed to, and so exclusive of, life in the Spirit.

At the same time, we must not overlook the fact that vulnerable persons who are fully capable of determining themselves are likewise responsible for fulfilling the vocation to love in truth. Should they willfully fail in their actions and lives to respond to that calling and thus become guilty of grave personal sin, they will not fulfill themselves as persons. They, too, will become subject to the personal disintegration that characterizes every life lived according to the flesh. By forsaking their authentic, human vocation, these vulnerable persons introduce the most serious kind of vulnerability, moral and spiritual vulnerability, into their own lives—a condition that absolutely no one else could have imposed on them, whether by depersonalizing attitudes and treatment or by any other means.

Of course, vulnerable persons who are subject to severe psycho-rational disintegration (serious mental retardation, for example) are incapable of determining themselves in a way that would make them personally responsible for anything they might do, and so they are equally incapable of committing personal sin. In certain instances, however, it is possible that such persons are, in fact, responsible for having brought their condition on themselves, though once afflicted, they might no longer be directly responsible for how they act.[60] In either case, they remain, essentially, subjects of truth and love, having been made in the image and likeness of God. The same is true of those who are vulnerable because of the psychosomatic immaturity that characterizes the early stages of human development (such as the embryonic period and infancy). Indeed, all human persons—whether vulnerable or "strong"—retain this heritage, even in cases where they threaten and contradict it in actions by which they freely and knowingly realize some counter-value and thereby subject themselves culpably to psycho-moral disintegration and spiritual ruin. Regardless of any of these conditions, every person remains the "object" of a Love that is "greater than sin, than weakness, than the 'futility of creation'; it is stronger than death.... [I]n man's history this revelation of love and mercy has taken a form and a name: that of Jesus Christ."[61]

60. Such is the case, for example, when someone abuses drugs knowingly and willingly and then suffers an incapacitating, perhaps irreversible loss of cognitive and volitional function as a result. Regardless of the cause, disintegration of that kind prevents persons from fulfilling (or perfecting) themselves in the psycho-moral sense.

61. *Redemptor Hominis* (March 4, 1979), 9, Vatican translation (Boston: St. Paul Editions, 1979).

## God's Creative Plan for "the Body" Fulfilled through Christ's Redemptive Love

Before we discuss the fulfillment of God's creative plan for "the body," we would note that John Paul II's actual scheme begins with Christ's words to the Sadducees regarding the resurrection (see Mt 22:24–30; Mk 12:18–27; Lk 20:27–40).[62] Based on that text, he elaborates on what Christ indicates there about the meaning of the body's masculine and feminine forms in the state of eschatological fulfillment.[63] After considering briefly some of St. Paul's complementary insights about the resurrection of the body in 1 Corinthians 15,[64] he goes on to discuss bodily continence for the sake of the kingdom of heaven (see Mt 19:11–12). He understands continence as a possible state in life that one undertakes voluntarily (in response to a special grace) to anticipate in one's own body (precisely through its spousal meaning), and thus to give witness to, the eschatological state of redeemed human beings.[65] John Paul rounds off that discussion by turning to 1 Corinthians 7 for St. Paul's pastoral reflections on the relation between virginity and marriage.[66] Only after all that does he discuss marriage and its sacramentality in the new economy of salvation in Christ. That rather detailed discussion begins and constitutes much of part 2 of his great catechesis on "the body."

While the theme of marriage, so central to John Paul II's reflections on God's original creative plan and on original sin, informs and guides his reflections on bodily resurrection and on continence for the sake of the kingdom, we will nevertheless reverse here his actual scheme of resurrection-continence-marriage. In that way, his reflections on marriage redeemed will immediately succeed the previously treated themes of the catechesis to form the following whole: (1) man and woman's original marital relationship "in the beginning"; (2) the threat that original sin and its consequences pose to that relationship; and (3) the redemption of the marital relationship in Christ. According to John Paul's scheme, this last set of reflections completes the groundwork for the final chapter of part 2: his treatment of Paul VI's 1968

62. Likewise, in the chapters of TOB corresponding to our previous two subheadings on God's original creative plan and on original sin, John Paul begins, respectively, with Christ's words to the Pharisees about God's institution of marriage "in the beginning" (Mt 19:3–9; Mk 10:2–12) and with his words in the Sermon on the Mount about adultery in the heart (Mt. 5:27–28). The words to the Sadducees about the resurrection complete the "triptych" of Christ's statements on the basis of which John Paul II constructs his theology of the body. See TOB 64:1.

63. See TOB 64–69.

64. See ibid., 70–72.

65. See ibid., 73–81.

66. See ibid., 82–85.

encyclical, *Humanae Vitae*. We will not, however, be including that chapter in our study. In addition to allowing us to form a coherent sequence on the theme of marriage as such, our rearrangement of John Paul's scheme will bring out the paradigmatic significance of the marital relationship, as lived according to God's eternal plan, for the state of continence for the sake of the heavenly kingdom—a state that is itself, in turn, preeminently an image of our definitive, eschatological, spousal union with God in Christ.

### Ephesians and the "Great Mystery"

Presupposing in his reflections God's self-revelation in Christ, John Paul II has already shown us, based on Genesis 2:24, that the authentic bodily expression of the marital union between man and woman is, from "the beginning," a visible reflection of the invisible mystery of God's intra-Trinitarian life. Turning his attention now to the fulfillment of God's creative plan through Christ's redemptive sacrifice on the cross, he offers an extensive exegesis of Ephesians 5:21–33 and related texts to deepen his reflections on the body's meaning for man and woman. God's eternal love for us was "consummated"—fully expressed and realized in time—by the redemptive sacrifice of Christ on the cross for the sake of the Church. In and through that salvific act, Christ has united the Church to himself in a spousal way as his Bride and his Body, with himself as Bridegroom and Head. In a real but mysterious way, the Bride/Body forms a single subject with her divine Bridegroom/Head through their mystical spousal union. At the same time, she acquires and retains her own authentic identity in virtue of that union, just as wife and husband each experience greater self-discovery and self-possession in the act of becoming "one flesh" according to God's original creative plan.

By giving himself spousally *to* the Church in the act of giving himself sacrificially *for* her, Christ adorned his Bride with the fullness of the gifts of salvation,[67] thus endowing her with new life—the grace of sanctification—in him. He thus reveals preeminently the way in which the total donation of self in the new economy of grace must be realized in the reciprocal relation of man and woman in marriage, if it is to constitute a true communion of persons—one that is both an effect and a sign of Christ's saving grace. In Christ, the spousal dimension of love has become fused with the redemptive one, so that the body, having originally been created to "speak" the language of

67. These salvific gifts are represented by "the washing of water accompanied by the word" (Eph 5:26)—that is, baptism. See Eph 5:29–30 for what is perhaps an oblique reference to the Eucharist, as John Paul suggests in TOB 92:8; 99:1.

spousal love, has been newly inscribed with a redemptive meaning as well.[68] Therefore, to be conformed to and incorporated into Christ's redemptive act, marital love must include the element of mutual self-sacrifice between spouses, each voluntarily subordinating his or her self-interest to the true good of the other.

John Paul tells us that the grace of original innocence in which the first man and woman were created was already an effect and a sign of the mysterious love of God that has eternally elected each of us in Christ to enter an adoptive, filial relationship with the Father. Constituted in holiness, the original couple saw in their nakedness the means of expressing their interpersonal, unitive love and of sharing in God's work of creation through procreation. In generating offspring, moreover, the couple would cooperate with the Creator in extending to their children the grace of original innocence, a supernatural endowment given in the sacrament of creation (with God's infusion of the rational soul into man and woman) as the fruit of the Father's having chosen us in Christ "before the creation of the world" to be "holy and immaculate in his sight" (Ep 1:4). That is why marriage, as instituted by God in the beginning, is the primordial sacrament, the privileged sign and vehicle of God's salvific initiative.[69]

However, once that initiative was rejected with the introduction of original sin and its consequences into human history, marriage was deprived of the grace, given with the sacrament of creation, that it was instituted to mediate as a gift to the generations and thereby to creation itself. It nevertheless retained its value as a sign of the supernatural gracing that would abound once more in human life through the redemptive union of Christ with his spouse, the Church. Ephesians 5:29–32 alludes to marriage "in the beginning" as a foreshadowing of the spousal relation of Christ and the Church, calling the link between type and fulfillment "a great mystery" (v. 32).[70] Anticipating this, the prophetic tradition (especially as elaborated in Isaiah, Hosea, and Ezekiel) seized on the analogy between the marital covenant and the covenant that Yahweh established with Israel, which served as a revelation of his eternal plan to unite his people definitively to himself.[71] John Paul

68. See TOB 90:1, 5–6; 91:1–6. See also 92:4–7; 102:4; and *LR*, 147.

69. See TOB 96:3–7; 97:1, 3.

70. See ibid., 93; 95b:5–7; 97:1–2.

71. Although the Old Testament legal tradition tolerated polygamy, monogamy gradually appears in the prophetic tradition as "the only right analogy of monotheism understood in the categories of the covenant, that is, of faith and trust in the only true God-Yahweh, Israel's Bridegroom." Ibid., 37:4.

suggests, therefore, that "marriage has remained the platform for the realization of God's eternal plans."[72]

In the redemptive act by which he indissolubly united the Church to himself as his beloved spouse, Christ newly, definitively, and permanently actuated and made "visible" the grace of our eternal election in him—the supernatural gift of sanctification first actuated at the world's creation and revealed as original innocence in the pure spousal love and unity of the first couple. By thus becoming the subject of this new supernatural gracing, the Church is a *new creation*.[73] The power of Christ's redemptive grace flowing through the Church enables husbands and wives to model their relationship on that of the divine Bridegroom and his Bride. Out of reverence for Christ, in whom they are eternally elected and to whom they are eternally subject, spouses voluntarily make themselves subject *to each other* (Eph 5:21).[74] Their capacity for mutual subjection for Christ's sake and each other's suggests that marriage is once again capable of communicating to them the grace of sanctification, whose source is the sacrament of redemption—the irrevocable and unsurpassable historical realization of our eternal election in Christ.

The salvific power of marriage in its primordial sacramental form is therefore renewed through and inserted into the new and definitive covenant in Christ. In a word, Christian marriage is a sacrament in the strict sense: it is one of the seven visible signs, instituted by Christ and administered by

72. Ibid., 97:1; see 98:2.

73. See ibid., 97:3–5; 98:8. Even if grace constituted man and woman originally in a state of innocence and justice, it can still "more abound" (Rm 5:20) as the fruit of Christ's redemptive love for the forgiveness of sins (see TOB 98:4; Aquinas, *ST* I 95, 4, *ad.* 1). The final dispensation of grace is therefore distinguished from the original in that it is directed toward the man of the threefold concupiscence. In either case, however, the state of grace signifies, in John Paul's view, a sharing, on the part of man and woman, in the divine nature through the personal indwelling of God, which is none other than the gift of adoptive sonship that the Father extends to us eternally in the Son (e.g., TOB 96:5). For Aquinas, Adam's original integrity and rectitude of will presuppose that God had endowed him with divine grace (see *ST* I, 95,1). However, John Paul seems to imply that the divine indwelling was fundamentally the same in Adam before sin as it is in Christians in the state of grace, whereas Aquinas (referring to Augustine) makes the following qualitative distinction: "It is not disputed that Adam, like other just souls, was in some degree gifted with the Holy Ghost; but *he did not possess the Holy Ghost, as the faithful possess Him now,* who are admitted to eternal happiness directly after death." *ST* I, 95, 1 *ad.* 2, trans. Fathers of the English Dominican Province (Westminster, Md.: Christian Classics, 1981). Indeed, the exaltation of the "fall" as the *felix culpa* that gained for us so great a Redeemer seems to reflect an intuition that we have received, in Christ, a grace that somehow surpasses even that of Adam in the original state—his preternatural and supernatural gifts notwithstanding. That same intuition is expressed in the Liturgy at the offertory: *Deus, ... humanae substantiae dignitatem mirabiliter condidisti et mirabilius reformasti.*

74. See TOB 89; 99:2.

his Church, that confer efficaciously the grace they signify. Because Christ opened marriage again to the saving power of God through the redemption of "the body" (that is, the whole human person, from whom the body's dignity derives), he could insist on the abiding validity of its original indissolubility "in the beginning" when questioned by the Pharisees about the lawfulness of a man's divorcing his wife (see Mt. 19:3–8). Through the redeeming grace of the sacrament, man and woman can master the threefold concupiscence of "the body" that followed in the wake of original sin, so that their conjugal union in the new economy of salvation will reflect, precisely by sharing in, the indissoluble union of Christ and his Church—a union "consummated" and ever sustained by his salvific love. Christian marriage thus issues from the Redemption as the new and definitive configuration of the original marital covenant.[75] In this way, John Paul shows that the institution of marriage "in the beginning" prepared our understanding for the new covenant in Christ, while Christ's spousal relationship with his Church is the source of renewal for marriage, bringing the inner meaning of the marital relation between husband and wife to full expression.[76]

### The Objective and the Subjective Language of the Body

Throughout his theology of the body, John Paul II has emphasized that the human body has an objective, spousal meaning because its sexual differentiation signifies the perennial complementarity of male and female *persons* and mediates their interpersonal exchange, particularly when man and woman freely give the gift of self to each other in marriage as the basis for the family. The body's spousal meaning is therefore "integrally inscribed in the very structure of the masculinity and femininity of the personal subject."[77] Coming from God "in the beginning," it is intimately tied to the mystery of creation. It is likewise tied to the mystery of redemption. Christ restored to the body its original spousal meaning—obscured and disfigured by sin—by personally employing its self-giving capacity in the very act by which he redeemed it, effecting thereby his spousal union with the Church, which has become his Body.[78]

While John Paul has referred often to the objective meaning, or "lan-

75. See ibid., 98:2–3, 5–8; 100:2–3, 6; 101:1; 102:2.

76. See ibid., 90:1–4; 95b:5. Wojtyła's 1974 article, "The Family as a Community of Persons," anticipates some of the themes in his theology of the body—a project that was apparently already germinating in his mind, if not already underway. See *PC*, 326.

77. TOB 105:5. See also 105:2.

78. See ibid., 105:4.

guage," of the body, he has also affirmed clearly that, insofar as the body expresses a personal subject, the language that it "speaks" is authored subjectively. It is a question of how man and woman decide to employ the spousal meaning inscribed in their very being as masculine and feminine persons, determining themselves accordingly. Will they consciously appropriate, or "reread" truthfully, the body's objective language for themselves so as to confirm and unfold its original, self-giving meaning through their voluntary activity? Or will they cause the body to utter a lie by authoring and acting on a meaning that falsifies its original language? In either case, man and woman authorize the meaning that they give to the body, and so they are personally responsible for the way in which they express themselves through it. In that sense, the body "speaks" with their authority and thus on their behalf, fulfilling a prophetic role, as it were. Depending on whether the subjective content that informs the body's objective, spousal language coincides with or contradicts the proper meaning of that language, the body gives witness, respectively, as either a true prophet or a false one.[79]

If, for example, spouses express bodily "the deepest words of the spirit—words of love, gift, and faithfulness"[80]—then their subjective conformity with the body's objective, spousal meaning allows the body to speak for them in a truthful and moral way. On the other hand, if the subjective language that one or both spouses express bodily is that of infidelity and lustful "appropriation," then the body utters a lie and acts immorally, in the name and with the authority of the person. Whenever man and woman employ the body to simulate love or authenticity for reasons that are ultimately self-serving and hence destructive of self and others, they falsify the language it was created to speak. That is what underlies the sin of adultery.[81]

Expressing, as it does, a person, the human body, in its masculine and feminine forms, has a unique dignity. Its objective, spousal meaning cor-

79. See ibid., 105:1–3, 5; 106:1–4. This is but another way of saying that the human act issuing from one's interior and expressing itself outwardly through the body ought to concur with, utilize, and support the spousal, or self-giving, meaning with which the Creator endowed the human body, as male and female, "in the beginning." By determining our way of being from our personal depths, the interior act is the inner "word," the "language," that ultimately establishes what we "say" in and through the body. To the extent that it does not fulfill the personal and moral responsibility of reinforcing the body's objective meaning, the interior act, expressed outwardly, will obscure and distort—garble and fracture—the body's inherently spousal language, thus falsifying it. Indeed, it will do the same, where the actor is concerned, even if not expressed outwardly, hence the possibility of committing adultery in the heart.

80. Ibid., 104:7.

81. See ibid., 104:4, 9; 105:1. In essence, such misuse of the body also underlies other sexual sins like contraception, masturbation, fornication, and homosexual acts.

responds precisely to that dignity, and so the personal subject is morally bound to uphold that meaning in actions relating both to his or her own body and to that of another. It is true that since the original fall from grace, man and woman remain subjects of concupiscence and so, too, ever prone to misreading and misusing the body's language. Through the power of Christ's redemptive grace, however, they become capable once more of rereading the truth of that masculinity and femininity so essential to the body's language, recognizing therein, as they did "in the beginning," the basis for establishing a true communion of persons. To the extent that they act accordingly by the grace of Christ, they insert themselves into and witness prophetically to God's creative and redemptive plan.[82]

### Continence for the Sake of the Kingdom of Heaven: A Sign of Bodily Redemption

Authentic human love has always a spousal (or unitive) and a redemptive meaning because it is always expressed through the language of the body, which is rooted in the mystery of creation and taken up into the mystery of redemption in Christ. That is why the example and the grace of Christ's giving himself up for the sake of his Bride, the Church, is necessary to help Christian spouses understand and live the meaning of the body in their marital life. But the salvific love of the divine Bridegroom is also necessary to help people of any state in life understand and conduct themselves in a deeply Christian way as persons living a bodily existence in the world. Within the horizon of our hope for the redemption of the body, any aspect of human experience, even suffering or death, can be transformed through the body and its spousal significance into a profound expression of self-giving love that bears within itself the salvific fruit of the Redemption. Indeed, the salvific dimension of love extends, in Christ, beyond the one who loves, so as to embrace other persons and even the whole of creation itself, whose own redemption is mysteriously taken up into the redemption of the body (see Rm 8:19–23).[83]

In particular, John Paul II draws attention to the fact that man and woman can express redemptive love through the spousal meaning of the body not only in the sacrament of marriage, so integrally linked with the sacrament of creation and of redemption, but also in the vocation to continence—celibacy or virginity—for the sake of the kingdom of heaven. By word and example,

82. See ibid., 105:2; 106:1–4; 107:2–3.
83. See ibid., 102:7–8.

and by the power of the Redemption, Jesus introduced the possibility of continence as a free response to a special grace of God, encouraging but not commanding those who receive it to accept it. In effect, they can voluntarily make themselves "eunuchs" for the kingdom (see Mt 19:11–12). In virtue of the charismatic choice for continence, the person who recognizes, values, and is naturally drawn to marriage and its procreative fruitfulness as a great good instituted by the Creator will nevertheless renounce the option to marry, so as to anticipate in his or her own body the definitive completion of the body's redemption in Christ at the final resurrection.[84]

When tested by the Sadducees, who were trying to discredit belief in the possibility that the dead will one day rise (see Lk 20:27–33), Jesus responded that God is God of the living, for the scriptures reveal that the patriarchs, who had long since died, are alive in him (see Ex 3:15). The children of the resurrection will therefore be beyond death. Moreover, they will take neither wife nor husband (see Lk 20:34–38). Indeed, Christ himself will be the divine spouse of all the elect, whose everlasting life in him eliminates the need for procreation. It follows that once "the marriage of the Lamb" to his Bride has been eschatologically "consummated" (Rv 19:7), the spousal meaning of the body will achieve its definitive mode of expression, as each of the elect enters an unsurpassable communion of love with God in Christ and with all the saints. The fruitfulness of physical generation will give way to the abounding spiritual fruitfulness of perfect charity.

Those who choose the lifelong vocation of virginity or celibacy bear witness to that future age by dedicating their lives exclusively to Christ now. They manifest their decision through the body by making a sincere gift of themselves to other persons for the sake of the heavenly kingdom. In doing so, they become spiritual "mothers" and "fathers" through works of charity born of life in the Spirit, whose power to generate supernatural fruit in willing subjects has found its surpassing expression in the divine maternity of the Virgin Mary—that is, in the mystery of the conception and birth of the eternal Son of God as man.[85] By thus fulfilling the call to communion that

84. See ibid., 73:4; 76:3–4; 81:2–3; and *LR*, 250–55.

85. Mary's "*consent to motherhood* is above all *a result of her total self-giving to God in virginity.* Mary accepted her election as Mother of the Son of God, guided by spousal love, the love which totally 'consecrates' a human being to God. . . . The words 'Behold, I am the handmaid of the Lord' express the fact that from the outset she accepted and understood her own motherhood as a total *gift of self,* a gift of her person to the service of the saving plans of the Most High. . . . [S]he perfectly unites in herself the love proper to virginity and the love characteristic of motherhood, which are joined and, as it were, fused together." *RMa,* 39. Because she was completely united

arises from their inner solitude before God and *with* God, those who direct the reciprocal "for you" of masculinity and femininity toward the heavenly kingdom for love of Christ in the life of continence fulfill the Trinitarian image of God in themselves through the body's spousal meaning. In the power of the redemption of the body, the freedom of the gift of self through continence accepts willingly the abiding self-sacrifice entailed in renouncing the natural inclination toward marriage, as well as that entailed in mastering the concupiscent inclinations of "the flesh." It does so with the explicit motive of reciprocating the spousal love that Christ expressed through his redemptive sacrifice, and in such a way as to be occupied only with pleasing the Lord (see 1 Cor 7:32). In all these ways, then, the life of virginity or of celibacy for the kingdom of heaven participates uniquely in the Redemption and thus contributes preeminently to the realization of God's kingdom in its earthly manifestation. While not identical with it, the temporal "incarnation" of the kingdom prepares for, reflects, and shares already in the mystery of the heavenly kingdom yet to be realized and revealed in its eschatological fullness.[86]

John Paul II's analyses both of marriage and of continence for the kingdom of heaven show clearly that the choice for either vocation is grounded in the same personal disposition to realize the spousal meaning of the body through the sincere gift of self. In virtue of that disposition, the two vocations are intrinsically ordered toward fruitfulness: marriage in both the physical and spiritual sense (through the procreation and education of children, the fostering of family unity, and so on), and continence in the strictly and perhaps more intensely spiritual sense (through observance of the evangelical counsels and the renunciations they entail, through the realization of new and broader forms of intersubjective communion, and so on). What is more, these two vocations have been instituted by God to participate in and witness to God's indissoluble love for his people, particularly as manifested and realized definitively in Christ's redemptive and spousal love for his Church. Insofar as the vocation to continence integrates a mature consciousness of the body's spousal, or self-giving, meaning as an ontological reality stemming from the two ways—male and female—in which the human body is structured to express a person and the communion of persons, it affirms

with the Person and mission of her Son, Mary, ever virgin, became the mother and the model of the Church. See nos. 40–47.

86. See TOB 75:1–3; 77:1–4; 78:5; 79:2–3, 8–9; 80:5–7; 84:1–2. See also *Lumen Gentium (LG)*, 48; *GS*, 39; *LR*, 255.

the vocation to marriage and family life even while renouncing it freely for the sake of the kingdom. In a word, marriage and continence for the kingdom of heaven, far from being mutually opposed, are *complementary*.[87]

### The Eschatological Fulfillment of the Body

According to John Paul II, the spousal meaning of the body, expressed in different but complementary ways through marriage and continence, will be fulfilled identically and definitively at the final resurrection. Reflecting on Christ's response to the Sadducees, "who say there is no resurrection" (Mt 22:23; Mk 12:18; Lk 20:27), John Paul concludes that the resurrected human body will retain the masculinity or the femininity proper to it, for this is what underlies the body's spousal meaning and so, too, the fact that the divine image is reflected in its authentic modes of expression. By telling the Sadducees that human beings accounted worthy of the bodily resurrection will no longer marry (see Mt 22:30; Mk 12:25; Lk 20:34–35), Jesus is suggesting that in the age to come, the body will still be either male or female, while the meaning and expression of masculinity and femininity will be different. In the resurrection, the psychosomatic nature of human beings, and hence their modes of expressing the body's self-giving capacity, will be wholly spiritualized, as Jesus indicates by analogically likening (or equating, according to Luke's Gospel) those who rise from the dead to the angels, whose nature is wholly spiritual (see Mt 22:30; Mk 12:25; Lk 20:36). John Paul explains that the spiritualization of resurrected human nature refers to the perfect reintegration of soul and body. The soul and its powers will utterly permeate and master the body and its energies, so that the body will be completely and naturally unopposed to the soul's direction. In that way, the children of the resurrection will be able to realize themselves fully as persons.[88]

The kind of spiritualization that the resurrection of the body will realize in human nature is something unprecedented in human experience, even before the fall of Adam and Eve, for its source is in the unsurpassable level of participation in the divine nature that God will grant to the whole psychosomatic subjectivity of the human person.[89] The fact that every redeemed

87. See TOB 76:6; 78:3–5; 80:5; 86:6; 102:6. Regarding spiritual parenthood, see also *LR*, 260–61.

88. See TOB 64; 66:1, 4–5; 67:1–2.

89. TOB 95b:4 makes it clear that participation only, in the divine nature, is possible for the creature, not identity with it. One might add that the depth of one's participation in the inexhaustible mystery of the Godhead will correspond in some way to the level of one's personal response on earth to grace in charity.

human being will thus enter the eternal mystery of infinite Love constituted by the intra-Trinitarian communion of the divine Persons does not mean, for the finite creature, the loss of individuality but, on the contrary, the full flowering of each one's personal identity through the highest possible experience of truth and love in God. In turn, and for that reason, the glorified human body, precisely in its masculinity or its femininity, will express perfectly—indeed, virginally (as "the eschatological fulfillment of the 'spousal' meaning of the body")[90]—the person's reciprocal response to God's Trinitarian self-communication, as each of the elect freely gives the gift of self unreservedly to God.[91]

Those resurrected to everlasting life in the body will discover in God the relations existing among all created things; that is, they will understand the divine order of the world. Above all, their perfect rediscovery and possession of self in God will include the understanding of their proper relations with one another, so that they form a perfect intersubjective communion: the communion of saints. The definitive revelation and expression of the body's spousal meaning in the eschatological age will therefore be "the source of the perfect realization of the 'trinitarian order' in the created world of persons."[92] Through the Spirit of Life at work in the soul, the human body, redeemed in Christ, conceals within itself even now something of the mystery of resurrected life and final incorruptibility.[93]

### The "Bodily" Fulfillment of the Vulnerable within the Horizon of Redemption in Christ

As we saw above, Christ expressed his redemptive, self-sacrificial love through the body and so also through the spousal meaning with which it was endowed from the beginning, based on its masculine and feminine forms. Redemptive love became transformed thus into unitive love, which, given the original language of the body, has always an analogously spousal character even when it is not spousal in fact. The sacrificial act by which Christ redeemed the Church is therefore identical with his spousal union *with* her, so that she is redeemed only insofar as she is united to him as Bride to Bridegroom, as Body to Head.

Conversely, the body took on a new redemptive meaning in Christ, apart from which authentic unitive love cannot be expressed. Christ gave himself

90. TOB 68:3.

91. See ibid., 67:3–4; 68:2–3.

92. Ibid., 68:4. See 69:2–6.

93. See ibid., 70:8; 71:3.

*to* the Church precisely by giving himself *for* her, the fusion of unitive and redemptive love in Christ having taken place through the medium of human vulnerability. Our redemptive union with Christ will therefore always entail a response, on our part, that includes some sort of reciprocal self-sacrifice, such as subordinating our concupiscent desires to his will by the power of his salvific grace. Self-sacrifice of that kind, for the love of Christ through life in the Spirit, is now essential to, and expressed chiefly in, the self-giving by which we each become united authentically with another or others, whether as a spouse, family member, friend, neighbor, caregiver, compatriot, and so on. The sincere gift of self has consequently become redemptive in Christ.

### The Sacramentality of Human Vulnerability through the Power of the Redemption

Already in the Incarnation, the relation between the redemptive and spousal dimensions of love was anticipated, inasmuch as the self-emptying of the eternal Son in taking human form involved at once the "wedding" of the divine and human natures in his divine Person. Redemptive union with Christ, then, means sharing not only in the glory that has been revealed in him but also in the self-emptying and the suffering—the vulnerability—through which he attained that glory.[94] Self-emptying, suffering, or vulnerability of any kind that is connected somehow with Christ's gracious activity in, through, and for the Church, and so inserted into the economy of the Redemption, has therefore a sacramental quality. It is a sign of Christ's glory and a means to that glory because it is a vehicle through which Christ *communicates* his glory. The broadly sacramental character of human vulnerability that has been infused with Christ's redemptive grace and that is lived in accordance with it is somewhat analogous to the dynamic at work in the vocation to continence, which seeks, signifies, and invites others to intimate union with Christ through the renunciations that it entails. In a mysterious paradox that only Christianity can sustain, the vulnerability of psychical, psycho-rational or somatic brokenness, of natural developmental weakness, of material poverty or social powerlessness, or of voluntary self-emptying for another's sake, as expressed through the body's unitive meaning, can be transformed into a life-giving gift of grace flowing from the power of the Re-

94. Cf. Gal 2:20; 2 Cor 4:8–10, 17–18; Rm 6:3–8; *SD*, 20–23. "Union with Jesus Christ, which we shall realize in Heaven in joy and vision, is already possible for us on earth in suffering." Elisabeth Leseur, *The Secret Diary of Elisabeth Leseur: The Woman Whose Goodness Changed Her Husband from Atheist to Priest* (Manchester, N.H.: Sophia Institute Press, 2002), 110.

demption to a world that often seems eager to travel the speedways of death.

Unfortunately, many of us have largely rejected that gift, or at least failed to appreciate its value. To the extent that we do not cooperate with the wonders that God's grace would otherwise accomplish in us through the various forms of vulnerability to which we or other persons are subject, weakness and suffering are unnecessarily wasted and increased because the opportunities that human vulnerability offers us to love and to be loved are lost. Suffering, in particular, will seem to be just an evil—a useless and meaningless one. Unlike the great good of marriage, suffering was clearly not part of God's original creative plan; however, once introduced into the world as a consequence of original sin, it did, like marriage deprived of its supernatural efficacy before the Redemption, serve didactic and other salutary purposes. These included teaching humility, testing faith, inspiring soul-searching and a deepening of faith, eliciting mercy and compassion (whether from God's side or ours), punishing transgressions of the covenant, signifying God's withdrawal from the midst of his people and their need for redemption, intensifying their hope for redemption, and foreshadowing the coming of the Redeemer as the Servant that the LORD will send as a covenant to the people, bringing them healing by bearing their iniquities and interceding for them. Also in a way analogous to marriage, which Christ, in the power of the Redemption, has newly endowed with grace and incorporated into his sevenfold sacramental economy to fulfill definitively its original purpose, human suffering (along with other forms of human vulnerability) has in its own, more general way become in Christ a sign and a vehicle of grace, drawing its efficacy from the power of the Redemption flowing through the Church. Only God can bring such good out of suffering, which, in violating the original integrity of God's good creation, is evil in itself.

Similarly, God alone can draw good out of the hardship or suffering that we experience from the personal sacrifices by which we voluntarily *make* ourselves vulnerable in opening ourselves to others for their sake. In some instances, such sacrifices entail personal risk: they might cause or even require us to endure an evil of one kind or another, perhaps to the point of martyrdom. In any case, our efforts would have no supernatural power to effect good were they not sustained by the gracious activity of God in Christ through the Church. Indeed, without that grace, we would make no such efforts at all.

Vulnerable human beings become a *new creation* by participating in the grace of our eternal election in Christ through their suffering, weakness, powerlessness, or voluntary self-emptying. Though original sin had deprived us of that grace, Christ has newly actuated it through his redemptive sacrifice. Therefore, without minimizing either the gravity of human suffering or our moral obligation to try and alleviate it where possible, suffering and other vulnerable persons can voluntarily conform themselves so fully to the once vulnerable Christ by the power of his redemptive grace that they become fully alive in him, not only despite their suffering or their helplessness, but precisely in and through it, even unto death. Similarly, in cases where suffering or helpless persons are psychosomatically incapable of conforming themselves to Christ voluntarily, he can nevertheless make his redemptive grace effective in and through them by the agency of his Church, bringing them to glory along the same path of vulnerability that he himself once trod. This uniquely Christian paradox is such a sign of contradiction, such a stumbling block, to worldly individuals that they see no purpose or meaning in weakness and suffering. They might even hold the same view of the *persons* who are weak and suffering, especially in proportion to their degree of dependency.

If that attitude prevents us from seeing in the weak, suffering, frail, disfigured, marginalized, or impoverished body of each vulnerable human being the revelation of a person having sovereign worth, then it will likewise prevent us from reading in that body's objective, spousal language the invitation and the means to interpersonal communion with the person whose body it is. Above all, it will cause us to overlook or to scorn the body's redemptive meaning and to interpret the significance of the body only subjectively, in terms of selective values such as health, strength, beauty, and self-sufficiency. Once the body's objective language is obscured by this reductive one, we dispose ourselves to reading into the body such lies as euthanasia and abortion. We then become disposed *to act* on those lies in relation to ourselves or others, as the case may be. Blinded by vincible ignorance, concupiscence, or sheer godlessness, we pretend or we falsely think that we are making our body speak the language of "mercy," of "compassion," or even of "moral obligation" when we destroy our life or the lives of others because of their vulnerability. But in fact, the language that we have subjectively authorized the body to speak is so radically opposed to the truth of its objective, unitive meaning that it is inherently devoid of any redemptive meaning as well. Since those two meanings have become one in Christ, we can be certain that any falsely unitive language that we might speak through the body's masculine or feminine—its spousal—structure does not flow from, but is inimical to, the power of the Redemption, and so it does not participate in the redemption of the body. It has no power to save, leaving one "vulnerable" to moral and spiritual ruin.

Those who are subject to serious, unavoidable suffering provide an indispensable witness to the power of the Redemption, to the hope of bodily resurrection, and so to the dignity and sanctity of human life, when they reject the lie of euthanasia and take up their suffering as an apostolate or even as a long-term vocation. They display the treasure of their courageous witness through the "earthen vessel" of a disintegrating body and a frail humanity, making it clear that its transcendent, salvific power comes from God and not from them (cf. 2 Cor 4:7). Those who care tirelessly for weak or suffering persons provide a similar witness by voluntarily making themselves subject to the vulnerable out of reverence for Christ—that is, by opening their lives to and sacrificing themselves for the needy, as Christ did for us. And far from losing their own identity by being so self-forgetful, these caregivers become more fully the unique person they were created to be: they fulfill their humanity through the proper exercise of the body's unitive meaning in the power of the Redemption. The same is true of mothers and fathers who reject the lie of abortion so as to welcome and care for their unborn child even in difficult personal circumstances, or when they learn beforehand that the child is seriously infirm. As in both marriage and the life of continence for the kingdom of heaven, absolute fidelity to these and similar apostolates/vocations testifies to the incomparable and invincible efficacy of the new economy of salvation in Christ, reflecting in that way Christ's indissoluble union with his Church.

### The Transformation of the Vulnerable State in the Eschatological State of Glory

For Pope John Paul II, the body is a sign, or "sacrament," of the person as an image of God. And precisely as the body of a person, it can serve as a conduit of divine grace. The catechesis on the body thus implies that the human person is a mystery whose full reality can never be exhaustively expressed in and through the body. Nevertheless, while in the grace of original innocence, man and woman could bodily express themselves in a fully authentic way—that is, according to the whole truth and value proper to them as personal beings. They were free to give the gift of self to each other completely and unreservedly. It was original sin that threatened their ability and their will to express their person freely and truthfully through the body, whose sacramental character was therefore compromised, and whose nobility as a vessel of grace was lost with the loss of grace. In part, the lack of authenticity that crept into the bodily self-expression of the man and the woman was due to the psycho-moral disintegration resulting from their concupiscent desires and acts after the fall. But concupiscence is itself a symptom of the disintegration of spirit and body that they experienced *because* of the fall and that has adversely affected the human condition ever since.

In a more fundamental way, psychosomatic disintegration as a threat to personal self-expression is especially evident in those vulnerable persons who are unusually limited in their capacity to express themselves *as* persons through their bodily structure. Precisely for that reason, though, they quietly stir in us the longing to be free with the interior freedom of the gift, the freedom that once enabled man and woman to give themselves away to each other unreservedly and thereby to express themselves authentically and to discover themselves more fully as bodily persons. In other words, the very condition of vulnerable human beings enkindles our deeply interior desire to experience the redemption of our whole being, soul and body. That sometimes secret hope abides in the heart of each of us because we are all mysteriously associated with, and called to fulfillment through, Christ and his Paschal Mystery.

Like all of the elect in the heavenly kingdom, formerly vulnerable human beings who have been redeemed definitively in Christ will receive, in overflowing measure, the inexhaustible gift of God's eschatological communication of himself to them in love; that is, they will participate in the intra-Trinitarian communion to the fullest extent possible for human beings as creatures of God. Thus divinized, they will enjoy the full freedom of the spirit. On the last day, therefore, their spirit will subject their risen body to itself so completely as to spiritualize it. This perfect integration of spirit and body, the result of their unsurpassable level of divinization, will coincide with their perfect *personalization*, which excludes all bodily and psychical constraints. In the first place, those once vulnerable persons will express themselves fully *as* persons by giving themselves fully to God in absolute freedom through the glorified body, thus reciprocating with their whole being the unreserved self-communication of God to them. Their fully personalized psychosomatic subjectivity will fulfill itself definitively in the ineffable joy of contemplating God eternally.

With the rest of the redeemed, formerly vulnerable human beings who rediscover themselves in God in the perfection of their fully integrated and divinized psychosomatic subjectivity at the final resurrection will also enjoy a perfect intersubjective communion with those who have been bodily glorified with them. For that reason, the saints of the eschatological age will reflect perfectly, on the level of humanity fully glorified, the intra-Trinitarian communion of the divine Persons. This does not mean that the identity of each one of the elect will be entirely revealed to the others, for something of the mystery of the person as an image of God will remain, a mystery that can be penetrated fully only by God himself.[95] At the same time, however, since "Christ retains in His risen body the marks of the wounds of the cross in His hands, feet and side,"[96] it is perhaps not too much to suppose that those among the elect who, by God's grace in Christ, have blazed the trail to glory through their vulnerable state on earth will be specially distinguished in heaven by some glorified sign of their former weakness, which was in fact their strength. For by the inscrutable wisdom of God in Christ, human vulnerability can become a glorious manifestation of the persons subject to it, insofar as they express through it, as far as possible, that invincible power whose effects radiate with everlasting splendor from time into eternity: Love.[97]

95. Taken together, the following texts seem to imply this: Rv 2:17; 3:12; 19:12.

96. *SD*, 25. See Jn 20:24–28.

97. "Just as the Resurrection transformed Christ's wounds into a source of healing and salvation, so for every sick person the light of the risen Christ is a confirmation that the way of fidelity to God can triumph in the gift of self until the Cross and can transform illness itself into a source of joy and resurrection." *Message of the Holy Father for the World Day of the Sick for the Year 2000: Contemplate the Face of Christ in the Sick* (August 6, 1999), 7. Vatican website.

# 5

# The Vulnerable and the Mystery of Jesus Christ

In the last chapter, we sampled something of the richness of Pope John Paul II's theology of the body and considered some of its implications relative to vulnerable human beings and their agency. However, John Paul's theology of the body does not elaborate every theological basis for his anthropological convictions. It would therefore be worthwhile for us to examine selected Christological texts from a few of his other important writings and to highlight their theological and anthropological import. As an interesting, though somewhat parenthetical, result of that effort, we will see more directly how the tri-personal understanding of God underlying the theology of the body is ultimately grounded, as it would have to be, in the revelation of Jesus Christ, in whom theology and anthropology converge. Our main focus, however, will be on the Incarnation and the Paschal Mystery, as these two events of Christ's life mark the moments of his greatest vulnerability, humanly speaking. In some contexts, moreover, John Paul relates those events explicitly to vulnerable human beings and their status as personal agents.

In that light, and drawing on the theological, Christological, and anthropological insights gained from the previous chapters, we will then proceed, much as we did in the second part of chapter 3, to consider successively four categories of vulnerable human beings, enriching further thereby our understanding of the vulnerable and their agency by following John Paul's leads. This time, however, we will slightly reconfigure the categories we presented previously. As before, we will consider persons who are suffering from oppressive conditions imposed from the outside. And once again, we will consider psychosomatically developing persons and persons with serious psycho-rational disabilities, but this time under a single heading. For the first time, we will categorize persons having mild-to-moderate psychical disabilities (such as those affecting the senses and perhaps affecting, in turn, certain perceptions and cognitive functions), together with persons having strictly somatic disabilities. We will begin, however, with a new category in which we will examine a wholly different order of human vulnerability based on what we learned explicitly from the catechesis on the body. We will call it *voluntary,* or *freely self-imposed,* vulnerability. This idea was clearly present in chapter 3 when we spoke of different kinds of intracommunal relationships that can form between vulnerable human beings and the persons caring for or acting in solidarity with them, but it became thematic only in the theological context of chapter 4.

More specifically, voluntary vulnerability is a form of vulnerability that we impose freely on ourselves from within. We dispose ourselves to offer ourselves sacrificially to and for others so as to invite them to communion with ourselves. Once we have developed that idea, we will show successively how, in the case of certain conditions that others have imposed on us from without or that have been imposed on us by our own psychosomatic structure, we can, by recourse to voluntary vulnerability, transform them into the very means by which we extend or answer the call to interpersonal communion in the effort to establish it reciprocally with others. We will then go on to consider, as our final category, those persons whose psychosomatic structure precludes their having an appreciable level of self-awareness or, therefore, of the kind of personal volition that underlies voluntary vulnerability. Even so, they offer themselves to others in a different yet still personally active way through their vulnerability, which thus serves both as an invitation to interpersonal communion and as the means by which those who accept that invitation can establish it with them. Whether through voluntary vulnerability or through their natural aspiration toward it, human beings express themselves as agents of love, though their differing modes of doing so come more fully to light only in the Person of Jesus Christ.

## Voluntary Vulnerability and Moral Vulnerability

Before we begin with our Christological explorations, we should say something about voluntary vulnerability as compared with what, in the previous two chapters, we have already termed or alluded to as "moral vulnerability." Both of these forms of vulnerability pertain directly to the moral and thus to the personal, or spiritual, order. Hence, they both entail the use of freedom and so are voluntary, though they head in radically different directions. The term "vulnerability" refers in each case to the way in which the subject decides to determine himself as a person relative to other persons. Either he voluntarily "subjects" himself selflessly to others for love's sake and thereby grows personally, or he refuses to do so and thereby becomes subject to personal disintegration. The term is therefore used on analogy with the somatic, the psychical, the psycho-rational, and the material/externally imposed forms of vulnerability that we have already discussed, and that we have generally understood as objective states or conditions that, while perhaps affecting the intersubjective relations of the persons subject to them, were not chosen voluntarily by their subjects. Still, we can expect to see certain similarities and relationships between the objective applications of the term and the two analogical, more subjectively oriented applications now being considered, precisely because the term lends itself to those analogies by relating in each case to the subjection of the personal subject to something or to someone—including oneself. In one way or another, each of these vulnerabilities will open the persons subject to them to the possibility of either personal fulfillment or personal desolation.

As for "voluntary vulnerability," the expression can apply to persons who are not presently subject to objective forms of vulnerability like those mentioned above but who "subject" themselves voluntarily to those who are, in the sincere effort to serve their true good and to foster *communio* with them. In some cases, they are morally bound to do so, though the motive for acting out of sheer obligation decreases in inverse proportion to the level of one's voluntary willingness to serve others—that is, in inverse proportion to one's love of neighbor. "Voluntary vulnerability" can also apply to persons who *are* subject to somatic, psychical, or material/externally imposed vulnerabilities, but who are nevertheless able, and so morally bound, to "subject" them to—that is, to integrate them voluntarily into—actions that somehow serve the true good of others. In that way, they transform their structurally or their externally imposed vulnerabilities into a freely *self-*

*imposed* vulnerability-for-others. When necessary, they must also voluntarily impose on themselves the additional "vulnerability" of opening themselves to receive the care and assistance of others. But this, too, is another way in which they raise their concrete structural or material/externally imposed vulnerability appropriately to the moral and spiritual plane so as to help establish with others a real communion of persons. Whatever form it takes, voluntary vulnerability is the indispensable condition for participating in the humanity of others for the sake of the true common good, and so it serves one's own true good as a person.

"Moral vulnerability," on the other hand, is the very antithesis of voluntary vulnerability, and so it leads necessarily to alienation from oneself and others. Some persons who are not presently subject to any of the objective forms of vulnerability seek to avoid having ever to *subject themselves* voluntarily to any vulnerable person making a claim on them here and now. They will sometimes go so far as to eliminate the person him- or herself to accomplish that end. In addition, morally vulnerable persons of this stripe might seek to assert their power or to maintain their advantages over others by imposing, exploiting, or refusing to ease certain types of vulnerabilities to which those others are subject. They are therefore unwilling to freely make the personal sacrifices necessary to fulfill their moral obligation to help others surmount their state of vulnerability. At the same time, such persons are often the ones who consciously and inordinately seek to avoid having ever *to be subject* themselves to any of the vulnerabilities that turn them away from or against others. Their mentality goes hand in hand with their subjection to the three forms of concupiscence, which they act on, according to that mentality, in any number of ways.

For example, persons yielding to their moral vulnerability might try to deny or to defy their own mortality by seeking the "fountain of youth" and by acting hedonistically. Or unbridled greed might lead them to deprive the vulnerable of their rightful share in the material goods to which all are entitled, even if they have to steal from or murder them to do it. And should their efforts to avoid physical, mental, or material vulnerability fail, they might attempt to usurp God's prerogative over their life by resorting to suicide or assisted suicide, lest they have to alter their way of life or allow others to see them fall from on high. It is clear, then, that such persons are vulnerable to final moral and spiritual ruin, as we indicated repeatedly in the last chapter. We will have occasion to note that persons subject to structural or material/externally imposed vulnerabilities who are nevertheless capable of mature human action are also subject to that same end, if, by willfully renouncing the task of determining themselves in a truly good way through the constructive integration of their vulnerable condition into their person, they opt instead to use their condition in ways that lead to their personal disintegration.

The persistent danger of culpably becoming subject to definitive moral and spiritual ruin is universal among human beings capable of rational decision;[1] however, the persistent effort to avoid that danger through voluntary vulnerability is not. The state of moral vulnerability signifies a precipitous slide away from what is truly human and personal in us. It signifies a vicious and ultimately cowardly way of life. Voluntary vulnerability, on the contrary, embraces all that we really are and are meant to be as human persons. It signifies a virtuous and heroic way of life, which means that it is also a task that we are obliged to undertake and see through to the end. And not all are willing to commit themselves to that task. Voluntary vulnerability, which underlies every other form of habitual self-mastery in the service of charity, is not a universally practiced virtue. Nevertheless, it remains the "goal" of somatic, psychical, psycho-rational, and material/externally imposed forms of vulnerability. That is, these concrete types of vulnerability call us to serve the persons subject to them, while those same persons are called to "subject" their vulnerabilities voluntarily to themselves, to the extent possible, and to serve others in some way by doing so. In that way, each side does good for the other and thereby helps foster a genuine communion of persons, which always serves the true good of each and all.

Given the close correlation between the objective and the analogous, voluntary forms of vulnerability, it is important for us to deal with both kinds in our forthcoming discussion of human vulnerability. However, we will not treat moral vulnerability as a separate category, since we have already discussed the concept sufficiently in the previous two chapters and above. We will simply allude to or mention it specifically in the context of the other

1. While we can legitimately acknowledge that this and other dimensions of human vulnerability are universally applicable, at least virtually, we must also avoid any tendency to stretch the term "vulnerability" so far as to eviscerate it of any meaning. A manifestation of moral vulnerability common in our day is for some persons or groups to exploit, contort, or invent certain facts or situations so as to portray themselves as victims when they have, in fact, no conceivable claim to that status. But they will use it as a platform for demanding either compensation for the abuses they have allegedly suffered or self-serving rights to which they claim entitlement. They sometimes do this with the intention of gaining power over other people, who end up becoming the *real* victims to the extent that they succeed. See related remarks in *DM*, 12, along with the corresponding paragraph in *DM*, 14, regarding a distorted notion of justice that would lead each person to claim "rights" relative to others, resulting in the oppression of the weak by the strong.

categories selected for discussion. Besides, we can grasp its meaning easily enough as the radical inverse of voluntary vulnerability, which we *will* treat separately in the light of the Christological discussions to which we now turn.

## Human Vulnerability in the Light of Jesus Christ

Because every human being has been chosen and willed into existence by God as a subject of truth and love, he lives "from the moment he is conceived beneath the heart of his mother" within the horizon of redemption in Christ.[2] For Pope John Paul II, it is precisely through the more evident forms of human vulnerability that some people bear living witness to that fact, even if only implicitly. Before an audience of disabled people in December 2000, he spoke as follows: "In your bodies and in your lives, dear brothers and sisters, you express an intense hope of redemption. In all this is there not an implicit expectation of the 'redemption' that Christ won for us by his death and resurrection?"[3] Vulnerable human beings therefore anticipate in a special way the possibility of sharing in the glory of Christ, who is the concrete and definitive expression in human history of God's everlasting love.

In order to attain to the glory of Christ, we must follow the path that Christ himself marked out for us by his life, suffering, and death. Christ came to serve, not to be served, and to give his life as a ransom for many (see Mt 20:28). He willingly became subject to us for the very purpose of redeeming us, submitting himself even to suffering and death at our hands. It was precisely in subjecting himself to death, in giving himself up for the sake of the Church, that Christ performed the ultimate act of obedience, or voluntary subjection, to the will of the Father.[4] The possibility of his fulfilling the Father's will in that way presupposes the Incarnation, in which the Son of God, though from eternity in the form of God and hence consubstantial with the Father, emptied himself and took the form of a slave, assuming the human state (see Phil 2:5–7). In other words, the invulnerable Son of God made himself vulnerable by becoming man, thus placing himself at our disposal for our sake. By doing so, he expressed definitively in time the invincible love

2. *RH*, 13.

3. *Homily of John Paul II: Jubilee of the Disabled* (December 3, 2000), 2. Vatican website.

4. "The gift of his love and obedience to the point of giving his life (cf. Jn 10:17–18) is in the first place a gift to his Father. Certainly it is a gift given for our sake, and indeed that of all humanity (cf. Mt 26:28; Mk 14:24; Lk 22:20; Jn 10:15), yet it is *first and foremost a gift to the Father.*" From John Paul II's last encyclical, *Ecclesia de Eucharistia* (April 17, 2003), 13, Vatican website.

of God,[5] who has from all eternity chosen us in Christ (see Eph 1:4–5). John Paul II has proclaimed this reality starkly as follows: in the Incarnation, God expresses his love for humanity "to the point of making himself vulnerable in Jesus."[6] The mystery of Christ is nothing less than the revelation and expression of divine love in the mode of human vulnerability.

## Unreserved Self-Giving: The Temporal Expression of the Son's Eternal Relation to the Father

We saw in chapter 4 that in the state of original innocence, man and woman, created in God's image, recognized fully the gift-character of creation and its origin in divine love. They consequently understood that they would find personal fulfillment only by existing and expressing themselves through the body as "gift-for-another." However, this essential meaning of human existence became obscured and distorted by sin. Christ's mission was to restore what was lost or darkened by sin, particularly by re-creating the divine image in us.

In voluntarily making himself vulnerable to suffering and death—that is, to the wages of human sin—Christ perfectly fulfilled the will of his heavenly Father, who expressed his love for us by giving us his Son to redeem us (cf. Jn 3:16). That is why the Son's sacrificial offering of himself to the Father through the Holy Spirit was simultaneously his supreme act of redemptive self-giving for the sake of the Church. It also explains why the redeeming love of the Son constitutes the supreme manifestation of the Father's love for us. "Making the Father present as love and mercy is, in Christ's own consciousness, the fundamental touchstone of his mission as the Messiah."[7] The Paschal Mystery reveals definitively and concretely the salvific will of the Father and so, too, his love and mercy. For Christ "makes [God's mercy] incarnate and personifies it,"[8] mercy being "love's second name," as it were.[9] Based on the Paschal Mystery, therefore, the disciples of Jesus understand their Master when he says, "He who has seen me has seen the Father" (Jn 14:9): "Believing in the crucified Son means 'seeing the Father,' means believing that love is present in the world."[10]

In this way and others, John Paul makes it clear that God reveals *himself*

5. Cf. *SgC*, 48–52.

6. General Audience (June 10, 1998), 2, Vatican website.

7. *Dives in Misericordia* (November 30, 1980), 3, Vatican translation, *Origins* 10, no. 26 (1980): 401–16.

8. Ibid., 2; cf. *RH*, 9.

9. *DM*, 7.

10. Ibid. See nos. 1, 4, 8.

in the very act of saving us through the temporal mission of the Son, and also of the Holy Spirit,[11] who brings forth salvific love from the Son's sacrificial suffering.[12] The temporal missions "involve and reveal the 'processions' in God himself,"[13] because the eternal "processions" that establish the relations of the Son and Spirit as subsistent in the divine nature are the same as those grounding the missions.[14] The Father's giving of the Son to the world in time is therefore grounded in the eternal begetting by which he gives the Son his filial identity in relation to himself as Father. It follows that the Son's temporal *self*-giving must be grounded in the eternal gift that he makes of himself, as Son, to the Father in response to the Father's eternal giving of *him*self, as Father, to him, the Son he eternally begets as his perfect image in personal self-giving. Whatever the Son does to fulfill his messianic mission from the Father presupposes this ontological ground in the immanent relation of his Person to that of the Father.[15] The immanent relation of the eternal Son's natural generation from, and reciprocal self-giving to, the Father is thus "prolonged" and "externalized" in the historical life of

11. "God reveals himself and his plan of salvation to mankind through the mission of the Son and the Holy Spirit.... However, the mission of the divine Persons to mankind is not only a revelation but also a work of salvation by which mankind becomes the People of God." Wojtyła, *Sources of Renewal: The Implementation of the Second Vatican Council,* trans. P. S. Falla (New York: Harper and Row, 1980), 206. See 53–65. See also John Paul II's Wednesday general audience on October 9, 1985, in *God, Father and Creator,* 153; *DetV,* 3, 11.

12. John Paul shows the close connection between the missions of the Son and the Holy Spirit throughout *DetV* (e.g., nos. 11, 40–41). While in our reflections on the vulnerable and their agency we will emphasize Christology, as John Paul did in his theology of the body, we should still be aware that his Christology is richly pneumatological, especially in relation to the Redemption. We should therefore understand upcoming references to the redemptive power of Christ's sacrifice, to the grace of Christ, and so on as implying the operation of the Holy Spirit, who extends the salvific power of the Son's redemptive sacrifice throughout human history. Conversely, "[a]ll invocation of the Spirit, all emphasis on the 'pneumatological' ... is in fact invocation of Christ himself as Redeemer and Bridegroom. 'And the Spirit and the Bride say: Come!', wrote St John (Rev 22,17; cf 1 Cor 16,22)." *SgC,* 98. For more on John Paul II's pneumatology and its originality, see Antoine Nachef, B.S.O., *The Mystery of the Trinity in the Theological Thought of Pope John Paul II* (New York: Peter Lang, 1999), 199–233.

13. Wednesday audience on November 13, 1985, in *God, Father and Creator,* 175.

14. See Wednesday audience on December 4, 1985, in ibid., 183. For more on the correlation between the eternal processions and the revelatory, temporal missions of the Son and the Spirit, see Aquinas, *ST* I, 43; Matthias Scheeben, *The Mysteries of Christianity,* trans. Cyril Vollert, SJ (St. Louis: Herder, 1946), 357–64.

15. For that reason, "there is an identity between the message and the messenger, between saying, doing and being." *Redemptoris Missio* (December 7, 1990), 13, Vatican website. Consequently, once all things have been made subject to Christ, he will, in turn, subject them, together with himself, to the Father, so that God will be all in all (see 1 Cor 15:27–28; *LG,* 36). "And this 'making subject' is inseparable from his own filial 'submission' [or self-giving] to the Father, as the Apostle teaches us (1 Cor 3, 23): 'You belong to Christ and Christ belongs to God.'" *SgC,* 177.

Christ,[16] which is why the Son is the perfect image of the Father, not just in eternity, but also in time (see Col 1:15; Heb 1:1–3).[17]

The incarnate Son of God therefore "goes forward in obedience to the Father, but primarily He is *united to the Father in this love* with which He has loved the world and man in the world."[18] This means that Christ's sacrifice of himself on the cross is an expression not only of the *Father's* love for us but also of *his own*—one and the same divine love reaching us personally, from eternity, through the humanity of Christ. He was given in love by the Father, and he simultaneously *gives himself,* through the Spirit, with that same love, since "all that the Father has is mine" (Jn 16:15).[19]

By the power of the Holy Spirit—who, as the personal expression of the mutual love of the Father and the Son, is the Love-Gift of God and the Source of all God's giving to creatures—the Son was conceived as man in the womb of the Virgin Mary and thus "sent," given to the world.[20] The Son's eternal relation of total self-giving, in love, to the Father would consequently come to be expressed through his human consciousness, will, and life as one of unconditional, filial obedience to the will of the Father. The incarnate Son has renewed the divine image in us accordingly, since we were created to reciprocate God's love for us in perfect obedience and thus find perfect fulfillment.[21] Through his human body, the Son of God expressed perfectly the radically self-giving nature of personal love, both human and divine. And he expressed it precisely in the mode of vulnerability. If it has been revealed to us in Christ that the redemptive will of God is effected through human vul-

16. In turn, the historical mission of Christ prolongs and "incarnates" itself in the Church: "As the Father has sent me, even so I send you" (Jn 20:21; see 17:18). The Son "does" with the Church what he has "seen" the Father "do" with him (cf. Jn 5:19): He sends her on her mission to the world, which is one with his. See *Sources of Renewal,* 206–7; *Redemptoris Missio,* 23.

17. The metaphysical content of the mission statements is especially pronounced in the fourth Gospel and expressed succinctly in its prologue (Jn 1:1–18), which affirms clearly that the Son's relation to the Father is eternal and at the level of the divinity. It is this same relation, or personal identity, that we meet "in the flesh."

18. *SD,* 16.

19. See Heb 9:11–14; *DetV,* 40–41.

20. As a creative work of God, the Incarnation is effected by the *ad extra* operation of the entire Trinity, although it is commonly attributed to the activity of the Holy Spirit by appropriation (see Aquinas, *ST* III, 32, 1). Still, it is the subsistence of the Holy Spirit in God as the personal Love-Gift of the Father and Son that establishes the basis of God's free giving, in love, to creatures. See *DetV,* 10.

21. "*Humanity, subjected to sin,* in the descendants of Adam, in Jesus Christ became *perfectly subjected to God* and united to him, and at the same time full of compassion towards men. Thus there is *a new humanity,* which in Jesus Christ through the suffering of the Cross has returned to the love which was betrayed by Adam through sin." *Dominum et Vivificantem* (May 18, 1986), 40, Vatican translation (Boston: Pauline Books and Media, 1986).

nerability, then vulnerable human beings serve as a special sign, not only of our hope for redemption, but also of the means by which we are to achieve it in and through Christ.

## Man as Re-expressed for Love in the Mystery of the Incarnation and the Redemption

In reciprocally expressing and experiencing love through the body, the first man and woman understood that the whole meaning of their existence was rooted in Love and in fulfilling the vocation to love that was uniquely theirs as living images of God in the world. They also understood that creation itself was an expression, a "radiation," of the Father's eternal love, and that they, in particular, were each created to be a special vessel and conduit of that love therein.

> THE REALITY OF THE GIFT and of the act of giving, which is sketched in the first chapters of Genesis as the constitutive content of the mystery of creation, confirms that the irradiation of Love is an integral part of this same mystery. Only love creates the good, and in the end it alone can be perceived in all its dimensions and its contours in created things and, above all, in man.... The first verses of the Bible ... speak not only about the creation of the world and about man in the world, but also about grace, that is, about the self-communication of holiness, about the irradiation of the Holy Spirit, which produces a special state of "spiritualization" in that first man.[22]

Once man and woman had alienated themselves from God through sin, they no longer radiated as fully the love of God in the world, nor did they communicate it as grace to others. They lost sight of Love as the ultimate Ground of their life and of the whole created order, and their ability to express love authentically through the spousal meaning of the body became gravely impaired. Yet, "Man cannot live without love. He remains a being that is incomprehensible for himself, his life is senseless, if love is not revealed to him, if he does not encounter love, if he does not experience it and make it his own, if he does not participate intimately in it."[23] Because God is faithful to his paternal love and hence to himself, he did not abandon us to a meaningless existence devoid of authentic love and self-understanding. Through the mystery of his love radiating from the truth about man and the world contained in the Son's Incarnation and act of redemption, the Father effected a new creation, consummating his original self-communication to the world.[24] Above

22. TOB 16:1.

23. *RH*, 10.

24. See ibid., 13; *DetV*, 50.

all, he restored us to the dignity that we had lost through sin, the dignity of being adopted children of God through the radiation of the Spirit in us.[25] Thus, the new expression of the Father's love for and truth in us, fulfilled in Christ's suffering and death, means that in the mystery of the Redemption, "man becomes newly 'expressed' and, in a way, is newly created."[26] That is to say, man is "newly created in Christ for the fullness of grace and truth," so that by becoming inwardly transformed through union with the incarnate Son, he lives "a new life that does not disappear and pass away but lasts to eternal life." And eternal life "is the final fulfillment of man's vocation."[27]

Having been re-expressed thus in Christ, we are capable once more of radiating the love and truth of the Father in the world through the spousal meaning of the body, which was created for that purpose "in the beginning." The Father's gift of the Spirit in Christ "restored to mankind—to human relationships, to marriage, to the family, to the various social groupings, to nations and to states—the fundamental sense of gift and of being 'bestowed.' This kind of awareness is a fruit of the Spirit of Christ; it results from irradiation by love, which puts a fundamentally different complexion on all these relationships and systems."[28] But if Christ re-expressed us fully through the mystery of the Redemption, then we know from chapter 4 that the radiation of God's love and truth in us through the interpersonal meaning of the body will always take the form of a sacrificial gift of self—a gift imbued with the redemptive power of Christ. Through his self-emptying on the altar of the cross, Christ revealed what would otherwise have been inconceivable to the human mind, namely, that even "suffering and death can express a love which gives itself and seeks nothing in return."[29] The self-giving love that

25. See *DM*, part 4, nos. 5–6, "The Parable of the Prodigal Son" (cf. Lk 15:11–32). In the parable, the father's fidelity to his fatherhood is expressed in his unwavering devotion to his son: "The father's fidelity to himself is totally concentrated upon the humanity of the lost son, upon his dignity" (no. 6). His merciful love has the interior form of *agape*, which "is able to reach down to every prodigal son, to every human misery, and above all to every form of moral misery, to sin" (ibid.). In this way, the person who is the object of mercy is "found" again: he is restored to value and reestablished in the truth about his own dignity. As the prodigal son became aware that his misbehavior could never alter his filial relationship to his father, he also became aware of the dignity he had lost by not living up to that relationship (see no. 5). He therefore resolved to change his ways. That is why, on the son's return home, the father "sees so clearly the good which has been achieved thanks to a mysterious radiation [*communicatio*] of truth and love" (no. 6). The love radiated by the faithful father somehow remained with and became newly active and reflected in the penitent son.

26. *RH*, 10.

27. Ibid., 18.

28. *SgC*, 58.

29. John Paul II, *Fides et Ratio* (September 14, 1998), 93, Vatican translation, *Origins* 28, no. 19 (1998): 317–47. See 1 Jn 3:16.

Christ expressed through his suffering and death is nothing less than the salvific love of God for us and the filial love of the divine Son for the Father.

By sharing in the mystery of the Redemption, therefore, human beings are reconstituted in Christ to radiate the love of God by expressing it just as Christ did. By obedience to the will of the Father in the power of the Holy Spirit, we, too, express our filial love for the Father when we sacrificially offer ourselves, in love, to and for others, and also to and for Christ in them. Because each of us has been incorporated in some way into Christ's redemptive sacrifice, "the question of man is inscribed [therein] with a special vigor and love." The mystery of the Redemption thus speaks a "rich universal language."[30] It is the language of love. It is the language of God, who *is* Love (1 Jn 4:8, 16). It is the same language, the same Word of Love, through which God created the universe and sustains it in existence.[31]

Among the creatures of the material world, human beings are utterly unique. Having been created in God's image and likeness, we not only reflect in some way the divine language: we can also understand it and speak it ourselves. We can dialogue through it with one another and, above all, with God. Sin entered the world precisely when we, in Adam, disrupted that dialogue by turning away from God, the Author of the language we had been created to speak. We were consequently thrown into confusion: the language of love was no longer fully comprehensible to us, and our ability to express it diminished. We thus became alienated from God, from our own self, from other human beings, and from creation at large.[32]

It is only when God re-expresses his love and truth in us that we regain our facility with the divine language. That is precisely what Christ accomplished fully in the mystery of the Redemption. And the reason why he was able to accomplish it is revealed in the mystery of the Incarnation, by which the eternal Son came into the world as man: God himself can speak his own language, the language of Love, using the "grammar" of human nature.[33] The Incarnation thus affirms definitively that "in the beginning" man and woman were created in the divine image (Gn 1:26–27), and it also reveals definitively the essential content of that affirmation.

Through frequent references to *Gaudium et Spes*, 22, Pope John Paul II has

30. *RH*, 18.

31. See ibid., 9–10.

32. E.g., Gn 3:9–11, 17–19, 22–24; 4:8; 6:5–7; 11:1–9.

33. It is precisely on this basis that sacred Scripture, using human words, can communicate the Word of God in a true and abiding way. See *Fides et Ratio*, 94 and 84; Vatican II, *Dei Verbum*, 13.

emphasized that the eternally begotten Son of God united himself in a certain way with every human being by his Incarnation. It follows, then, that from the first moment of its creation, the complete human nature (soul and body) assumed by the divine Son subsisted in his Person, the substantial bearer of that nature, thus marking the first moment of the Son's existence as man: "When at the moment of the Annunciation Mary utters her 'fiat': 'Be it done unto me according to your word,' she conceives in a virginal way *a man*, the Son of Man, *who is the Son of God*. By means of this 'humanization' of the Word-Son the self-communication of God reaches its definitive fullness in the history of creation and salvation.... 'The Word became flesh.'"[34] The Incarnation was therefore the beginning of the Son's personal history as a man among men, of his temporal contact with the human race and, indeed, with creation itself, which is somehow also taken up into this mystery. Through the Incarnation, we come to understand that our personal bonds with other human beings begin from the moment of our conception. Because he is a person, man has

> a history of his life that is his own and, most important, a history of his soul that is his own. [I]n keeping with the openness of his spirit within and also with the many diverse needs of his body and his existence in time, [he] writes this personal history of his through numerous bonds, contacts, situations, and social structures linking him with other men, beginning to do so from the first moment of his existence on earth, from the moment of his conception and birth.[35]

From conception, each of us relates to other human beings in various ways so as to develop *as* a person; but none of us develops thereby *into* a person. Our personal contacts with one another presuppose our personal being; however, it is precisely because we are personal beings that we must fulfill ourselves through personal relations with others, through love.

## Summary Reflections on Human Vulnerability in the Light of Jesus Christ

Given that the Person of the Son of God has united himself in a certain way with every human being on assuming human nature "in the fullness of time" (see Gal 4:4; Eph 1:10), the Incarnation reveals that the personal subject is the substantial bearer of his distinctly human nature from the moment of conception. In our case, that is the moment when God infuses the spiri-

34. *DetV*, 50. Indeed, the angel Gabriel had announced to Mary that she would *conceive* a Son in her womb, the Son to whom she would later give birth. See Lk 1:31.

35. *RH*, 14.

tual soul into the "bodily" matter contributed by the parents, so as to create a new, utterly unique and unrepeatable human person.[36] The Incarnation also reveals that human nature was created "from the beginning" to be the "grammar" through which the human person "speaks" the universal language of love, the "language" of God himself. Because love is an exclusively personal reality that orders persons toward each other and unites them for the true good of each and all, human beings are inherently social beings, whose contacts with the world and with one another begin to form as soon as we begin to exist. Such contacts are, of course, necessary if the material needs of our bodily existence in the world are to be met. But the Incarnation reveals, above all, that our first contacts with others are part of our genuinely personal history and, as such, reflect the dynamic openness of the human spirit to the world in general and to the world of persons in particular.

The dynamism of the human spirit is always expressed through the body, into which Christ has inscribed a new dignity. In the Incarnation, Christ himself "has taken up the human body together with the soul into union with the person of the Son-Word."[37] What is more, Christ has inscribed a new redemptive significance into the human body, through which he expressed his eternal, filial relation to the Father by offering himself freely, in his humanity, as a sacrificial victim for our salvation, both in obedience to the Father's will and in accordance with his own identity as the personal image and bearer of the Father's love for us. By his self-sacrifice, he has newly created us for the grace of sanctification—that is, for the radiation of the Holy Spirit in us through our regeneration in the waters of baptism. These waters introduce us into the very Life of the Holy Trinity, which Christ has revealed to us as our salvation precisely in the act of redeeming us. Baptized Christians living fully according to the Spirit radiate the eternal love of God on earth in the highest possible way prior to the state of glory.[38]

36. The dogma of the Immaculate Conception implies the same thing. In view of Christ's merits, God preserved Mary from all stain of original sin from the first moment of her conception (i.e., of her personal existence). This singular privilege—a work of sanctifying grace—could pertain and so could have been granted only to a human *person*; therefore, Mary was a human person from the instant she was conceived in the womb of her mother. Then and ever after she belonged to Christ. See *RMa*, 10; Pius IX, *Ineffabilis Deus* (December 8, 1854), Denzinger-Schönmetzer, 2803 (Denz.,1641).

37. TOB 56:4.

38. In connection with this, we can also *experience* the eternal love of God and the knowledge of its Source contemplatively through the transforming union with God that faith effects in us through charity by the illuminating activity and the additional gifts of the Holy Spirit—and this to a degree essentially identical with that attained in the definitive union of the soul with

That having been said, John Paul II asserts repeatedly, nonetheless, that Christ has in some way united himself with *every* human being through the mysteries of the Incarnation and the Redemption. On account of the former, human nature has been supernaturally elevated, "raised up to a divine dignity." And on account of the latter, "we ought to believe that the Holy Spirit in a manner known only to God offers to every man the possibility of being associated with [the] paschal mystery."[39] This new situation applies to everyone even prior to baptism, though it is inherently ordered toward baptism and finds its fulfillment therein.[40] If we are each a bodily person from the moment of our conception, and if, by his Incarnation, the Son of God is in some way united with us, then from the beginning of our existence, we must each be in some way associated with the Paschal Mystery as well. In *Salvifici Doloris,* John Paul brings out this idea of universal incorporation into the Redemption explicitly in relation to human vulnerability: "The Redeemer suffered in place of man and for man. Every man has *his own share in the Redemption.* Each one is also *called to share in that suffering* through which the Redemption was accomplished.... Thus each man, in his suffering, can also become a sharer in the redemptive suffering of Christ."[41] Because we have been re-expressed in Christ—that is, re-created to be bearers of God's Spirit, not just in spite of, but precisely in and through, our vulnerability—even those with a high level of psychosomatic immaturity or disintegration can mediate the radiation of the Father's love and truth in a uniquely human and personal way, and with renewed power, regardless of appearances to the contrary. We will explore that profound mystery further in due course.

---

God in glory, though in the present life the contemplative experience remains always general and obscure. Believing, in the light of faith, and seeing (beatific vision), in the light of glory, are therefore rooted in the same divine reality and hence continuous, the one ordered toward the other. Because God's self-communication to us in knowledge and love exceeds the soul's natural state and powers, one's cooperation with it in faith involves a painful but welcome spiritual purgation (which, we might add, would invariably be related to, manifested in, and expressed through the body and its new redemptive significance in Christ). See Wojtyła, *Faith according to St. John of the Cross,* 183–201, 257–59.

39. *GS,* 22.

40. Avery Dulles, SJ, situates John Paul's remarks on grace in the unbaptized within the context of passages from Vatican II like the one cited above, along with relevant pronouncements from his immediate predecessors. Taken together, the official teachings imply that the Church serves as both the instrumental and the final cause of salvation in non-Christians—that is, as both the mediator of saving grace (through her indissoluble union with her divine Head) and the goal (beginning with baptism) toward which that grace is ordered (the Church being the divinely willed, ordinary means of salvation for all). See Dulles, "The Church as Locus of Salvation," in McDermott, *Pope John Paul II,* 169–87.

41. *SD,* 19.

## A New Creation in Christ: Human Vulnerability as a Revelation of the Person

We will now look at the four categories of human vulnerability mentioned at the beginning of the chapter, showing, in the light of Jesus Christ, how human beings can express themselves as agents of love and truth, and hence as persons, in and through their vulnerability. To aid our understanding as we proceed, we will include additional passages from the writings of Karol Wojtyła/John Paul II, and also a few from the works of other authors. As we noted in chapter 3, the particular mode of human agency that we will highlight in each category is not necessarily exclusive to or exhaustive of it, nor are the categories themselves definitive.

### The Personal Expression of Love through Freely Self-Imposed Vulnerability

In Ephesians 5:21, St. Paul exhorts his spiritual children, especially husbands and wives, to be subject to one another out of reverence for Christ. The subjection about which he speaks is the voluntary entrusting of oneself to another (or others) in self-giving love. Opening oneself to someone in that way is the precondition for receiving him or her on an interpersonal level, thereby placing one in a vulnerable position relative to that person. Vulnerability of that kind is properly balanced only when the voluntary subjection of an *I* to a *thou* is fully reciprocated, with each side looking out for the genuine interests of the other (cf. Phil 2:4). One then discovers and fulfills the truth of one's own existence. Thus, "[t]he capacity to entrust oneself and one's life to another person and the decision to do so are among the most significant and expressive human acts."[42]

It is in Christ and out of reverence for Christ that we find the inspiration, the motivation, and, above all, the grace to live according to the type of freely self-imposed vulnerability by which we make an offer of our lives to and

42. *Fides et Ratio*, 33. Indeed, it expresses the divine image in us: "[I]t was God himself, the Eternal Father, who *entrusted himself to the Virgin of Nazareth*, giving her his own Son in the mystery of the Incarnation" (*RMa*, 39)—the Father and the Son having chosen her "before the creation of the world" (Eph 1:4), "entrusting her eternally to the Spirit of holiness" (*RMa*, 8). In turn, the incarnate Son, who does "only what he sees the Father doing" (Jn 5:19), "entrusts Mary to John because he entrusts John to Mary. At the foot of the Cross there begins that special *entrusting of humanity to the Mother of Christ* [cf. Jn 19:26–27]" (*RMa*, 45). For, as the one who was "full of grace" (Lk 1:28), Mary "entrusted herself [in faith] to God without reserve and 'devoted herself totally as the handmaid of the Lord to the person and work of her Son'" (*RMa*, 13, quoting from *LG*, 56).

for the sake of others, fulfilling ourselves thus as persons. Since we are doing what we have "seen" the Son do when we subject ourselves to others for their sake, we are likewise subjecting ourselves to Christ and so fulfilling the Father's will. For that reason, whenever we invite other persons to interpersonal communion with ourselves by directing some form of sacrificial self-giving toward them, it is ultimately for Christ's sake that we do so. Following John Paul II's lead, we can take this even further. The fact that God has chosen us in Christ from all eternity (see Eph 1:4–5) has been made manifest in the Incarnation and the Redemption, through which the Son of God has "*in a certain way united Himself with each man.*"[43] Because Christ bears a mysterious relation to each one of us, the sacrificial gift of self that we offer to and for other persons is simultaneously referred directly to him.[44] Therefore, by opening ourselves personally, in love, to others, we also open ourselves to personal communion with Christ: "As you did it to one of the least of these my brethren, you did it to me" (Mt 25:40).[45] Conversely, it is ultimately Christ who invites those "least of His brethren" to personal communion with himself in those of us who, by the grace of his Spirit, offer ourselves sacrificially to and for them as an invitation—perhaps only an implicit one—to personal communion with *us*. There is consequently a general sense in which Christ might say of us, "He who receives you receives me, and he who receives me receives Him who sent me" (Mt 10:40). Indeed, Christ intended that the vocations of celibacy and virginity for the sake of the kingdom of heaven should rest explicitly on the set of interpersonal dynamics just described: "For truly, I say to you, whoever gives you a cup of water to drink because you bear the name of Christ, will by no means lose his reward" (Mk 9:41).

Only when we live by the power of Christ and thus remain in communion

43. *GS*, 22, as quoted in *RH*, 8; see nos. 13–14, 18. Though Christ's ineffable union with baptized Christians through the divine indwelling and the devout reception of Holy Communion is absolutely distinct from and ontologically superior to his mysterious union with all human beings through the Incarnation and the Redemption, John Paul never seems to provide a clear account of the difference in *RH*. In *DetV*, 52, he distinguishes between (1) the filiation of divine adoption based on the Incarnation, and (2) the rebirth in the Spirit that implants it in the soul. But clarity is still lacking.

44. Note, too, that every sin has reference to the cross of Christ because of the universality of the Redemption, in which the innocent Lamb of God bore the whole weight of human sin and death (see *DetV*, 29, 32). At the same time, the Resurrection and the sending of the Holy Spirit for the forgiveness of sins reveal Christ's victory over sin and death. The gift of the Spirit exposes sin for what it is by demonstrating, in the depths of one's conscience, its relation to Jesus' suffering and death (ibid., 31). The Spirit thus opens the possibility of repentance and conversion to each of us (ibid., 42), the precondition of our opening our heart to our neighbors, and to Christ in them, in self-giving love.

45. See *RH*, 16; *SD*, 30; *MD*, 14.

with him are we capable of subjecting ourselves freely to another in self-giving love. Self-subjection to another for love of "neighbor" implies that we have subjected the works of death—lust, greed, and pride—*to ourselves* by sacrificially dying to our sinful desires and placing them under our personal control. In this we follow Christ, who won this grace for us by subjecting *our* sins and the death they merit to *him*self. Indeed, he did so in the very act of *subjecting himself* freely *to us* on the altar of the cross for the sake of our salvation and in obedience to the will of the Father, with whom he is perfectly united in love for us. Fully mature, self-giving love is therefore always a freely assumed, self-transcending form of vulnerability by which we make ourselves subject to others for their sake, precisely by renouncing and overcoming any subjection that we might have to sin; for the egotistical nature of sin would militate against that kind of selfless activity by making us vulnerable, instead, to forms of behavior that are alienating and destructive to others and to ourselves. Self-possession of the highest order is absolutely necessary for ensuring the freedom of the gift of self. "In order to be able to serve others worthily and effectively we must be able to master ourselves, possess the virtues that make this mastery possible."[46]

The fact that we must strive to realize our personal essence in freedom indicates that we are as yet in a state of "becoming" and hence *always* vulnerable in at least some respect. It is through the freely given gift of self by which we relate harmoniously to others that we *find* and so *become* ourselves. Through the same self-mastery that this requires, we can also relate harmoniously to the natural world, which we must subject to ourselves only in ways that truly advance the good of *persons* and so promote human dignity. Should we fail to renounce and to conquer the form of vulnerability that is "of the world" (that is rooted in lust and hence dehumanizing) and thereby reject the vulnerability that is "of the Father" (that is rooted in grace and hence consonant with human dignity and the vocation to love), we will become alienated from and threatened by our own self, other persons, and certain products of our own activity.[47] It is only by sharing in the fruits of Christ's redemption through union with him as the Crucified and Risen One that our true freedom to fulfill our eternal vocation to love is restored. Once we have been re-created thus, we live as heirs to the promise of sharing Christ's ultimate victory over death in the glory of the resurrection.

46. *RH,* 21.
47. See ibid., 15–16.

### The Personal Expression of Love through Externally Imposed Vulnerability

Pope John Paul II's analysis of Ephesians 5:21–33 shows that our re-creation in Christ opens the possibility of our subjecting ourselves to others through a self-imposed form of vulnerability by which we freely offer ourselves to them and for them out of love for them. It therefore also indicates, by way of analogy, how persons whose subjection to others is *imposed* rather than *self*-imposed can nevertheless appropriate an oppressive situation actively by freely making an offering of themselves to and for other persons through it, thus subjecting the situation to themselves and fulfilling themselves as persons. Having been newly created in Christ and thus sharing in the redemptive efficacy of his life, suffering, death, and resurrection, they can voluntarily express redemptive love bodily under externally imposed conditions that cannot otherwise be immediately changed. They do not ignore, accept, or cooperate with the evil being perpetrated against them and others. On the contrary, they act efficaciously to overcome it by allowing the power of Christ's redeeming grace to work through them in the midst of it. In that way, they go from being victims to victors, mysteriously transforming an apparently hopeless condition of oppression by others into an invincible power for effecting good—a power to which only true inner freedom has access. By doing so, they bear extraordinary witness to their transcendent worth as persons and to the power at work in them, thereby inviting others—even their victimizers—to enter communion both with themselves and, if only implicitly, with Christ *through* themselves. For Jesus Christ is the Source and model of the redemptive power of human vulnerability.

#### Freedom in Christ as Expressed through Externally Imposed Constraints

From the standpoint of the external events surrounding his crucifixion and death, Christ's vulnerability was imposed from without: "The Son of man will be delivered to the chief priests, and they will condemn him to death, and deliver him to the Gentiles; and they will mock him, and spit upon him, and scourge him, and kill him" (Mk 10:33–34). Yet, from the standpoint of the interior freedom through which he sacrificially offered his life for our salvation, Christ's vulnerability was self-imposed: "No one takes [my life] from me; I lay it down of my own accord" (Jn 10:18. See 12:27; Is 53:7–12). After the public ministry during which he bore witness, in words and deeds, to the truth that the Father's love and mercy were incarnate and available to us in his own Person, Jesus uttered that truth most eloquently in the suffering and death that he freely endured to reconcile the world to the Father. In obedience to the Father's will, Christ did not evade suffering by destroying his persecutors with the power that he had at his disposal. For how, then, would the Scriptures be fulfilled (see Mt 26:53–54)? Instead, he freely took on himself the suffering that they imposed on him from without, expressing thereby that he, the Innocent One, had also freely taken on himself the very sinfulness by which they imposed it. Christ's suffering and death was the means by which, and the sign that, he himself would satisfy for the punishment due to our sins.[48] By thus determining himself supremely at his supreme moment of self-deprivation, he restored us to the grace of our eternal election in him and so to the dignity that was ours "in the beginning." Through this incredible paradox, Christ has given us, at once, the quintessential example of the power of active passivity and the ultimate sign of contradiction.

It is true that there are various conditions in the world today that pose a tremendous threat to human freedom. As a result, man "rightly fears falling victim to an oppression that will deprive him of his interior freedom, of the possibility of expressing the truth of which he is convinced, of the faith that he professes, of the ability to obey the voice of conscience that tells him the right path to follow."[49] But when he avails himself of the truth that Christ proclaimed by his life, suffering, death, and resurrection, that same man becomes interiorly free "from what curtails, diminishes and as it were breaks off [his] freedom at its root, in man's soul, his heart and his conscience."[50] As a result, if we become subject to external constraints imposed on us unjustly by persons stronger than we or by circumstances beyond our control, we can still testify to the truth, even in lonely silence, by a supremely free interior act that expresses the sovereign value of our person through our bodily vulnerability.

One way that we can transcend the limitations on our freedom that others have imposed on us unjustly from without is through the prayer that this injustice evokes from the depths of our heart: prayer that is inspired and sustained by the grace of Christ; prayer that is consequently offered in union

48. Of course, our participation in this grace depends on whether or not we live and die for love of Christ by the power of his Spirit.

49. *DM*, 11. This is the most radical form of alienation, "by which I mean deprivation of that which constitutes man's human nature." *SgC*, 121.

50. *RH*, 12.

with him; prayer that contains within it the voice of Christ himself. "Many times, through the influence of the Spirit, prayer rises from the human heart in spite of prohibitions and persecutions and even official proclamations regarding the non-religious or even atheistic character of public life. Prayer always remains the voice of all those who apparently have no voice—and in this voice there always echoes *that 'loud cry'* attributed to Christ by the Letter to the Hebrews" (cf. Heb 5:7).[51] As we transcend our vulnerability more consciously thus, we more actively—that is, freely—appropriate our external constraints in such a way as to affirm through them the very truth that our oppressors had tried to suppress by imposing them, or that our circumstances might otherwise have obscured. This concerns, above all, the truth about the dignity of the human person, each one of whom shares a divine calling to redemption and eternal life in Christ.

It is Christ's revelation of this truth that sets us free (see Jn 8:31–36). "What a stupendous confirmation of this has been given and is still being given by those who, thanks to Christ and in Christ, have reached true freedom and have manifested it even in situations of external constraint!"[52] Here, as in the preceding quotation, John Paul is almost certainly speaking out of his lived experience as a young man and later as a priest under the barbarism of Nazism and then communism in Poland. That same experience undoubtedly underlies also the words he spoke during the canonization Mass of St. Maximilian Kolbe—words having a similar force and significance.

> In that death, terrible from the human point of view, there was the whole definitive greatness of the human act and of the human choice: He spontaneously offered himself up to death out of love. And in this human death of his there was the clear witness borne to Christ: The witness borne in Christ to the dignity of man, to the sanctity of his life and to the saving power of death, in which the power of love is made manifest.[53]

When we witness to the truth of human dignity by refusing to reciprocate, to compromise with, or to cower before the injustice of our oppressors, it is not merely for our sake or for that of others that we do so, but for Christ's sake. To affirm by our actions both our own personal dignity and the inherent personal dignity of even our oppressors, we must sacrificially die to ourselves, to our inclinations toward vengeance, hate, and despair, so as to live

51. *DetV*, 65.

52. *RH*, 12.

53. "The Canonization of Maximilian Kolbe," *Origins* 12, no. 19 (1982): 292. Pope John Paul II canonized Father Kolbe as a martyr for the faith at St. Peter's Basilica on October 10, 1982.

in Christ and for Christ. When, through our vulnerability, we make such a sacrifice freely in the service of truth and out of love for the truth, we do, in analogous fashion, what Christ did. And we do so precisely in virtue of the redemptive efficacy of Christ's own sacrifice, which radiates through ours. Saint Paul reminds us that the power of Christ "is made perfect in weakness." He therefore boasted gladly of the weaknesses, hardships, and persecutions he endured "that the power of Christ may rest upon me." He bore with everything "for the sake of Christ" (2 Cor 12:9–10).

### Redemptive Effects of the Sacrificial Gift of Self through Externally Imposed Constraints

We give witness to the truth in freedom not only when we are fully conscious of our reasons for acting nobly under conditions of adversity, but even when the conviction that moves us to do so is more intuitive. For in either case, our actions derive their power from Christ, whether through his sacramental union with us or, in the case of the unbaptized, through his general union with every human being in virtue of the Incarnation and the Redemption, made effective in their lives by a grace of the Spirit.[54] The universal extension of Christ's union with the human race situates him as the ultimate referent of every moral action. As such, he accepts the sacrifices that we offer through our vulnerability for love of authentic truth and justice, even when that motive remains partially hidden from us as we act, and even when we have no explicit knowledge of Christ as the final, personal end of our actions.

What is more, Christ endows our sacrificial self-offering with salvific power because it conforms to his own supreme and all-sufficient redemptive sacrifice. Consequently, the value of our self-sacrificial act is not contingent on anyone else's accepting us for the witness that we have borne through it. Indeed, Christ's redemptive sacrifice was itself a sign that the human race had, on the whole, rejected him.[55] Still, the Father accepted the self-oblation of the Son so that it became the source of a new giving on God's part, especially with respect to the glory of the resurrection, the gift of the Holy Spirit,

54. "Man—every man without any exception whatever—has been redeemed by Christ, and ... with each man ... Christ is in a way united, even when man is unaware of it: 'Christ, who died and was raised up for all, provides man'—each and every man—'with the light and the strength to measure up to his supreme calling.'" *RH*, 14, quoting from *GS*, 10.

55. "In the torment of the cross [Christ] did not obtain human mercy." *DM*, 8. Still, his sacrifice was received perfectly into the heart of Mary, his mother. See ibid., 9; *RMa*, 18–19.

and the Eucharist.[56] Likewise, when Christ (and the Father through him) accepts our sacrificial self-offering, which he himself inspires, he transforms it into a source of new redemptive grace capable of inspiring a new giving of self. The act of self-giving thus becomes charged with redemptive significance for each of us as an actor. In a conditional way, depending on the response, it also becomes redemptive for those in behalf of whom and before whom we act, to say nothing of persons of whom we might be entirely unaware. We might not be conscious of these salvific effects; however, in every self-sacrificing activity offered in the service of authentic truth and justice as discerned through right reason, the grace of Christ's Paschal Mystery becomes operative, transforming our very lives into powerful, transcendent signs and prayers that touch the lives of others, if in no other way than by secretly echoing those "loud cries" that Christ uttered on the cross for our sake and on our behalf. Solidarity—that "firm and persevering determination to commit oneself ... to the good of all and of each individual, because we are all really responsible for all"[57]—is the name that we give to this dynamic reality when fully conscious of it.

Our experience of oppression at the hands of others might take place on the physical, the psychological, or the moral and spiritual level, or it might include any combination of these. It is even possible that we might unintentionally incite our oppressors to treat us more harshly because of our unflagging fidelity to the truth despite their efforts to oppress us. On the other hand, we might succeed thereby in moving them to show mercy toward us. If so, they will thus have affirmed our true dignity as persons, even if not yet completely, suggesting that they have accepted, to an extent, the sacrificial self-offering that we have expressed through the condition of vulnerability that they themselves have imposed on us. That is, they have accepted, at least partially, our implicit invitation to genuine dialogue as a step toward interpersonal communion—and not only ours, but that of Christ *in* us. Because the self-sacrificial actions by which we upheld the truth of human dignity were inspired and sustained by Christ's redemptive grace and hence impressed with his image, our oppressors were drawn, perhaps unwittingly, to Christ through us. Their affirmative response to us was at once an affirmative response to Christ. In that way, the actions that we were able to execute freely under oppressive conditions for love of truth and justice conduced not

56. See *RH*, 20.

57. John Paul II, *Sollicitudo Rei Socialis* (December 30, 1987), 38, Vatican website.

only to our own salvation, but also to that of our oppressors, who, if they, too, persevere in the service of authentic truth and justice, will likewise come in some way to share in and radiate Christ's glory.

The life of Elisabeth Leseur illustrates in profound and unexpected ways how the exercise of human agency through physical and, above all, externally instigated psychological and spiritual suffering can, when united to Christ, bring about dynamic personal and communal effects like those just described. Besides serious physical illness, Elisabeth suffered under the oppression of her husband Felix's militant atheism, which asserted itself a few years after their marriage in Paris in 1889. This psychological and spiritual trial was compounded by the unbelief of all their social contacts. After pulling back from the brink of unbelief herself and then applying herself diligently to the study of the Catholic faith, she knew that she could not, for the most part, lead all these unbelieving souls to Christ and to spiritual solidarity with herself by the sheer force of lucid argumentation, of which she had become exceedingly capable. Rather, Elisabeth became convinced that, "To refrain from action is sometimes the greatest sacrifice, and the most fruitful of all actions."[58] She discovered that she could act in a hidden and more powerful way by suffering in silence, by offering herself to Christ through her physical, personal, and spiritual trials, principally for the conversion of her husband and other unbelievers. In this way, she developed a rich interior life, which expressed itself outwardly in her serene, dignified bearing and in her total respect for and self-giving to others.

The truth of Christ revealed to Elisabeth her vocation: the hidden apostolate of prayer, penance, and suffering that she accepted and lived with supreme freedom. That same truth became somehow transparent to her husband and to those around her through her visible activity, which secretly bore within it the image of the "fruitful inactivity" of Christ's Passion.[59] Thus, through the exterior signs of her unwavering fidelity to the truth, Elisabeth gradually won the respect and admiration of those whose beliefs were radically opposed to her own. Indeed, shortly after her untimely death at age forty-seven, the impact of her life of grace so transformed her atheistic husband that he went on to become a Dominican priest. In fact, she had offered her suffering and her very life to God for that intention, predicting before her death that God would fulfill it, so sure was she that he had accepted her self-sacrifice.[60] Such an outcome testifies to the truth of her conviction that the

58. Leseur, *Secret Diary*, 176.

59. Ibid., 128.

60. See ibid., xl–xli.

"*active and truly fruitful passivity*" of trials well borne is the most powerful form of intercessory prayer,[61] so that even the least of one's good thoughts and acts (however hidden) resonates profoundly in other souls, whether near or far, through the gracious action of God.[62]

In this context, the comments of philosopher Kenneth Schmitz on Wojtyła/John Paul's understanding of human action are particularly relevant: "Consummate action may take form as the quiet acts of prayer, meditation and contemplation open to all [self-]conscious beings, and which are of the highest importance and value, attaching us to our transcendent source, and by means of its inner bonds attaching us also to our fellow creatures."[63] We have just seen the effects of such "consummate action" in the life of Elisabeth Leseur and those around her. Because every charitable, self-sacrificial act is inspired and sustained by the redemptive power of Christ's sacrifice and directed toward him as its ultimate referent, it can have a redemptive effect even when the person performing it and the person(s) benefiting from it have no knowledge of or direct contact with each other. All that is required is the good will of the giver and the openness of the receiver(s) to the salvific power of grace unleashed by the actor's selfless expression of love.

### Christ Witnesses with Witnesses of Truth Condemned Unjustly by Oppressors

When, by the redemptive power of Christ's grace, persons subjected to externally imposed oppression are interiorly set free to transform their vulnerability into an instrument of truth, it is not only they who bear witness to the truth before their oppressors. It is the Truth in Person that accompanies them in their witness. "Is it not often Jesus Christ Himself that has made an appearance at the side of people judged for the sake of the truth? And has He not gone to death with people condemned for the sake of the truth? Does He ever cease to be the continuous spokesman and advocate for the person who lives 'in spirit and truth'?"[64] It is often as victims of injustice that people find occasion to offer their lives sacrificially as the means of proclaiming the truth for which they were condemned. Though their proclamation might not be verbal or mainly so, their fidelity, in action, to the truth speaks powerfully, while also affirming the truth of their dignity as human persons, who can exercise authentic freedom even under the most unjust and oppressive con-

61. Ibid., xxxi.

62. See ibid., 149, 155, 178.

63. Schmitz, *At the Center,* 119.

64. *RH,* 12. See *SgC,* 122.

ditions by upholding what is objectively right and good. The witness-unto-martyrdom of St. Thomas More is an excellent case in point.[65] Nevertheless, the ways in which people suffer unjustly for the truth are myriad. But Christ stands by such as these, even if they have no explicit belief in him.[66] If in no other way, he makes himself "known" in the depths of one's conscience. Hence, "[i]n man's estimation the silent but positive approval given him by his own quiet conscience far outweighs the most appalling suffering."[67]

By sacrificially expressing themselves as subjects of truth and love amid the injustice imposed on them from without, vulnerable human beings appeal to the inherent capacity for truth and love that founds the existence even of their oppressors, affirming implicitly the personal dignity of the latter in the act of affirming their own. When oppressors oppose that witness, they also oppose themselves to the truth about human dignity and its disclosure through human vulnerability. They thus oppose themselves to Christ himself, who revealed and re-created human dignity precisely by bearing witness to the truth of the Father's love and mercy toward us through his own vulnerability, both in the Incarnation and, above all, on the cross. Though "the 'price' of our redemption is ... proof of the value that God Himself sets on man and of our dignity in Christ,"[68] the cross of Christ, and of those who manifestly share in it, is for many a sign of contradiction. While it actually "indicates the lengths to which the battle to save man's dignity must go,"[69] the cross might seem to negate the truth of our surpassing dignity rather than to affirm and uphold it. That is why it stands ever as "a sign that will be opposed" (see Lk 2:34; 1 Cor 1:18) or, at the very least, avoided.[70] So, when human beings who witness to the truth through the cross of oppression are nevertheless rejected, or when they have that cross imposed on

65. The revelation of true human freedom and hence of true human dignity "acquires a particular eloquence for Christians and for the Church in a state of persecution ... because the witnesses to divine Truth then become a living proof of the action of the Spirit of truth present in the hearts and minds of the faithful, and they often mark with their own death by martyrdom the supreme glorification of human dignity." *DetV,* 60.

66. The glory of Christ hidden in human suffering "must be acknowledged not only in the martyrs for the Faith but in many others also who, at times, even without belief in Christ, suffer and give their lives for the truth and for a just cause. In the sufferings of all of these people the great dignity of man is strikingly confirmed." *SD,* 22. See *SgC,* 122.

67. *SgC,* 182. See John Paul's treatment of martyrdom in *Veritatis Splendor,* 90–94.

68. *RH,* 20; see 1 Cor 6:20; *SgC,* 77.

69. *SgC,* 102.

70. Weighted with the oppressive burden of human sin, the cross of Christ seemed to deprive him of all that was human and personal in him: "his appearance was so marred, beyond human semblance, and his form beyond that of the sons of men" (Is 52:14).

them precisely because of that witness, Christ is put on trial and judged with them. Whatever injustice we do to them we do to him (see Mt. 25:41–46; Acts 9:1–5; 26:14–15). For that reason, Christ's description of the Last Judgment (Mt 25:31–46) "must always be made the 'measure' for human acts as an essential outline for an examination of conscience by each and every one."[71]

### Overcoming Oppressive Social Structures by Christ's Grace and Truth

Before proceeding to the next category of vulnerable persons, we should note first that the external constraints to which some persons are subject derive from unjust social "situations" rather than from overt oppression by specific people or groups of people.

> Man's growth in this life is hindered by the conditionings and pressures exerted upon him by dominating structures and mechanisms in the various spheres of society. It can be said that in many cases social factors, instead of fostering the development and expansion of the human spirit, ultimately deprive the human spirit of the genuine truth of its being and life—over which the Holy Spirit keeps vigil—in order to subject it to the "prince of this world."[72]

While the injustice embedded in certain institutions, structures, and systems (political, economic, social, cultural, legal, educational, and so on) is always "the result of the accumulation and concentration of many *personal sins*,"[73] it can nevertheless take on an almost anonymous character, for the individual sins at the root of it lie hidden in the seemingly impersonal, concrete societal forms through which it is perpetuated on a vast scale.[74] For that reason, the forms of external constraint impinging on the person because of unjust situations of that kind are particularly insidious. They can make vulnerable persons appear to be merely "victims of circumstance," as if, for example, they just happened to have been "born into" poverty, or into a particular racial or ethnic group that, for no other reason, leaves them at a "disadvantage" or renders them so "different" as to be content with things as they are.

Once they have been interiorly freed by Christ, however, such persons can appropriate their state of vulnerability and transcend it in ways similar to those discussed above. An example of that would be when persons living by the grace and truth of Christ refuse to use the unjust circumstances of

71. *RH*, 16.

72. *DetV*, 60.

73. *Reconciliatio et Paenitentia*, 16.

74. See *DetV*, 56.

their life as an excuse for becoming apathetic or dejected; or for blaming, envying, or hating others; or for perpetrating their own acts of injustice in response to the situation. By working instead in a spirit of solidarity with those who can help effect constructive change, or perhaps by confronting them with a legitimate spirit of opposition (itself a form of solidarity), they will witness to their inherent dignity and worth as human persons, bringing the injustices against them into relief so as to inspire others to help them right the wrongs and to make the sacrifices necessary to do it properly. Even an apparent failure in that regard will secretly sow the seeds of positive change, since vulnerable persons who witness thus are sustained by and radiate the redemptive power of Christ's sacrifice.

## The Personal Expression of Love through Structural Vulnerability

We will now discuss a third category of vulnerability, this one involving persons subject to severe somatic disintegration or to some lesser form of psychical/cognitive disintegration. Either of those conditions might be the result of congenital abnormalities or the natural aging process, but it might also be acquired at any stage during or after the course of normal development, for example, by means of an injury inflicted accidentally or perhaps even purposely. Our examination of the present category will proceed along the lines of the previous section. There, it was a question of external constraints, which, being incapable of undermining the interior freedom that Christ has set free, became the language through which the persons subject to them expressed themselves precisely *as* persons. Here, it is a question of structural constraints of the somatic or the psychical order, which can likewise be used as the language expressing the person whom Christ has interiorly freed.

In order to transform severe somatic or milder psychical/cognitive constraints into an efficacious means of personal expression, the persons subject to them must be transformed inwardly by the redemptive power of Christ's sacrifice, so that their structural limitations and the effects of these do not weaken or break their inner resolve to surmount them to the extent that God would allow. Believers have the advantage of being able to recognize the redemptive value of their condition, which helps strengthen and encourage them to offer themselves sacrificially through it to others and for the sake of others. They subject to their personal control any tendency toward attitudes of self-pity, bitterness, despair, or the like, living instead by the power of

Christ and hence *for* Christ and in union with him. It is this that leads to love of neighbor.

Still, whether they are aware of it or not, human beings are motivated and sustained by Christ's redemptive grace and hence united with him in some way whenever they offer themselves sacrificially to and for others through their somatic or their psychical vulnerability. Such actions conform them to Christ's sacrificial offer of himself on the cross and have him as their ultimate referent.[75] As a result, they are never performed in vain, even if people reject both the ones who offer themselves thus and, consequently, the salvific efficacy of Christ's grace at work in the action *by which* they offer themselves thus. He who inspires the sacrificial action accepts both the offering and the person who offers it, imparting to them a share in the redemptive power of his own sacrificial action on the altar of the cross. John Paul tells us that "the weaknesses of all human suffering are capable of being infused with the same power of God manifested in Christ's cross"—that is, with the invincible power of love.[76] As a result, vulnerable actors who are inserted thus into the salvific economy of Christ, and so united with him, are inspired to perform further acts of disinterested self-giving through their vulnerability. In doing so, structural disintegration and its effects become the means through which human beings, even at the point of death, attain and express their spiritual maturity, their perfection as persons. "*In suffering there is concealed a particular power that draws a person interiorly close to Christ,* a special grace.... [Therefore, when the body] is gravely ill, totally incapacitated, and the person is almost incapable of living and acting, all

75. The authentic self-giving of even the unbaptized involves a favorable response to the grace of Christ. John Paul II frequently alludes to this implicit acceptance of Christ by non-Christians, but he does not always indicate how the mode and operation of grace might differ in unbaptized persons as compared with Christians, in whom the grace of baptism effects an ontologically superior union with and conformity to Christ and his Church. Surely *LG*, 16, and *GS*, 22, are key texts for his general view of the matter. In *Redemptoris Missio*, 10, he is a little more specific. For those who have been brought up in other religious traditions or who have not had the opportunity to come to know or accept the Gospel or to enter the Church, "salvation in Christ is accessible by virtue of a grace which, while having a mysterious relationship to the Church, does not make them formally part of the Church but enlightens them in a way which is accommodated to their spiritual and material situation. This grace comes from Christ: it is the result of his Sacrifice and is communicated by the Holy Spirit. It enables each person to attain salvation through his or her free cooperation."

76. *SD*, 23. "[T]he Redemption, accomplished through satisfactory love, *remains always open to all love* expressed *in human suffering*." Though the Redemption "was completely achieved by Christ's suffering, [it] lives on and in its own special way develops in the history of man" (ibid., 24). In the end, "it is [Christ] Himself who acts at the heart of human sufferings through His Spirit of truth" (ibid., 26).

the more do interior *maturity and spiritual greatness* become evident."[77] The fact that the person's interior solidarity with Christ is effected through the instrumentality of structural disintegration serves to remind us that it is always the *whole* person, soul and body, who is encompassed and transformed by the salvific power of his redemptive sacrifice.

The sacrificial offering that a person makes of him- or herself through certain types of psychical or somatic disintegration can become a gift for others who allow themselves to be transformed by Christ's power working through it. "In the spiritual dimension of the work of Redemption *[the suffering person] is serving,* like Christ, *the salvation of his brothers and sisters.* Therefore, he is carrying out an irreplaceable service."[78] We might add that he is also building up communion among persons, if only invisibly. Human suffering fosters communion in another way as well, perhaps as a salvific effect of Christ's redemptive grace flowing through the sufferer. It calls others to make themselves immediately present, in love, to the suffering person. For example, we might be able to do something great or small to make the person more comfortable. If not, we can at least "suffer with" the person, for that is the true meaning of compassion, that sympathetic "sensitivity of heart" that is sometimes "the only or principal expression of our love for and solidarity with the sufferer."[79] While it is true that "no heart can penetrate deeply enough another's pain,"[80] one can still make an offering of the compassionate suffering that one experiences *because of* another's pain.[81] It is simply a question of opening one's *I* to the sufferer, whose suffering is meant "*to unleash love in the human person,* that unselfish gift of one's 'I' on behalf of other people, especially those who suffer."[82] In that way, a communion of persons is established between those who suffer and those who express their care for them by willingly, even self-sacrificially, entering into their suffering, if in no other way than by the witness of their concrete presence to them. The reciprocal exchanges that take place between suffering persons and those who care for them embody what Christ has taught us, namely, that

77. Ibid., 26.

78. Ibid., 27.

79. Ibid., 28.

80. Leseur, *Secret Diary,* 47.

81. E.g., ibid., 42–43.

82. *SD,* 29. See no. 30. John Paul told André Frossard that when he was young, he used to shy away from looking directly at suffering people until he later understood the meaning of the "dread mystery" that they bore in their bodies: "[P]eople who are ill bring charity into being, 'the weak are a source of strength.'" Frossard concludes, "People used to talk about the 'sacrament of the sick.' I think that in his own way of looking at things, the Holy Father considers every sick person to be ipso facto a kind of sacrament." Frossard, *Portrait,* 68.

man is "*to do good by his suffering* and *to do good to those who suffer.* In this double aspect He has completely revealed the meaning of suffering."[83]

A communion of persons can also exist on a wholly *spiritual* level between structurally disabled persons and others who might or might not be afflicted so. The sufferers who make a sacrificial offering of their lives through their structural vulnerability and the persons who, being well disposed, benefit from the redemptive power of Christ at work in that self-offering might be completely unknown to each other and yet powerfully transformed by their spiritual solidarity. But regardless of whether this kind of *communio* is concretely perceptible, it involves, for the participants, an encounter with Christ, whose grace underlies every instance of genuine human solidarity, and whose Person is the ultimate "object" of each one's positive response to that grace.

We see, then, that in God's plan for human salvation, persons having severe somatic or less radical psychical/cognitive constraints can *voluntarily* perform the indispensable service of cooperating with Christ through their suffering—whether explicitly or implicitly—by responding favorably to his grace so as to extend the fruits of his redemptive sacrifice to others. Accordingly, Elisabeth Leseur states that "*[s]uffering is the higher form of action, the highest expression of the wonderful Communion of Saints.*"[84] And John Paul II tells us why: "Those who share in the sufferings of Christ preserve in their own sufferings a very special *particle of the infinite treasure* of the world's Redemption, and can share this treasure with others."[85] This could not but follow from the special solidarity between Christ and the vulnerable implied in his self-emptying in the Incarnation and the Redemption. Since persons subject to somatic or to psychical disintegration share mysteriously in the human vulnerability that Christ assumed during his earthly life, he is mysteriously present to them in theirs. Christ himself "is the one who in each individual experiences love; He Himself is the one who receives help, when this is given to every suffering person without exception. He Himself is present in this suffering person, since His salvific suffering has been opened once and for all to every human suffering."[86] Christ's intensely personal identification

83. *SD*, 30.

84. Leseur, *Secret Diary*, xxxi. In *Reconciliatio et Paenitentia*, 16, John Paul II quotes Leseur when referring to this mysterious Communion: "Every soul that rises above itself, raises up the world" (cf. *Secret Diary*, xxxv).

85. *SD*, 27. As we saw in chapter 1, John Paul understood well this meaning of human suffering and lived it accordingly.

86. Ibid., 30.

with suffering human beings is so strong that he regards our care for or neglect of them (or any vulnerable persons) as determining our attitude toward *him*. He will judge each of us accordingly (cf. Mt 25:31–46).

### Expressing Personal Love through Structural Vulnerability in the Absence of a Developed Self-Awareness

The last category of vulnerable human beings that we will examine involves persons who are incapable of sacrificially offering themselves to and for others through their vulnerability in a conscious and voluntary way. They are prevented from doing so either by severe psycho-rational disintegration or by the psychosomatic immaturity that is natural to the early stages of human development. This is not to suggest that they have no means of communicating themselves to other persons or of receiving them in an exclusively human and personal way. But it is more true of this category of human beings than of any other that the specific mode by which they express themselves as persons through their particular form of vulnerability can be adequately understood only in the light of Jesus Christ. By revealing the Father's love for us in his own Person, Christ has revealed us to ourselves and has made clear to us our supreme calling to everlasting life.[87] Man must therefore "'appropriate' and assimilate the whole reality of the Incarnation and Redemption in order to find himself."[88] Pope John Paul II's own appropriation of that reality, to the extent that we have detailed it so far, has enriched our general understanding of the human person and of the dynamic subjective relations that can and do exist between persons. It has likewise enriched our more particular understanding of the three categories of vulnerable human beings that we have already examined in this chapter. And it will help us appreciate more fully his profound contribution to our understanding of personhood and agency in our final category of vulnerable human beings, while also giving us a sense of how his thought on human agency might have developed since the original publication of *Person and Act* in 1969. So let us now consider the subtle but real, intracommunal language of the most vulnerable of the vulnerable in the light of Jesus Christ.

In Jesus Christ, God has definitively revealed himself to us as Love. It follows, therefore, that if the image of God has been renewed in us through the Incarnation and the Paschal Mystery of the divine Son, then we have

87. Cf. *GS*, 22; *RH*, 8.

88. *RH*, 10. The "way" of man that Christ himself traced out "leads invariably through the mystery of the Incarnation and the Redemption" (ibid., 14).

been re-created for and recalled to our original vocation to love. Love is an exclusively personal reality. Historically, we first encountered that reality concretely and definitively as the reality of God himself when, in the Incarnation, the eternal Person of the Son of God became the substantial principle of the human nature that he assumed in the womb of his virgin mother once she uttered her *fiat*. In that way, the Incarnation reveals to us that our mission to fulfill the vocation to love begins from the first moment of our existence, from conception, for that is when God establishes us as persons. As such, we are always worthy to receive love and always capable of giving it in some way.

From the Incarnation through the Redemption, the Son of God radiated the Father's love in the world personally through a human nature, both perfecting that nature and bringing the infinite love of God to perfect expression on the human plane. In an analogous way, every creature radiates the Father's love in virtue of, and in proportion to, the specific dynamism by which it projects, through its nature, the gift of its own existence in the world. That is to say, the love of God is revealed to us in the very "act" by which each creature reveals *itself* to us as a work and a gift of the Creator. It is the Holy Spirit, as the personal Love-Source of all God's giving to creatures, that "speaks through the testimony of every creature, for it is he who has given them a voice with which to speak."[89]

However, it is only in Christ that the love of God is communicated to the world directly and absolutely in the Person of the divine Son. The mystery of the incarnate Son tells us, moreover, that our spiritual nature possesses an unlimited openness to all reality, since it is capable of accommodating the utterly unique, infinitely transcendent reality of God himself. For that reason, the human spirit alone is referred to, capable of aspiring toward, and capable of receiving, through the body, the inexhaustible Love of God that expresses itself finitely in every creature as the divine Source of "the gift," of the creative donation of the world. But that is not all. Though it is itself a created reality, the human spirit—precisely *as* spirit, made in God's image and capable of accommodating the reality of God himself—has an unlimited creative capacity to radiate the love of God in the world and so manifest its glory through the body. That is why our contact with other persons from the moment we are conceived transcends the merely physical order so as to be taken up into the very history of souls—both ours and theirs. Human beings

89. *SgC*, 56. See Ps. 19:1–4; Wis 13:1–5; Rm 1:19–20.

are therefore distinctly *personal* beings based on their soul-body existence and the singular nature of both its relation to God and its reflection of God in the world.

Because of our special relation to God as persons, we radiate his love in the world in a concrete yet uniquely personal way through the body. It is this that stands at the basis of our relations with one another. From that perspective, we can see more clearly that in virtue of the dynamic act of existence by which they project, through their bodily nature, their personal being into and seek contact with the world, vulnerable human beings having a high degree of psychosomatic immaturity or psycho-rational disintegration are nevertheless capable of revealing themselves personally to others. For the dynamic relational thrust of their spirit through the body it informs is already the self-expression—the radiation—of their person, precisely because each of them is the highest, most qualitatively intense expression in the visible world of God's radiative love. Each of them is a created good of such concentrated splendor that it takes the form of a creaturely person. The self-enactment of their being has a definite end. It is the act by which the self-transcending spirit aspires toward, so as to be filled with, God's love, initially as radiated through the concrete presence of other persons. In them, too, the radiation of that love transcends the strictly material level and arrives at the personal. In effect, then, the spirit of the most vulnerable human beings opens out to other persons and invites them to communion with itself by radiating the love of God through its bodily self-expression, while it is simultaneously drawn, through the body, to other human beings because they likewise radiate most fully the love of God toward which it aspires. In that way, a subtle, perhaps wordless, though profoundly real and meaningful dialogue can take place reciprocally between those who are psychosomatically most vulnerable and those who are not.

To summarize, the ontological constitution of a human being as an utterly unique and superior radiation of God's creative love is what allows him to present himself, objectively and from the beginning of his existence, as a person to other human beings. This is, in turn, the basic condition that opens the way to us for an authentic exchange of persons in love. (Likewise, our personhood opens us also to such exchanges with persons angelic or divine.) While certain physical, psychical, psycho-rational, or moral conditions might impede or incline someone to resist the fundamental human dynamism toward full human development in the communion of persons, it is nevertheless true that the vocation of every human being—even when newly conceived, when disabled, or when chronically ill—is to express his humanity fully as a person.[90]

On the other hand, regardless of how "person-like" we might consider our pets or other higher animals to be, the projection of their being into the world through their own, natural dynamism reflects only, and cannot transcend, the nonpersonal kind of being they are. They are gifts for us to appreciate, to enjoy, and to wonder at as effects and signs of God's creative love, but they do not exist for their own sake. That distinction belongs only to persons. Consequently, they have no calling to, nor therefore do they actually aspire toward, the Love itself that created them. We can speak of their aspiration toward God's love only analogously, insofar as they sense in other creatures certain goods with which that Love has endowed them. In turn, this leads these living but nonpersonal creatures to imitate, according to an analogous mode inscribed in their nature, the mystery of communion in God himself, insofar as they interact with other creatures for their mutual good and thus form various types of communities among themselves. But they do not aspire toward communion itself as a fulfillment of their being. So much less, then, do they aspire to fulfill their being in some higher and definitive way by entering communion with God.

Human beings alone can perceive and aspire toward the Creator through the signs and effects of his handiwork in the creation because we alone are distinguished by an inner, spiritual life that revolves around truth and goodness, that is ordered toward interpersonal communion in love, and that develops in virtue of the fact that each one of us is a person. The animals have no such inner life.[91] The living principle that animates them must therefore be produced by their body. In consequence, it is not an independent spiritual principle. Being essentially material, it cannot transcend itself. It can neither accommodate nor aspire to the reality of God, who is Spirit. Nor, therefore, can it radiate the love of God in the unlimited way that persons can. In contrast, the spiritual dynamism of the human soul radiates through the body to express a person in such a way as to penetrate the being of another person with one's own personal presence and thus establish the condition for a communion of persons. And in communicating themselves, they communicate the image of God in which each of them was made. By giving themselves to and receiving each other in a truly personal way, they perfect that image in

90. See *LF*, 11.
91. See *LR*, 21–24.

themselves. The lack of a developed self-awareness does not prevent a person from taking part in this interpersonal dynamic with others in a way perfective of all, nor does it prevent them from receiving and serving as instruments of God's grace in Christ.

Karol Wojtyła's last dramatic play, *The Radiation of Fatherhood: A Mystery* (1964),[92] presents ideas germane to our discussion of interpersonal relations involving the most vulnerable of persons. The play's main speaker, representing every human being, is Adam, recalling him through whom we have inherited both our humanity and the wound of original sin. Because of that wound, Adam tends to exile himself to a life of loneliness, even in the presence of other people. He is unwilling and feels ill-suited to take the "risk" of love and to assume the responsibilities that go with it. Still, he cannot suppress fully the radiation of the Father's love in himself, for original sin did not efface completely the image that God implanted of his Fatherhood in the very soil of Adam's soul.[93] It is through this "fissure" in Adam's depths that God enters quietly to try and reshape him according to the pattern of Love in which he was made. And the way in which God "takes aim" at Adam is through a child, Monica.[94]

Monica is never identified explicitly in the play as Adam's daughter in the immediate sense. Just as Adam represents "every man," Monica seems to represent "every child," the perennial sign of new life generated creatively through the radiation of God's Fatherhood in Adam. Because Adam's fatherhood—flawed though it might be—is a real participation in the Fatherhood of God, we can understand his reflections on the meaning of fatherhood relative to the child as referring either to himself or to God. For example, as Adam leafs through an album of photographs from Monica's early childhood, he notes that her "Daddy" does not appear in the album because he is "far away." At the same time, he is like the (radiating) sun, which, though unseen in an outdoor picture of Monica, is known by its effects: it warms the child from without and within.[95]

The radiation of Adam's (and of God's) fatherhood is impressed indelibly in Monica's being and in the history of her soul, so that he (like God) is somehow present even in his absence.[96] "My father's history in me begins with

92. The plays of Karol Wojtyła are collected in the following work: *Karol Wojtyła: The Collected Plays and Writings on Theater*, trans. Boleslaw Taborski (Berkeley: University of California Press, 1987).

93. See Part 1, Scene 2.

94. See ibid., Scene 3.

95. Part 2, Scene 1.

96. Much as in the Prodigal Son. See note 25 above.

his absence, yet he must have been there all the time, though I did not feel him at all" because "his roots were embedded in me."[97] Though it seems to Monica that her Daddy is "not on earth," she tries to "give birth" to him by leaving flowers on his desk so that, seeing in this expression of love that he is present in her heart, he might look for her in his.[98] Perhaps she would grow in him as he had in her: "I did not know for many years that you had grown so much in me ... until the day I linked the immense longing in my soul precisely with you, until the day the absence had to become the presence it had once been."[99] Here, we can understand the child's reflections as referring, on another level, to God's Fatherhood as well.

Adam struggles to cut his way through the "thicket" that is in him: will he continue to abide in loneliness, or will he "risk" opening his heart to the child in love, that he might receive her as his own? It is precisely the vulnerability of the child that finally penetrates the seeming *in*vulnerability of Adam's self-imposed isolation. While they are working their way together through the "forest" of their tangled relationship in search of a clearing, an agitated viper (or *serpent*) appears suddenly, eliciting from the core of Adam's being the response that expresses the very essence of his fatherhood: "one must protect this child."[100] His responsibility for the child extends not only to her physical well-being: he must protect her also from moral and spiritual danger. And so he takes her to a stream, symbolizing the waters of baptism, that the radiation of God's Fatherhood might be born in her anew (that the "absence" might become the "presence" it once had been before the fall of Adam). At the same time, she asks that the radiation of Adam's fatherhood might also be renewed in her: "Be water for me!"[101] So, he enters into her heart through the "many doors" she has opened for him, instructing her that the love by which one can say "mine" of another person means accepting and giving oneself to that person through the integration of emotion by reason and will. It means assuming responsibility for the meaning of the word "mine"—something that Adam had refused to do until now.[102] So, through her vulnerability, Monica entered Adam's heart and helped him recapture the meaning of his fatherhood (of his very self), while Adam's acceptance of

97. Part 2, Scene 2, soliloquy 2.

98. Ibid. Similarly, God's children light candles in Church to symbolize their abiding presence before and their mindfulness of him, that he might, in turn, be mindful of and present to *them*.

99. Part 2, Scene 2, soliloquy 3.

100. Ibid., Scene 3.

101. Ibid.

102. Ibid., Scene 4.

his paternity in relation to Monica will help her "evade the vicious viper."[103]

On the pole opposite Adam's loneliness is Christ, the Son of God, who wholly contains in himself and communicates—radiates—the love of the Father. The Church makes the love of the Bridegroom available through the waters of baptism, allowing Adam to give himself away in love and thus to recapture his fatherhood, precisely by becoming again a "child" reborn in the Spirit.[104] As a child in the literal sense, Monica represents one's rebirth into that newness of life, and she embodies its meaning by summoning Adam implicitly through her vulnerability to accept her self-offer by opening his heart to her in self-giving love. In that way, the child restores "the bridegroom in the father."[105] And as a father, Adam represents the Source of the new life in Christ and of life itself. Thus, Adam and Monica are drawn in love both to each other and to God through the radiation of the Father's love in each of them.[106]

It bears repeating that the psychosomatically vulnerable persons presently under consideration "speak" their language—they communicate themselves to us—through the mediation of their bodily structure, which, as an expression of the human spirit and its radiation of the Father's love, is specially configured for giving and receiving love. This meaning of the body is reinforced by the fact that the whole psychosomatic dimension of human vulnerability has been assumed and redeemed by Christ, in whom it has become an objective sign of a "someone" offering himself to us and for our sake, even—and perhaps especially—when he presents himself to us in the form of a weak, helpless, radically dependent gift of love. Vulnerable human beings who lack an appreciable self-awareness of their identity as persons neither confirm nor contradict the objective meaning of their vulnerability subjectively, since they are incapable of subjectively determining themselves in a way that either corresponds to or diverges from that meaning.

Still, the act of existence by which they present themselves to us in the uniqueness of their person as a qualitatively superior radiation of the Father's love is itself an objective act of their entrusting themselves to us. And we should be able to reread correctly, in the light of Christ (at least implicitly, through the hidden action of his grace), the objective language of human

103. Ibid., Scene 5.

104. Part 3, Scenes 1, 2.

105. Part 1, Scene 5.

106. Original sin tries to abolish fatherhood by destroying the "rays" (the radiation) of God's Fatherhood that permeate creation and human history. See John Paul II, *Crossing the Threshold,* 227–28.

vulnerability and to recognize therein a word of love calling out for nothing less than a loving response. The radical dependency of these vulnerable persons requires that we who, on "hearing" their call, are drawn by love to *respond* in love must "subject" ourselves to them in their need. Whatever service we render to them we render simultaneously to Christ (see Mt 25:40), who has united himself with them in a special way by his Incarnation and Paschal Mystery (and, where baptism and perhaps also confirmation have been administered, by sanctifying grace). In virtue of that union, it is not only the vulnerable who entrust themselves to us through their vulnerability, but also Christ who entrusts both them and himself *in* them to us. For that reason, "whoever receives [a little] child in my name receives me" (Mt 18:5). And whoever receives Christ receives the Father. Therefore, when we give ourselves to, so as to receive, the vulnerable, the radiation of God's Fatherhood is realized more perfectly in us and through us.

Because psychosomatically vulnerable persons lacking full self-awareness are nevertheless open in spirit to the fullness of truth and love, their spiritual dynamism refers them, through their vulnerability, to God in Christ, who is mysteriously united with them. We can suppose that Jesus accepts their dynamic aspiration toward God as their personal self-offering *to* God, associating it with his Paschal Mystery and leading them to everlasting life (cf. Mk 10:13–16). As a result, any human neglect or abuse that would deprive them of their personal dignity cannot deprive these "least" of Christ's brothers and sisters of their ultimate personal fulfillment in God's kingdom. On the other hand, the radiation of God's love will necessarily diminish in and thus impoverish ontologically those who willfully neglect or abuse the vulnerable—so much so that they themselves might end by being deprived of their ultimate eschatological fulfillment if they persist in their ways. To neglect the most vulnerable of the vulnerable is to neglect Christ himself (see Mt 25:45).

In the conscious expression of love by which we serve these vulnerable persons, we also open ourselves to receive the love of the Father that radiates through, and in the form of, their distinctly human vulnerability. It thus becomes clear that our relation to the vulnerable is never simply unilateral: "the one who gives is also a beneficiary."[107] Through the existential act by which they make their person present to us as a uniquely intense radiation of God's love in the form of human vulnerability, the most vulnerable persons

107. *DM*, 14.

provide the invaluable service of drawing us out of ourselves and toward them, that we might fulfill ourselves personally in loving them. Conversely, the love that the vulnerable receive from us can help bring to personal fulfillment in them the love that they both radiate and aspire to naturally as persons, moving them toward greater self-expression and thus drawing them, too, further out of themselves, to the extent that their psychosomatic vulnerability will allow. And because we have each been re-expressed through the Incarnation and the redemptive love of Christ to radiate and to aspire toward the love and truth of the Father with renewed vigor, the ultimate term of every authentic exchange of love between the vulnerable and us is, for each and all, God himself through Christ.

# 6

# The Vulnerable as Actors in the Social Encyclicals of Pope John Paul II

In the last chapter, we focused our discussion on four different categories of vulnerable human beings and their personal agency in the light of our key anthropological, theological, and Christological reflections to that point. In the present chapter, together with the next, we will have occasion to revisit each of those categories, as well as the one we have termed "moral vulnerability." We will proceed even more concretely than before, drawing from the four encyclicals in which John Paul II addresses specifically the most urgent contemporary threats against the vulnerable and their agency. Those encyclicals—namely, John Paul's three commemorative social encyclicals and *Evangelium Vitae*—will affirm yet again the personal dignity of the vulnerable, as well as their ability to exercise their agency personally in and through their vulnerability. What is more, the social encyclicals in particular will show us how the types of vulnerable persons on whom they focus can act, not only despite the forces that threaten their acting, but even so as to prevail over them.

In his social encyclicals, the focus of this chapter, John Paul expresses special concern for laborers and poor people, particularly insofar as their vulnerability is imposed on them from the outside. These people suffer from various forms of oppression and injustice that deprive them of their intrinsic human rights in systematic and institutionalized ways that are often controlled, as the case may be, by their own employers, by prevailing social and economic structures and practices, by the state, or by rich and powerful persons, groups, and nations whose selfish decisions have a direct, negative impact on their lives. A twisted ideology of some kind typically underlies the exploitive activity of the persons, structures, and systems adversely affecting the lives of workers and the poor (including the working poor). The ones who live by such an ideology have made themselves vulnerable to moral and spiritual ruin because the actions by which they harm and exploit others originate interiorly from a perverse will. This self-inflicted, personal disintegration is even more pernicious than the kind of vulnerability that its subjects impose on others from the outside, for in actively disregarding or violating the humanity of their victims, they end up destroying their own. The materialistic and narcissistic greed that often motivates their actions so enslaves them to "things" that they would prefer to sacrifice their own *being* to the cult of *having*.[1] Both externally imposed and moral vulnerability figure prominently in the social encyclicals of John Paul II. Indeed, we could not in practice find the one without the other.

But that is not all. We will see that John Paul employs the concept that, in chapter 5, we called "voluntary (or freely self-imposed) vulnerability" for the sake of others. In the present context, he employs it on a highly collective level, summoning employers, powerful sociocultural, economic, and political institutions, whole nations, the international community, and certainly also the Church to make the sacrifices necessary to help improve the lot of workers and the poor. That means striving voluntarily to eliminate all forms of vulnerability imposed from without by transforming the attitudes, systems, and structures that foster and perpetuate the violation of human dignity and the alienation that goes with it. When workers and the poor are invited, as they should be, to participate in the process by which they are integrated fully and justly into the human community, the path to true solidarity is opened. Solidarity allows for the collaborative exercise of each one's personal agency for the sake of the true common good, which always serves one's own true good as well. As circumstances allow, the vulnerable must personally contribute to eliminating the unjust and dehumanizing condi-

1. See *SRS*, 28. Citations to *SRS* are from the Vatican translation available on the Vatican website.

tions to which they have been subjected and commit themselves resolutely to the free and constructive—though always challenging—activity of true solidarity with one another and with those who are obliged to respond in a morally appropriate way to their just cause. We will follow John Paul through his social encyclicals in considering all three forms of vulnerability—externally imposed, moral, and voluntary—in the light of his profound understanding of the human person.

In the three social encyclicals, we will discover that John Paul II's philosophical and theological understanding of the human person undergirds his defense of the inviolable dignity of the vulnerable not only by allowing him to affirm the essentially personal character of both their humanity and their agency, but also by allowing him to critique the sociocultural, economic, and political structures that alienate them or that even endanger their lives, in either case denying them their rightful place in society and the world community. We will see John Paul apply his anthropology in this wide-ranging way in the next chapter as well, when we examine his great encyclical on the dignity and sanctity of human life, *Evangelium Vitae*. We will thus come to understand more clearly that his characteristic focus on the human person, together with the inextricable link between the moral quality of one's actions and the person one "becomes," entails something more than just individual morality, and hence something more than just the personal merit or guilt that accrues to each person for either fulfilling or forsaking the moral obligation to help the vulnerable as he or she can. Because the actions that issue from our personal core also establish, condition, and are conditioned by the way we structure and live together in society and the world, John Paul's anthropology leads naturally, in the four encyclicals, to an assessment of the various kinds of societal, national, and international structures and relations that are built on and that influence, in turn, the personal decisions and actions of many individuals. That is why we will also find John Paul speaking, in one way or another, of our collective moral conscience and of our collective responsibility for any structures that violate the personal dignity of many to the material advantage of a few.

Before we proceed, let us take a moment to reintroduce briefly the social encyclicals of Pope John Paul II. The first one, *Laborem Exercens*, was issued on September 14, 1981, to commemorate the ninetieth anniversary of Pope Leo XIII's encyclical *Rerum Novarum*.[2] Leo's landmark document formally

2. Citations to *LE* are from the Vatican translation available on the Vatican website.

inaugurated the Church's social magisterium by systematically addressing the condition of workers during the growth of the industrial age. In his own document, John Paul reflects on the nature of human work and on the dignity and rights of the worker.

*Sollicitudo Rei Socialis,* dated December 30, 1987, commemorates the twentieth anniversary of Pope Paul VI's encyclical *Populorum Progressio.* In the earlier document, Paul stressed the moral duty of more fortunate individuals and of developed nations to assist needy people and developing nations. True human development is not just a matter of economic prosperity, for the social, cultural, and spiritual dimensions of human existence are also essential to human flourishing. Therefore, the effort to promote development must concern itself with the whole person. John Paul expands on that theme in the light of the conditions that arose during the twenty-year period between the publication of the two documents.

Finally, *Centesimus Annus,* issued on May 1, 1991, commemorates the centenary of *Rerum Novarum.*[3] After calling attention to the key principles of Leo XIII's renowned encyclical, particularly those bearing on the rights and dignity of the human person, John Paul uses them as a basis for interpreting the unfolding of world events from Leo's time onward. He includes an incisive analysis of the dramatic collapse of communism in central and eastern Europe beginning in late 1989. John Paul II sees the human person, the subject of work, at the center of those events. From that perspective, he considers the problems, the uncertainties, and the promise of the contemporary world and its future. The economic factors adversely affecting the condition of workers and the poor will not improve unless workers, society, the state, and international organizations fulfill their respective moral obligations and coordinate their efforts, with a view toward ensuring that everyone can freely participate to an appropriate degree in the social, economic, political, cultural, and religious spheres of human existence.

It is beyond the scope of the present chapter to give an exhaustive account of John Paul II's social encyclicals or to evaluate them critically.[4] Rather, we will take a somewhat synthetic and thematic approach to our examination of the documents so as to highlight, against the defective anthropologies treated therein, the original contribution that he makes to an authentic understand-

3. Citations to *CA* are from the Vatican translation available on the Vatican website.

4. For a brief indication of some of the strengths and weaknesses of each of the three encyclicals, see Weigel, *Witness to Hope,* 419–21, 557–60, 612–19.

ing of vulnerable human beings and their personal agency. Even from that perspective, we cannot claim to be exhaustive.

## The Catholic, Capitalist, and Marxist Views of the Human Person and Human Labor

Because human labor is so closely connected with the identity of the human person, one understands it rightly only insofar as one understands the *person* rightly. It follows that a false anthropology leads to a false view of work and, by extension, of how society ought to be constituted culturally, economically, and politically. That is precisely what has happened in the capitalist and Marxist systems. We will see that more clearly if we begin by looking at the biblical understanding of human beings and their labor as John Paul II elaborates it in the light of Catholic social teaching. This will also provide the background for our reflections in the third part of the chapter.

### John Paul II on the Personal and Social Aspects of Human Labor

Pope John Paul II's reflections on human labor begin with the book of Genesis, which reveals indirectly that the human vocation to work belongs to God's original covenant with man and woman in the mystery of creation. In order to carry out the divine command to "fill the earth and subdue it" (Gn 1:28), we must act in and on the world, whose vast resources present themselves to us as a gift and a trust. We must consequently appropriate a part of nature's riches so as to transform them, through work, into the means by which we achieve our legitimate ends. Confirming and advancing our dominion thus, we express ourselves as persons and so reveal our lofty dignity. As a distinctly human form of activity, our work of dominating the earth responsibly is one of the ways in which God's image in us manifests itself. Indeed, human work reflects and unfolds God's original act of creating the world, the "work" from which the Creator "rested" when he completed it (see Gn 2:2). We, too, must rest from our work—that is, from exercising our strength in external actions—so as to take up another "work," namely, that of preparing for the "rest" that God has reserved for those who do his will.[5]

While it is true that the objects of the external world serve as our "workbench,"[6] human work originates from *within* the human subject, for we act

5. See *LE*, 4, 12, 25; *CA*, 31; *GS*, 34.
6. See *LE*, 12.

consciously to adapt our natural environment according to our needs. That is why John Paul II understands the exercise of our dominion as a transitive activity consisting of both a subjective and an objective dimension.[7] Work expresses itself *objectively* in the various ways that we dominate the world—for example, through agriculture, industry, research, and the instruments of technology.[8] The objective dimension of work serves to advance our dominion only insofar as we, the subjects of work, realize ourselves as persons through it. That is what determines the ethical value of work.[9] Any form of work that does not express and promote human dignity is unworthy of us.[10] For that reason, the *subjective* dimension of work has priority over the objective.

Having been created in God's image, each of us is a person, "a subjective being capable of acting in a planned and rational way, capable of deciding about himself and with a tendency to self-realization."[11] That is why, in the very act of transforming the world around us (however modestly), we transform *ourselves* in some way.[12] Since our creative activity is also *self*-creative, human beings are themselves the primary purpose of work. If work is the explicit object of our activity, it has nevertheless a bearing on how we realize ourselves as subjects by doing it. We are for work only insofar as work is for us. The objective content of work must therefore be ordered toward our self-fulfillment as persons, our becoming *more human*, as it were.[13] In a real sense, we each become our own work *through* our work, which is always, in its subjective aspect, a personal act.[14] We can thus understand why industriousness, properly expressed, is a virtue.[15]

As the first "Gospel of work," the book of Genesis reveals that work is an original blessing by which human beings refer themselves and the world back to the Creator through the proper exercise of their dominion, thus sharing in the unfolding of God's creative plan.[16] On the other hand, Genesis also reveals that because of original sin, we must exert ourselves considerably before our efforts bear any fruit, and sometimes very little at that (cf. Gn 3:17).[17] The toil that is our lot anticipates the death we will undergo as the final "reward" that sin has earned for our labors (cf. Gn 3:19).[18] Yet, even when

7. See ibid., 4.
8. See ibid., 5.
9. See ibid., 6. See also *GS*, 35.
10. See *LE*, 9.
11. Ibid., 6.
12. See ibid., 9, 26; *GS*, 35.
13. See *LE*, 9–10.
14. See ibid., 24; Leo XIII, *Rerum Novarum* (May 15, 1891), 44, Vatican website. Hereafter *RN*.
15. See *LE*, 9; *SgC*, 139.
16. See *LE*, 25, 27; *GS*, 34.
17. See *LE*, 9.
18. See ibid., 27.

compounded by the certainty of our own death, the seeming futility of human work is not an insoluble riddle for us. Through the "Gospel of work" that Christ lived and proclaimed, and, above all, through the Paschal Mystery, human labor has been endowed with new meaning and value.

In his humanity, the Son of God spent most of his earthly life as a craftsman, a manual laborer. "This circumstance constitutes in itself the most eloquent 'Gospel of work,' showing that the basis for determining the value of human work is not primarily the kind of work being done, but the fact that the one who is doing it is a person."[19] In addition, Christ showed his regard for human work by referring to various kinds of laborers in his parables: the shepherd (e.g., Jn 10:1–16), the sower (e.g., Mk 4:1–9), the doctor (Lk 4:23; 5:31–32), the servant (e.g., Mt 24:45), the steward (Lk 16:1–8), the merchant (Mt 13:45–46), and so on. He referred to his Father as "the vinedresser" (Jn 15:1), and he compared the apostolic mission to the manual work of harvesters (Mt 9:37; Jn 4:35–38) and fishermen (Mt 4:19).[20] Jesus also declared that his Father (and he, too) is working even now (see Jn 5:17).[21]

For the final word on the "Gospel of work," however, John Paul turns to Christ's Paschal Mystery. By entering solidarity with human laborers, Christ opened for them the possibility of uniting their toil with the work of salvation he accomplished through his suffering and death on the cross. As a result, when we dutifully accept whatever hardship our work entails, we collaborate somehow with Christ's redemptive act. Christians see in their own work a small share in the cross of Christ, which has conferred on human labor an unimaginable potential for good. Because that good bears also a relation to the Resurrection, we not only realize and sanctify our humanity by applying ourselves to our work: we simultaneously contribute to human progress in a way that anticipates the kingdom of God.[22]

John Paul II's biblical reflections on the "Gospel of work" have shown us that human labor accords with the Creator's will, and so it is good for us despite its toil.[23] While the objective value of different types of work might vary, the criterion on the basis of which we must judge work of any kind is always the same: the surpassing dignity of each person as the subject of work.[24] Still, human labor involves more than just solitary subjects and achieve-

19. Ibid., 6; see no. 26.

20. See ibid., 26.

21. See ibid., 25.

22. See ibid., 27; *GS*, 39. See *SRS*, 48, for John Paul II's reflection on the Eucharist as the highest realization, this side of heaven, of the kingdom of God, to which human work contributes. See also *SRS*, 31.

23. See *LE*, 9, 11.

24. See ibid., 6.

ments. So, true to form, John Paul considers not only the personal, the subjective, dimension of work, but also its *social* dimension.

In the first place, work is a condition of family life, since we ordinarily obtain through work the means of subsistence necessary for establishing a family. Work also plays an indispensable role in helping the family fulfill its purpose as the first and foremost school of virtue. The formation of genuinely *human* persons is an essential element of the whole process of education. One of the ways in which we become more fully human is by applying ourselves industriously to our work. When we do, the value of work and the values inculcated *by* work are assimilated into the life of the family. At the same time, the family "constitutes one of the most important terms of reference for shaping the social and ethical order of human work."[25]

Within the larger society, human beings contribute to the common good by their work. Ideally, we will place ourselves at the service of the society to which we are historically and culturally linked, our own nation having, in a sense, a greater claim on our labor.[26] The great community to which we belong includes and reflects the work of all preceding generations. By laboring together with our compatriots for the true common good, each of us adds to that heritage and, by extension, to that of the whole human family.[27] We thus work not only *with* others but also *for* others.[28] That is especially true when we sanctify our work by uniting it with the saving work of Christ.

In view of its personal and social significance, work is a duty that we are morally obliged to fulfill;[29] therefore, anything interfering with our ability to fulfill the obligation to work, or even with our ability to express ourselves freely *through* work, will threaten the possibility of our self-realization as persons. Left unchecked, the situation will inevitably threaten the integrity of the whole social order as well, eventually to the detriment of the human family itself.

Deriving from the Church's sound understanding of human beings and their work is her understanding of two complementary principles, namely, the right to private property and the universal destination of goods. These principles are central to the Catholic critique of both the capitalist and the Marxist systems. According to John Paul II, the book of Genesis suggests that

25. Ibid., 10. See *CA*, 49; *Familiaris Consortio*, 45.

26. See *LE*, 23.

27. See ibid., 10.

28. See *CA*, 31.

29. See *LE*, 16; Paul VI, *Populorum Progressio* (March 26, 1967), 17, Vatican website. Hereafter, *PPro*.

the acquisition of private property is closely connected with the exercise of our dominion—that is, with our development as free and intelligent beings through work. In order to subdue the earth and thus establish it as a fitting home, we must take over part of nature's riches. These comprise our workbench. On the other hand, the right to private property is not absolute. Private ownership of the means of production is no longer legitimate when it deprives workers of their due. Again, John Paul looks to the book of Genesis, which reveals that created reality is God's gift to us all, excluding no one. Everything that we use in our work, even technological know-how, has its basis in the resources that we have received as a gift in the mystery of creation. We simply discover what has been given and use it in the process of production, which includes the intellectual workbench. Hence, the human goods produced through our work, like the goods of the earth from which they derive, belong to all for the *benefit* of all. They are the result of an effort encompassing all previous generations of labor, and they are meant, in turn, to *serve* human labor so that all might gain access to every truly human good. The right of private ownership is therefore subordinate to the principle of *the universal destination of material goods.*

It remains true that we must each make the world's resources our own through work, transforming them in a way that increases their nobility, fulfills our needs, and extends our dominion. That is the appropriate human response to God's original gift. But the human vocation to work includes *working with others* and also *for* others, so that no one is deprived of a rightful share in that gift. This means that the private property acquired through work is naturally ordered toward a social purpose, namely, the common use of goods.[30] Accordingly, John Paul states that private property "is under a social mortgage."[31]

Human labor is the primary *efficient cause* in the process of production. Man is *homo faber,* the "maker," precisely because he alone is a person capable of acting deliberately—that is, as an efficient subject. It follows that "capital"—understood here as all the tools and means of production—is itself the product of human labor. As such, it serves only as an *instrumental cause* of the production process. At the same time, by utilizing the instruments of production in our work, each of us "enters into the labor of others" (see

30. See *LE,* 12, 14; *CA,* 30–31, 43; *Christifideles Laici* (December 30, 1988), 43, Vatican website; *GS,* 69, 71; Paul VI, *PPro,* 23; Leo XIII, *RN,* 8, 22; Aquinas, *ST* II–II, 66, 2.

31. *SRS,* 42.

Jn 4:38), and we avail ourselves of the historical heritage of human labor.[32] Thus, while labor has priority over capital, the two are inseparable and must never be opposed. The production process becomes "subjective," serving our good as persons, only when we truly participate in our labor. We must be able to take initiative and to express ourselves creatively, knowing that as we work, each of us is working *for himself*, sharing responsibly in his labor and its fruits.[33] He can then "consider himself a part-owner of the great work-bench at which he is working with every one else."[34] Work must always be organized to respect authentic personal values, especially the freedom to act in truth at one's workbench.

### The Concept of Work in Early Capitalism: Subordinating the Person to the Employer

With the birth and growth of industrialization in the nineteenth century, a conflict arose between capital and labor in the socioeconomic system known as liberalism, or capitalism. Here, the term "capital" refers to the owners or holders of the means of production; however, we have seen that it is also used to denote the means themselves, which include natural resources, manufactured goods, and the whole collection of increasingly refined work-instruments made from them. The term "labor," in the present context, refers to the workers who contribute to the production process by their work, but who do not themselves possess the means of production. The same term is also used to denote the function performed or the effort expended by workers in their work.[35] Thus understood, early capitalism regarded labor as a kind of "merchandise" that the worker (especially the *industrial* worker) would "sell" to the employer (who was also the owner of the means of production, the "capital") in exchange for a wage.[36] The worker is then viewed merely "as some kind of instrument, with a work capacity and physical strength to be exploited at low cost and then discarded when no longer useful."[37]

John Paul observes that, by understanding "capital" and "labor" solely according to the secondary meanings given above, we risk reducing them conceptually to impersonal forces, though in reality they necessarily pre-

32. . See *LE*, 7, 12, 13.

33. See ibid., 15; *CA*, 43.

34. *LE*, 14.

35. See ibid., 11–13. According to the conditions of its time, *Rerum Novarum* seems to identify "capital and labor" with "rich and poor." See nos. 2–3.

36. See *LE*, 7; *CA*, 4.

37. *SRS*, 39.

suppose "living, actual people."[38] Applying the biblical view of work to the contemporary situation, therefore, he reaffirms Catholic social teaching by declaring that capital—that is, the privately owned means of production—must always serve workers and their work. Only then will human dominion advance in a way that corresponds to our dignity as creatures made in God's image. The divine order became inverted when the owners of the means of production, driven by the prospect of rapid material gain, violated the natural rights of their laborers, viewing human labor solely in terms of its economic significance. John Paul calls that "the error of economism," which, by placing products before persons, is also "an error of materialism."[39] This degrading estimation of human labor had two major consequences for workers. First, it led employers to deny laborers the right to economic initiative, thus suppressing their creative subjectivity. Second, it led employers to exploit and impoverish them both materially and humanly, effectively forcing labor into a position of dependence on capital. Thus, employers sought to maximize profits by denying their employees fair wages, decent working conditions, and the opportunity to improve their lot. In a sense, labor was separated from capital while remaining wholly dependent on it. Nevertheless, John Paul II reaffirms that Catholic social teaching does not regard the errors and abuses of capitalism as reason to reject, in principle, private ownership of the means of production.[40]

## The Concept of Work in Marxist Socialism: Subordinating the Person to the State

During the early industrial period, the conflict between capital and labor was interpreted by some as a socioeconomic class struggle. This interpretation was given ideological expression in Marxism, also known as scientific socialism and later as "real socialism"—communism—once Marxism (particularly as taken up by Lenin) crystallized into a state system. Against the ideology of liberal capitalism and the political systems based on it, Marxist socialism proposed and politically promoted the collectivization of the means of production, which workers were to seize from private hands and transfer to the state. By eliminating private property through the uprising of the "proletariat," or working class, the collectivist system was supposed to eliminate class differences and, consequently, the class injustices that ac-

38. *LE*, 14.

39. Ibid., 13.

40. Ibid., 14. See *RN*, 6–15; 46.

companied them. John Paul reminds us that according to the Marxist interpretation, socialism sees no need to restrain class conflict out of ethical or juridical considerations, nor out of respect for human dignity—even one's own. Given its utter disregard for reasonable boundaries, Marxist socialism will resort to any means—lies, force, terror, weapons—to impose its way, not only on the society engaged in class struggle, but also on nations and, ultimately, the whole of humanity. Thus, the Marxist doctrine of class struggle is inherently related to the imperialistic militarism of its time, and both are rooted in "atheism and contempt for the human person, which place the principle of force above that of reason and law."[41]

Because socialism is based on a false anthropology,[42] it has a negative impact on human acting and development. Like unbridled capitalism, socialism stifles worker creativity and initiative by subordinating legitimate personal interests to the operation of the socioeconomic system, which in this case is controlled by the state. Under socialism, each citizen is viewed as "a molecule within the social organism" or as "a 'cog' in the State machine,"[43] so that human labor is deprived of its dignity as a free activity of the person. Workers are supposed to realize their personal good without reference to their own freedom. But then "the concept of the person as the autonomous subject of moral decision disappears, the very subject whose decisions build the social order."[44]

In addition, since workers are deprived of the right to private property under the socialist system, they do not benefit from the fruits of their own labor. Having nothing to call their own, they become dependent on the social system and on those who presume to control it on their behalf. As the only body governing and deciding about society's goods and its means of production, the bureaucratic apparatus is also effectively their sole "owner." That is why the socialist system is really just a form of "state capitalism" that perpetuates class inequalities under a different guise.[45] At the same time, it reduces human beings to a series of socioeconomic relationships, making them less conscious of their surpassing personal dignity, while also disposing them to "opt out of national life" either by physically emigrating or by adopting a form of "psychological" emigration.[46] Psychological emigration

41. *CA*, 14. See *LE*, 11.

42. See *CA*, 13.

43. Ibid., 13 and 15 respectively. See *LE*, 15.

44. *CA*, 13.

45. See ibid., 35; *SRS*, 15.

46. *SRS*, 15. The element of "psychological emigration" underlies the attitudes of conformism and avoidance described in *Person and Act*. See *AP*, 344–48.

implies passivity and submissiveness, which means that those who succumb to it will not contribute actively to the formation of an authentically human community to the extent that conditions will allow. On the contrary, Marxist socialism fosters only the alienation of human existence.[47]

## The Consequences to Society of Disregarding Its Members as Persons and Free Agents

The relationship between employer and employee in liberal capitalism and that between the state and the working class in Marxist socialism were marred by the same underlying disorder, namely, a total disregard for the human person as the subject of work. In *Rerum Novarum*, Pope Leo XIII foresaw the danger of "the worker question" expanding to the state level as Marxist ideology sought to exploit and aggravate the conflict between capital and labor.[48] Once Marxist socialism did, in fact, take concrete form as communism established itself in various countries, it was not long before workers were caught in the middle of distorted, contentious, and exploitive international relationships, as the competition between the systems of East and West grew to global proportions. This resulted in the inordinate use of human, material, scientific, and technological resources for military purposes, which had a negative impact on national economies and so, too, on the nature of work, its availability, and the availability of crucial forms of assistance for the poor. Third World countries were among the most seriously affected by this situation.[49]

Leaving aside the military aspects and consequences of the historical conflict between East and West, however, we will now look at collectivism and capitalism according to the forms they assumed during the second half of the twentieth century, showing how a flawed anthropology has led in each case to disastrous social, economic, political, cultural, moral, and spiritual consequences that continue to plague us today. This means that the worker question, which is inextricably tied to the question of human development, remains unresolved. When we consider that peoples' lives are increasingly intertwined economically in today's world, we can expect that the persistence of the worker question will yield a personal and a social fallout that extends universally. It would therefore seem that workers, radically poor

47. See *CA*, 41.

48. See *RN*, 2, 4.

49. See *SRS*, 20–24; *CA*, 18.

people, and, indeed, the general population are more vulnerable than ever.

But for that reason, the principles that Leo XIII has set forth in *Rerum Novarum* can serve as a guiding light to the world today, beset as it is by seemingly insuperable socioeconomic difficulties, political corruption, cultural disintegration, moral uncertainty, and spiritual emptiness. Recognizing this, Leo's successor, Pope John Paul II, examines all these problems through the lens of Catholic social teaching and offers a coherent vision for solving them, one that centers firmly on the person, the subject of work. Further on, we will consider the challenging yet hopeful possibilities that John Paul holds out to workers and the poor as actors in a community of acting that extends as far as the human family itself.

## The Communist System: Depersonalizing Society by Suppressing Free Participation and Truth

True to its roots in "scientific socialism," communism is essentially atheistic. By denying the existence of God, the communist system suppresses people's awareness of their transcendent dignity while simultaneously depriving them of their inherent rights as persons. For example, communism will not permit people to act freely in their own interest, because its denial of God implies also a denial of transcendent truth, leaving no objective, mandatory basis for regulating human activity. From that perspective, it follows that competing interests would cause conflict between individuals, groups, and nations. Those claiming to have a deeper knowledge of society and immunity from error therefore take it on themselves to impose the communist order on others by exercising absolute power. There is no question here of trying to balance legitimate personal interests with a view toward the common good. Rather, it is a question of dominating others through the use of force, without regard for reason or law.[50] As John Paul II points out, however, "where self-interest is violently suppressed, it is replaced by a burdensome system of bureaucratic control which dries up the wellsprings of initiative and creativity."[51] The state nevertheless justifies its recourse to violence and domination in the belief that it will succeed in creating the perfect society, one that is free of evil. Given this utopian or perhaps tendentiously convenient view, politics becomes a kind of "secular religion."[52] Since the Church might appeal to an objective criterion of good and evil to judge the activity of the state managers, they must reject her or force her to submit to their ideological agenda.[53]

50. See *CA*, 14, 29, 44.
51. Ibid., 25.
52. See ibid.
53. See ibid., 45.

Because the people are not permitted to express their subjectivity freely in the political, social, economic, and cultural spheres of the totalitarian state, society is robbed of its personal, or subjective, character.[54] Thus denied the possibility of participating in society, those living under totalitarian dictatorships are not free to control their own destiny. They are not even permitted to retain a real sense of their own identity, as state efforts to destroy their historical memory and cultural roots have made clear.[55] The human person, made in God's image and possessing inviolable rights, is thus reduced to a mere instrument of production in the state machine. According to the state's ideology, human beings are not the efficient cause of production but rather the mere products of their economic or production relations.[56] Consequently, the state managers maintain that the needs of workers can be satisfied materially, without reference to a spiritual dimension within or beyond them.

Because the political and socioeconomic systems of these societies presuppose a false anthropology rooted in atheism, the relationship between the state that manages the means of production and the working class forced to use them is distorted, depriving society of the personal quality necessary for its continued survival. In turn, this explains the state's economic inefficiency and, consequently, its inability to supply the people's material needs—even the most basic ones. All that notwithstanding, the communist states of central and eastern Europe in the twentieth century continued to impose their way of life and their atheistic worldview on the people, who were not free to question or to change anything, even if it violated the norms of reason and moral conscience. They consequently experienced a spiritual void in their lives and a corresponding loss of the sense of life's meaning. The communist state thus sought to strip human beings of their dignity by violently suppressing, even destroying, all that is most personal in them, especially the right to seek the truth (both natural and revealed) and to act freely and intelligently in accordance with it. Yet, the search for personal identity and the meaning of life would continue to assert itself in the hearts of the people, a sure sign that change was in the offing.[57] At the same time, the Church would continue to defend her freedom of mission, precisely so as to defend the proper freedom of the human person, of the family, and of authentic social and national life.[58]

54. See ibid., 13.

55. See ibid., 18.

56. See *LE*, 13.

57. See *CA*, 24, 29.

58. See ibid., 45.

## The Capitalist System: The Danger of Placing Profits over Persons

Given their antithetical positions on human freedom, private ownership, and the organization of labor and society, the collectivist and capitalist systems are ideological opposites. Yet, in a different and perhaps more insidious way, the same problems that have undermined collectivism threaten the capitalist societies of the West. Like the totalitarian regimes inspired by Marxism, Western societies operate according to a materialistic view of human beings and their needs. Consistent with this is the false view that economic activity is free to create and to satisfy human needs artificially, without reference to or responsibility for the true good of the person as a bodily and spiritual whole. As a result, Western societies tend to see the human person "more as a producer or consumer of goods than as a subject who produces and consumes in order to live."[59]

The driving force behind an economic system that fosters the consumer mentality is greed, which seeks to maximize profits even at the cost of our humanity.[60] In a system like that, the value of laborers tends to be judged solely on the basis of their productivity—their ability to yield profitable results—regardless of whether their work enriches them as *persons*. The value of consumers is also degraded. Instead of trying to identify and satisfy authentic human needs so that we might experience ourselves more fully as persons, many producers try to maximize profits with products designed to arouse our instinctive human desire for purely material forms of immediate gratification. They might even enlist the mass media to help them achieve that aim.

The communications media are capable of exerting a dangerous influence on human behavior by manipulating human needs, tastes, and opinions.[61] In that way, economic activity creates consumer attitudes and lifestyles that are "objectively improper and often damaging to [man's] physical and spiritual health."[62] The consumer becomes preoccupied with possessing and enjoying things as an end in itself, without freely and rationally assessing their proper place in the objective order of values. Our desire to *have* more thus loses its connection with our vocation and our moral obligation

59. Ibid., 39.
60. See John Paul II, *Ecclesia in America* (January 22, 1999), 56, Vatican website.
61. See *CA*, 41.
62. Ibid., 36.

to *be* more.[63] The needs that we want to satisfy and the ways that we satisfy them become increasingly self-centered and materialistic as instinct and passion begin to control our behavior. Because we cannot fulfill ourselves as persons through self-centered materialism, our efforts to do so leave us spiritually empty and at a loss to understand life's meaning. We might then try to fill the void with artificial forms of consumption like drugs and pornography, which inevitably violate the well-being and personal dignity of anyone involved with or affected by them in any way.[64]

As always, John Paul II insists that the family, founded on the self-donation of a man and a woman to each other in marriage, is the structure most suited to the formation of a genuinely human environment. It is a sacred place in which children are conceived, welcomed, protected, nurtured, and educated. Here they learn their first lessons about truth and goodness, and about how to love and to *be* loved. Thus, each of us learns within the family what it means to be a person.[65]

Yet, negative elements within the social structure are discouraging the formation of true family life and attacking its integrity. In addition, people are coming to regard children as just another "thing" that one might or might not opt to "have." As a result, "human ingenuity seems to be directed more towards limiting, suppressing or destroying the sources of life—including recourse to abortion, which unfortunately is so widespread in the world—than towards defending and opening up the possibilities of life."[66] Worse still, wealthier nations that are hellishly bent on undermining the role of the family as the "sanctuary of life" are apparently not satisfied with confining their efforts to their own societies. They are also conducting coercive anti-childbearing campaigns abroad, disregarding the freedom of the world's poorest populations and pressuring them into accepting methods of demographic control that amount to a "new form of oppression."[67] Recently developed techniques carry this "to the point of poisoning the lives of millions of defenceless human beings, as if in a form of 'chemical warfare.'"[68] As we become more intent on "having," we become equally intent on depriving others of "being," lest they lay claim to a rightful share in what we want or

63. See *SRS*, 28; *RH*, 16; *GS*, 35. Elsewhere, John Paul II reminds us that "value comes not from what a person 'has' even if the person possessed the whole world!—as much as from what a person 'is': the goods of the world do not count as much as the good of the person, the good which is the person individually." *CL*, 37.

64. See *CA*, 36.

65. See ibid., 39.

66. Ibid.

67. Ibid., quoting *SRS*, 25.

68. Ibid., 39.

have already.[69] In that way, we unwittingly become less the being that *we* should be.

John Paul is careful to note that an economic system based on production and consumption is not, as such, the cause of these problems. Rather, it is when society absolutizes the role of economic life to the neglect of the social, ethical, and religious dimensions of human life that economic freedom oppresses and alienates us instead of contributing to our personal growth. In other words, the problems are cultural. Absolute freedom in the economic sphere not only subordinates our intrinsic value to the value of "things": it also encourages our futile attempt to satisfy ourselves materially and without any reference to objective truth. As a result, our *personal* freedom withers and our culture slides inevitably into decline. Society must work toward overcoming the "individualistic mentality" feeding the "culture of death," first of all, by reestablishing the family as the "sanctuary of life" founding a true *culture* of life.[70]

### Losing Our Sense of Self as We Lose Our Sense of God: Totalitarian Seed in Capitalistic Soil

According to the conditions prevailing at the time of its release, *Centesimus Annus* states that in terms of economic efficiency, capitalist societies have triumphed over Marxist ones. As we have already indicated, however, the encyclical finds disturbing parallels between the two types of society, such that the "triumph" of capitalism is by no means certain. While not officially atheistic and perhaps even claiming the contrary, Western consumer societies are exhibiting and sanctioning a practical atheism in the most crucial areas of social life. By denying "an autonomous existence and value to morality, law, culture and religion," they agree with Marxism in reducing human beings "to the sphere of economics and the satisfaction of material needs."[71] Society reinforces that vacuous anthropology by psychologically bludgeoning us through the mass media, which, by relentless appeal to our instincts and passions, erode our reason and will to the point where we accept and adopt ways of thinking and acting that wholly contradict our transcendent dignity as persons. In that way, the consumer society seeks "to convince man that he is free from every law and from God himself, thus imprisoning him within a selfishness which ultimately harms both him and others."[72]

69. See *Familiaris Consortio*, 30.

70. See *CA*, 39, 49.

71. Ibid., 19.

72. Ibid., 55. John Paul warns of "*the slavish conformity of cultures*, or at least key aspects

Given the manipulative and subversive power of the media, we can say without exaggeration that in Western consumer societies, force predominates over reason in a way different from, but in the end just as brutal as, that of the former communist regimes. Behavioral conditioning amounts to a subtle but powerful form of coercion by which society suppresses the natural human need to pursue truth, goodness, beauty, and the meaning of life. This makes us unmindful of our historical heritage—that is, of the legal, ethical, cultural, and religious foundations on which our society was originally built, and from which it derived its stability. However, it is only by exercising self-control in obedience to the truth about ourselves and about God that we become free to participate constructively in the formation of an authentic human community ordered toward our final destiny in God.

The inverted order of force and reason in the West, as in Marxist societies, is based on false anthropological presuppositions that extend into the political realm. Because our consumer societies have largely convinced us that we are most free when freed *from* the truth rather than *for* the truth about ourselves and God, there is now a widespread tendency to identify that notion of freedom with democracy, "a tendency to claim that agnosticism and sceptical relativism are the philosophy and the basic attitude which correspond to democratic forms of political life."[73] A democratic system based on that understanding regards truth as variable according to time and circumstance, or as that which is determined by the majority. Morality, law, and the notion of human rights and dignity then become subject to arbitrary interpretations and hence devoid of any real meaning. The same thing happens to the concept of the true common good, if it is ever even considered at all. In that kind of atmosphere, political figures are inclined to make and to justify decisions aimed at satisfying the demands of groups wielding electoral or financial power, while ignoring the demands of justice and morality.[74] John Paul therefore observes rightly that "if there is no ultimate truth to guide and direct political activity, then ideas and convictions can easily be manipulated for reasons of power. As history demonstrates, a democracy without values easily turns into open or thinly disguised totalitarianism."[75]

---

of them, to cultural models deriving from the Western world," summarizing the basic dangers inherent in contemporary Western "models." See "Message of His Holiness Pope John Paul II for the Celebration of the World Day of Peace" (January 1, 2001), 9, Vatican website.

73. *CA*, 46. See *Fides et Ratio*, 5.

74. See *CA*, 47.

75. Ibid., 46. See *Ecclesia in America*, 19; Leo XIII, *Libertas* (June 20, 1888), 16, 31, Vatican website.

We have seen that in totalitarian collectivist systems, the people are forcibly subjugated to the state. In the democratic capitalist systems of the West, there is a preliminary phase in which the people are manipulated, in the name of freedom, to reject the true and abiding order of values and to become slaves of their own passions. In addition, many people refuse to participate in the political process, either because civic spirit is lacking or because they are disillusioned by repeated violations of the public trust on the part of elected officials.[76] Unless reversed, the resulting social disintegration will directly precede and precipitate subjugation to the state.

We should note here that in *Centesimus Annus*, 42, John Paul II makes some favorable remarks about capitalism, at least relative to Marxism. But those remarks are clearly cautious and qualified. "[C]an it perhaps be said that, after the failure of Communism, capitalism is the victorious social system, and that capitalism should be the goal of the countries now making efforts to rebuild their economy and society?" Moreover, is capitalism the model that ought to be proposed to Third World countries seeking "true economic and civil progress?" After indicating that the answer is complex, John Paul continues:

> If by "capitalism" is meant an economic system which recognizes the fundamental and positive role of business, the market, private property and the resulting responsibility for the means of production, as well as free human creativity in the economic sector, then the answer is certainly in the affirmative.... But if by "capitalism" is meant a system in which freedom in the economic sector is not circumscribed within a strong juridical framework which places it at the service of human freedom in its totality, and which sees it as a particular aspect of that freedom, the core of which is ethical and religious, then the reply is certainly negative.

If one reads to the end of the paragraph (or considers the encyclical as a whole), John Paul gives us absolutely no reason to think that, in his view, the kind of capitalist system he would find acceptable as a model for other countries actually exists. On the contrary, he says that "there is a risk that a radical capitalistic ideology could spread," one that does nothing to help eliminate the marginalization, the exploitation, the alienation, and the "great material and moral poverty" that remain in the world, even in the more advanced countries.

It is true that a capitalist society has the potential to enable all its members to participate freely and creatively in the economic sector. That is a key

76. See *CA*, 47.

issue for John Paul II, along with the regulation of the economy according to truly just moral principles so that it will operate in a way that promotes the true good of each and all. But it is also fair to say that John Paul would not have been opposed in principle to other economic models on which to build society, as long as they satisfied the conditions he has laid out. And so he says in the very next paragraph, "The Church has no models to present; models that are real and truly effective can only arise within the framework of different historical situations, through the efforts of all those who responsibly confront concrete problems in all their social, economic, political and cultural aspects, as these interact with one another."[77]

### Capitalism's Socioeconomic Impact on Third World Workers as Persons and Actors

While advanced capitalistic societies have largely overcome the kind of opposition between capital and labor that existed in the early period of industrialization, history is, unfortunately, in some ways repeating itself in countries trying to develop along the lines of a free market system. In Third World settings, workers are still being deprived of necessities such as adequate wages, humane working conditions, unemployment insurance, and retirement benefits.[78] Beyond the question of workers' rights, a distinctly modern problem is adding to the difficulties facing developing countries. The old subsistence economies of most of the world's populations can neither compete with nor be suitably integrated into the advanced economic activities taking place at the international level. Few people have access to the knowledge and training that would enable them to modernize their methods of production and to fulfill their potential as human resources whose initiative, creativity, organizational skills, and entrepreneurial ability would qualify them to enter the international market. "[E]conomic development takes place over their heads, so to speak."[79]

Many people who, through no fault of their own, cannot improve their condition by themselves enter crowded Third World cities in the desperate hope of finding lucrative opportunities; however, they often find themselves culturally displaced and sometimes even "exposed to situations of violent uncertainty, without the possibility of becoming integrated."[80] What is more, their struggle to provide for their most basic needs takes place "in conditions

77. Ibid., 43.

78. See ibid., 34.

79. Ibid., 33.

80. Ibid.

of 'ruthlessness' in no way inferior to the darkest moments of the first phase of industrialization."[81] Thus, the poor in the Third World are especially vulnerable to being exploited, both because of their material poverty and because of a poverty of knowledge and training that "prevents them from escaping their state of humiliating subjection."[82]

Workers in Third World countries are threatened not only by internal conditions such as underdevelopment, lack of higher education, sociocultural displacement, and exploitation, but also by labor policies regulated by developed countries. On the one hand, trade establishes interdependent economic relations among individual states, which is in itself a normal and potentially positive development. However, it also allows powerful states and especially the big corporations directing production to fix the highest possible prices for their products, while reducing prices to the lowest possible level for the raw materials and semi-manufactured goods that come from poorer societies for use in production. That injustice is a significant cause of the great disparity between national incomes, and workers in the disadvantaged countries invariably get caught in the middle because their employer keeps the working conditions of his laborers at a substandard level so as to secure for himself the highest possible profit in a system manipulated by foreign interests to their *own* advantage.[83]

While economic, financial, and social mechanisms seem often to function almost automatically, they are ultimately manipulated by people, particularly those of the more developed countries. Consequently, as the economic gap between rich and poor widens, workers in poor countries might be tempted to react violently.[84] At the same time, the injustice caused by international relations lacking an ethical foundation ultimately recoils on the rich countries themselves, which begin to manifest signs of underdevelopment such as widespread unemployment and homelessness. Clearly, then, "development either becomes shared in common by every part of the world or it undergoes a process of regression even in zones marked by constant progress."[85]

81. Ibid.

82. Ibid.

83. See *LE*, 17; *SRS*, 43.

84. See *CA*, 10; *LE*, 18; and Paul VI, *PPro*, 30.

85. *SRS*, 17. In *SRS* 14, 16, and 17, and in *CA*, 33, John Paul II makes passing references to the "Fourth World." According to note 31 in *SRS*, "The expression 'Fourth World' is used not just occasionally for the so-called less advanced countries, but also and especially for the bands of great or extreme poverty in countries of medium and high income." This "World" within our world knows no boundaries. It is characterized by poverty so extreme that its victims lack—indeed, they are

It is therefore imperative that wealthy nations that have made loans to help Third World countries invest in development defer, lighten, or even cancel the debt as the only ethically proper response to situations where the debtor nations, to service their loans, have no choice but to export the very resources they need for their own development. Short of that, whole peoples might be reduced to hunger and despair,[86] perhaps provoking them to respond with violence against those perpetrating the injustice.[87] "At the root of war there are usually real and serious grievances: injustices suffered, legitimate aspirations frustrated, poverty, and the exploitation of multitudes of desperate people who see no real possibility of improving their lot by peaceful means."[88] Here again, John Paul II's words serve as a sobering reminder that the only sure path to peace is through equitable and genuinely human development.

We must also heed John Paul's frequent reminders that poverty or underdevelopment is not just an economic matter, nor therefore is development merely a function of economic growth.[89] While it is true that the poor are hindered from "being" because they have too little, it is also true that the rich are often hindered from "being" because they have *too much*.[90] Possessed by the need to possess, they become enslaved to "things" and to profits, the desire for which leads to a thirst for power over others.[91] This can happen not only to individual persons, but also to whole nations, which introduce "structures of sin" to solidify their standing over other nations. In that case, we find that "behind certain decisions, apparently inspired only by economics or politics, are real forms of idolatry: of money, ideology, class, technology."[92] This is a real moral and spiritual poverty, born of a social, cultural,

often systematically deprived of—even the most basic resources necessary to improve their lot. And they are often ostracized and treated as though they are without dignity because of their situation. Father Joseph Wresinski (1917–1988), who dedicated his whole priestly life to living among and advocating for the poorest of the poor, coined the expression "Fourth World." Together with poor families and a group of committed volunteers, he founded the international movement, ATD Fourth World. His ideas about the poor coincide on many points with those of John Paul II. See Alwine de Vos van Steenwijk, *Father Joseph Wresinski: Voice of the Poorest*, trans. Charles Sleeth (Santa Barbara, Calif.: Queenship Publishing, 1996).

86. See *SRS*, 19; *CA*, 35.

87. See *SRS*, 10; *LE*, 18.

88. *CA*, 52.

89. See ibid., 13, 29, 39, 40, 57, 60, 61; *SRS*, 9, 15, 17, 27–29, 32, 33, 46; *LE*, 15. See also Paul VI, *PPro*, 13, 14, 34.

90. See *SRS*, 28; *Redemptoris Missio*, 59.

91. *SRS*, 37. See Jas 4:1–2.

92. *SRS*, 37. "The acquisition of worldly goods can lead men to greed, to the unrelenting desire for more, to the pursuit of greater personal power. Rich and poor alike—be they individuals, families or nations—can fall prey to avarice and soul-stifling materialism." Paul VI, *PPro*.

and religious poverty that precludes the true freedom and development of both the dominating societies and those subject to them.[93]

As John Paul points out in *Sollicitudo Rei Socialis*, 28,

> the difference between "being" and "having," the danger inherent in a mere multiplication or replacement of things possessed compared to the value of "being," need not turn into a contradiction.... The evil does not consist in "having" as such, but in possessing without regard for the quality and the ordered hierarchy of the goods one has. Quality and hierarchy arise from the subordination of goods and their availability to man's "being" and his true vocation. This shows that although development has a necessary economic dimension ... it is not limited to that dimension. If it is limited to this, then it turns against those whom it is meant to benefit.

The tenor of John Paul II's social encyclicals does, in fact, indicate that this limited concept of development dominates contemporary societies, that a contradiction between authentic "being" and "having" really exists on a wide scale. The reason is this: we have widely become unmindful of God, which means that we have also become, inevitably, unmindful of man and his true good. Only a truly Christian society—or, minimally, a society based thoroughly on the natural law and responsive to the invisible movement of grace—is capable of overcoming the contradiction that has arisen in today's world between "being" and "having." And one would be hard pressed to find such a society today, unless we scale down to consider some of the smaller "societies" therein, including certain religious communities and, of course, exemplary individual families. Fundamental to John Paul's vision for resolving this crucial problem is the widespread acceptance and practice of a genuinely human solidarity.

## Human Solidarity and Its Expression in Authentic Human Action

Drawing on Pope John Paul II's social encyclicals, we have examined various social, cultural, political, economic, moral, and spiritual threats to human persons and their agency—threats that often result in or from the degradation of workers through the deprivation of their legitimate rights. While these different threats impinge seriously on the person's freedom of self-determination, John Paul insists that human freedom cannot ultimately be

93. Recalling the words of St. Augustine, Cardinal Wojtyła noted that the "'amor sui usque ad contemptum Dei' in its various forms and dimensions lies at the root of all the ruthless exploitation of men by other men." *SgC*, 58–59.

overcome. Nor, therefore, is it subject to "blind" economic forces. Constructive socioeconomic change is possible when human beings become the protagonists of development—that is, when they engage their freedom in mature, personal action. But such change also requires the collaboration of the actors. According to John Paul's understanding, genuine solidarity among vulnerable workers, the poor, and those who are, comparatively speaking, economically independent is inspired by a common resolve to act (indeed, to *labor*) for the true common good. Solidarity of that kind leads to the transformation of dehumanizing structures into their opposite and to the self-realization of each and all as persons.

Solidarity is a specifically personal trait, not a vague feeling of closeness, compassion, or pity.[94] We saw in chapter 3 that it is rooted in the shared humanity by which we each have reference to every other human being as our *neighbor.* Because solidarity grounds our efforts to secure the common good in love, truth, and freedom, it is a dynamic principle of action that gives rise to new human relationships of mutual service. That is why it transforms unjust or inadequate forms of social organization into structures that foster human dignity and development, inviting and facilitating the creative participation of all.

Human labor utilizes the riches of the earth intended for everyone, which is one reason why, over time, it links people together on a universal scale. Accordingly, John Paul observes that work bears "the mark of a person operating within a community of persons."[95] Human labor is meant to draw people together, not drive them apart.[96] Once individuals, peoples, and nations recognize their radical interdependence and the dignity of one and all, they will also recognize "the need for a solidarity which will take up interdependence and transfer it to the moral plane."[97] Therefore, to address the various threats against the development of peoples and, more fundamentally, against the worker as a person and an actor, John Paul proposes that all individuals, peoples, and nations cultivate and act according to the moral and social attitude—the *virtue*—of solidarity.[98] In *Sollicitudo Rei Socialis,* he defines solidarity essentially as he does in *Person and Act.* It is "a firm and persevering determination to commit oneself to the common good; that is

94. See *SRS,* 38.

95. *LE,* opening remarks.

96. See ibid., 20; *CA,* 27.

97. *SRS,* 26.

98. See ibid., 38. See also Kevin P. Doran, *Solidarity: A Synthesis of Personalism and Communalism in the Thought of Karol Wojtyła/Pope John Paul II,* American University Studies, Series 7: Theology and Religion 190 (New York: Peter Lang, 1996), 155–57, 192–93, 239.

to say to the good of all and of each individual, because we are all really responsible for all."[99] John Paul II presents the attitude of solidarity as the antidote for our excessive desire for profit and our thirst for power. The sinful attitudes that give rise to those dispositions underlie the exploitation of workers and the underdevelopment of peoples because we end up concretizing them in the many "structures of sin" that perpetuate injustice and impede true human development. For that reason, we must effectively counter them by their inverse, namely, the attitude of solidarity and the actions that flow from it.[100] History has already confirmed the need for and the effectiveness of genuinely human solidarity, which is "the path to peace and at the same time to development."[101]

### Workers' Unions as an Expression of Solidarity

The "worker question" of the nineteenth century and the problems connected with it "gave rise to a just social reaction and caused the impetuous emergence of a great burst of solidarity between workers, first and foremost industrial workers."[102] The reaction of the workers was just and, indeed, "eloquent" from the standpoint of social morality because it represented a united effort to uphold the dignity of the person as the subject of work. In the early industrial period, these subjects of work were fast becoming subordinated to the industrial machines on which they *performed* their work, and so depersonalized in that respect.[103] At the same time, employers were exploiting and impoverishing workers by denying them just wages, decent working conditions, and social security for themselves and their families. The workers' movement therefore "began as a response of moral conscience to unjust and harmful situations."[104]

For their part, workers were obliged to respond within the bounds of justice and morality. Indeed, they would not have otherwise succeeded in forming an authentic community of acting capable of effecting constructive change in the socioeconomic sphere. The history and experience of Marxist socialism would ultimately verify that. Marxism framed the worker's struggle for social justice in terms of a *class* struggle that could be resolved only through violence. Social upheaval was supposed to usher in a new political and socioeconomic order marked by equality and justice. But by applying

99. *SRS*, 38. See *AP*, 341–42; Doran, *Solidarity*, 203–5.

100. See *SRS*, 36–38.

101. Ibid., 39.

102. *LE*, 8.

103. See ibid, 5, 8.

104. *CA*, 16.

the military doctrine of "total war" to internal conflicts, Marxism sought to achieve its ends without any ethical or juridical restraint, thus excluding the possibility of reasonable compromise.[105] When human beings exercise their freedom without regard for truth, goodness, and the just demands of law, they neither care to act in a way that is truly collaborative and self-actualizing nor are they able to do so, for they disregard thereby the very conditions by which alone they can perform such an act. Freedom is then used arbitrarily and ends up "submitting itself to the vilest of passions, to the point of self-destruction."[106] Solidarity movements in the sphere of work (or in any other sphere) must, on the contrary, remain open to genuine dialogue and collaboration with others.[107]

In particular, John Paul II is speaking here about the role and responsibility of trade or labor unions in upholding the rights of workers. If we have a duty to fulfill the Creator's will, our own needs, and the needs of others through work, then we have also an implicit *right* to work.[108] At the same time, our work and everything connected with it must correspond to our dignity as persons. It follows that certain rights are due to workers—rights that flow from and uphold those connatural to them as human beings. Labor unions are themselves an expression of the right of workers to form free associations aimed at securing and protecting their legitimate rights and interests as persons. Human beings have, for example, a natural right to a decent level of subsistence and hence to a just wage in return for the work they perform. In most cases, the wage is the means of assuring that workers have access to the goods intended for all, with something left over for savings.

What is more, human beings have a natural right to found a family, entitling workers to a *family wage* sufficient for supporting their dependents in all their essential needs. A just wage is therefore the principal indicator of whether a socioeconomic system is functioning in a just way. It is also the most important means of securing a just relationship between workers and their employers.[109] Worker solidarity in the form of unions is the key to achieving that end. It is equally indispensable for persuading businesses to invite greater worker initiative, participation, and responsibility, so that each business becomes a "society of persons" where, through dignified work, laborers can fulfill their own needs while serving the needs of society.[110] In the end, this will contribute to the success of the business itself.

105. See ibid., 14.

106. Ibid., 4. See Leo XIII, *Libertas*, 1, 16.

107. See *LE*, 8.

108. See *CA*, 43.

109. See *LE*, 19.

110. See *CA*, 35, 43.

Among other workers' rights, John Paul (basing himself on *Rerum Novarum*) mentions the right to compensation for work-related accidents and to health insurance for workers and their families, the right to an adequate pension for retirement, the right to working conditions that do not jeopardize a person's health or moral integrity, the right to periods of daily rest, to Sunday rest (so that workers can fulfill their religious duties), and to annual vacation periods,[111] and the right of women who freely choose to work to fulfill their irreplaceable mission within the family as mothers, without their being penalized in the workplace as a result.[112] By negotiating on issues such as labor contracts, wages, working conditions, and social legislation, labor unions can help bring about needed reforms in the socioeconomic life of society. Though traditionally associated with industrial workers, labor unions have become a necessary expression of solidarity among workers in manual, artistic, scientific, and agricultural occupations, to name a few. Even groups of intellectuals whose field of employment is saturated, whose educational background does not correspond to available employment opportunities, or whose professional expertise is no longer in demand require the protection afforded by workers' unions. Among other things, union organizations can provide workers with educational and training opportunities that will make them capable not only of *having* more but of *being* more.[113]

When labor unions fulfill their proper role, they help secure the just good of workers and also the good of society. By aiming at true social justice and not the elimination of the opponent, union activity can restore work's power to unite capital and labor into a community of persons, one dedicated to the formation of a just social order. This is not to say that the struggle for social justice will never have its confrontational moments. But even these social tensions can and must be transformed by a true spirit of solidarity, which includes openness to dialogue, respect for and collaboration with others, and genuine concern for the common good. From that standpoint, the struggle inherent in true solidarity "is not a struggle against other persons, but the struggle of a person with himself, and of a society with its own values and structures."[114]

Workers' unions manifest their concern for the common good when they consider realistically the limitations imposed by the country's general economic condition, even as they seek to improve the worker's lot and to correct defects in the socioeconomic system. In addition, they must use the right of

111. See *LE*, 19; *CA*, 7, 9, 15.

112. See *LE*, 19.

113. See ibid., 8, 20.

114. Doran, *Solidarity*, 222. See *LE*, 20.

workers to strike only as a last resort, and in the event of a strike they must never violate the demands of justice by preventing crucial services from being delivered to the community or by paralyzing society's socioeconomic life. Thus, when the activity of workers' unions is motivated by a just cause, the end sought must still be achieved by just means. Short of that, union activity will serve neither the true common good nor, therefore, the cause of advancing the self-realization of each worker as a person through work. To put it another way, if either capital or the state is exploiting labor, workers will truly *act* to improve their situation and thus grow humanly only through a genuine spirit of solidarity, one that extends to employers, to society, to the state, and ultimately to the whole of humanity.

### Society, the State, and the International Community in Solidarity with the Worker

Pope John Paul II affirms that society, the state, and even international organizations, governed as they are by real people, are obliged to enter solidarity with workers by supplementing and supporting the legitimate efforts of their associations. Both society and the state have an active role to play in regulating economic activity so as to promote healthy economic growth, fair business practices, and the creation or the continuation of dignified forms of work, all in keeping with the true common good. In the event of unemployment, societal and state intervention might be necessary to assist those affected, for example, by providing unemployment benefits and retraining programs that prepare unemployed workers to enter vigorous sectors of the economy. The duty to assist unemployed workers and their families with grants for their subsistence stems from the principle of the universal destination of goods and, even more fundamentally, from the right to life.[115] While economic activity must enjoy a certain autonomy, the state has nevertheless a legitimate role in overseeing and regulating that activity. *Indirectly* and according to the principle of *subsidiarity*, the state must create and safeguard the conditions of a free economy, thus stimulating employment opportunities and an increase in the sources of wealth. *Directly* and according to the principle of *solidarity*, it must defend the most vulnerable workers, including immigrants, by limiting the autonomy of those who determine working conditions. And it must ensure adequate training and support for the unemployed.[116]

The state has also the task of defending and preserving collective goods

115. See *LE*, 18.
116. See *CA*, 15; *LE*, 23.

such as the natural and the human environments. Free market mechanisms do not satisfy the need for goods pertaining to those orders, though such goods are necessary for the integral development of human persons and for enabling them to attain legitimate personal goals.[117] It is especially important for the state to encourage the growth of authentic family life, in which husband and wife commit themselves to each other, to their children, and to elderly family members in a spirit of solidarity and charity. As a "community of work and solidarity,"[118] the family unit is essential to the integrity and human character of social life, as well as to overcoming the widespread individualism of the day. It also strengthens the relations between generations. The state has therefore an interest in formulating social policies that will help the family fulfill its indispensable role in society.[119]

In view of the economic interdependence of different societies and states in today's world, international collaboration is also necessary for overseeing the economy and directing it to the true common good.[120] Toward that end, nations working together in a spirit of solidarity should establish treaties and agreements that promote work as a fundamental human right. Such efforts would also have to ensure the rights of the person as the *subject* of work, so that the people of every society would be able to enjoy a truly decent standard of living. Universal progress in the area of human development is the prerequisite for universal justice and peace, especially insofar as it eliminates tensions leading to conflict and encourages reconciliation among peoples.

Since "it is always man who is the protagonist of development,"[121] true progress "must be made through man and for man and it must produce its fruit in man."[122] That is why the nations of the world must accept the responsibility of transforming their interdependence into a real display of solidarity that aims to achieve an equitable distribution of the goods meant for all.[123] Above all, they must accomplish this by ensuring that those capable of work have the opportunity to make a meaningful contribution to the common good through their labors. In that way, workers can also achieve their *own* good and thus realize themselves as persons. John Paul warns us that when

117. See *CA*, 40.

118. Ibid., 49.

119. See ibid. See also no. 48, regarding other tasks of the state, which include guaranteeing the right to private property, preventing monopolies from hindering development, and direct (though instrumental and temporary) intervention when social sectors or business systems are too weak to fulfill their proper roles.

120. See ibid., 58.

121. *SRS*, 30.

122. *LE*, 18.

123. See *RH*, 16.

the interdependence of nations is divorced from its ethical requirements, disastrous consequences follow for the weakest members of society.[124]

### The Sacrificial Demands of Solidarity between the Rich and the Poor

Those who "have" will be more inclined to help those who "have not" when they stop viewing them as "a burden, as irksome intruders trying to consume what others have produced."[125] The poor, after all, have a right to survive. What is more, they are entitled to a rightful share in the material goods intended for all, along with the opportunity to work for and to help produce those goods. To an extent, poor people provide an opportunity and an incentive for *others* to act in a generous spirit of solidarity, especially when persons more fortunate regard them properly as sources of greater enrichment for everyone. Likewise, by thinking more kindly of the poor, prosperous nations will be more inclined to recognize their moral obligation to make appropriate sacrifices to help lift them out their poverty.

To begin with, the interdependence of nations demands "the sacrifice of all forms of economic, military, or political imperialism, and the transformation of mutual distrust into collaboration."[126] In the context of "the politics of blocs" (referring to the antagonism between East and West during the Cold War), John Paul II stated that this kind of sacrifice "is precisely the act proper to solidarity among individuals and nations."[127] The sacrificial act of solidarity necessarily precedes the mobilization of resources that encourage economic growth and common development. Vast resources could be freed up by military arms reductions, by resolving conflicts through diplomatic intervention, and by arms control.[128]

At the same time, prosperous nations must reorder their values so that economic and political choices affecting the poor and the marginalized will reflect the demands of morality and justice rather than pure self-interest. That, too, requires a great spirit of sacrifice and solidarity. It is ultimately "respect for the objective rights of the worker ... that must constitute *the adequate and fundamental criterion* for shaping the whole economy, both on the level of the individual society and State and within the whole of the world economic policy and of the systems of international relationships that derive from it."[129] International organizations like the *International Labor Organiza-*

124. See *SRS*, 17.
125. *CA*, 28; see no. 58.
126. *SRS*, 39.
127. Ibid.
128. See *CA*, 28.
129. *LE*, 17.

*tion* and the *Food and Agriculture Organization,* both agencies of the United Nations, can exert a constructive influence here.[130] Once the path to true human development has been cleared by voluntary, sacrificial means, the poor will have greater opportunities to exercise their capacity for work, contributing in their own way to the material, cultural, and moral growth of their nations, while also enriching, by extension, the whole of humanity.

For their part, the people in each developing country are obliged to make appropriate use of the opportunities that the developed countries provide. In solidarity with one another and with the more advanced nations, poorer nations must work to overcome the underdevelopment and deterioration that have been caused, in part, by the serious failures of their own economic and political leaders.[131] Their efforts must aim at achieving economic and political stability, increased food production, greater literacy and access to information, the improvement of workers' skills, and the training of responsible business leaders. In addition, poorer nations must carefully ascertain the true needs of society and initiate ways of supplying them.

In these ways, and by combining their productive capabilities, poorer nations will become less dependent on more powerful producers.[132] They will also prepare themselves to enter the international market, an opportunity that the international community, if imbued with the spirit of solidarity, will open to them. Once the more advanced economies come to value the human potential and contribution of the poor, they might be more willing to sacrifice income, positions of power, and lifestyles wasteful of resources intended for all.[133] The spirit of solidarity also implies the willingness of the poor to assume responsibility for their own development, and hence to sacrifice the passive attitude that would perpetuate their dependence on wealthier nations. What is more, poor people united in true solidarity will sacrifice the *destructive* attitude that sees violence as the answer to injustice, corruption, and inefficiency. Instead, they will seek to advance their cause through peaceful public demonstrations, mutual support, and unwavering commitment to the true common good.[134] Getting right to the heart of the matter, Pope John Paul II declares that "solidarity demands a readiness to accept the sacrifices necessary for the good of the whole world community."[135]

130. See ibid.
131. See *SRS*, 16.
132. See *CA*, 35; *SRS*, 44, 45.
133. See *CA*, 52.
134. See *SRS*, 39.
135. Ibid., 45.

### Worker Solidarity as an Active Stance against Communism

Underlying the attitude of solidarity is one's awareness that one is a person and that every other human being is equally a person. The fall of oppressive regimes worldwide in the 1980s and beyond was often linked to that awareness. People recognized that their personal dignity was being violated under those regimes, but they also understood that they would have to address the situation in ways that respected the dignity of others—even that of their oppressors. In that light, John Paul II examines the collapse of communism in central and eastern Europe beginning in 1989.

For John Paul, the decisive factor leading to that remarkable outcome was the violation of workers' rights by totalitarian systems claiming to speak for the working class. The "crisis of systems" reached its peak with the Solidarity movement in Poland, where, "on the basis of a hard, lived experience of work and of oppression," the people "rediscovered the content and principles of the Church's social doctrine."[136] He finds it particularly noteworthy that the collapse of the Eastern bloc was accomplished largely through peaceful protest marked by dialogue and a willingness to negotiate. Armed only with the weapons of truth and justice, the people renounced the way of violent confrontation characteristic of Marxism, while yet refusing to bow to the threat of force. They appealed instead to their adversary's conscience, "seeking to reawaken in him a sense of shared human dignity."[137] By faithfully bearing witness to the truth of human dignity in a genuine spirit of solidarity, oppressed workers acted powerfully to disarm the adversary, since they did not give violence an opportunity "to justify itself through deceit, and to appear, however falsely, to be defending a right or responding to a threat posed by others."[138]

John Paul identifies economic inefficiency as the second factor in the crisis of Marxism. He points out that the problem with the collectivist economic system was not so much technical as "a consequence of the violation of the human rights to private initiative, to ownership of property and to freedom in the economic sector."[139] He is also quick to add that a distorted economic

136. *CA*, 23.

137. Ibid.

138. Ibid. The liberty of conscience by which man obeys the will of God despite the state's defiance of divine law "nobly maintains the dignity of man and is stronger than all violence or wrong." Leo XIII, *Libertas*, 30.

139. *CA*, 24.

structure is not enough to explain the dissolution of communism in east central Europe. We must also take into account how the moral and cultural life of the communist countries became corrupted through the state's effort to eliminate both the question of God from society and the implications of that question for understanding and ordering human life in society.

Ironically, all these threats to the worker's person and agency ended up threatening and defeating communism itself, which could neither completely nor indefinitely suppress the truth about man and about God in the human heart. Those who remained faithful to God despite oppression and persecution bear eloquent witness to that. Their lives also prove that human freedom has the power to transcend factors that condition and impinge on its exercise. Our ability to act in a truly human way is so intimately personal that coercive efforts to constrain our free activity are ultimately doomed to fail, with dire consequences for the society that presumed to try and constrain it so.[140] Human freedom strives to express itself not only in the economic sphere, but also in the spheres of culture, morality, and religion, as we grapple with the meaning of our existence. That is why "the struggle to defend work was spontaneously linked to the struggle for culture and for national rights."[141]

Sometimes "the irrepressible search for personal identity and for the meaning of life" underlying the triumphant reassertion of human freedom in its struggle against the depersonalizing injustices of totalitarian oppression led the spiritually hungry "to rediscover the person of Christ himself as the existentially adequate response to the desire in every human heart for goodness, truth and life."[142] Indeed, the "Gospel spirit" was necessary "in the face of an adversary determined not to be bound by moral principles."[143] It provided clarity of vision in a time of moral darkness, thus serving as a moderating influence when the temptation to meet violence with violence might easily have overwhelmed people's willingness to act with proper restraint. Every human being must give due regard to the demands of justice and morality in order to act freely for the true good and thus to realize him- or herself as a person. That is no less true when acting in solidarity with others. Those who unite in action can realize themselves freely as persons only by serving the true common good, and they can realize that good only by means corresponding to the dictates of right reason expressed as practical truth in conscience.

140. See ibid., 25; Paul VI, *PPro*, 15.

141. *CA*, 24.

142. Ibid.

143. Ibid., 25.

The struggle leading to the 1989 downfall of communist regimes in Europe was sustained by great personal suffering and sacrifice born of the Gospel spirit of solidarity with the crucified Christ. That same spirit is always bound to solidarity with one's "neighbor." The seemingly passive condition of those burdened under the yoke of communism was thus transformed into a powerful—indeed, an irresistible—form of genuine human activity, or "fruitful passivity." "It is by uniting his own sufferings for the sake of truth and freedom to the sufferings of Christ on the Cross that man is able to accomplish the miracle of peace and is in a position to discern the often narrow path between the cowardice which gives in to evil and the violence which, under the illusion of fighting evil, only makes it worse."[144] John Paul acknowledges rightly that this prayer-inspired method of struggle with and peaceful victory over communist tyranny would have been inconceivable "without immense trust in God, the Lord of history."[145] The faith in Christ that the Church imparts to others "not only helps people to find solutions; it makes even situations of suffering humanly bearable, so that in these situations people will not become lost or forget their dignity and vocation."[146]

John Paul II wisely advised the people living in European countries trying to rebuild themselves after the downfall of communism that they could not afford to slacken the moral commitment and conscious witness to the truth that inspired their successful stand against their oppressors. Economic rebuilding must be complemented by *moral* rebuilding.[147] He warned, moreover, that the temptation to resort to violence still looms in human hearts wounded by past injustices between individuals, groups, and nations. That is why he expressed the hope that "all people will grow in the spirit of peace and forgiveness."[148] When people overcome hatred by forgiving one another, they each perform a most personal and truly self-fulfilling act, without which their efforts to rebuild society will ultimately fail.[149] The experience with communism had already proven that violence and injustice cannot found a lasting social order. What is more, John Paul encouraged the creation or the consolidation of international structures that could arbitrate dis-

144. Ibid. See *LE*, 27.

145. *CA*, 25.

146. Ibid., 59. "The man who is strong with the strength given him by faith does not easily allow himself to be thrust into the anonymity of the collective." *SgC*, 200–201.

147. See *CA*, 27.

148. Ibid., 27.

149. "From the Christian point of view [the path of forgiveness and reconciliation] is the only path which leads to the goal of peace." John Paul II, "World Day of Peace" message, 21.

putes arising between nations about the legitimate rights of each. Of course, these "structures" would have to consist of competent groups of people acting in solidarity with and for the sake of others.

Beyond that, the formerly communist countries of east central Europe would be entitled to receive material assistance from wealthy nations, whose abundance obliged them to share their own resources. This would also represent a debt of justice on the part of the European countries that bear some responsibility for the historical events leading to the violent imposition of communism on their neighbors. Under the communist system, the subjugated countries were often regarded as "objects" and so prevented from acting as *subjects* of their own development.[150] As a result, they now struggled with material shortages and demoralized spirits. While the formerly communist countries would have to take on the responsibility of becoming the primary agents of their own development, the aid that they would receive from other nations would serve as a means toward achieving that end.[151] For their part, the wealthy nations would do well to understand that peace and prosperity are goods that belong to the whole human race. "It is not possible to enjoy them in a proper and lasting way if they are achieved and maintained at the cost of other peoples and nations, by violating their rights or excluding them from the sources of well-being."[152] That is why the more prosperous countries must act to assist not only the post-communist countries but also the countries of the Third World, which often labor under the most desperate conditions of all.

## Cultural Development as the Prerequisite of Solidarity

It bears repeating that economic growth alone does not constitute authentic human development. On the contrary, when human life is reduced to a mere function of the prevailing economic system, we become enslaved *to* it and *by* it.[153] The proper medium of human development is culture. Within the cultural sphere of human existence, people seek the answers to life's big questions concerning birth, love, work, and death, among other things.[154] The search for truth and the effort to *live* according to the truth endows each

150. See *CA*, 28; *SRS*, 15.

151. See *CA*, 28.

152. Ibid., 27. "Peace is indivisible. It is either for all or for none. It demands an ever greater degree of rigorous respect for justice and consequently a fair distribution of the results of true development." *SRS*, 26.

153. See *SRS*, 28, 33, 47; *RH*, 15; Paul VI, *PPro*, 19.

154. See *CA*, 24.

nation with its character, one that bears the imprint of former generations and extends toward the future. The more adequate our self-understanding is, the more adequately we will collaborate with others to build up a decent society, one that fosters true human dignity, creativity, and participation.[155]

That is why the apex of human development is the freedom to seek and to know God, and to live according to a true knowledge of God.[156] No authentic progress is possible when people are denied this fundamental right and duty, nor when they are hindered or prevented from discovering and freely accepting Jesus Christ, their true good.[157] Human interiority must therefore be the measure of human development and the end toward which we direct it.[158]

It is precisely the cultural and religious poverty of economically developed nations that perpetuates and exacerbates the material poverty of nations that are underdeveloped in the economic sphere. In order to help the poor develop both economically and humanly, those benefiting from advanced economies must work to overcome the forms of poverty to which they themselves are vulnerable. Fundamentally, their task would consist in subordinating what is material and instinctive in themselves to what is properly spiritual when identifying their needs and the means of satisfying them. Otherwise, they would thwart their personal growth by forfeiting their transcendent ability to act in a truly human way. That is perhaps the most pernicious form of poverty, for it is self-inflicted, blind or hostile to truth and goodness, and grievous in its personal and social consequences.

Concretely, the spiritual and cultural renewal of wealthy societies demands that they act to educate consumers on how to exercise their power of choice responsibly. It also demands that those who produce goods and those in the mass media learn to appreciate and to exercise their respective moral responsibilities to consumers and to society.[159] Elevating the culture would

155. See ibid., 51.

156. "The individual's relation to God is a constitutive element of the very 'being' and 'existence' of an individual." *CL*, 39.

157. See *CA*, 29. John Paul mentions the danger that religious fundamentalism poses in this regard.

158. See *SRS*, 29. John Paul II exhorts the particular Churches in America to extend their missionary efforts beyond their continental borders, since there are "many millions of men and women who, without faith, suffer the most serious kind of poverty." *Ecclesia in America*, 74.

159. See *CA*, 36. *Ecclesia in America* acknowledges not only the dangers of the social communications media (nos. 20–21) but also their great potential for the new evangelization and for helping to shape positively the culture and mentality of people today (no. 72). On the responsibility of media professionals, see *CL*, 44.

therefore mean changing inferior and harmful patterns of production and consumption. Secondly, it would mean abandoning extravagant and corrupt lifestyles and replacing them with ways of life that take truth, beauty, goodness, and human solidarity into account when making consumer choices or personal decisions affecting the common good and the development of the poor. Thirdly, it would mean making appropriate changes to disordered economic and political power structures. Above all, it would mean adopting genuinely ethical and religious values and cooperating freely with God's grace. By developing their own culture thus, materially wealthy nations will grow in the spirit of solidarity, which reaches out to assist those members of the human family who are burdened by an overall lack of development.[160]

### The Church's Solidarity with Humanity

As the sacrament of unity for all mankind,[161] the Church expresses her solidarity with the whole human race in various ways. For one thing, she makes an indispensable contribution to the formation of culture through her preaching, which guides the nations along the path of truth and peace. She preaches about the human vocation to dominate the world that God has entrusted to us, so that it becomes more fruitful and perfect through our work. She also preaches about God's saving deed in Christ, which has united all people and made them responsible for one another.[162] Central to her message is the clear and forceful affirmation that "every individual—whatever his or her personal convictions—bears the image of God and therefore deserves respect."[163] By thus revealing us to ourselves and making us aware of our incomparable dignity, the Church prepares the way for truly human development, which is essential to the human vocation, the means to human perfection, and a foremost expression of God's image in us.[164]

The Church's expression of solidarity with mankind is not limited to her preaching. She also offers and communicates the life of God through the sacraments. She directs human life according to the commandments of love of God and neighbor.[165] As an "expert in humanity," she offers her social doctrine as a guide for human development,[166] one that gives rise to a commitment to justice because based on the two great commandments to

160. See *CA*, 58–60; *SRS*, 9.

161. See *LG*, 1; *SRS*, 31.

162. See *CA*, 50–51.

163. Ibid., 22.

164. For a brief but clear and comprehensive overview of Wojtyła/John Paul's understanding of the relationship between faith and culture, see Cardinal Avery Dulles, SJ, *The Splendor of Faith* (New York: Crossroad Publishing, 2003), 153–69.

165. See *CA*, 55.

166. See *SRS*, 41.

love. Knowing that her social doctrine, as well as her vocation to charity, demands the witness of actions, the Church exercises a "preferential option for the poor," embracing "the immense multitudes of the hungry, the needy, the homeless, those without medical care and, above all, those without hope of a better future."[167] As "a special form of primacy in the exercise of Christian charity,"[168] the Church's solidarity with the poor includes the offer of material assistance "in ways that neither humiliate nor reduce them to mere objects of assistance, but which help them to escape their precarious situation by promoting their dignity as persons."[169] The Church also counts among the poor those trapped in cultural, spiritual, or other forms of poverty, knowing that she must serve Christ in them too.[170]

Because Christian solidarity is imbued with charity, the two are identical in many respects.[171] Like charity, solidarity moves out toward others gratuitously and in a spirit of forgiveness and reconciliation. Solidarity's transcendent character flows from our seeing each person as a neighbor in the specifically Christian sense: as someone who is made in God's image, redeemed by Christ, and under the action of the Holy Spirit. This demands that we love each person as the Lord does. Such love expresses itself in our willingness to sacrifice ourselves for another—even an enemy—to the point of death, if necessary. Christian faith thus provides a new model of unity for the human race, one that reflects God's ineffable intra-Trinitarian life. In a word, solidarity in the fullest sense is based on the Christian vision of *communion*, which goes beyond merely human and natural bonds.[172] Only when human beings seek earnestly, with God's help, to cooperate with the divine plan by sacrificing themselves and their extravagant lifestyles for the sake of their needy brothers and sisters will they succeed in building a world marked by true justice and peace—a real civilization of love.[173]

In the civilization of love, vulnerable laborers and poor people are not—

167. Ibid., 42. 168. Ibid.

169. *CA*, 49. See no. 26; Leo XIII, *RN*, 29–30; Paul VI, *PPro*, 12.

170. See *CA*, 57; Leo XIII, *RN*, 28.

171. As a relationship of persons, grounded in their shared humanity and flowing from love, solidarity is expressed as social charity. In *CA*, 10, John Paul equates the terms "solidarity," "social charity" *(socialis caritas)*, and "friendship," the latter two of which were used by his predecessors. See Doran, *Solidarity*, 77–121 for an analysis of these and other related terms. Leo XIII's exhortation to charity for resolving the social problems of his own day is germane (see *RN*, 63). John Paul II mentions the lack of "social love" *(amor socialis)* characterizing the human situation in the modern world, suggesting that solidarity is not being expressed concretely on a wide scale (*RH*, 16).

172. See *SRS*, 40; *GS*, 24.

173. Paul VI used the expression in his homily during the Mass closing the Holy Year (Decem-

or at least ought not to be—merely "objects" of the transcendent solidarity that Christians seek to establish with them. For one thing, the offer of Christian solidarity expressed by others gives them an opportunity to take an active role in improving their lot with the help they receive. This implies that the vulnerable are invited to enter solidarity with those who are offering their assistance, and that the invitation requires a deliberate response. As they rise above their condition, vulnerable laborers and the poor can express their positive response to the call to solidarity more concretely by offering their skills, talents, and resources for the betterment of others.

At the same time, the vulnerable should see in the transcendent offer of Christian solidarity not only an invitation to participate in it themselves, but also an invitation *to discern God's loving presence* therein. When social solidarity issues from Christian charity, it constitutes a call to communion with God through communion with the Body of Christ. As human beings and human agents, the vulnerable have to reckon with that call when Christians turn to them in a real spirit of solidarity. It is a spirit that stirs up the deepest questions of the human heart, questions that demand an answer if human beings are to be most fully themselves.

Apropos of this, Gerard Beigel shows how Wojtyła/John Paul II's anthropology grounds the link between faith and social justice.[174] Christian social action is an active response of faith, inspired by God's grace. As we now know so well, we always express such a response through the body, which thus becomes a luminous sign and instrument of God's glory in the visible world. Inwardly transformed by grace, we share once again in God's creative vision of the world and of humanity. This deepens our perception of value and our realization of freedom in love. Our social action is therefore ordered toward extending to all people the communion that we already enjoy with other Christians and with God in Christ.

> The sacramental dimension of Christian social action is not simply a luminous symbol of God's love, but is also an efficacious presentation of God's love to others. Through their faith and ecclesial life, Christians can love others, especially the poor, with the same love with which the Lord himself loves them. The efficacy of the sacramental

---

ber 25, 1975; see "Close of the Holy Year," *Origins* 5, no. 30 [1976]: 481–82), and also in the *Message of His Holiness Pope Paul VI for the Celebration of the Day of Peace* (January 1, 1977), Vatican website. John Paul II relates it to "solidarity" in *CA*, 10. In his own *World Day of Peace* message on January 1, 2001, he used the expression several times, as well as "civilization of love and peace" (nos. 10 and 19). *LF* employs the expression extensively and thematically.

174. See Gerard Beigel, *Faith and Social Justice in the Teaching of Pope John Paul II* (New York: Peter Lang Publishing, 1997).

activity of Christians is ... a true *human presentation* of God's redeeming love, which invites others to recognize and receive that same love.[175]

Our capacity to radiate the power and glory of God in the sphere of social justice finds its ultimate model in the Incarnation.[176]

Similarly, in *Christifideles Laici,* John Paul emphasizes that "communion with Jesus, which gives rise to the communion of Christians among themselves, is an indispensable condition for bearing fruit."[177] By "fruit" he means not only the extension of communion among Christians,[178] but also its expression in the world through social solidarity,[179] which has the evangelical effect of inviting others to the fullness of ecclesial communion.[180] Christians have therefore a "mission to communion," where communion represents both the source and the fruit of mission.[181] At the root of each aspect of communion is the Christian's call to holiness,[182] that is, to conversion. As Peter Casarella observes in a related context, it follows that "the implications for social solidarity are present [temporally and ontologically] from the very beginning of one's conversion to Christ. In other words, a dualism of private beliefs and public life even in the name of fostering the pluralistic values of liberal society is fully excluded."[183] To sum up, then, Christian social solidarity springs naturally from the concrete yet mystical communion of persons born of conversion to and life in Christ. In turn, it fosters the extension of that communion to the whole human race—and this precisely because the conversion that urges solidarity "makes us aware that whatever we do for others, especially for the poorest, we do for Christ himself."[184]

We saw earlier that Christians themselves are sometimes reduced to a seemingly hopeless condition of vulnerability and yet, imbued with the love of God, they offer the witness of an extraordinary solidarity and serenity in the face of "evil mechanisms" and "structures of sin" that are ultimately overcome by their often "silent" (or largely hidden) proclamation—their *radiation*—of Christ's Gospel. In this connection, John Paul mentions "St. Maximilian Maria Kolbe who offered his life in place of a prisoner unknown to him in the concentration camp at Auschwitz."[185] We see, then, that in ex-

175. Ibid., 97. See 59–80.

176. See ibid., 116–19.

177. *CL*, 32.

178. See ibid., 18–31.

179. See ibid., 40–44.

180. See ibid., 33ff.

181. See ibid., 32.

182. See ibid., 16–17.

183. Peter Casarella, "Solidarity as the Fruit of Communion: *Ecclesia in America*, 'Post-Liberation Theology,' and the Earth," *Communio* 27 (Spring 2000): 111.

184. *Ecclesia in America*, 26. See no. 52.

185. See *SRS*, 40.

pressing solidarity toward others through their communion with Christ, poor and oppressed Christians can powerfully exercise their agency in a heroic, ultimately victorious confrontation with injustice and evil by embracing the cross against all odds. In that way, they raise ultimate questions in people's minds about the transcendent Source of their activity and thus invite others to solidarity and communion with themselves in Christ and with Christ in themselves. By docility to the mysterious prompting of God's Spirit, non-Christian poor and oppressed persons can also participate, in ways known only to God, in Christ's victory over injustice and evil when, in a spirit of solidarity with others, they actively, though without explicit awareness, take up their share of the cross, which is the eternal expression of God's invincible love at work in the world.

# 7

# The Vulnerable as Persons and Actors in *Evangelium Vitae*

In this chapter, we will focus on Pope John Paul II's historic 1995 encyclical, *Evangelium Vitae*. In it, John Paul reiterates the main lines of his anthropological enterprise. But he does so with the explicit intention of providing a framework in which to develop the essential features of an "anthropology of the vulnerable"—an anthropology that resoundingly affirms the personhood and genuinely human agency of both psychosomatically developing human beings and those undergoing disintegration of any kind. The encyclical's thoroughly biblical character will help us clarify the grounds on which John Paul seems, long before its promulgation, to have modified the understanding of human agency that he presented in *Person and Act*, even to the point of his ascribing genuinely personal actions to human beings whose undeveloped level of consciousness and rationality or whose advanced state of disintegration would seem to preclude any possibility of their performing them. In *Evangelium Vitae*, John Paul II's reflections on, and his expressions of concern for, psychosomatically developing and variously disintegrated human persons give him occasion to speak also about moral vulnerability and voluntary vulnerability, which we will consider further as we proceed.

## Introduction to the Persons and Themes Central to *Evangelium Vitae*

Before we take a detailed look at the biblical anthropology that John Paul II lays out for us in *Evangelium Vitae,* we would do well, first, to look more specifically at the persons who are the main "objects" of his concern in the document, and, second, to give an overview of the reciprocal relation between the document's general anthropology and its anthropology of the vulnerable. This will help us avoid serious misunderstandings about the meaning we attach to the latter expression.

### The Vulnerable in *Evangelium Vitae*

Of the persons most occupying his attention in *Evangelium Vitae,* John Paul mentions, in the first place, "the great multitude of weak and defenseless human beings, unborn children in particular, whose right to life is being trampled upon."[1] He refers here explicitly only to human life at its earliest stages, perhaps because the widespread legalization, promotion, acceptance, practice, institutionalization, and imposition of abortion have placed unborn lives, beyond all others, at an unprecedented risk. But he is well aware that the detestable mentality behind abortion threatens the existence of every other human life that the "strong" members of society regard as inconvenient, useless, burdensome, costly, or dispensable. As with the unborn, the lives of persons who are approaching the final stage of their earthly existence because of advanced years or terminal illness are easily exploited and extinguished. Accordingly, euthanasia is on the rise in various countries, and John Paul is deeply troubled about the trend. Attacks against the unborn, the elderly, and the dying are especially unjust, not to mention cowardly, because they "strike human life at the time of its greatest frailty, when it lacks any means of self-defense."[2] In *Evangelium Vitae,* then, the "attacks affecting life in its earliest and in its final stages" are of foremost concern to Pope John Paul II.[3]

But that is not all. He is also clearly disturbed about contemporary threats against the lives and needs of sick, suffering, and disabled persons throughout the range of human existence.[4] The foul attitude by which physically

1. *EV,* 5.

2. Ibid., 11.

3. Ibid. John Paul points out a contradiction that betrays an enormous hypocrisy: "Precisely in an age when the inviolable rights of the person are solemnly proclaimed and the value of life is publicly affirmed, the very right to life is being denied or trampled upon, especially at the more significant moments of existence: the moment of birth and the moment of death." Ibid., 18.

4. E.g., ibid., 15.

healthy, "self-sufficient" people regard as "useless" any persons whose condition renders them radically dependent on others has opened wide the door to eugenic abortion, infanticide, and euthanasia. These murderous practices testify to the fact that human life is frequently not accepted nowadays unless it conforms to arbitrary standards of normality and physical well-being.[5] In a climate like that, the "strong" are not likely to value vulnerable human beings for *who they are*—namely, unique, unrepeatable, and inviolable *persons*. Rather, having overturned the objective order of goods, they tend to value them only for *what they have*, as when the "strong" take organs from dying human beings whom they have prematurely pronounced dead, so as to transplant them into persons whose lives they have decided are comparatively more valuable or worth living.[6] They even go so far as to produce human embryos and fetuses by in vitro fertilization for the express purpose of "harvesting" their tissues and organs for transplanting into others, or for supplying researchers with "objects" of experimentation.[7] On the whole, then, John Paul II expresses concern, in *Evangelium Vitae*, for all vulnerable persons whose very right to life is being threatened both directly and indirectly on a vast and ever widening scale: the unborn (human embryos and fetuses), the newly born (especially when sickly, crippled, or deformed), the severely disabled, the suffering, the incurably ill, the elderly (especially when no longer independent), and the dying—in short, the weakest, the neediest, and the most defenseless members of society.

## Anthropology in *Evangelium Vitae*

In *Evangelium Vitae*, we can distinguish the main elements of a general anthropology from a more specific anthropology of the vulnerable. The general anthropology highlights the basic features constitutive of *every* human life. John Paul II's purpose in presenting it, therefore, is to show unequivocally that vulnerable human beings are not essentially different from, and certainly not inferior to, persons who are "strong"—that is, persons who are not presently subject to the same kinds of vulnerabilities. The general anthropology thus serves as the foundation for the anthropology of the vulnerable contained in the document.[8]

5. See ibid., 14–15, 19, 63.

6. See ibid., 15.

7. See ibid., 63. John Paul declares that "the use of human embryos or fetuses as an object of experimentation constitutes a crime against their dignity as human beings who have a right to the same respect owed to a child once born, just as to every person" (ibid.).

8. While *EV*'s general anthropology takes Wojtyła/John Paul II's basic anthropological

There are two constants that establish each of us as a personal being and that define the ultimate meaning of our existence in time, namely: (1) our origin in God according to the divine image; and (2) our divine calling to a supernatural end, in which the divine image is fulfilled in us by our eschatological participation in the life of God himself. If God has created every human being in his image and calls each one of us in Christ to share eternally in the divine life, then human life is absolutely sacred and inviolable, regardless of its stage of development or its condition—that is, regardless of how vulnerable it might be. Our origin and end in God reveals God's unconditional love for us, which guarantees the dignity of every human life and prohibits its devaluation under any circumstances.[9]

The two constants identified in *Evangelium Vitae*'s general anthropology enable and oblige us to conduct our life in a particular way as it dynamically unfolds in virtue of them: we can and must fulfill the meaning of our existence by welcoming our own life and that of our "brother"—whose "keeper" we are—as a gift.[10] And we do that precisely by *giving* the gift of our life *to* others and *for the sake of* others. By lovingly receiving and serving life thus, we gratefully acknowledge it as a sacred trust bestowed on us by the Creator and sole Lord of life. That becomes especially clear when the life in question is so weak and defenseless that others must assume responsibility for its care. For their part, vulnerable human beings likewise witness to the intrinsic meaning and value of human life when, in a manner corresponding to the capabilities of each, they bestow the gift of self on other persons through their vulnerability as a sign of their having accepted both their own life and the lives of those to whom they have thus entrusted themselves.

Sin undermines the image of God in us, thus threatening our attainment of the supernatural end for which God has created us, and to which he unceasingly calls us. Accordingly, *Evangelium Vitae*'s general anthropology warns us that we gravely endanger the gift of our own life by adopting perverted attitudes that, together with the "structures of sin" created on account of them, conspire against the vulnerable. For in these ways, we reject the very ones who are most in need of being accepted and served in love—we to whose care they have entrusted themselves in some way. Likewise, some vulnerable persons reject *themselves*, when capable of doing so, by concurring with or actively taking part in the conspiracy against them.

themes and develops them with a view to the encyclical's specific concerns, we will find no substantial advance in John Paul's reflections on those themes.

9. See *EV*, 38; *CL*, 37; *GS*, 29.

10. See *EV*, 19; Gn 4:9.

We see, then, that the constitutive aspects of *Evangelium Vitae*'s general anthropology pertain to and determine the life of vulnerable human beings as much as anyone else's. As persons made in God's image, they are called to eternal life. They must therefore exercise their intrinsic capacity to love and serve the gift of human life as far as their condition allows, while avoiding sin where sin is possible. So, even if we can distinguish, up to a point, between a general anthropology and an anthropology of the vulnerable in *Evangelium Vitae*, we must remain mindful of the fact that the one cannot really be separated from the other.

Indeed, the link between those two inseparable aspects of the document's anthropology is evident from the other direction as well. The life of every human being has a definite beginning, from which it passes through the earliest stages of human existence. And it sooner or later passes over the threshold of death. These two events, which correlate with the two constants discussed above, define the boundaries of every person's life-history, and so they are among the more significant moments of human life. They also constitute the moments of its greatest vulnerability. Similarly, the vulnerability caused by suffering of one kind or another is an inescapable fact of human existence.[11] A truly integral anthropology must therefore always include the aspect of human vulnerability. Consequently, as we later consider *Evangelium Vitae*'s anthropology according to the aspect of vulnerability in particular, we will be presupposing its wider relevance for the understanding of the human person in general.

## *Evangelium Vitae*'s General Anthropology

Let us now consider the general aspects of *Evangelium Vitae*'s anthropology in more detail. Following that, we will examine the document's analysis of the widespread, culturally institutionalized crimes against life that numerous members of society perpetrate against the weak, to their own temporal, and possibly also their eternal, detriment. We will then elaborate *Evangelium Vitae*'s "anthropology of the vulnerable," which will provide the basis for some final reflections on the uniquely personal character of the agency exercised by the most vulnerable human beings of all.

11. See *SD*, 5–8.

## Our Origin and End in God

By the special creative action of God, human beings are made in the divine image and likeness (Gn 1:26): "The life which God offers to man [when he is created] is a gift by which God shares something of himself with his creature."[12] For one thing, this means that we are entrusted with exercising a responsible dominion over the earth. To the extent that we obey the divine law, we will fulfill that charge and thus reflect God's absolute dominion.[13] Our superior place in the world constitutes "a clear affirmation of the primacy of man over things; these are made subject to him and entrusted to his responsible care, whereas for no reason can he be made subject to other men and almost reduced to the level of a thing."[14] The exalted dignity that we have as stewards of the earth presupposes the unique gifts with which the Creator has endowed us. The Lord "filled them with knowledge and understanding, and showed them good and evil" (Sir 17:7). Our spirit and its faculties of intellect and will constitute each of us as a living image of God's eternity (see Ws 2:23), so that our earthly existence already contains "the seed of an existence which transcends the very limits of time."[15] We are therefore "naturally drawn to God,"[16] and so never fully satisfied with our life in the world.

Among the world's living creatures, human beings radiate, and thus manifest, the glory of God most splendidly. The capacities of our spiritual nature far exceed the natural capacities of plants and animals, indicating our superior level of participation in the gift of life that comes from Life itself.[17] Because of our unique correspondence to the Creator, moreover, we are each the subject of inherent rights and values that safeguard our dignity and that must therefore never be questioned, transgressed, or opposed, but always acknowledged, respected, and promoted.[18] In a word, God has endowed human life with "a sacred and inviolable character, which reflects the inviolability of the Creator Himself."[19]

Even so, the origin of human life in God, distinguished by that "breath of

12. *EV*, 34.

13. See ibid., 42, 52.

14. Ibid., 34.

15. Ibid. See *GS*, 18. In referring to Sirach 17:7 and Wisdom 2:23, we are following *EV*, 34, which quotes both texts. The biblical quotations in the official English translation of *EV* being used in this chapter come, for the most part, from the Revised Standard Version. Likewise, any biblical texts quoted in this chapter beyond those contained in the document are from the RSV.

16. *EV*, 35.

17. See ibid., 84.

18. See ibid., 71.

19. Ibid., 53; see nos. 81, 87.

life" (or spirit) by which God made each of us "a living being" (Gn 2:7),[20] does not alone explain the profound, "almost divine dignity of every human being."[21] Rather, the "abundant life" (see Jn 10:10) that Christ offers to each person through his redemptive mission gives all aspects of human existence in time their full meaning.[22] From all eternity, the Son is given "life in himself" by the Father, who has life in *him*self (Jn 5:26).[23] With the coming of the Son in the flesh (see Jn 1:14), this life became manifest (see 1 Jn 1:1–2), and the Son gives it to all who live by faith in him.[24] Communion with Jesus, then, means that the gift of life that we receive from God at the beginning of our existence becomes open to *eternal* life by our sharing in the life of God through the grace of the Spirit bestowed by the Father in, through, and with the Son. In that way, "[e]very person is freely called in the Son by the power of the sanctifying Spirit" to "communion with the Father"—that is, to eternal life.[25]

Our supernatural vocation "reveals the greatness and the inestimable value" of our earthly life, which constitutes "the fundamental condition, the initial stage and an integral part of the entire unified process of human existence."[26] Because human beings are made in the image of God's eternity (see Ws 2:23), we already anticipate a certain fullness of life in our earthly existence.[27] Indeed, it is precisely because God is our definitive goal and fulfillment that we experience our greatest temporal satisfaction through genuinely interpersonal dialogue with other human beings, in each of whom "there shines forth a reflection of God himself."[28] In Christ, our inner dynamism toward eternity is fulfilled: first, by the enlightening promise and the renewing gift of participation in the divine life through grace; and, finally, in the eternal life that consummates the communion with God that human beings in the state of grace presently enjoy. Against the backdrop of our ultimate end, temporal life has just a relative significance.[29] We might, after all, be called some day to give up our life voluntarily for a friend (see Jn 15:13) or, more explicitly, for the sake of Christ and his Gospel (see Mk 8:35).[30] Yet, human life in its earthly state remains sacred, since it is from here that "eternal life already springs forth and begins to grow."[31] More specifically, it is "the 'place' where God manifests himself, where we meet him and enter into com-

20. See ibid., 35.

21. Ibid., 25; see no. 84. See also Ps 8:5–6.

22. See *EV*, 1–2, 30, 38, 80.

23. See ibid., 29.

24. See ibid., 30, 80.

25. Ibid., 1; see nos. 2, 37, 83.

26. Ibid., 2.

27. See ibid., 31, 81.

28. Ibid., 34; see no. 35.

29. See ibid., 2.

30. See ibid., 47, 55, 86.

31. Ibid., 38.

munion with him."[32] For that reason, "the life which Jesus gives in no way lessens the value of our existence in time; it takes it and directs it to its final destiny: 'I am the resurrection and the life.... Whoever lives and believes in me shall never die' (Jn 11:25–26)."[33]

## The Sincere Gift of Self: An Affirmation of Life

The blood that Christ poured out as a sacrificial offering for the forgiveness of sins is the source of human redemption and the gift of new life. It therefore speaks eloquently and eternally of the sacredness of human life. "The blood of Christ ... shows how precious man is to God's eyes and how priceless the value of his life."[34] As the sign of Christ's self-giving love, his precious blood also "reveals to man that his greatness, and therefore his vocation, consists in the sincere gift of self."[35] In obedience to the will of the Father, Christ gave his life on the cross for those "who were his own in the world" (Jn 13:1). Though they were yet sinners (see Rm 5:8), he "loved them to the end" (Jn 13:1), proclaiming in this way "that life finds its center, its meaning and its fulfillment when it is given up."[36] The glory of Christ, which first radiated "from the house of Nazareth and from the manger at Bethlehem,"[37] is manifested in all its fullness and power with the death of Christ on the cross.[38] It was precisely then that the Roman centurion recognized and explicitly proclaimed the divine identity of the Son of God (see Mk 15:39), whose life became, through death, our own life and salvation. "The redemptive obedience of Christ is the source of grace poured out upon the human race, opening wide to everyone the gates of the kingdom of life."[39] By the gift of the Spirit of Christ, we are given a "new heart" (see Ez 36:25–26; Jer 31:33), enabling us to follow the example of Christ and to achieve thus the authentic meaning of life by becoming a gift for others.[40]

In giving ourselves to others in love, we simultaneously accept the gift of life and serve it.[41] This affirmation of life is "an indispensable condition for being able 'to enter life.'"[42] It is precisely because God has entrusted human beings to one another according to the law of reciprocal self-giving and other-receiving that he has also entrusted us with the gift of freedom, "which possesses an inherently relational dimension."[43] We can fulfill our-

32. Ibid.
33. Ibid.
34. Ibid., 25.
35. Ibid.
36. Ibid., 51.
37. Ibid., 33.
38. See ibid., 50.
39. Ibid., 36.
40. See ibid., 49.
41. See ibid., 54, 86.
42. Ibid., 54. See Mt 19:16–19.
43. *EV*, 19.

selves in freedom only insofar as we open ourselves to others through the sincere gift of self, that is, through love.[44] By adhering to the law of reciprocity in the power of Christ's Spirit, we build up a genuine communion of love, one that serves as "a true reflection of the mystery of the mutual self-giving and receiving proper to the most holy Trinity."[45] The selfless love of neighbor reaches heroic proportions when, while valuing our own life, we give it up freely to save that of another (or others). Actions like that proclaim the "Gospel of life" by the total gift of self, and so "they are the radiant manifestation of the highest degree of love."[46] Giving the gift of ourselves to and for others is therefore the means by which we become conformed to the image of the incarnate Son (see Rm 8:29), who is, in turn, "the image of the invisible God" (Col 1:15).[47] In a special way, we receive the strength to fulfill our original vocation to love when we partake of Christ's blood in the Eucharist, which draws us into the dynamism of his love and his gift of life.[48]

### Radical Individualism: A Threat to Life

Of course, when we reject the lives of others by withholding the sincere gift of self, we contradict the essential meaning of our own existence, which finds its fulfillment only in the vocation to love. It is the specific task of human freedom to pursue that vocation through the unequivocal affirmation of life. "There is no true freedom where life is not welcomed and loved; and there is no fullness of life except in freedom."[49] The individual who prefers instead to understand freedom as the absolute right to pursue personal interests and desires without reference to the objective and universal truth flowing from human life and indelibly marking it as a supremely good gift of the Creator, whose image it bears, "not only deforms the image of God in his own person, but is tempted to offenses against it in others as well, replacing relationships of communion by attitudes of distrust, indifference, hostility and even murderous hatred."[50]

We cannot promote ourselves independently of others without thereby denying them their inherent rights as persons and violating the fundamental purpose of our own freedom, which we have received as a gift so that we might realize our true good through genuinely interpersonal relationships founded on the law of reciprocal giving and receiving. Individuals seeking

44. See ibid., 96.
45. Ibid., 76.
46. Ibid., 86; see no. 55.
47. See ibid., 36.
48. See ibid., 25.
49. Ibid., 96.
50. Ibid., 36; see nos. 19, 48, 71, 96. See also *LF*, 14.

autonomy of action to the point of disregarding the essential truth about human existence always oppose themselves in some way to the fundamental values of life and love, with the result that their freedom is no longer truly free. "When freedom is made absolute in an individualistic way, it is emptied of its original content, and its very meaning and dignity are contradicted."[51]

By failing to understand and to exercise our freedom according to its inherent meaning, we invariably fail to grasp the authentic meaning of our own existence. The proper sense of our own human identity undergoes an eclipse that can typically be traced back to the eclipse in us of the proper sense of God.[52] "When God is not acknowledged as God, the profound meaning of man is betrayed and communion between people is compromised."[53] In this state of eclipse, we do not perceive human life as a transcendent reality. Instead, it becomes reduced, in our view, to a mere "thing" over which we claim ownership, along with the right to control and manipulate it as we will.[54] This most dire consequence of practical materialism, of which individualism, utilitarianism, and hedonism are offshoots, reveals the abysmal depths into which human beings plunge when we choose to live as if God did not exist. Once we subordinate the unconditional values deriving from the truth of human existence to conditional values like usefulness, productivity, pleasure, and material well-being,[55] the transgression of the moral law, particularly where the inviolability of human life is concerned, is inevitable. This results in a "progressive darkening of the capacity to discern God's living and saving presence."[56]

On the other hand, human conscience remains ever the sanctuary of our encounter with God, whose voice does not cease to resound therein.[57] Because it is "only before the Lord that man can admit his sin and recognize its full seriousness,"[58] our dialogue with God within the depths of conscience can provide the point of departure for "a new journey of love, openness and

51. *EV*, 19. As John Paul put it to André Frossard, "Liberty is the measure of how much love we are capable of giving." Frossard, *Portrait*, 90. It follows, therefore, that our love, or our lack thereof, is the measure of how much liberty we have.

52. See *EV*, 21–24.

53. Ibid., 36. See *GS*, 36; *Reconciliatio et Paenitentia*, 18.

54. See *EV*, 22. See also William Brennan, *John Paul II: Confronting the Language Empowering the Culture of Death* (Naples, Fla.: Sapientia Press of Ave Maria University, 2008), 51–79. Of course, "the *sacredness of the human person* cannot be obliterated, no matter how it is devalued and violated because it has its unshakable foundation in God as Creator and Father." *CL*, 5.

55. See *EV*, 23.

56. Ibid., 21.

57. See ibid., 24; *GS*, 16.

58. *EV*, 21. See *Reconciliatio et Paenitentia*, 18.

service to human life."[59] By acknowledging our dependence on God and following his commandments in the true spirit of the law of love, we can each fulfill our freedom to the highest degree without infringing on either the life or the authentic freedom of any other person.[60] On the contrary, we will freely promote those values.

It is the *whole* law of God, and not just the fifth commandment, that fully protects the sacredness and inviolability of human life by revealing "that truth in which life finds its true meaning."[61] Inasmuch as "the meaning of life is found in giving and receiving love,"[62] the divine law is summed up in the law of love[63]—the Gospel of life, which Christ proclaimed through his own words, actions, and Person. This Gospel has been written since "the beginning" in the human heart—that is, in each person's conscience—and so it can be grasped in its essential traits by the light of reason and observed with the assistance of the Spirit, "who, blowing where he wills (cf. Jn 3:8), comes to and involves every person living in this world."[64] Therefore, if the person is reminded in the depths of conscience that human life is sacred and inviolable, then he is likewise reminded that life is "something which does not belong to him, because it is the property and gift of God the Creator and Father."[65] But that all presumes our good will as we each stand before God. "Every person *sincerely open to truth and goodness* can, by the light of reason and the hidden action of grace, come to recognize in the natural law written in the heart (cf. Rom 2:14–15) the sacred value of human life from its very beginning until its end, and can affirm the right of every human being to have this primary good respected to the highest degree."[66] That is so "even in the midst of difficulties and uncertainties" that might otherwise obscure the unconditional value of and right to life.[67]

When we ignore the prompting of conscience and violate God's law in some way, we gravitate precipitously toward committing crimes against life, or at least condoning them.[68] The eclipse, in the moral conscience, of our authentic sense of self and of God takes place in corresponding measure. Each person is ultimately responsible for the fact that his or her conscience has become darkened in the sight of God regarding the value of human life. However, it is also true that the many individual consciences that have undergone a

59. *EV*, 24.
60. See ibid., 96.
61. Ibid., 48.
62. Ibid., 81.
63. See ibid., 40–41.
64. Ibid., 77; see no. 29.
65. Ibid., 40.
66. Ibid., 2 (italics added).
67. Ibid, 2.
68. See ibid., 48.

similar eclipse constitute collectively what John Paul II calls "the 'moral conscience' of society,"[69] which is also, in a way, responsible for the widespread conditioning of individual consciences against life. That is so "not only because it tolerates or fosters behavior contrary to life, but also because it encourages the 'culture of death,' creating and consolidating actual 'structures of sin' which go against life."[70] As a result, both the individual and the social conscience are increasingly subject to "confusion between good and evil precisely in relation to the fundamental right to life."[71] This grave danger is compounded by the pervasive influence of the mass media, which are often implicated in the "conspiracy against life."[72] In such instances, the media have abandoned their responsibility to exercise that "scrupulous concern for the factual truth" that balances "freedom of information with respect for every person and a profound sense of humanity."[73]

## The Strong against the Weak: Exploiting the Vulnerability of the Vulnerable

Pope John Paul II acknowledges that certain cultural, social, economic, and psychological factors can sometimes mitigate subjective responsibility and culpability for the objectively evil crimes that some people commit against life.[74] But he is also keenly aware that a widespread moral decline is taking place at the level of individual persons who, conceding "to the 'thinking' of the evil one,"[75] defy God and attack their neighbor, just as Cain did (see Gn 4:2–16).[76] Above all, John Paul expresses alarm at the "structures of

69. Ibid., 24; see no. 70.

70. Ibid., 24.

71. Ibid; see nos. 4, 58. "Man receives from God his essential dignity and with it the capacity to transcend every social order so as to move towards truth and goodness. But he is also conditioned by the social structure in which he lives, by the education he has received and by his environment. These elements can either help or hinder his living in accordance with the truth. The decisions which create a human environment can give rise to specific structures of sin which impede the full realization of those who are in any way oppressed by them. To destroy such structures and replace them with more authentic forms of living in community is a task which demands patience and courage." *CA*, 38.

72. See *EV*, 17, 24.

73. Ibid., 98.

74. See ibid., 12, 18, 66. "There are [cultural] agendas which 'play' on man's weaknesses, and thus make him increasingly weak and defenceless." *LF*, 13. The mass media often take advantage of this form of vulnerability, manipulating and falsifying the whole truth about man and woman as persons. See *LF*, 20.

75. *EV*, 8.

76. See ibid., 7–9.

sin" that have been incorporated into the social, cultural, legal, political, and economic institutions of many countries, as well as into the scientific, technological, and medical fields.[77] Likewise, "one cannot overlook the network of complicity which reaches out to include international institutions, foundations, and associations which systematically campaign for the legalization and spread of abortion in the world.... We are facing what can be called a 'structure of sin' which opposes human life not yet born."[78] These and other structures of sin are responsible for the systematic implementation, on an unprecedented scale, of "a conspiracy against life."

## Individual and Societal Attitudes That Threaten Life

Characteristic of the conspiracy against life is the idealization of the value of efficiency, even to the point where "a life which would require greater acceptance, love and care is considered useless or held to be an intolerable burden, and is therefore rejected in one way or another. A person who, because of illness, handicap or, more simply, just by existing, compromises the well-being or lifestyle of those who are more favored tends to be looked upon as an enemy to be resisted or eliminated."[79] According to this view, the intrinsic dignity of the person is of no account. Human "value" stands or falls on the arbitrary criterion of self-sufficiency, a criterion deriving from a radically individualistic notion of autonomy. "Only the person who enjoys full or at least incipient autonomy and who emerges from a state of total dependence on others" is regarded as being a subject of properly human rights.[80] This outlook presupposes that a certain level of psychosomatic integrity and development is constitutive of the person's value, and perhaps even of the person as such. It also underlies the tendency "to equate personal dignity with the capacity for verbal and explicit, or at least perceptible, communication."[81] To "merit" the right to life, then, a person would have to demonstrate the ability or, minimally, a sufficient capacity to function and communicate in a way that is generally regarded as useful, productive, and distinctly human. In other words, one would have to possess, either now or in the foreseeable future, the personal (and even the material) resources needed to live independently of others. Short of that, human life would not, in this view, serve any real purpose; it would not fulfill the criteria for meaningfulness or "quality" that the "strong" have settled on through purely practical, ulti-

77. E.g., ibid., 4, 12, 17. See Brennan, *Confronting the Language*, 1–28.

78. *EV*, 59.

79. Ibid., 12; see no. 64.

80. Ibid., 19.

81. Ibid.

mately selfish considerations that fail to take into account the whole reality of the person.[82]

When human beings "are considered not for what they 'are,' but for what they 'have, do and produce,'"[83] the weak become subject to those having the power to force their own will on them. A "completely individualistic concept of freedom ... ends up by becoming the freedom of 'the strong' against the weak who have no choice but to submit."[84] Those who assert themselves over and against the vulnerable take as their only reference point their own subjective and changeable opinion about what constitutes good and evil.[85] However, the freedom that emancipates itself from all forms of tradition and authority "shuts out even the most obvious evidence of an objective and universal truth,"[86] so that "any reference to common values and to a truth absolutely binding on everyone is lost, and social life ventures on to the shifting sands of complete relativism."[87] By ignoring or denying their fundamental relationship to God, the "strong" become their own rule, insisting that society grant them the legal warrant to dispose freely, as they will, of both their own lives and those of the vulnerable.[88] But once the state arrogates to itself, as a matter of "public interest," the power to eliminate the lives of its weakest and most defenseless members, democracy violates its own basic principles and so heads ineluctably in the direction of totalitarianism.[89] "The 'right' [to life] ceases to be such, because it is no longer firmly founded on the inviolable dignity of the person, but is made subject to the will of the stronger part."[90]

82. See Brennan, *Confronting the Language*, 81–106. Though referring specifically to people with mental illnesses in the following passage, John Paul might just as well be referring to any radically dependent person vulnerable to being dismissed by the "strong" as unproductive and hence burdensome: "When God turns his gaze on man, the first thing he sees and loves in him is not the deeds he succeeds in doing, but his own image, an image that confers on man the ability to know his own creator, to rule over all earthly creatures and to use them for God's glory. And that is why the church recognizes the same dignity in all human beings and the same fundamental value, regardless ... of the fact that this ability cannot be utilized because impeded by mental illness." John Paul II, "The Image of God in People with Mental Illnesses," *Origins* 26, no. 30 (1997): 496.

83. *EV*, 23.

84. Ibid., 19; see nos. 12, 20, 23, 66, 70.

85. See ibid., 19, 68, 70. Apropos of this, John Paul observes that some forms of humanism "exalt the individual in such a manner that these forms become a veritable idolatry." *CL*, 5.

86. *EV*, 19.

87. Ibid., 20.

88. See ibid., 4, 18, 64, 68.

89. See ibid., 20.

90. Ibid., 20. "The appearance of the strictest respect for legality is maintained, at least when the laws permitting abortion and euthanasia are the result of a ballot in accordance with what are generally seen as the rules of democracy. Really, what we have here is only the tragic caricature of legality; the democratic ideal, which is only truly such when it acknowledges and safeguards the dignity of every human person, is betrayed in its very foundations." Ibid.

What is more, any "democratic" system that has in this way forsaken its responsibility to found its civil law on the objective moral law written in the human heart is incapable of ensuring a stable peace.[91] Its pursuit of morally illicit ends by morally illicit means, particularly where the value of human life is concerned, is certain to undermine the possibility of authentic solidarity between people by destroying the mutual bonds that would otherwise have united them.[92] Instead of promoting the harmonious coexistence of its citizens and even that of nations, the governing body becomes merely a tool for regulating interests to the advantage of the most powerful. It sometimes does that under the guise of "regulating different and opposing interests on a purely empirical basis,"[93] ostensibly to maximize the level of freedom that each individual expects as his or her due, irrespective of any reference to objective truth and objective moral rectitude—especially where the right to life is concerned. The true foundation of democracy is therefore betrayed the moment the state transfers the foundation of human rights from the person to itself, allowing force to become "the criterion for choice and action in interpersonal relations and in social life."[94] This contradicts the very meaning of a state ruled by law, where communal life is supposed to be governed by the force of reason, not by the reasons of force.[95] Human laws that are contrary to right reason are not only inherently unjust: they are acts of violence. In violating the natural moral order and its basis in the eternal law of God, "they are completely lacking in authentic juridical validity."[96] That is, they cannot bind conscience, which, instead, obliges the person to oppose unjust

91. "Peace and Life. They are supreme values in the civil order. They are also values that are interdependent. Do we want Peace? Then let us defend Life!" Pope Paul VI, *Celebration of the Day of Peace.*

92. See *EV,* 20, 70.

93. Ibid., 70.

94. Ibid., 19.

95. See ibid. In a homily given in the Archdiocese of Newark, New Jersey, during his apostolic journey to the United States in 1995 (just six months after *EV* was issued), John Paul spoke as follows: "When *the unborn child*—the 'stranger in the womb'—is declared to be *beyond the protection of society,* not only are America's deepest traditions radically undermined and endangered, but a moral blight is brought upon society. I am also thinking of threats to the elderly, the severely handicapped and all those who do not seem to have any social usefulness. When innocent human beings are declared inconvenient or burdensome, and thus unworthy of legal and social protection, grievous damage is done to the moral foundations of the democratic community. The right to life is the first of all rights. It is the foundation of democratic liberties and the keystone of the edifice of civil society. *Both as Americans* and *as followers of Christ, American Catholics* must be committed to the defense of life in all its stages and in every condition." *Homily of His Holiness John Paul II: Eucharistic Celebration for the Faithful of the Archdiocese of Newark* (October 5, 1995), Vatican website.

96. *EV,* 72; see no. 73.

laws nonviolently, in obedience to God—especially those inimical to the inviolable right to life of vulnerable human beings.

## The Crimes against Life

Perpetrating and legalizing the crimes against life as it does, the domination of the weak by the "strong" is nothing other than practical atheism aiming to usurp God's absolute sovereignty over life and death. When we attempt to "be like God" (Gn 3:5) by exercising power over human life, our "foolish and selfish way of thinking" inevitably leads us to use that power for injustice and death, thereby undermining the very foundation of authentic human relationships: mutual trust.[97] The breach of interpersonal trust within families is particularly grave. In the climate of the culture of death, the attacks on the lives of the most vulnerable are most often "carried out in the very heart of and with the complicity of the family, which by its nature is called to be the 'sanctuary of life.'"[98]

### Contraception and Abortion

The temptation to destroy life when it has barely begun frequently stems from the trivialization of human sexuality in societies that promote materialism, individualism, utilitarianism, and hedonism as primary values.[99] In a context like that, we no longer perceive the human body as a properly personal reality that signifies and makes possible our relations with other persons, with God, and with the world. Instead, it becomes reduced, in our understanding, to a purely material reality that we can control and manipulate as we please. At the same time, human sexuality becomes depersonalized and depersonalizing, exploited and exploitive. "From being the sign, place and language of love, that is, of the gift of self and acceptance of another in all the other's richness as a person, it increasingly becomes the occasion and instrument for self-assertion and the selfish satisfaction of personal desires and instincts."[100]

It is then but a small matter for us to disrupt the integrity of the conjugal act by artificially separating its unitive meaning from its procreative meaning through the use of contraception. "Procreation then becomes the 'enemy' to be avoided in sexual activity."[101] That is why the contraceptive mentality leads so often to abortion when an "unwanted" child is conceived.[102] A cou-

97. Ibid., 66.
98. Ibid., 11; see nos. 6, 92, 94.
99. See ibid., 23, 97.
100. Ibid., 23.
101. Ibid.; see no. 14.
102. See ibid., 13. "If an individual is exclusively concerned with 'use,' he can reach the point

ple that is not open to the possibility of new life is likely to regard a newly conceived child more as an obstacle to personal fulfillment than as a personal gift to be welcomed with love.[103] On both the personal and the public level, innocuous terms like "interruption of pregnancy" are employed to facilitate or even to encourage the decision to destroy the life of the child in the womb. Linguistic deceptions like that represent an effort to "distract attention from the fact that what is involved is the right to life of an actual human person," suggesting that "conscience does not cease to point to [life] as a sacred and inviolable value."[104]

Procured abortion constitutes the most fundamental and flagrant violation of interpersonal trust, since "the unborn child is totally entrusted to the protection and care of the woman carrying him or her in the womb."[105] It often reflects a breach of trust between the parents themselves, undermining the inherent nature of the family as a community of love and a sanctuary of life.[106] The parents, of course, are directly responsible for the care of the child entrusted to them, but there are others who serve in capacities that oblige them to play a significant role in encouraging and supporting parental efforts to ensure the child's welfare. Chief among these are legislators and members of the medical profession. Thus, when legislators promote and enact laws that deny the fundamental right to life to the unborn, and when medical personnel become "agents of death" rather than servants of life, they all bear a serious moral responsibility for the direct involvement of one or both parents in exploiting the absolute vulnerability of the child and in thus violating a sacred trust.[107]

In some instances, certain members of the health care profession will recommend an abortion when prenatal diagnostic techniques—fallible though they might be—detect some abnormality in an unborn child. Underlying the acceptance of eugenic (or selective) abortion is a shameful and reprehensible

---

of killing love by killing the fruit of love. For the culture of use, the 'blessed fruit of your womb' (Lk 1:42) becomes in a certain sense an 'accursed fruit.'" *LF*, 21.

103. See *EV*, 13.

104. Ibid., 11. See no. 58; Brennan, *Confronting the Language*.

105. *EV*, 58. "Therefore, by the authority which Christ conferred upon Peter and his successors, in communion with the bishops—who on various occasions have condemned abortion and who, in the aforementioned consultation, albeit dispersed throughout the world, have shown unanimous agreement concerning this doctrine—*I declare that direct abortion, that is, abortion willed as an end or as a means, always constitutes a grave moral disorder*, since it is the deliberate killing of an innocent human being." Ibid., 62.

106. See ibid., 59.

107. See ibid., 59, 89.

attitude that "presumes to measure the value of a human life only within the parameters of 'normality' and physical well-being."[108] Once we have arrived at the point of accepting life only conditionally—that is, only as long as it is not affected by any serious limitation, handicap, or illness—we find it easy to justify not only eugenic abortion but also infanticide (whether or not the baby is healthy) and euthanasia, leading us back to a state of barbarism.[109] In addition, when we presume to separate procreation "from the fully human context of the conjugal act" by using methods like in vitro fertilization, we are sure to become indifferent to the risks posed to the development of the embryos artificially produced thus.[110] Worse still, we might even destroy some of them or exploit them for medical or scientific purposes, reducing human life "to the level of simple 'biological material' to be freely disposed of."[111]

The pharmaceutical industry has heavily invested itself in the attack against the unborn by researching and developing an array of products that suppress life in the womb and that might eventually dispense with any need for medical assistance to kill a newly conceived life, thus "removing abortion from any kind of control or social responsibility."[112] When contraception (including abortifacients), along with sterilization and abortion, is promoted and even imposed by wealthy countries in their dealings with poorer ones, we see more clearly that the attack on the unborn is not simply directed at them alone. Many of the "powerful" people in developed parts of the world regard population growth among the world's poor as a threat to their national interests and security. In addressing the demographic question, therefore, they persuade or even coerce less privileged peoples to accept massive birth control programs, instead of helping them develop in ways that genuinely respect the life and dignity of individuals and families.[113] Developed countries have thus targeted the poor in underdeveloped countries by launching an offensive against the *unborn children* of the poor.

108. Ibid., 63. On the other hand, prenatal diagnostic techniques are morally licit when "they do not involve disproportionate risks for the child and the mother, and are meant to make possible early therapy or even to favor a serene and informed acceptance of the child not yet born." Ibid.

109. See ibid., 14.

110. Ibid., 14.

111. Ibid. See no. 63; Brennan, *Confronting the Language*, 29–50.

112. *EV*, 13.

113. See ibid., 16, 18, 91.

### Euthanasia

The trust that should characterize familial, societal, and even international relations is shattered by the attacks committed against human life in its earliest stages. It then becomes impossible to forestall similar attacks from occurring against a life that for any reason finds itself weak and defenseless at a later stage. As soon as values such as pleasure, material opulence, and efficiency become the governing principles of both the family and society, we will be less apt to recognize, appreciate, and protect the intrinsic value of human life itself. Instead, we will tend to regard as burdensome, useless, meaningless, or even intolerable any life marked by constant suffering, severe handicaps, terminal illness, or the limitations of old age.[114] Attitudes like that often reflect the absence of a genuinely religious outlook.[115] Having thus lost our sense of the transcendent, we seek to assume full control over our own life and that of others, particularly by taking control of death itself.[116]

In *Evangelium Vitae*, euthanasia is defined as "an act or omission which of itself and by intention causes death, with the purpose of eliminating all suffering."[117] It is particularly despicable when carried out for "the utilitarian motive of avoiding costs which bring no return and which weigh heavily on society" and on the family.[118] But even when motivated by "a misguided pity at the sight of the patient's suffering,"[119] euthanasia amounts to nothing more than "a false mercy and indeed a disturbing 'perversion' of mercy."[120] It is never justified under any circumstances.[121] Conscience testifies to that by our need to use ambiguous language, as we do in the case of abortion, to

114. See ibid., 23, 64. "Unquestionably, the quality of a society or civilization is measured by the respect it has for its weakest members. A technically perfect society where only fully productive members are accepted must be considered totally unworthy of human beings, perverted as it is by a type of discrimination that is no less reprehensible than racial discrimination. The handicapped person is one of us and shares in our humanity. To recognize and promote his or her dignity and rights is to recognize our own dignity and rights." John Paul II, "The Handicapped in Modern Society," in *Origins* 14, no. 15 (1984): 233.

115. See *EV*, 15.

116. See ibid., 64.

117. Ibid., 65.

118. Ibid., 15; see nos. 64, 94.

119. Ibid., 15.

120. Ibid., 66.

121. "[I]n harmony with the magisterium of my predecessors and in communion with the bishops of the Catholic Church, *I confirm that euthanasia is a grave violation of the law of God*, since it is the deliberate and morally unacceptable killing of a human person." Ibid., 65; see no. 66. "Regardless of the intentions and circumstances, euthanasia is always an intrinsically evil act, a violation of God's law and an offence against the dignity of the human person." *Letter of His Holiness Pope John Paul II to the Elderly* (October 1, 1999), 9, Vatican website.

disguise the true nature of this kind of attack on human life.[122] Behind the act itself of euthanasia, like that of abortion, is a perverted notion of human autonomy, which we presume to think should include "an absolute power over and against others."[123] The perversity of euthanasia as such is especially evident when it is performed either by relatives, "who are supposed to treat a family member with patience and love," or by doctors, "who by virtue of their specific profession are supposed to care for the sick person even in the most painful terminal stages."[124] A more subtle but no less serious form of euthanasia occurs when organs needed for transplants are removed from the donor before an objective and ethically sound effort has been made to determine whether the person is really even dead.[125]

Euthanasia takes the form of murder when it is inflicted on someone who neither requested nor consented to it. "The height of arbitrariness and injustice is reached when certain people such as physicians or legislators arrogate to themselves the power to decide who ought to live and who ought to die."[126] Even if perpetrated at the victim's request, the act of euthanasia is never morally justified. It would thus also be morally illicit for anyone to carry out the act against him- or herself, regardless of any subjective factors that might mitigate personal guilt. Suicide always constitutes an objective denial of God's absolute sovereignty over life and death. It is also a rejection of charity toward oneself and a "renunciation of the obligation of justice and charity toward one's neighbor, toward the communities to which one belongs and toward society as a whole."[127]

### The Vulnerability of the "Strong"

Jesus told the rich young man, "If you would enter life, keep the commandments" (Mt 19:17). He mentioned first the commandment, "You shall not kill" (v. 18), which is "included and more fully expressed in the positive command of love for one's neighbor."[128] One cannot enter or remain in communion with Jesus without fulfilling the law of love, receiving him thus so as to be "born of God" into that life which is the light of men (see Jn 1:4, 12–13). "Unless one is born anew, he cannot see the kingdom of God" (Jn 3:3).[129] That is why the "strong" who prey on the weak and subject them to any of the crimes against life become, in that very act, the most highly vulnerable

122. See *EV*, 11.
123. Ibid., 20.
124. Ibid., 66.
125. See ibid., 15.
126. Ibid., 66.
127. Ibid.
128. Ibid., 41; see no. 54.
129. See ibid., 37.

of all. By depriving others of temporal life, they risk depriving themselves definitively of *eternal* life in Christ.[130] At the same time, they deprive themselves of any meaningful fulfillment in the present life. On a larger scale, authentic peace, justice, development, freedom, and happiness will evade everyone's grasp as long as the attack on the vulnerable continues. If we do not advance the true common good by respecting, protecting, loving, and serving human life, then we will undermine the very foundation of society. In that case, neither we nor the sociocultural world of which we are a part will long endure.[131]

## *Evangelium Vitae*'s Anthropology of the Vulnerable

Having reviewed *Evangelium Vitae*'s general anthropology, as well as its treatment of certain attitudes and actions destructive of vulnerable human life, we will now take a thorough look at the "anthropology of the vulnerable" that John Paul II develops in the encyclical. His express purpose in writing *Evangelium Vitae* is "to reaffirm with the authority of Peter the value of human life and its inviolability, in the light of present circumstances and attacks threatening it today."[132] This concerns, above all, the most vulnerable members of society, whose intrinsic right to exist is being unjustly threatened or denied simply because their lives are at the point of greatest weakness, need, dependency, and defenselessness, especially at the beginning and final stages of their earthly existence.

### The Innocence of the Vulnerable

The attacks against the most vulnerable human persons are never justified because their victims can never be credibly regarded as posing a real threat to anyone. That is particularly evident in the case of the unborn. They are absolutely innocent.[133] The same can be said of the newly born, whose

130. It is likewise true that a vulnerable person who commits or consents to a crime against his or her own life (to say nothing of anyone else's) also risks the loss of eternal life.

131. See *EV*, 5, 101. "We are facing an immense threat to life: not only to the life of individuals but also to that of civilization itself. The statement that civilization has become, in some areas, a 'civilization of death' is being confirmed in disturbing ways." *LF*, 21. Rocco Buttiglione's remark in another, not wholly unrelated, context is highly relevant here: "The drama of modern man is that of having physically survived his own spiritual extinction." Buttiglione, *Karol Wojtyła*, 11.

132. *EV*, 5.

133. "The moral gravity of procured abortion is apparent in all its truth if we recognize that we are dealing with murder. . . . The one eliminated is a human being at the very beginning of life. No one more absolutely innocent could be imagined. In no way could this human being ever be

right to life is also being called into question or denied outright.[134] John Paul refers to the innocence of vulnerable human beings and to innocent human life some thirty times in *Evangelium Vitae*. In doing so, he is not denying that the lives of the vulnerable are affected by the consequences of original sin, or that some vulnerable persons might even be guilty of personal sin. Rather, he is speaking in a manner akin to the Old Testament proscriptions against the shedding of "innocent" blood.[135] That is, he intends to convey the idea that the victims of any of the crimes against life have a just cause before God, given their defenselessness in the face of the unprovoked attacks unleashed against them simply because they *are* defenseless.[136] In that sense, they are "righteous," reflecting the "innocence" of Abel and Job.[137]

We see, then, that the attacks against the elderly (whether or not they are self-sufficient), the severely handicapped, and the seriously or the terminally ill are likewise wholly unjustified. It is unlikely, in most cases, that they are capable of acting as aggressors or of adequately defending themselves against aggressive acts directed at them, and so they are "innocent" in at least that respect. But even more fundamentally, the attacks that others direct against them because they are *vulnerable* to attack constitute, in every case, grave violations of their intrinsic dignity as persons created in God's image and called to eternal life in Christ. That is why their cause before God cries out for justice. We must therefore conclude that the very weakness to which the condition of any vulnerable human being subjects him or her entitles that person—precisely *as* a person—to receive the greatest acceptance, love, and care. The frailty alone of the vulnerable qualifies them as "innocent." And so John Paul states unequivocally that "[t]o defend and promote life, to show reverence and love for it, is a task which God entrusts to every man"—and, by extension, to the whole of society.[138]

---

considered an aggressor, much less an unjust aggressor!" Ibid., 58. See John Paul II, *Crossing the Threshold*, 206.

134. See *EV*, 14–15. Against this inexcusable attack on new human life, John Paul affirms that newborns communicate to their parents "the newness and freshness" of their humanity even when "born with mental or physical disabilities." *LF*, 16.

135. E.g., John Paul refers to Exodus 23:7 in *EV*, 40, and to Jeremiah 19:4 in *EV*, 49.

136. E.g., see Proverbs 22:22–23.

137. See *EV*, 25 and 31. This would also apply, in a way, even to persons who have made *themselves* vulnerable to the crimes against life through their own vicious habits (e.g., through drug abuse), whose effects have so devastated their physical or mental well-being that their disability has left them at the "mercy" of others. Of course, these persons would certainly be morally accountable for having put themselves in that position in the first place, whereas that could not be true in any way of unborn or newborn children, nor of many other vulnerable persons.

138. Ibid., 42; see no. 81.

## The Vulnerable in the Sanctuary of the Family

We accept life (including our own) with love to the same extent that we love with our life, giving it generously in service to and for others.[139] The revelation and communication of love is first and foremost the vocation of the family, which has been divinely constituted as "the sanctuary of life" and consequently charged in a singular way with the responsibility of welcoming and defending human life. For that reason, family members who are newly conceived, young, old, sickly, or dying should be, above all, the special "objects" of a love that readily receives them by giving the gift of self generously *to* them. "Within the family each member is accepted, respected and honored precisely because he or she is a person; and if any family member is in greater need, the care which he or she receives is all the more intense and attentive."[140] In this way, the whole family learns that love reciprocally received and given is what ultimately gives life and the mysteries of life—procreation, suffering, and death—their true meaning.[141]

## Human Vulnerability as a Means of Seeking and Actively Expressing Love

From the moment that he personally entered the drama of human history and began "sharing in the lowliest and most vulnerable conditions of human life,"[142] Jesus gave himself to us in obedience to the will of the Father.[143] In a special way, he proclaimed "to all who feel threatened and hindered that their lives too are a good to which the Father's love gives meaning and value."[144] And the healings he performed for them signified not only "God's great concern even for man's bodily life,"[145] but, above all, the salvation that

139. E.g., ibid., 86.

140. Ibid., 92. Regarding disabled children in particular, John Paul reminds us that "when children are more vulnerable and exposed to the risk of being rejected by others, it is the family that can most effectively safeguard their dignity, equal to that of healthy children.... Illness, indeed, must prompt an attitude of special attention to these persons who belong in every way to the category of the poor who will inherit the kingdom of heaven.... When families [John Paul includes here those that welcome disabled children in foster care or adoption; see also *EV*, 93] are properly nourished by the Word of God, miracles of genuine Christian solidarity take place within them. This is the most convincing response to those who consider disabled children a burden or even as unworthy to live the gift of their life to the full. To welcome the weakest, helping them on their journey, is a sign of civilization." *Address of the Holy Father to the Congress on Integration of Disabled Children* (December 4, 1999), 2–3, Vatican website.

141. See *EV*, 81, 97.

142. Ibid., 33; see Phil 2:6–7.

143. See *EV*, 51.

144. Ibid., 32.

145. Ibid., 47.

they would receive through the forgiveness of sins and "the 'gift of the Spirit' by which Jesus ransoms us from death and opens before us a new life."[146] It was through his death on the cross that Jesus made this new life available to everyone, thus revealing all the splendor and value of human life. "Truly great must be the value of human life if the Son of God has taken it up and made it the instrument of the salvation of all humanity."[147] By the power of the Spirit, Jesus has endowed us with a "new heart," making it possible for us "to appreciate and achieve the deepest and most authentic meaning of life: namely, that of being a gift which is fully realized in the giving of self."[148] By giving ourselves in love to and for others, each of us follows the example of Christ in response to his grace, coming thus to share in his risen life—the eternal life of God, which he won for us at the price of his own blood.

In revealing the meaning of love by offering us the gift of his own life, Jesus sought to reclaim our love through the vulnerability of his wholly innocent humanity. By the gift of the Spirit, he would restore us to ourselves, to our original vocation to give ourselves in love, and thus save us. Similarly, human beings subject to the forms of vulnerability treated in *Evangelium Vitae* seek and express love through the "innocence" that their vulnerability confers on them. To the extent that others respond to the possibilities of Christ's grace hidden in the self-offer of the vulnerable, their own humanity undergoes a restoration as it opens up to new life in the Spirit, leading them toward salvation and hence away from their vulnerability to moral and spiritual ruin. At the same time, the vulnerable benefit in some way from the love they receive when others accept them—perhaps in virtue of the implicit offer they make of themselves through their condition of vulnerability—in the grace of the Spirit of Christ. Let us now consider more precisely what John Paul II teaches us in *Evangelium Vitae* about how vulnerable human beings invite the love of other persons while actively expressing their own, and about how the exchange of love between the vulnerable and others is reciprocally enriching and ultimately salvific.

### Suffering and Dying Persons

It is a fact of human experience that life's value is discovered through love. On the one hand, the vulnerability of persons who are gravely ill and for whom death approaches is often compounded by the temptation to give

146. Ibid., 51; see no. 50.

147. Ibid., 33.

148. Ibid., 49.

in to despair.[149] At the same time, however, it is frequently the very prospect of death that elicits in them a powerful urge to resist the annihilation of their own person. Human life, after all, contains within it the seed of eternity.[150] And so there arises in the heart of sufferers facing death the request for companionship, sympathy, and support—a request that is, at once, a plea to those around them to help sustain their hope that life will triumph over death.[151]

In seeking the love and acceptance of others, suffering and dying persons are also seeking an affirmation of their life. They receive that in the true compassion of those of us who are willing to share their distress rather than hasten their death out of a misguided sense of pity or a selfish refusal to be burdened with a life that we deem to be meaningless.[152] It is precisely our display of solidarity and our outpouring of genuinely merciful love that enables sufferers to face their condition with remarkable peace and fortitude. Indeed, "the courage and serenity with which so many of our brothers and sisters suffering from serious disabilities lead their lives when they are shown acceptance and love bears eloquent witness to what gives authentic value to life and makes it even in difficult conditions something precious for them and for others."[153] When suffering persons—in this case, seriously disabled ones—summon from within themselves the willingness and the determination to persevere under the weight of their condition, they often do so as an active response to the love they have received from us in response to their sometimes implicit plea for support. In that way, they provide a compelling witness to the life-giving power of love. For love bestowed and accepted illuminates the meaning and purpose of human life by awakening its latent vitality and by infusing it with new energy and resilience, while strengthening one's will to press on. Suffering persons discover the meaning and the incommensurable goodness of human life when we accept and give ourselves to them in love, and they help *us* discover it when they lovingly accept us and make a gift of their own life to us through their vulnerability. The deepest significance of their self-gift and the scope of its possibilities are fully revealed and realized only by their sharing in the life, death, and resurrection of Jesus Christ.

149. See ibid., 67. Likewise, see John Paul II, *Address to the Sick, the Elderly and the Handicapped* (November 23, 1986), Vatican website. John Paul delivered the address during his pastoral visit to New Zealand.

150. See *GS*, 18; *EV*, 7, 31, 34, 35, 67, 81.

151. See *EV*, 67.

152. See ibid., 66.

153. Ibid., 63.

By making an offering of themselves first of all to Christ through their suffering, the vulnerable become more fully conformed to him and thus more fully incorporated into his redemptive sacrifice. United thus with Christ's passion and his sacrificial death on the cross, the suffering they experience becomes a saving event, an act of love that promotes their personal growth and fills their life with meaning and value.[154] In the same way, their suffering becomes an efficacious instrument of salvation for the members of the Church (see Col 1:24) and for the larger world of persons as well.[155] By making it possible for us to transform suffering so, God has revealed to us, in Christ, his power over life. Therefore, even "[w]hen every hope of good health seems to fade ... the believer is sustained by an unshakable faith in God's life-giving power,"[156] neither despairing nor seeking death, but rather witnessing to the hope of redemption. The display of genuine hope born of persevering faith is a true and indispensable form of agency that sufferers or persons with disabilities might exercise.[157]

When a sufferer's condition is such that death is just on the horizon, "the certainty of future immortality and hope in the promised resurrection cast new light on the mystery of suffering and death, and fill the believer with an extraordinary capacity to trust fully in the plan of God."[158] This means that, in response to God's grace, believers facing death will freely and consciously accept their condition as a means of sharing in the Lord's passion. They will sometimes even forgo treatment with painkillers so that their consciousness of what they are doing will not be diminished, though they are certainly not morally bound to do so in cases of unbearable suffering.[159] By the grace of the Spirit, dying persons conform their lives to Christ filled with faith, hope, and love, so that they experience death as participating in the mystery of the Lord's own death and resurrection.[160] When they freely assimilate and thus "live" their own death in this way,[161] believers transform it into an event that is both meaningful and salvific.[162] "It is the door which opens wide on eternity."[163] Like Christ himself, they accept death at the time willed and chosen by the Father (see Jn 13:1), so that it becomes their supreme act of obedience to him.[164] In the face of death, as in life, the faithful must place themselves

154. See ibid., 81, 23.
155. See ibid., 67, 97; *CL*, 54.
156. *EV*, 46.
157. See John Paul II, *Jubilee of the Disabled.*
158. *EV*, 67.
159. See ibid., 65.
160. See ibid., 97.
161. See ibid., 22.
162. See ibid., 81.
163. Ibid., 97.
164. See ibid., 67.

completely in God's hands and accept from him this integral part of his loving plan.[165]

To sum up, then, persons subject to intractable suffering or imminent death can transform their condition into a salvific act of self-giving love by accepting it and offering themselves to Christ (and thereby to the Father) through it. Thanks to the mission of the divine Son and the grace of the Spirit, they can radiate the life of glory through the weakness of their cross, giving powerful testimony amid the culture of death that the cross of Christ is truly "the center, meaning and goal of all history and of every human life."[166]

The preceding examples of Christian suffering and death indicate that vulnerable persons can contribute in an almost unilateral way to the salvation of others when, by God's grace, they actively associate their condition with Christ's redemptive sacrifice. Such acts of self-giving love toward others might voluntarily or even necessarily remain concealed from the sight of all but God. "Many different acts of selfless generosity, often humble and hidden, [are being] carried out by men and women, children and adults, the young and the old, the healthy and the sick."[167] Interior or other hidden acts of unilateral, selfless generosity certainly constitute a genuine fulfillment of the true meaning of life, at least for the person who performs them and in virtue of the fact that the diffusion of their goodness can benefit the lives of others, even if in ways just as hidden as the acts themselves. Nevertheless, life is most completely fulfilled when there is an ongoing reciprocity of giving and receiving love. The passage quoted earlier suggested to us that disabled persons are inspired to live serenely and courageously with their sufferings precisely in response to the love and acceptance that they receive from others, bearing witness thereby to what makes life truly meaningful, even when it is beset by serious problems.[168] Life is therefore impoverished for everyone when vulnerable human beings are dismissed or rejected by those around them. When that happens, the possibilities for meaningful and mutually enriching exchanges between the vulnerable and the "strong," as well as all the good that this would accomplish, are significantly decreased or eliminated.

165. See ibid., 46. As we saw in chapter 1, Pope John Paul II lived fully to the end the message he proclaimed here.

166. Ibid., 50. See *GS*, 10.

167. *EV*, 86.

168. See ibid., 63.

### The Elderly

Pope John Paul II makes that point effectively when he considers the elderly. Within the climate of the culture of death, the elderly are likely to be viewed as a useless burden, and so left to suffer the pain of loneliness and the strain of having to fend for themselves. John Paul denounces the neglect and the rejection of the elderly as intolerable.[169] Their presence within (or at least their proximity to) the family is particularly important. For one thing, children learn the attitudes of togetherness, sharing, and service by seeing the example of their parents caring for elderly family members. In addition, when the elderly are accepted by other family members, a "covenant" between generations is formed, by which different age groups interact and communicate in mutually enriching ways.[170] That kind of atmosphere helps foster in children the sort of attitude that will move them to accept and care for their own parents as the years pass, in obedience to the fourth commandment. It is also an atmosphere that alleviates the loneliness and anxiety that the elderly might otherwise experience.[171] Finally, such an atmosphere permits the elderly to contribute to the family—to *give* of themselves in ways that their exclusion from family life would render impossible. For example, "thanks to the rich treasury of experiences they have acquired through the years, the elderly can and must be sources of wisdom and witnesses of hope and love."[172] In that way, they perform the invaluable and indispensable service of promoting the Gospel of life down through the generations.[173]

169. See ibid., 94.

170. See ibid., 92, 94. "[T]he signs of human frailty which are clearly connected with advanced age become a summons to the mutual dependence and indispensable solidarity which link the different generations, inasmuch as every person needs others and draws enrichment from the gifts and charisms of all." *Letter to the Elderly,* 10. In *LF,* 10, John Paul comments on the modern tendency to restrict family units to two generations (the "nuclear family"): "*Families today have too little 'human' life.* There is a shortage of people with whom to create and share the common good."

171. See *EV,* 88. In the unfortunate absence of this intergenerational solidarity, John Paul reminds the elderly (and us) that with God's help, they can actively participate in his saving plan by uniting themselves more closely to Christ's sacrifice, precisely in and through their loneliness and suffering. See *Letter to the Elderly,* 13.

172. *EV,* 94.

173. John Paul had spoken of this more specifically and rather profoundly as he addressed the elderly in Perth, Australia: "You are able to teach the young that it is important to value life in itself and for itself. You invite other age groups to realize that feverish activity is not the measure of a useful life. Your ability to cherish life for its own sake, in spite of a lessening of energy and mobility, challenges others to reflect not only on the value of doing but on the value of being. Your lives are directed towards the Kingdom of heaven, and this challenges those whose interests are all bound up with the passing world. As you gradually detach yourselves from certain possessions,

### The Weakest of the Vulnerable: The "Silent" Actors

The condition of some persons can make them so delicate, especially at the very beginning and end of life, that they cannot give the gift of self through their vulnerability using verbal or other easily perceptible and intelligible means of communication. But that does not preclude the possibility of their actively communicating themselves to and enriching the lives of other people in and through the utter helplessness that places them among the most vulnerable of the vulnerable. Even though the weakest members of the social structure—persons like the unborn and those at the point of death—appear to be "completely at the mercy of others and radically dependent on them," they can still "communicate through the silent language of a profound sharing of affection."[174] John Paul II gives us good reason to believe that he regards this "silent language" as a distinctly human and personal mode of communication, of which the most vulnerable human beings are among the agents. In that case, they are not only *persons* but also *actors*.[175]

In the broadest sense, the silent language to which John Paul refers can be expressed by persons in any condition according to their command of

---

you help others to reflect on their own relationship to material things. In this way your lives can be an eloquent witness to the essential values taught by Christ." *Address of John Paul II to the Elderly* (November 30, 1986), 7, Vatican website. See also *Letter to the Elderly*, 13; *CL*, 48.

174. *EV*, 19.

175. In his article entitled "Euthanasia and John Paul II's 'Silent Language of Profound Sharing of Affection': Why Christians Should Care about Peter Singer" (*Christian Bioethics* 7, no. 3 [2001], 359–78), Derek S. Jeffreys (rightly) describes the "silent language" passage in *EV*, 19, as "moving" (372), but he seems partially to misinterpret its clear meaning. He reads the passage as affirming only the self-giving and solidarity that *others* (e.g., family members, caregivers) might extend to the most vulnerable members of society rather than as affirming a special mode of agency that these vulnerable persons are capable of exercising themselves. Admittedly, the case he presents is especially difficult, namely, the relation between parents and their anencephalic infant. Though he speaks of the parents' "interaction" with their disabled child (e.g., through prayer, touching, or pure presence; see 372–73), Jeffreys describes only the unilateral action of the parents toward their child; that is, it is the *parents'* exercise of the "silent language" that transforms or redeems the suffering that *they* experience over the child's condition. In the case he proposes, Jeffreys does not give due consideration to the active, personal presence of the child and to how that child's suffering might consequently be redemptive through its inclusion in the suffering of Christ, about which he speaks on pages 364–66 (quoting from *SD*). Moreover, in his concern to refute Singer's utilitarian endorsement of euthanasia for children such as these (see 368–69), Jeffreys seems to overlook the fact that there are contexts other than that of suffering in which the "silent language" might be spoken, whether by a person who is exceedingly vulnerable or by one who is not. Still, he is quite right to recognize the importance of refuting Singer (359–60), and his effort to do so by appealing to John Paul II's insistence on the priority of spiritual goods over material ones (while affirming the value of both) is welcome. For his application of this hierarchy of goods to the political order, see *Defending Human Dignity*.

their personal capacities, in which case it might be expressed either more fully or less so. It is the language of a baby who, having experienced only the most tender maternal care, quietly rests her head on her mother's shoulder with a warranted sense of unconditional trust. It is, reciprocally, the language of that mother, who fostered such trust by giving herself to and for her child in so many quiet, unspoken ways. It is the language of the dying person, who, though completely debilitated and perhaps seemingly unresponsive, summons every last ounce of strength left in his body to squeeze the hand of a family member one last time before death. And it is the language of that family member, who quietly communicated with the dying person by taking his hand in the first place, giving physical substance to the bond of love that unites them here, and that will continue to unite them after the one crosses over the threshold of death.

The silent language to which John Paul refers is also the language of Christ's blood, the "voice" of which "cries out" or "speaks" silently but eloquently to the Father and to humanity about a supremely self-giving and life-giving love (see Heb 12:22–24; Gn 4:10). "Precisely because it is poured out as the gift of life, the blood of Christ is no longer a sign of death, of definitive separation from the brethren, but the instrument of a communion which is richness of life for all."[176] At the moment of his greatest weakness, Christ gave the most complete and most powerful testimony about his Person, his Life, and his mission, thereby illuminating "the meaning of the life and death of every human being."[177] Each person, from the one newly conceived to the one crossing the threshold of death, is a divine gift so ineffably precious that he or she is called in Christ through the "silent testimony" of his blood to share eternally in the Life and Love of God himself. In many cases, it is when the most vulnerable persons speak through the "silent language" of their weakness and defenselessness that this "Gospel of life"—which is also "the Gospel of God's love for man" and "the Gospel of the dignity of the person"[178]—is most powerfully and wondrously proclaimed.

Given the sublime subtlety of the "profound sharing of affection," it is not easily perceived or understood by those who have accepted or adopted the ways of the culture of death. A real sensitivity is needed here, born of a contemplative outlook arising from faith in the God of life. Once life is grasped and accepted as an utterly gratuitous gift of the Creator, we are more

176. *EV*, 25.

177. Ibid., 50.

178. Ibid., 2.

disposed to see his living image in every human person.[179] "The glory of God shines on the face of man,"[180] who has been created with a dignity that is almost divine.[181] What is more, "the Son of God has united himself in some fashion with every human being" by his Incarnation,[182] "which enables us to see in every human face the face of Christ,"[183] in whom God's image in us has been fully revealed and renewed.[184]

It was, above all, in and through the most humble and vulnerable conditions of human life that Christ manifested and restored God's glory in us.[185] Therefore, while every human being is "a sign of the living God, an icon of Christ,"[186] the Master identifies himself in a special way with the vulnerable, in whom he expects to be seen, loved, and served.[187] By radiating his glory through their fragile, bodily existence, they invite the love that he himself wants to receive in them from others. That is why it is ultimately Christ himself who is rejected when human life is rejected in any way.[188] Conversely, the real rejection of Christ invariably takes the form of attacks against the lives of the vulnerable.[189]

The infant, the sick, the suffering, the disabled, the elderly, the dying: vulnerable persons of every kind challenge the "strong" to perceive in their face "a call to encounter, dialogue and solidarity."[190] The manner in which these persons lay down the challenge varies. In some cases, they "cry out" for help in an audible way.[191] However, in the case of the unborn, and per-

179. See ibid., 83.

180. Ibid., 35. See Irenaeus, *Adversus Haereses,* IV, 20, 7.

181. See *EV,* 25, 84.

182. *GS,* 22. See *EV,* 2, 104.

183. *EV,* 81.

184. See ibid., 36. In *Totality and Infinity: An Essay on Exteriority* (trans. Alphonso Lingis [Pittsburgh: Duquesne University Press, 1969]), philosopher Emmanuel Levinas uses "the face" as a metaphor for the *one* finite image that overflows with the infinite. Among other things, he reflects on the infinity—the transcendence—revealed in the "naked" human face insofar as the latter is, of itself, the premier expression of human vulnerability, silently uttering the primordial word, "thou shall not commit murder." If this "word" did not implicitly precede every other word, the possibility of human relationality—and so, too, the very reason for human language itself—would disappear. This and other aspects of his thought, as elaborated in *Totality and Infinity,* suggest that persons lacking the capacity for verbal dialogue can nevertheless actively express their transcendence as they "face" others. See John Paul II, *Crossing the Threshold,* 210–11.

185. See *EV,* 33, 50, 51.

186. Ibid., 84.

187. See ibid., 43.

188. See ibid., 104. "Whoever attacks human life in some way attacks God Himself." Ibid., 9.

189. See ibid., 22, 104. The preeminent biblical example of this is Herod's effort to eliminate the Christ Child by attacking the Holy Innocents (see Mt 2:1–18). See *LF,* 21. Thus, the "conspiracy against life" is really, in the end as in the beginning, a conspiracy against God and so, necessarily, against truth. See John Paul II, *Crossing the Threshold,* 64–65.

190. *EV,* 83.

191. See ibid., 32; Lk 18:35–43.

haps that of others, their complete helplessness excludes even the possibility of perceptible cries and tears, the most basic and poignant means by which human beings, especially infants, express their need.[192] Still, this does not necessarily imply that only inferior forms of communication remain open to them, or that they are incapable of any communication at all. On the contrary, as persons created in the divine image and renewed in Christ, the glory of God radiates in them, so that they enrich the life of others by their very presence, bodily expressed.[193] Their very life is a sign and an offer of love, as well as an invitation to love, communicated "through the silent language of a profound sharing of affection."

Let us consider in particular the silent self-communication in love of unborn children. Like every other human person, each unborn child is an image of God's glory and an icon of Christ. But he is perhaps the most vulnerable of the vulnerable, since, hidden from view in his mother's womb, others cannot directly see in his "face"—that is, in his humanity—the face of Christ inviting them to accept, love, and serve him in this least one among his brethren. Still, though unseen, this little one is by no means unannounced. John Paul II attributes even to the unborn a "silent language" by which they actively communicate their affection in a distinctly human and personal way. On what anthropological basis does he support such a startling position?

In *Evangelium Vitae,* John Paul seems to intuit the truth of his position and does not seem expressly concerned about defending it.[194] Nevertheless, the theological and anthropological convictions that he sets forth in the document give us some direction as we ponder the meaning and basis of his affirmation about the agency of the unborn (and of all the weakest members of the social structure). At the most fundamental level, the claim that the unborn child can communicate through the silent language of human affection follows from the fact that he is a human person. God involves himself directly in human procreation by creating the spiritual soul, which, together

192. See *EV,* 58.

193. See ibid., 35, 98.

194. We are referring here to a *rational* intuition. While the expression, "the silent language of a profound sharing of affection," is beautifully poetic, it is by no means a mere metaphor. John Paul II, philosopher and theologian, is expressing a profound truth about which he is convinced. And even if the expression as such was not actually authored by John Paul himself (since *EV* is "the fruit of the cooperation of the episcopate of every country of the world" [no. 5]), it is utterly consistent with his thought (perhaps even echoing that of John of the Cross) and has received his authoritative stamp by its inclusion in the document.

with the body that expresses it, constitutes the newly conceived life humanly and personally as God's image. Thus, "the life which parents transmit has its origins in God."[195] Since God's care also preserves the human spirit (see Jb 10:12),[196] we can affirm, from that standpoint, that it is he who "sets in order the elements" of every unborn child (see 2 Mc 7:22); that is, it is he who "knits" each one together in his mother's womb (see Ps 139:13).[197]

The special action of God at the initial moment of life reveals that "the life of every individual, from its very beginning, is part of God's plan."[198] What is more, his ongoing attention to the formation of children in the womb reveals that "they are the personal objects of God's loving and fatherly providence."[199] Modern genetic research on human embryos provides a firm basis for discerning this personal presence from the moment that new human life is conceived,[200] lending empirical support to the biblical view that God "gazes on [all human beings] when they are tiny shapeless embryos and already sees in them the adults of tomorrow whose days are numbered and whose vocation is even now written in the 'book of life.'"[201] John Paul gives us an oblique reminder of the biblical and theological grounds for discerning a personal presence in the unborn when he invites every woman who has had an abortion to commend her baby, with hope, to the Father and his mercy.[202] For only a person, whose spiritual soul survives the death of the body, can be entrusted to God's care after death.

In our general anthropology, we saw that "man is naturally drawn to God,"[203] who made the human soul "in the image of His own eternity"

195. *EV*, 44.

196. See ibid.

197. See ibid., 61.

198. Ibid., 44.

199. Ibid., 61.

200. See ibid., 60.

201. Ibid., 61, referring to Ps 139:13–16. "'Before I formed you in the womb I knew you, and before you were born I consecrated you' (Jer 1:5). The genealogy of the person is thus united with the eternity of God, and only then with human fatherhood and motherhood, which are realized in time. At the moment of conception itself, man is already destined to eternity in God." *LF*, 9. Cf. *EV*, 43.

202. "Infantem autem vestrum potestis Eidem Patri Eiusque misericordiae cum spe committere." *EV*, 99; *AAS* 87 (1995), 515. Note that the English translation of the text diverges rather dramatically from the Latin, reading as follows: "You will come to understand that nothing is definitively lost, and *you will also be able to ask forgiveness from your child, who is now living in the Lord*" (italics added). Still, the translation implies that God sustains in existence, for all eternity, the little soul he created, such that the reciprocal, interpersonal relation of mother and child is not completely ruptured with the latter's death. In many cases, a pregnant mother's own vulnerability is directly linked to her unborn child's vulnerability to being aborted, since she might be the victim of poverty, unbearable pain, violence, abandonment, and other enormous pressures that make "the choice to defend and promote life so demanding as sometimes to reach the point of heroism." *EV*, 11; see. no. 59.

203. *EV*, 35.

(Ws 2:23).[204] Therefore, every human being, even if yet unborn, is moved from within toward eternal existence with God as his or her definitive goal and fulfillment. "The life which God bestows upon man is ... a drive toward fullness of life; it is the seed of an existence which transcends the very limits of time."[205] This is the very dynamism that spurs our personal growth from the beginning. We strive naturally to realize our initially secret drive toward the Infinite—the supernatural end for which we were created—by communicating with other human beings, for in virtue of the spiritual soul, created and given directly by God as the principle of our life, there is in each of us "a reflection of God himself, the definitive goal and fulfillment of every person."[206] In seeking thus to "satisfy the need for interpersonal dialogue, so vital for human existence,"[207] we express our inner striving for communion with God himself.

In one way or another, therefore, we offer ourselves in love to other persons because, having been made in God's image, they are capable of *accepting* us in love. In that way, we express also our fundamental openness to *receiving* the love that *they* offer *to us*. Since all human beings share the same personal dignity, there is an ineffable "'spiritual' kinship uniting mankind in one great family."[208] It is this that ultimately underlies the unique character of communication between persons, making possible that silent but profound sharing of affection to which alone the most weak and defenseless human beings have recourse, and which expresses their natural spiritual drive toward God.

Motherhood provides a particularly striking example of spiritual solidarity and interpersonal exchange, for it

> involves a special communion with the mystery of life, as it develops in the woman's womb. The mother ... "understands" with unique intuition what is happening inside her .... [She] accepts and loves as a person the child she is carrying in her womb. This unique contact with the new human being developing within her gives rise to an attitude toward human beings—not only toward her own child, but every human being—which profoundly marks the woman's personality.[209]

In virtue of that experience, "women first learn and then teach others that human relations are authentic if they are open to accepting the other person: a person who is recognized and loved because of the dignity which comes

204. See ibid., 34.
205. Ibid., 34.
206. Ibid., 35.
207. Ibid.
208. Ibid., 8; see no. 57.
209. *MD*, 18. *EV*, 99, quotes from this same passage, but a little more sparingly.

from being a person and not from other considerations such as usefulness, strength, intelligence, beauty or health."[210] Women teach this, above all, through the unique, sacrificial sharing that authentic motherhood entails, which is how they "give voice," in their own way, to the language of love that their children have secretly taught them from the hidden sanctuary of the womb. The heroic, self-giving actions of mothers constitute a "silent but effective and eloquent witness" to what it is that builds up an authentic culture of life.[211] And like the child in her womb, a mother often makes her personal presence known and enriches the lives of others just by "being there."

In a most remarkable scriptural passage (see Lk 1:39–56), John the Baptist and Jesus communicate silently but effectively with each other and with their respective mothers while still in the womb. It is particularly astonishing that the event took place just days after Jesus, eternal according the his divinity, was first conceived according to his humanity. The scene unfolds as follows. The angel Gabriel announced to Mary that she would conceive and give birth to the Son of God (see Lk 1:26–33). As a sign that this would be accomplished by "the power of the Most High"—that is, by the Holy Spirit—the angel also revealed to Mary that her aged kinswoman, Elizabeth, was already six months pregnant, for such things are possible with God (vv. 34–37). Mary believed Gabriel's word and, shortly thereafter, she "arose and went in haste" from Nazareth to a city of Judah, where she entered Zechariah's house and greeted Elizabeth (vv. 39–40). Upon hearing the greeting, Elizabeth immediately felt John, the baby in her womb, leap for joy (vv. 41, 44). At the same time, "Elizabeth was filled with the Holy Spirit" (v. 41), recognizing Mary as the mother of the Lord (v. 43) and proclaiming prophetically, "Blessed are you among women, and blessed is the fruit of your womb" (v. 42). She declared Mary blessed a second time for having believed that the things promised her by the Lord would be fulfilled (v. 45). With that, Mary herself began to prophesy (vv. 46–55).

In *Evangelium Vitae,* Pope John Paul II calls attention to the real dynamic at work behind this whole scene by quoting from the section corresponding to it in the *Expositio Evangelii Secundum Lucam* of St. Ambrose.[212] While Elizabeth was first to hear Mary's voice with her ears—that is, "according to

210. *EV,* 99.

211. Ibid., 86.

212. See Ambrose, *Expositio Evangelii Secuundum Lucam,* II, 22–23, Corpus Christianorum, Series Latina, vol. 14 (Turnhout, Belgium: Typographi Brepolis Editores Pontificii, 1957), 40–41. The translation used here of passages from this text is that found in par. 45 of the official English translation of *EV,* except where noted.

the order of nature"—John leaped in her womb because of the mystery of the Lord's presence, having been first to experience the new order of grace.[213] "She recognized the arrival of Mary; he, the arrival of the Lord. The woman recognized the woman's arrival; the child, that of the child." After John, filled with the Holy Spirit (see Lk 1:15), leaped for joy at the arrival of Jesus in the womb of Mary, Elizabeth, in turn, became filled with the Spirit *through her son* and began to prophesy. Whereas she communicated to John her joy at the greeting of Mary, he communicated to her the joy *and the grace* that he received from the Lord's presence *within* and *radiating through* Mary.[214]

Mary, too, rejoiced in the Spirit after John leaped in his mother's womb (see Lk 1:47). And like Elizabeth, she began to prophesy (vv. 46–55). But Mary's response, to continue with Ambrose's exposition,[215] was not the result of her having been filled suddenly with the Holy Spirit, as was the case with Elizabeth. While Elizabeth was filled *after* the conception of John, Mary was filled *before* the conception of Jesus (see v. 28). Still, her joyful response to John's hidden activity does indicate that "the Incomprehensible One was indeed mysteriously active in His mother."[216]

Thus, both Mary and Elizabeth speak of grace because their children, acting from within them, are unfolding its very mystery for their benefit. By a "double miracle," the mothers "prophesy under the inspiration of their children."[217] John Paul summarizes the matter well: "It is precisely the children who reveal the advent of the Messianic age: In their meeting, the redemptive power of the presence of the Son of God among men first becomes operative."[218]

213. Where John is concerned, Mary's greeting "gave voice" to her Son's announcing himself.

214. In virtue of John's sharing that grace with his mother, Mary "became in some way a 'tabernacle'—the first 'tabernacle' in history—in which the Son of God, still invisible to our human gaze, allowed himself to be adored by Elizabeth, radiating his light as it were through the eyes and the voice of Mary." *Ecclesia de Eucharistia*, 55.

215. Here we are taking up Ambrose's text at the point where *EV*, 45, leaves off. The additional material reinforces the part of the text translated in the encyclical. The sentences excluded there read, in the original, as follows: "Exsultauit Iohannes, exsultauit et Mariae spiritus. Exsultante Iohanne repletur Elisabet, Mariam tamen non repleri spiritu, sed spiritum eius exsultare cognouimus—incomprehensibilis enim incomprehensibiliter operabatur in matre—et illa post conceptum repletur, ista ante conceptum." *Expositio*, 41.

216. "When Mary exclaims, 'My soul magnifies the Lord and my spirit rejoices in God my Saviour', she already bears Jesus in her womb. She praises God 'through' Jesus, but she also praises him 'in' Jesus and 'with' Jesus. This is itself the true 'Eucharistic attitude.'" *Ecclesia de Eucharistia*, 58.

217. *EV*, 45. Quite literally, they prophesy by the *spirit* of their children. The original text reads as follows: "Istae gratiam loquuntur, illi intus operantur pietatisque mysterium maternis adoriuntur profectibus duplicique miraculo prophetant matres spiritu paruulorum." Ambrose, *Expositio*, 41. Thus, each mother gives voice to her child.

218. *EV*, 45. In John Paul II's apostolic exhortation on St. Joseph, *Redemptoris Custos*

If the children were able to communicate with each other and with their mothers from the womb by means of "the silent language of a profound sharing of affection," that was because each mother had already communicated to her child, in a silent and profound way, her own affection for *him*. From the first, the children were gratefully and unconditionally accepted by their mothers as wholly unexpected gifts. "The exaltation of fruitfulness and the eager expectation of life resound in the words with which Elizabeth rejoices in her pregnancy: 'The Lord has looked on me ... to take away my reproach among men.'"[219] In a singular way, Mary is the one "who accepted 'Life' in the name of all and for the sake of all ... through her acceptance and loving care for the life of the Incarnate Word."[220] Contained in each mother's welcoming response to her child is her lifelong willingness to give herself to him and for him, and even *with* him.[221] Hidden beneath the heart of their mothers, the children received, reciprocated, and elicited further this silent communication of love. Using that same form of expression, the children communicated mysteriously with each other. In their humanity, they were naturally drawn to and disposed to receive the love of God as expressed by their mothers, and they radiated that love themselves (Jesus by his divine nature, John by grace), in virtue of their personal presence in the womb from the moment of their conception.

## Human Action and the "Silent Language"

Having examined *Evangelium Vitae*'s "anthropology of the vulnerable" at length, we will now try to clarify the relation and the distinction between human action as strictly understood in *Person and Act* and the silent language of shared affection, which, though expressible on different levels at

([August 14, 1989], Vatican website), he mentions "the influence Jesus exercised upon John the Baptist when they were both in their mothers' wombs (cf. Lk 1:41–44)," owing to his divinity operating through his humanity, its "efficacious instrument" in "sanctifying man" (no. 27). Further on, he says that St. Joseph—the "Guardian of the Redeemer"—experienced "that pure contemplative love of the divine Truth which radiated from the humanity of Christ" (ibid.). During his earthly life, therefore, not only were Christ's manifestly human actions sources of grace for us, but so, too, was the "hidden" action by which the radiance of his divine being shined through his humanity such a source.

219. *EV*, 45; see Lk 1:25.

220. *EV*, 102. In the motherhood of Mary, the Theotokos, "the vocation to motherhood bestowed by God on every woman is raised to its highest level." Ibid., 103.

221. "'Standing by the cross of Jesus' (Jn 19:25), Mary shares in the gift which the Son makes of himself: She offers Jesus, gives him over and begets him to the end for our sake." *EV*, 103.

any stage of life, is the only mode of communication open to certain persons. Among them, we would have to include at least some, probably many, seriously infirm or dying persons, and certainly every unborn, newly born, or very young child. Granting that the act of their own existence is (1) a radiative communication of their concrete, personal presence, (2) a personal reflection of God's creative love, (3) a possible vessel and vehicle of grace, and (4) dynamically ordered toward God as its ultimate end: can we still qualify this mode of activity, this act of personally being, as being personal? Based on texts that we have examined in this chapter and earlier ones, it seems that sometime after the publication of *Person and Act* in 1969, Karol Wojtyła/John Paul II modified his own response to that question, moving from a definite "no" to a qualified "yes."

In *Person and Act,* as we know, the author's aim was to uncover, through our self-experience in performing moral acts, the personal structure by which we perform them. He identifies such acts as voluntary, distinguishing them, appropriately, from involuntary acts (activations or "happenings"), which arise spontaneously from human nature (for example, organic functions, emotional surges, or reflexive, physical reactions to sensory stimuli). Wojtyła insists, nonetheless, that each of us remains the subject of nature's "acts." By actualizing the personal structure of self-possession and self-governance that establishes the transcendent core of human existence from its beginning, the actor can integrate certain of those otherwise involuntary acts of the natural psychosomatic dynamism into the voluntary, self-determining moral act as the condition for performing it, whereas any appreciable level of psychological and rational immaturity or disintegration would prevent one from actualizing the personal structure in that way. Cardinal Wojtyła's original position, in the latter case, is that we are dealing with a person who, nevertheless, cannot perform personal acts.

However, consistent with the sound anthropological principles that he laid out in *Person and Act,* Wojtyła/John Paul seems later to have concluded rather explicitly that it is a mistake to dismiss the involuntary activity of human beings as strictly "nonpersonal"—as dynamized solely by nature—precisely because even human beings who are presently capable only of such activity are persons, strictly speaking. Every involuntary operation that follows on the act by which one comes to exist personally, though often analogous to the purely natural operations that we see in other living beings of the material world, is nevertheless on a qualitatively and incomparably higher level, for it is rooted in, perfects the existence of, expresses, reveals, and communicates a human person. This means that the dynamic spiritual act of existence underlies, and so places the person at the center of, the derivative, natural dynamisms, which consequently tend toward and serve as the foundation for the full self-expression of the person in action. The implications of that idea, coupled with complementary theological considerations based on the biblical revelation, seem to have helped Wojtyła/John Paul arrive at his later affirmations about personal agency in vulnerable human beings having an underdeveloped or a seriously impaired self-awareness and rationality.

John Paul II's thinking on this matter reached something of a peak with his reflections on the inexhaustible mystery of the eternal Person of the Son of God initiating the new and definitive dispensation of grace by acting through the humanity that he had only just assumed, in time, in the womb of the Virgin Mary. The Visitation scene, as interpreted in *Evangelium Vitae,* 45, seems to illustrate what John Paul meant when he spoke earlier, in paragraph 19, of "the silent language of a profound sharing of affection," by which alone the weakest members of society, including the unborn, can communicate. Through that revelation, we learn unequivocally that one's personal self-communication to other persons proceeds immediately from one's personal act of existence as expressed by the concrete, "self-determining" humanity of which the person is the subject.

From the purely empirical standpoint, we now know that just sixty to seventy days after conception, the nervous system, together with the rest of the body's other major systems and structures, is so highly developed that human sensation has already begun. Where human beings are concerned, to have a sensation means to be aware of it. Cardinal Wojtyła has made it clear that human sensation manifests itself in the field of human consciousness. So, even at this early stage of development, sensory cognition and human consciousness (which, according to Wojtyła, is itself rooted in, and forms an organic whole with, our cognitive potentiality) are operative, at least in a rudimentary way. This suggests, moreover, that the fetus is fast approaching, even then, the threshold of experiencing those deeper feelings and emotions that issue from the emotive core of the human psyche.

Even if the child cannot yet rationally objectify the meaning of the emotions radiating from the innermost psychical stirrings that happen in him, and consciousness cannot, therefore, relate that meaning back to him so that he can integrate the emotions deliberately into his person and determine himself in a personally self-fulfilling way, his experience of stirring emotions conduces, nevertheless, to making the child aware of himself as their subject. It conduces to the self-experience by which the child will come to recognize his objective subjectivity. He will consequently come also to recognize the concrete subjectivity of other persons, and likewise the objectivity of nonpersonal beings, as realities distinct from his own concrete existence. In addition, his emotions will orient him toward the objective values to which they relate, preparing, indirectly, for the intellectual apprehension of the truth about the good or evil of the values themselves. Indeed, the increasingly purposeful activity that we can now observe in the unborn child suggests that both cognitive intentionality and volition, at the incipiently rational level, along with memory, are developing simultaneously with the growth of incipient self-experience. Divine revelation would seem to confirm this.

If not so easily in Jesus' case, we can see fairly clearly in that of John the Baptist—though still three months from birth—that incipiently conscious, rational, and volitional activities begin much closer to the time that we first come to exist than we might tend to think. Newly imbued with the grace of the Messiah, John expressed himself purposefully in his mother's womb. At the very least, he experienced a deep, emotional stirring that radiated throughout his inner being and expressed itself bodily as joy. John's was a deeply felt religious experience rooted in the spiritual side of his being, while eliciting, and thus expressing itself through, a somatic response.[222] In view of the biblical testimony about the Baptist, it seems fair to say that this experience marked his whole life and personality. But there is more. Following Ambrose, John Paul II tells us the reason for John's spiritual elation: the child recognized the Savior's concrete presence in Mary's womb. By grace, he knew the source of his joy. And he communicated that grace, that knowledge, and that joy to his mother. The whole scene thus reveals John's awareness of himself and of the other persons present to him, and it consequently also reveals the integral engagement of all his cognitive and appetitive powers to the extent that they had already developed in him at the time.

The Visitation account confirms John Paul II's conviction that the child's active, personal presence in his mother has a deep impact on her personality, heightening her awareness of the mystery of human life and disposing her to be more open to it. What is more, given John Paul's complementary conviction that the mother, "even before giving birth, *does not only give shape to the child's body, but also, in an indirect way, to the child's whole*

222. Cf. *AP*, 231–32, 238–42.

*personality,"*[223] we might justifiably infer that the blamelessness with which Elizabeth (along with her husband, Zechariah) walked before God (see Lk 1:6) so marked her personality that she somehow communicated her virtue to John as he grew within her. Subtle but most real, a reciprocal relationship of that kind presupposes that a profoundly personal bond exists between a mother and her prenatal child, as each experiences and responds to the intimate presence of the other. It suggests, moreover, that even from the womb, a child soon begins to act according to the way in which his or her own personality is already taking shape.[224] That would be consistent with the original and purposeful activity that we can observe more easily in the postnatal infant or the young child—activity that cannot credibly be reduced to mere "activations" such as wholly involuntary instincts, reflexive responses, or modes of imitation. Indeed, the rapid development in and the child's coordinated use of the different senses in relation to a particular object, if not already signifying an incipient understanding of the object, is at least indicative of a dynamic seeking for such an understanding. And the very deployment of the senses—and so, too, of the body—in this guided *act* of seeking indicates the involvement of the will. But in order to perceive such realities in all their marvelous truth, and to be transformed by the equally marvelous exchanges of love between the vulnerable and us that can take place through them, we require that "contemplative outlook," born of faith in the God of life, of which John Paul II speaks in *Evangelium Vitae,* 83.

In harmony with Cardinal Wojtyła/Pope John Paul II's anthropology, the

223. *LF,* 16.

224. In his *Message of John Paul II on the Occasion of the Congress of the "Biological and Psychological Foundations of Prenatal Education"* ([March 20, 1998], Vatican website), John Paul praises the research that examines "the child still in his mother's womb, not only to monitor and observe his physical growth and to listen to the beat of his tiny heart, but also to study his emotions and record the signs of his psychological development. In this research there is an implicit respect for the person in whom an immortal spirit already pulsates and the Creator's image is revealed" (no. 1). For that reason, the interest of the researchers before him is ultimately "directed to the inmost depths of the new being, a guest in his mother's womb" (no. 2). John Paul observes further that "it is important to identify the connection between the psychological development of the unborn child and the family context in which he lives. The harmony of the married couple, the warmth of the home, the tranquility of daily life affect his psychology, fostering growth: it is not only genes that hand on the parents' hereditary traits, but also the repercussions of their spiritual and emotional experiences" (ibid.). Research "on the physical, psychological and spiritual elements of human life from its beginnings" is essential to "defending and promoting life, especially if it is frail and defenceless." Anyone concerned about that must therefore be "committed to creating a culture based on science, 'by offering serious and well-documented contributions, capable of commanding general respect and interest by reason of their merit'" (no. 4, ending with a quote from *EV,* 98).

preceding paragraphs have suggested that consciousness, intellect, and will are not necessarily completely latent once the basic structure of the body has been adequately formed and hence disposed for their rudimentary operation. This means that from a very early stage of existence, human beings are not exclusively receptive—even less, always passively so—but can act in a way that somehow intends to communicate their presence as persons to other persons, who can receive that communication and reciprocate it. The movement of the child toward others, and implicitly toward God therein, forms a continuum with the moral actions that one is normally capable of performing only later in life, when one understands the goal of communion with others and with God explicitly and seeks it by specific means through fully voluntary activity.

Of course, it might be that the self-conscious, voluntary actor seeks communion with God, and possibly even with other human beings, only implicitly, in the proximate end of his deliberate actions—in that sense detracting from the "personal fullness" that those actions might otherwise have if the person were to direct the natural dynamism of the spirit explicitly toward interpersonal communion with God and neighbor. However, this does not mean that the actions of such a person have no moral import. On the other hand, while we must acknowledge that the activity of the structurally developed fetus, of the newborn baby, of the young child, and, analogously, of the person suffering from severe psychical or psycho-rational disintegration falls far short of the level of voluntariness that would qualify it as moral, our foregoing considerations still give us good reason to believe that it transcends the strictly "natural" realm and falls squarely on the side of the personal. Right from the womb, vulnerable persons can and do express themselves *as* persons to others, even if their mode of radiative self-communication has not yet reached its "personal fullness," as Cardinal Wojtyła would put it when his thinking on the matter developed sometime after *Person and Act* was first published.[225]

As just indicated, our reflections apply also to persons who are suffering from a severe disintegration of their consciousness and rationality. Though they might never have been, or are no longer, capable of acting with personal fullness or even in an outwardly perceptible way, they can still communicate with other persons through the radiative expression of their own person through their living activity, which itself issues from their personal act of be-

225. See "Parenthood"(1975), in *PC*, 333.

ing and its dynamism toward freely giving the gift of self. While the developmentally mature persons with whom they communicate thus can make their presence known to these extremely vulnerable human beings in a voluntary and perhaps more demonstrative way, their actions still presuppose as their foundation the same basic mode of communication by which the most vulnerable persons express themselves. It is always a matter of the intimate radiation of one's ontologically personal depth into that of another.

Our reflections hold a fortiori for vulnerable persons whose consciousness and rationality remain intact, but who can communicate their personal, ontological depth freely only through the silence of the interior act. In that regard, we would do well to recall that in some persons who experience "unconscious experience," self-consciousness and rationality seem to operate somewhat independently of the disintegrating body, so that their interior acts (for example, their thoughts, prayers, or intentions) surpass by far what their psychosomatic condition would seem to allow, though such acts are perceived fully by no one but themselves. However, this does not mean that the intensity of those acts cannot radiate from the living presence of the actor into the deepest levels of the sympathetic, personal presence of another, and vice versa. So, we must never dismiss the possibility that persons suffering from this type of psychosomatic disintegration are silently communicating themselves and responding to us through a body that just "refuses" to heed their commands, but that is nevertheless a living testimony to—a radiation of—their active, personal presence.

As for the embryo at the earliest stages of existence, we must constantly return to that astounding datum of divine revelation wherein we see the incarnate Son of God operating in a personally communicative way through his newly conceived humanity. We learn here that we, as human beings, have and can exercise, from the first, the uniquely personal capacity to give ourselves away as a gift to and for others. Biblically, we know that one of the very first acts of historical self-giving performed by the eternal Son after his becoming flesh was the radiative communication of his concrete, personal presence—the incarnation of Love—to John the Baptist, who actively received it with joy while still in the womb and then communicated it, as grace, immediately to his mother in the very act of communicating to her the deepest dimension of his own personal being, now welling over with a spiritual elation born of that grace. We are thus made privy to that moment when the eternal image of the self-communicative Father began restoring universally, through the newly conceived humanity that he assumed personally and immediately in Mary's womb, the divine image in *us*, that we might likewise give ourselves away more fully in love from the very beginning of our existence. While it is true that we cannot do so in the ways proper to the Son of God become man, it is also true that the fullness of the mystery of human existence and activity is revealed only in him. The Incarnation has therefore something to tell us about how we relate to others intersubjectively from the very beginning of our existence, particularly in the new and definitive order of grace in Christ.

We have seen that, in keeping with our concrete, bodily existence in the world, we tend naturally to give ourselves away in love to other human beings, who alone among the world's creatures can perceive, receive, and reciprocate, in a manner corresponding to our personal dignity, the love that we radiate as personal, bodily beings. This mutual kinship among souls establishes the basis for a real communion of persons through a real sharing of affection; for the particular sensitivity that allows us to be humanly affected by the very presence of other persons is, by definition, a *personal* sensitivity: it is actualized by the love radiating from others through their humanity and it is ordered naturally to the activity of loving them through ours.[226] On the other hand, neither side can ever rest fully in any communion formed of human persons because, however deep, rich, meaningful, and satisfying that communion might be, it is only an anticipatory participation in, and so merely a reflection of, the Love that is its source and end—the Love that alone, therefore, can satisfy the human quest for love. For that reason, our every experience of love on the human plane propels us naturally outward, even if only implicitly, to a greater love—to Love Itself: to God, who is the supreme measure of personal love. Human nature's potential for the Incarnation and for sanctifying grace confirms the infinitude of our receptive capacity for

226. Our earlier remarks on the true compassion that we ought to extend to suffering and dying persons, along with Bishop Wojtyła's reflections on tenderness in *LR*, are apropos here, as both compassion and tenderness—closely related emotional attitudes of a very deep kind—seem to factor heavily in expressions of the silent language of a profound sharing of affection. Wojtyła goes so far as to say that "tenderness is the right of all those who have a special need for it—the weak, the sick, those who are in any way afflicted physically or morally. It would seem that children, to whom it is the natural way of showing love (though this is true not only of them), have a special right to tenderness. We must therefore apply to all [inward but especially outward] manifestations of tenderness one single criterion, that of love and love of the person." *LR*, 204. Based on Wojtyła's understanding of tenderness in *LR*, we can conclude that children exhibit a special sensitivity to, or awareness of, the inner state of other persons, and they are particularly spontaneous and uninhibited in expressing it outwardly. And in expressing toward children (or toward anyone else) the tenderness to which they have a special right, we must be sure that it is informed by the same, authentic love that is natural to them.

Love. We see in the jubilation of John the Baptist, Elizabeth, and Mary during the Visitation that their quest for Love, for God himself, had encountered its goal. They experienced the most personal love of the divine Son radiating through the humanity of which he became the substantial principle on assuming it at the moment of its creation in his mother's womb.

To conclude this part of our reflections on the profoundly personal way in which human beings, even when extremely vulnerable, can reciprocally share their affection with others, let us consider some particularly relevant insights of philosopher Kenneth L. Schmitz. He writes: "The transformal character of intimacy is the reason why it is not unconditionally necessary for intimates to communicate the meaning of their association to one another in ordinary words."[227] Words or nonverbal signs might be exchanged, but "it is not easy to find adequate words, for intimacy may surprise us too deeply for anything but wordless joy or grief, or it may consist of a felt shared presence that is all but ineffable."[228] One can see how Schmitz's reflection might pertain to the silent communication between a mother and the child in her womb, to the powerful bond between mutually devoted spouses, or perhaps to the reciprocal "self-presencing" of a dying loved one and the person attending him or her. Further on, Schmitz gets to the heart of the matter. Through intimacy, "we simply acknowledge our attunement with another personal presence; and the self we come to know in and through intimacy is just this *presencing*. In knowing this presencing, we come to the root of the person, to *personal existence* as such."[229] He adds immediately that "this self-presence is not formless, since its presence is interwoven with features that express the character of the person and are grounded in that self-presence."[230]

In a word, the utter uniqueness of the person is inseparable from his personal being. It is therefore communicated in and with the act of existence by which he presents himself. This means, for example, that the vulnerable person who is so incapacitated as to be unable to gesture or to speak nevertheless reveals his unique identity and dignity as a person simply by his act of "being there," precisely in that condition. In this way, he invites others to share his singular, personal presence. Moreover, the absence (or perhaps the imperceptibility) of a particular trait does not abolish or neutralize that pres-

227. Kenneth L. Schmitz , "The Geography of the Human Person," *Communio* 13 (Spring 1986): 41–42.

228. Ibid., 42.

229. Ibid., 43.

230. Ibid.

ence. "Metaphysically speaking, intimacy is not grounded in the recognition of this or that characteristic a person *has*, but rather in the simple unqualified presence the person *is*."[231] The following passage summarizes well just how profoundly intimate our relations with vulnerable human beings of any kind might be.

> The presence in which intimacy is rooted is nothing short of the unique act of existing of each person. Presence is but another name for the being of something insofar as it is actual, and in intimacy we come upon and are received into the very act of existing of another. We are, then, at the heart, not only of another person, but at the heart of the texture of being itself. No doubt it is true that the person is incommunicable in objective terms insofar as he or she is existentially unique. But in intimacy, as we approach the very act of self-disclosure, we approach the center of all communicability.... Put in the most general terms—though we must not forget that each intimacy is through and through singular—the "secret" that we discover through intimacy is this: that *reality is not indifferent to the presence of persons.*[232]

With that, let us continue in our final chapter to explore the inherent possibilities of Karol Wojtyła/Pope John Paul II's "anthropology of the vulnerable."

231. Ibid., 44.
232. Ibid.

# 8

# Developing the Philosophical Foundation of Pope John Paul II's Anthropology of the Vulnerable

Though we have given examples in previous chapters of Cardinal Wojtyła/Pope John Paul II's unequivocal and striking affirmations that vulnerable human beings—like the newly conceived child and the sufferer at the point of death—exercise a truly human and personal agency, we have also had to concede that he does not ever really explain fully the anthropological basis of those affirmations. However, this is not to say that his insights are invalid or that he ends up blurring the distinction between human actions performed deliberately and those performed by persons whose capacity for deliberate activity cannot fully be actualized because of developmental immaturity or some form of psychosomatic disintegration. In fact, we saw in chapter 3 that even while characterizing the newly conceived child as actively presenting himself as a person and a gift to his parents and to any older siblings he might have, Wojtyła states that the child is "deprived for a long time of the personal fullness of activity."[1] It would therefore seem that he

1. "Parenthood," in *PC*, 333.

had simply come to acknowledge that activities worthy of the designation "personal" or distinctly "human" cover a much broader range than he previously thought, even if the mode of activity and its level of personal fullness vary according to the person's condition. Above all, his reflections on parenthood (especially motherhood) and on human suffering, in the light of faith (and perhaps also with the biblically inspired philosophers of dialogue in mind), seem to have convinced him that even persons whose psychosomatic condition imposes significant limitations on their activity participate with others, perhaps subtly but no less truly, in forming the genuinely interpersonal dynamic of self-giving and other-receiving constitutive of the communion of persons.

In *Person and Act*, as we know, Wojtyła argues, on the one hand, that human beings perform distinctly personal actions only because they are already personal beings from the first moment of their existence, though he also argues, on the other hand, that human beings are only virtually, not actually, capable of performing such actions when they first come to exist, or when, for any other reason, their consciousness and rationality are not sufficiently operative. Nevertheless, the foundational anthropological principles undergirding *Person and Act* do, in fact, support Wojtyła/John Paul's later affirmations of personal agency in vulnerable human beings like these. Our purpose in this chapter will be to explore further how that is so. After having reviewed those principles on both the philosophical and the theological level, we will examine how the work of philosopher William Norris Clarke, SJ (1915–2008) brings out some of the latent aspects of Wojtyła/John Paul's work in such a way as to align it explicitly with his later, more developed thinking on human agency. Finally, we will consider the results of our effort in the light of the early childhood experiences of Helen Keller, prior to her acquisition of formal language as the principal means by which she would eventually express herself as a person.

## Key Principles underlying John Paul II's Anthropology of the Vulnerable

Two key principles in Cardinal Wojtyła/Pope John Paul II's anthropology seem, at least implicitly, to undergird his affirmations of personal agency in the most vulnerable persons. They concern (1) our ontological identity as persons and its bearing on our development and activity, and (2) our self-communication as persons to other persons based on the intrinsic dynamism of our ontologically personal identity. Here, we will review those principles as Wojtyła/John Paul has elaborated them both philosophically and theologically.

## The Ontologically Personal Character of Human Activity and Self-Communication

Karol Wojtyła/John Paul II's philosophical anthropology is founded on the principle that every human activity derives from the dynamic act by which each of us comes into existence as a personal being *(operari sequitur esse),* from which it follows that every human activity has, at least fundamentally, a personal character. In *Person and Act,* Wojtyła emphasizes the link between our natural psychosomatic activities and the proximate end toward which they tend as a whole, namely, rational, self-determining activity. He shows that self-determination of the most mature kind presupposes the integration of certain somatic and psychical dynamisms into fully moral actions, particularly in the interpersonal and social contexts. But this implies that those same dynamisms must somehow first be realized out of their antecedent potencies in preparation for their integration into the higher act in which they "seek" to terminate and for which they serve as the condition. Therefore, the teleology of the lower dynamisms toward the higher points back necessarily to their rooting in the personal act of being, since they establish the basis, the "raw material," for transcendent acts that require a sufficient cause. Exclusively in the case of human beings, then, teleology reveals itself to be autoteleology. The text we cited in chapter 2 from Wojtyła's 1976 article on person and community, which complements the text we cited with it from his 1961 article on Thomistic personalism, tells us clearly that the activity of the whole psychosomatic dynamism contributes to the constitution of the subject as a self-conscious personality, as a fully mature actor, and that this activity is based on all that is already contained in one's personal being.[2] Consequently, somatic and psychical activities are personally revealing, while self-revelation implies and necessarily entails self-communication.

Thus, the second key principle of Wojtyła/John Paul's philosophical anthropology is that we communicate—give—ourselves naturally to other persons, seeking, if only at the most rudimentary level, to find fulfillment in

2. In *PC,* see "Thomistic Personalism," 168–69, and "The Person: Subject and Community," 225.

the *communion* of persons. This principle, like the first, from which it flows, is indispensable to Wojtyła/John Paul's anthropology in general and to his more specific statements about personal agency in the most vulnerable human beings. Indeed, in his 1974 article, "The Family as a Community of Persons," Cardinal Wojtyła states explicitly that the uniquely personal dynamic of self-giving to and for others—the very condition of human fulfillment in the community of persons—originates in the act of personal being. Giving oneself as a gift is an order of activity that "is itself rooted in the order of existence, in the personal being *(esse)* of the human being," since action follows on being.[3] "If the 'gift of oneself' characterizes human activity," he continues, "it does so always because of this personal *esse,* which is capable of a disinterested gift of itself."[4] Wojtyła says that this gift rests entirely on the autoteleology proper to the dynamism of personal *esse.*[5] In other words, our personal *esse* directs itself, from the start, to the end of disinterested self-giving and interpersonal communion, which is proper to human persons. It follows that this dynamic self-directedness, already contained, as it is, in the subject's psychosomatic constitution from the very outset, flows immediately into the psychosomatic activity of that same subject. This suggests, in turn, that mature human actions, in which we fully actualize our intrinsic personal structure of self-possession and self-governance, are a matter of specifying how we will achieve our properly personal end, insofar as they appropriate, contain, imitate, and creatively guide, in continuous fashion, the natural dynamism of our own personal being toward self-fulfillment in interpersonal self-giving.

In the present context of "The Family as a Community of Persons," Wojtyła states that he discussed the same matters in *Person and Act* "in a more detailed and analytic way."[6] To some extent, that is true. For one thing, the basic premise of his book is that a being performs certain kinds of actions because it is already, from the first, the kind of being from which such actions can flow as the realization of its inherent possibilities. Accordingly, his 1974 article on the family tells us that the giving of self that typifies properly human activity is the realization of a potentiality inherent in personal being. In the final chapter of *Person and Act,* moreover, the author states (based on our experience of living and acting together) that "the mark of the communal—or social—trait is firmly imprinted on human existence itself."[7]

3. "Family," in *PC,* 318.

4. Ibid., 318–19.

5. See ibid., 319.

6. Ibid., in *PC,* 319.

7. *AP,* 318. While Wojtyła did not, perhaps, intend this particular statement in a strictly onto-

That leads him to posit in us the personal property of participation as an ontological predisposition to communicate ourselves to and for the sake of other persons, an essential condition of both our own personal fulfillment and theirs.

On the other hand, Wojtyła makes a statement in the article that suggests his thinking is moving forward. He says not only that spouses, "as mature persons capable of transmitting life," seek to fulfill themselves through disinterested self-giving, but that "every child who receives life from them also seeks this, coming into its parents' lives—from the very moment of conception—as a human being, as a 'creature ... that God willed for itself.'"[8] The question of exactly *when* the child actually begins seeking self-fulfillment through disinterested self-giving is not clearly expressed here and so subject to debate. However, in his follow-up article called "Parenthood as a Community of Persons (1975)," Wojtyła makes the astounding, unequivocally clear statements, quoted in chapter 3 and recalled above, about the newly conceived child actively, and not merely virtually, making a gift of his personal humanity to his parents and to any siblings that he might already have. The author says that from conception, this child "is already operative," immediately extending "the circle of giving that existed before its birth [meaning conception]" and bringing "to this circle a new and wholly unique content."[9]

We cannot but see in this a definite development in Wojtyła's thinking on personal agency, especially as it affirms that one gives the gift of self in some way from the very beginning of one's existence. He is too careful a thinker simply to have contradicted his own philosophical-anthropological principles with respect to this matter. In fact, we have shown above that he reaffirms those same principles intentionally in a context that includes his new and explicit statements about personal agency in the most vulnerable of all persons, though he does not seem to explicate the link. It is significant, though, that Wojtyła's remarks in both of the aforementioned articles represent his effort to penetrate more deeply certain anthropological statements

logical way, his study of the person and the act to that point demands the conclusion that the self-evident fact of human beings living and acting together with other human beings presupposes a ground in the person as such. Indeed, Wojtyła goes on to say that the communal or the social nature (lit. "character") of the actions that we perform with others "is rooted in the nature ["character"] of the person and not vice versa" (ibid., 319; cf. *Persona e atto,* 618, 619). Human beings are not, therefore, the product of their intersubjective activity but rather its source.

8. "Family," in *PC,* 316–17.

9. "Parenthood," in *PC,* 333. Both the present context and subsequent clarifications in the article indicate that "birth" means "the transmission of life to new human beings," i.e., conception. Ibid., 340; cf. 339.

in *Gaudium et Spes*, 12, 24, and 48. These statements are all inspired by the revelation of our unique likeness to the triune God, particularly as we realize that likeness united with others in truth and love, or in the unity of marriage and the family—the premier reflection of Trinitarian Love in the world.[10]

We have tried to show that Cardinal Wojtyła's grounding of the personal act of self-giving in the act of personal existence allows us to make sense of his statements about the self-giving activity of persons, like the newly conceived child, whose psycho-moral personality is not yet operative, or at least not so fully as to explain those statements. Though Wojtyła seems to imply the connection between his ontology and his statements on incipient self-giving if we regard his companion articles on the family and on parenthood as a single whole, we must admit that he never does so explicitly. To complicate matters, he tells us in the article on the family that "only a being that possesses itself can give itself" as a gift to another in a disinterested way,[11] establishing thereby the basis for forming that "rational community"—that *communio*—in which people live and act in mutual relation so as to "*confirm and affirm one another as persons*."[12] While every human being is essentially endowed with the interior structure of self-possession and self-governance as that which really defines the personal *esse* and its self-giving capacity, Wojtyła seems to imply here that this capacity remains in potency until the personal structure is fully engaged by the subject having a mature psycho-moral personality. But that brings us right back to his position in *Person and Act*.

Yet, in his companion article on parenthood the following year, Wojtyła affirms clearly that the newly conceived child is an integral, participating member of the family as *communio*, though he adds by way of qualification that this child does not yet enjoy "the personal fullness of activity." So here, it seems that Wojtyła is allowing for degrees of personal, self-giving activity, where the *disinterested* gift of self would represent that *personal fullness* of

10. The author seems to have achieved his deepest insights into the authentically personal, self-communicative agency of the most vulnerable human beings as he considered the matter more fully in the light of: (1) the biblical datum of our creation in the image of the triune God; and (2) the anthropological import of the divine revelation in Christ. If Wojtyła had already been thinking explicitly along these lines when he first wrote *Person and Act*, we would be at a loss to explain why he did not philosophically develop the anthropological insights gained from divine revelation, as he did relative to other matters throughout the work as a whole, so as to affirm the personal agency of human beings whose self-awareness and rationality are present only "virtually" or in a rudimentary way. It would therefore seem that his more comprehensive understanding of human agency developed gradually in his mind as he elaborated theologically on his philosophical anthropology in the years following its original publication in 1969.

11. "Family," in *PC*, 322.

12. Ibid., 321; cf. 319.

activity of which the child is deprived for a time. Later on, we will take up the question of "self-possession" as the basis for self-giving in the communion of persons, understanding it, first of all, in relation to the dynamic act of personal existence. This will allow us to see, in a way consistent with Wojtyła's own anthropological principles, that the most vulnerable persons are also fundamentally in possession of themselves as the subjects of their own being and so in a position to give themselves away to others. Though Wojtyła does not express this himself, his thinking on the personal agency of the most vulnerable human beings is by no means groundless. On the contrary, it presupposes a well thought-out philosophical and theological anthropology, intuitively applied.

Before we move on, let us review Wojtyła's brief treatment of potency and act in *Person and Act,* as it will provide us with another helpful contribution to our understanding of how personal, self-giving activity is possible in the most vulnerable human beings. As we saw in chapter 2, Wojtyła tells us that potency and act are strictly correlative terms, where "potency" refers to the inherent state of readiness in an actual being for a specific fulfillment of an accidental kind, while "act" refers to the proper fulfillment itself of that potency. "Actualization," on the other hand, refers to the transition from potency to act. In an already existing being, it links a real possibility with the real fulfillment of that possibility. Something could not accidentally come to be in a being if the capacity for it were not somehow contained already in the ontological structure of that being when it first came into existence.[13]

Since a being's dynamic act of existence is the abiding ground of all its secondary (or derivative) activity, we must conclude that the foundation on which rests any accidental "something" that comes to be in an existent is always already, to some degree, in a state of actualization until it reaches complete fulfillment (the natural upper limit of which is predetermined by what is given with the original ontological structure), barring some impediment. That is why we suggested earlier that the dynamic self-directedness of personal being toward conscious self-giving is already at work in the psychosomatic dynamism prior to the emergence of the mature, psycho-moral personality, and it is *still* at work, for that matter, after the personality has disintegrated for any reason. In this and other ways, then, we can understand in terms of his own anthropology how Wojtyła/John Paul II can affirm that newly conceived, newborn, or very young children, as well as persons

13. See *AP,* 63–64.

with serious mental disabilities and persons on the brink of death, can all give themselves to others as persons and as gifts, even if they cannot do so according to the full measure of personal activity.

### Love as Ground of the Activity and Self-Communicability of the Person, Made in God's Image

In terms of Wojtyła/John Paul II's theological anthropology, the initial coming to be of the human person *as* a person requires the direct action of God, who, acting through the procreative capacity of man and woman, creates the substantial, spiritual soul by which every newly conceived human being corresponds essentially to God's own image and likeness. This brings out much more clearly than does his philosophical treatment of our ontologically personal identity that even the most rudimentary activity of a human being cannot simply be equated with that of a nonpersonal being, however similar the activity of both might sometimes appear to be. Indeed, in virtue of our uniquely personal correspondence to God among the creatures of the material world, we, as human beings, are drawn toward him naturally, even before our personal subjectivity has emerged through the development and integrative exercise of our inherent, though initially unrealized, capacity to perform actions consciously and freely.

This exclusively spiritual trajectory toward God himself, and not merely toward his reflection in created beings, seems to underlie the soul's activity of "building" the body, which thus becomes disposed (assuming normal development) to accommodate the full range of the soul's powers, that we might eventually direct ourselves to God deliberately. In other words, the natural activity proper to the soul-body composite—to human nature—has a personal value in itself, unfolding so as to direct the person, secretly at first, toward fulfillment in the eternity of God. Rational activity is the proximate end toward which the soul-body's natural dynamisms tend as a whole, precisely because God is implicitly the *ultimate* end of their striving.

From a purely natural point of view, human beings cannot reach God himself, though we are made in his image and thus drawn toward him naturally by our inner dynamism and, most fully, by its highest expression in the explicit knowledge and love of God. So we seek, at least implicitly, to fulfill the transcendent dynamism of our spirit concretely in relation to the created reality that most closely approximates God, namely, other human beings (leaving aside the angels, whom we cannot directly perceive). This is perhaps a complementary way of understanding philosophically the unique basis of human sociality, of our intrinsic need to fulfill ourselves through participation in the humanity of others. In any case, it means that the whole human dynamism finds its fulfillment, and hence its purpose, in the deliberate act of self-giving culminating in a true communion of persons—that is, in love mutually given and received. The intrinsic principles of our concrete, personal being are therefore ordered toward that specific end. But then that same end, love, must already be somehow anticipated in our personal being from the beginning as the secret impulse that guides the unfolding of our soul-body structure in a distinctively self-giving and other-receiving—in a truly personal, hence loving—way. Indeed, if we have been made in the image of God, who *is* Love, and so have love as our vocation, then we must also be naturally suited to fulfill that vocation.

John Paul II reminds us frequently that we are called to live out our vocation to love in direct relation not only to one another but also to God, who invites us to fulfill our natural dynamism toward him in a definitive way. The Father offers us the supernatural, wholly gratuitous possibility of eternal communion with himself in Christ, his Son, through our sanctification in the Spirit. The fact that we can be incorporated thus into the intra-Trinitarian communion of Persons by God's free initiative presupposes that we, too, are persons. Regardless of our age or condition, therefore, we radiate the glory of God in a uniquely personal way both naturally and, by divine grace, supernaturally: naturally, because our whole spiritual dynamism, as created by God, is ordered toward the personal fullness of self-giving and interpersonal communion in love, thus reflecting both God's image in us and the divine meaning behind our uniquely personal mode of existence; and supernaturally, because, in virtue of God's self-communication to us in Christ, our existence and activity are permeated by a power that is not merely a created similitude of Love but *is* that Love itself. God is not just the origin and preserver of our existence and activity: he is also their ultimate end in the order of grace, guiding them to himself, without prejudice to the causality proper to our nature.[14]

Given our distinctly personal nature and the fundamental vocation for which God has created it, the self-constituting, self-communicative activity of our soul-body structure will not attain its personal fullness unless our journey to God is mediated by other persons with whom a reciprocal rela-

14. Note 19 of the English edition of *LR* contains an apt way of summarizing our reflections under this subheading so far: "God ... creates man, whose person the Divine Persons summon to communion with other persons, and above all with themselves. It is this summons which permits the constitution in man of a subjectivity strictly personal in the natural and the supernatural order" (294).

tionship of authentic love is concretely established. And in a world tainted by the consequences of original sin, there is always the sad possibility that this essential human need will not be met. That would impede or possibly even smother to death our natural, outward trajectory toward personal growth through love.[15] Where it is a matter of a person's reversing his natural outward dynamism later in life because of his willful compliance with sin, he will inevitably collapse in on himself. His personal "implosion" will leave him suspended in the dark and lonely void of egoism.

So, the obstruction of the natural human progression toward fully personal expression in relation to other human beings and to God can always be traced back to sin, because of which we exploit, misdirect, or pervert the basic human need to love and to be loved, thus depriving ourselves and others of its proper fulfillment. As this need underlies the very dynamism by which we seek to fulfill our fundamental human vocation, it constitutes the source of our greatest vulnerability, since our desire or our attempts to satisfy it fully in this life, which is impossible, can easily become distorted by sin or make us prey to the sins of those who would exploit us on account of it, always to the detriment or destruction of persons.[16] At the same time, the very quest to fulfill, in ever greater measure, our need to love and to be loved reminds us that we are yet in a state of becoming, that we have not yet achieved our proper perfection as persons or reached the Goal of our love. So even when our efforts to achieve happiness through love become misguided, twisted, or exploited, they confirm our basic desire to transcend ourselves, to achieve our highest

15. "For by his innermost nature man is a social being, and unless he relates himself to others he can neither live nor develop his potential." *GS*, 12. Here, we will leave aside the issue of developmental impediments to personal maturity that are related more remotely to the consequences of original sin. We have already shown, however, that such impediments do not necessarily hinder the growth and radiance of love in a person's life, particularly when that person is the "object" of the love of others.

16. In this context, we might mention a different category of vulnerable human beings about which John Paul II has expressed concern, namely, that of persons, especially children, who can easily fall prey to religious sects, with their "*aberrant forms of religious sentiment* which exploit the deepest needs and aspirations of the human soul, offering perspectives of deceptive and misleading gratification." *Address of John Paul II to Pilgrim Groups and Members of Various Associations* (December 23, 2000), Vatican website. See also *Ecclesia in America*, 73. If in no other way, the ones vulnerable to such deceit and exploitation express themselves, by their act of personal existence, as subjects of truth and love who thereby make a claim on others to *meet* them in authentic truth and love—and all this precisely because we have an innate dynamism toward *ultimate* Truth and Love, toward God. The manner in which we define and direct that dynamism as we mature typically reflects the influence of those around us. It is therefore an unspeakable betrayal of a sacred trust for any person or group to deprive the vulnerable of what their personal nature aspires to and requires by misleading, manipulating, abusing, exploiting, and controlling them with self-serving perversions of truth and love.

possible end, to become more than we presently are. Certainly no one wants to be less—not without contradicting one's innermost dynamism and one's own self. That is why we invariably get frustrated, at some level, when our personal growth is held back by anything or by anyone, including oneself.

## Deepening the Metaphysical Substructure of Wojtyła/John Paul II's Anthropology

The metaphysical foundation on which Cardinal Wojtyła/Pope John Paul II's understanding of the human person rests is clearly that of St. Thomas Aquinas. Central to that understanding is Thomas's dynamic ontology. For that reason, Wojtyła/John Paul's anthropology inherently contains elements of Thomas's more general ontology that he does not really develop, but that would be well worth considering as we try to deepen our understanding of human action in the most vulnerable human persons. We can approach that task through the work of Thomistic philosopher W. Norris Clarke. Father Clarke's studies include and develop some of the broader aspects of Thomas's dynamic understanding of being, especially being's intrinsic thrust toward self-revelation and self-communication, and the relationality that this implies. While we must be brief and selective in our examination of Clarke's engaging treatment of these themes, we will nevertheless see a remarkable consonance and complementarity between his work and that of Wojtyła/John Paul. To a large extent, we will let that speak for itself, but it should not surprise us, given the familiarity of both authors with Aquinas himself and with renowned Aquinas interpreters such as Joseph Maréchal, Etienne Gilson, Joseph de Finance, and Cornelio Fabro. What is more, like the work of many Catholic thinkers before them (including St. Thomas), the philosophical work of our two authors draws inspiration from the Christian revelation, which guides the process of independent intellectual inquiry. Clarke acknowledges explicitly that the revelation of the one God as a trinity of divine Persons informs the whole direction of his reflections on being and its attributes, particularly its dynamism toward self-communication as the basis for establishing relations with other beings. This is a perfectly legitimate—indeed, a laudable and necessary—way to proceed, for as John Paul II reminds us in *Fides et Ratio*, "reason needs to be reinforced by faith, in order to discover horizons it cannot reach on its own."[17]

17. *Fides et Ratio*, 67, quoting John Paul's letter of September 30, 1995, to the International Congress of Fundamental Theology on the 125th Anniversary of *Dei Filius*. In some instances, reason is capable of arriving at certain truths on its own, though revelation is still necessary to bring

## W. Norris Clarke on the Nature of Being, Its Self-Communicability, and Its Relationality

So, let us now survey some of the relevant themes of what Norris Clarke calls his "creative completion" of St. Thomas on being and person. We will then reflect on how the insights that Clarke achieves from developing implicit aspects of Thomas's thought help deepen the metaphysical substructure of Cardinal Wojtyła/Pope John Paul II's anthropology of the vulnerable.

### Being In-Itself

Father Clarke's point of departure is the medieval adage *agere sequitur esse* ("To act" follows on "to be"), as it is for Cardinal Wojtyła in *Person and Act*. In virtue of its act of existence, every being exhibits a drive toward its natural perfection through its proper operations, which lead to the actualization of its natural potencies: "Each and every thing shows forth that it exists for the sake of its operation. Indeed operation is the ultimate perfection of each thing."[18] Based on its proper operations, we distinguish one being from another and perceive that it exists "in itself" as an undivided whole, divided from every other. This indicates that each being has an essential determining principle, a central governing form, by which it inwardly unifies, in a manner proportioned to its level of existence, the parts of which it is composed. That is, it actively constitutes its own identity as the abiding center of its actions, attributes, and properties, while yet remaining in potency for the nonessential, or "accidental," changes open to it naturally. Ontological unity is therefore a transcendental (or universal) property of every real being.[19] So, in virtue of its single act of existence and its form, a being subsists in itself, and not in another, as the unified subject of existence, action, and predication. That is what it means to be a substance.[20]

---

them to term in the human mind by "directing them toward the richness of the revealed mystery in which they find their ultimate purpose." Ibid.

18. Aquinas, *Summa Contra Gentiles* I, ch. 113, as quoted by Clarke in "To Be Is to Be Substance-in-Relation," in *Explorations in Metaphysics: Being—God—Person* (Notre Dame: University of Notre Dame Press, 1994), 106. The book collects some of Clarke's key articles. See also W. Norris Clarke, *Person and Being*, Aquinas Lecture 57 (Milwaukee: Marquette University Press, 1993), 8; and his *The One and the Many: A Contemporary Thomistic Metaphysics* (Notre Dame: University of Notre Dame Press, 2001), 129. Since the same basic themes recur throughout many of Clarke's writings (with the author frequently quoting or paraphrasing himself), any cross-references in subsequent notes will be merely representative, not necessarily exhaustive, of the places where similar or identical material can be found.

19. See Clarke, *The One and the Many*, 60–71, 293.

20. Ibid., 99–102, 129–33, 144–45, 154. See also Clarke, "Substance-in-Relation," in *Explorations*, 104–5, and the relevant remarks by Schmitz in *At the Center*, 131–32.

### Being as Self-Communicative and Relational

But for St. Thomas, the operations of a being are not just for its own sake: "It is the nature of every actuality [or real being] to communicate itself [its actual good, or perfection] insofar as it is possible."[21] Every being is therefore inclined to share the good that it possesses or acquires,[22] to give of itself to other beings through its activity. This implies further that every being has also the capacity to *receive* the good of other beings, to be acted on by them.[23] Thus, various kinds of beings form a network, a system, of relations, in which each being enriches, and is enriched by, the others through the mutual exchange of goods perfective of each. For that reason, Clarke declares: "*To be* in the world of real existents is to be *substance-in-relation*."[24] Though presupposing substantiality as its ground, relationality (relatedness to other beings) is nevertheless an equally primordial, and not merely an accidental, dimension of being. It is the direct consequence of being's intrinsic self-communicability.[25]

The diffusion of goods between beings takes place in proportion to each being's specific mode of goodness and its natural capacity (whether conscious or not, autonomous or not) to give and to receive through its operations.[26] We must therefore understand terms such as "goodness," "giving," and "receiving" analogously, since the term "being" itself, as applied to many different kinds of existents, is analogous. Nevertheless, it remains true across the whole range of finite, real beings that each one is dynamically inclined to share its own goodness (even to the point of generating another like itself, where possible), and that new, accidental modes of being (nonessential modifications that do not destroy a being's self-identity, or substantial integrity) are actualized in each being as a dynamic center of action "seeking" to fulfill its finitude, its incompleteness, by active interchange with others—that is, by some mode of the giving and receiving dynamic characteristic of all beings.[27]

21. Aquinas, *De Potentia*, q. 2, art. 1, as quoted by Clarke in "Substance-in-Relation," in *Explorations*, 106.

22. See Aquinas, *ST* I, 19, 2. The relevant text is quoted in "Substance-in-Relation," in *Explorations*, 106.

23. So there are two types of potency open to limited beings: the capacity to act from within and the capacity to receive from without—both of these in proportion to each nature, and so analogously in each case. See Clarke, *The One and the Many*, 118; Clarke, *Person and Being* , 82–83.

24. Clarke, "Substance-in-Relation," in *Explorations*, 114. See Clarke, *Person and Being*, 14.

25. See Clarke, *Person and Being*, 13–15, 71.

26. An example would be the exchanges that take place between plants and their pollinators.

27. See Clarke, *The One and the Many*, 109–22.

To sum up, then, a being exists not merely as raw presence, or "in-itselfness," but as active, self-communicative presence to others.[28] If beings did not manifest themselves to other beings in some way by their actions, each would be to the others as if it did not exist at all. But as Clarke aptly puts it, "To be *real* is to *make a difference*" in the community of existents, in the universe.[29] This difference is an effect of the self-manifestation and the self-communication of each being to other real beings through the activity that flows from it naturally as an intrinsic property.[30] Every being is present to and affects other beings precisely because "[t]o be is *to be an actor*" of a particular kind.[31] It follows that self-revelatory, self-communicative action, and not just unitary, self-subsisting "in-itselfness," is a transcendental property of all being as such.[32]

### The Self-Luminosity of Personal Being

For St. Thomas, the act of existence, *esse,* is the root of all perfection. Since every real being participates in *esse,* all creatures manifest, in various ways and degrees, the self-expressiveness and the self-communicability of being as they strive to actualize their inherent possibilities both through the natural operations proper to each and in relation to one another. According to Clarke's reading of Thomas, the nature, or essence, defining an existent's type and activity restricts the intensity of its being—that is, its level of existence, self-expression, and self-communication.[33] It follows that the less a being is limited in its existence by its essence, the more it can exhibit the perfection proper to being in its fullness as dynamic, self-communicating act. If we affirm with Thomas that "*person* signifies what is most perfect in all nature,"[34] then we must conclude that the perfection of being is most clearly manifested to us in ourselves, whose particular mode of being can transcend

28. See Clarke, "Substance-in-Relation," in *Explorations,* 119; Clarke, *Person and Being,* 13.

29. Clarke, *The One and the Many,* 32. See Clarke, *Person and Being,* 12–13.

30. See Clarke, *The One and the Many,* 31–36; Clarke, *Person and Being,* 6–19.

31. W. Norris Clarke, *The Universe as Journey,* ed. Gerald McCool (New York: Fordham University Press, 1988), 72. See pp. 68–75. See also Clarke, "Action as the Self-Revelation of Being: A Central Theme in the Thought of St. Thomas," in *Explorations,* 45–64.

32. See Clarke, *The One and the Many,* 60.

33. Ibid., 72–91; *Person and Being,* 28. In *Explorations,* see Clarke's "The Limitation of Act by Potency in St. Thomas: Aristotelianism or Neoplatonism?" 65–88, and his "The Meaning of Participation in St. Thomas," 89–101. For some of the insoluble linguistic and conceptual problems that arise from this position, see Clarke, "What Cannot Be Said in Saint Thomas's Essence-Existence Doctrine," in *The Creative Retrieval of Saint Thomas Aquinas: Essays in Thomistic Philosophy, New and Old* (New York: Fordham University Press, 2009), 129–31.

34. *ST* I, 29, 3. See Clarke, *Person and Being,* 25.

the limitations imposed by the body, by matter. In the human person, being achieves, to a degree, what it is in itself when not limited by a specific essence: not just active presence, but luminous *self*-presence—the prerequisite of self-possession in the order both of knowledge (allowing me to refer to myself meaningfully as "I") and of free, self-determining action (allowing me to say meaningfully, "I am responsible for this action"). Clarke sums it up as follows: "To be fully is to be personally."[35]

Accordingly, luminosity is an exclusive property of personal being—human, angelic, and divine. It is the property that allows persons to present and to communicate themselves self-consciously, hence freely, to other beings. In material beings, the act of existence is dispersed spatially in matter to a greater or lesser extent, diminishing the luminosity, the concentrated intensity, that would otherwise characterize it. For that reason, the creatures of the visible world can never present and communicate themselves exhaustively to one another—or, in our case, be fully self-present—at any one time through a single act.[36] Still, human nature is not so restrictive of its act of existence that the latter cannot transcend its union with matter, at least virtually, if not always in fact. To the extent that it does, it exhibits a proportionally greater depth of interiority, or luminosity to self, and so greater self-possession. Being is then concentrated into a self-present *I* so as to become the subjective center of a field of reference capable of encompassing the full range of beings that manifest and communicate themselves. As the interior of personal being becomes more luminous to self, its relatedness to reality widens and deepens, while that same relatedness stimulates and helps intensify the person's self-luminous interiority in the first place.[37]

In knowing any being, the intellect knows it implicitly as just one "stop" on the way to the knowledge of being as such. This indicates that the intellect has a natural dynamism toward universal knowledge (or truth), which presupposes the intrinsic intelligibility of all being. Intelligibility is therefore a transcendental property of being. The will, for its part, corresponds to the *goodness* of being. In *loving* any being for its true goodness (in accor-

35. Clarke, "Person, Being, and St. Thomas" (1993), in *Explorations*, 218; Clarke, *Person and Being*, 25–28, 42–63. Much of the material in the article appears in *Person and Being* (sometimes identically), published later the same year. See also *Journey*, 78–79.

36. See Clarke, *The One and the Many*, 90. Besides, even if one creature *could* communicate itself exhaustively to another at once, its act could be received by the receiver only in proportion to the *mode* of the receiver—that is, only in a limited way corresponding to the recipient's nature. See ibid., 35; Clarke, *Journey*, 72.

37. See Clarke, *Person and Being*, 45, 65, 69.

dance with the intellect's objective judgment), the will loves it implicitly as just a limited instance of the goodness of being as such. And this indicates that the human will has a natural dynamism toward universal *love,* which presupposes the intrinsic goodness of all being as lovable. Thus, goodness, too, is a transcendental property of being.

### The Self-Communicability of Personal Being

The self-present *I* communicates itself mainly through the activity of intellect and will. Given the extroverted thrust of love toward the objective goodness of being, when the self-present *I* is *morally* good by acting freely in accordance with the exigencies of its own existential truth and goodness, it will lovingly seek the true good of other beings, in some way communicating something of its own goodness freely to them—especially to other *I*'s. At the same time, it will be open to receiving actively the kind of goodness offered by other beings, fulfilling itself in both the giving and the receiving. Through such exchanges, therefore, the light of the *I*'s subjective center intensifies (presuming the objective goodness of the exchange), newly equipping the personal subject to express and to communicate himself even more fully as good to other beings, while receiving more fully as good the self-communication (however limited) of their being as well.[38] Among human beings, it is necessary that this kind of dynamic exchange take place interpersonally, where an *I* relates to me as a *thou* so that my own *I* can emerge in consciousness.[39]

When persons express their luminous interiority to one another in the free, mutual exchange of their goodness, they achieve not only a community of being (toward which *all* being is directed, at least implicitly, in virtue of its intrinsic self-communicability, such that *to be* means *to be together*),[40] but the highest mode of community: communion in love.

> Despite all the conflicting drives within our flawed human nature, it is still connatural for a human person to be a lover, to go out towards others we love, sharing what we have and wishing them the good they need for their own flourishing, for they too are good by a participation in being similar to our own.
>
> To be an actualized human person, then, is to be a *lover,* to live a life of interpersonal self-giving and receiving. Person is essentially a "we" term. Person exists in its fullness only in the plural.[41]

38. See ibid., 68.
39. See ibid., 45–46, 58–59, 65–76.
40. See ibid., 23.
41. Ibid., 76.

Since personal being is the *highest* mode of being, the end toward which *every* being strives implicitly is nothing less than personal self-communication in love, even if it can fulfill its dynamism only according to some analogous mode of communication proportioned to its nature.

### The Spiritual Nature of Personal Beings

If we consider our acts of knowing, we notice that we can abstract universal meanings from particular sense objects. Such knowledge transcends the concrete, particularizing limitations of matter—that is, its dispersal in space and time. In our acts of self-knowledge, moreover, we notice that when referring to ourselves meaningfully as "I," we are at once the knower and the object known, the speaker and what is spoken about, revealing an absolute identity that also transcends material dispersal. Our intellectual activities must therefore be immaterial—that is, spiritual. This means, in turn, that we must always already *be* essentially spiritual. "Now if the characteristic activities of the human mind are spiritual (transcending matter) in nature,... then the nature from which they proceed, which we call the soul,... must itself be spiritual in nature. The higher cannot proceed from the essentially lower."[42] In other words, spiritual acts cannot derive from our corporeality, for the effect cannot surpass its cause. Therefore, while the soul is perfected (more fully enacted) by purely spiritual acts of knowledge and love, such acts could never be actualized in the first place unless their spiritual source already contained them—whether potentially or in some limited mode of actuality—as the end of its dynamism. As Clarke states: "Gradual development of the ability to express a power that one has in no way implies that the power itself was not present until it reached its full and evident expression."[43] On the contrary, it is precisely because the powers of intellect and will are

42. Clarke, "The Immediate Creation of the Human Soul by God and Some Contemporary Challenges," in *Creative Retrieval*, 176. This previously unpublished article is a somewhat reworked, updated, and elaborated version of a paper that Clarke gave at the APA Convention in Philadelphia, 1997, during the International St. Thomas Society session. The original paper was entitled, "St. Thomas on the Immediate Creation of the Human Soul by God." Father Clarke was kind enough to make it available to me some years ago.

43. From the unpublished paper cited in the previous note, Clarke, "Immediate Creation," 10–11. Though fully applicable in the present context, the quotation, as Clarke originally intended it, refers to the gradual unfolding of human intelligence in human history once God infused the spiritual soul directly into the body of a higher animal that had evolved adequately to receive it. Compare the published version in *Creative Retrieval*, 186–87. While Clarke's speculations on human evolution here and elsewhere are highly questionable (measured though they are), we can nevertheless appreciate his unflagging insistence on the irreducibility of spirit to matter, and hence on the necessity of the immediate creation of every human soul by God.

present in some way from the first that our spiritual nature (actuated by our spiritual *esse*) strives to be what it is when fully actualized. "From the first moments of our human existence we are living out implicitly, though not yet consciously, these two basic drives," namely, the mind's drive to know all being in truth, and the will's drive to love all being as truly good.[44] The dynamism toward knowledge and love is therefore operative in personal being from the start, moving us to express and to communicate ourselves actively in the world through the body.

### The Final Cause of the Activity of Finite Beings

Since all finite beings "seek" their own perfective good in analogous ways, there is likewise an analogous sense in which they "value" or "love" that which helps perfect them. The perfective good of each being is thus the end, the *final cause,* determining its operations—again, in analogous ways. Free, personal beings can rationally evaluate the possible ends for which they might act, but the particular end, or goal, to which they ultimately determine themselves still serves as the final cause of their action (or a related series of actions). Thus, the end-in-view appeals to their inner, predetermined inclination to realize the good, moving them to produce *this* effect rather than that one—ideally, so that the action by which the particular good is achieved contributes to their own perfection. From our experience of performing deliberately executed, goal-directed actions, we come to understand that even where nonpersonal beings are concerned, the effects that each of them causes must in some way have a goal—one that is already somehow contained, or predetermined, in that same being. Were that not so, there would be no sufficient reason for a being to produce specific effects, in which case it would never execute, in the first place, the actions by which to produce them. It is true that a being lacking consciousness is incapable of intending either consciously or consciously *and freely* the end for which it acts as agent. Still, "every dynamic natural property of a non-conscious agent is an innate ontological 'intentionality' toward a determinate type of effect, which it will carry out whenever the conditions of the surrounding environment permit."[45]

Thus, the final cause resides in beings as an intrinsic, dynamic inclination toward a future effect-to-be-produced, guiding them through their proper powers to cause a predetermined effect redounding to their own good. The final

44. Clarke, *The One and the Many,* 15.
45. Ibid., 205.

cause *does not* reside in an agent in the mode of real being, for it is the guiding form of an effect (the mode of being or the determinate being that comes to be) that does not yet really exist in or by the agent, which has still to cause it. Therefore, the only way to explain final causality, or future-as-present effect, in an existing being is in terms of that being's participation in *mental* being, in some really existing, self-present intelligence that can presently think up future effects as ends for each being, as well as appropriate means by which that being will achieve them. The ideas originated by this intelligence are projected outside it and received, in a less perfect way, into creatures that participate in their guiding influence according to a measure suited to each nature. The final cause is thus present in each being in the mode of idea, of mental being. All this bespeaks a Master Planner at work in the world.[46]

God is the intelligence that projects ideas beyond itself to establish beings that participate in them. If the being is nonconscious, it is naturally predetermined to produce particular effects according to the principle of final causality, which Clarke, following St. Thomas, has traced ultimately to the mind of God. If the being is conscious but not free, it is aware of several goods that exert an influence as a possible final (or determining) cause of its activity, of its efficient causality. It must therefore select (instinctively) the good that leads it to produce *this* effect rather than others that are open to it (the effect, we would add, by which this being tries best, albeit involuntarily, to fulfill its nature according to God's idea of it). And if the being is conscious *and* free, it is aware of numerous goods, any one of which might serve as a final cause, or goal, of its actions. And so it must deliberately choose *this* one from among them, determining itself accordingly, so as to produce the effect that achieves the goal. (Here, we must add that this leaves open the possibility of actions that do not lead to the perfection of the free, finite being that performs them, insofar as the ends sought therein conflict with the exigencies of its own nature as predetermined by the Intelligence that created it.)[47]

Despite the differences in their modes of operation, the beings in each of these categories, originating from the same Infinite Source, "actively unfold their diverse dynamic natures as finite participations in the divine perfection and as centers of self-expressive and self-communicating action and interaction with each other, thus forming a universe."[48] At the same time, they

46. See ibid., 199–205.

47. See Clarke, *Journey,* 76.

48. Clarke, *The One and the Many,* 303–4. See Clarke, "Thomas's Essence-Existence Doctrine," in *Creative Retrieval,* 123–29.

are "drawn by this same Source through the pull of the Good built into the nature of every being through the mediation of final causality, which draws each being toward the fulfillment of its own nature, as far as it can, as toward its own good."[49] By striving in its own way toward the good proper to it, therefore, each creature strives implicitly to imitate as far as possible, or even to be united with, God himself, the ultimate Good and the Source of all goodness.[50] But it is only when brought to consciousness in personal beings and offered, in gratitude and love, to God *by* them that the rest of the universe of beings can, in a sense, reach its Source so as to achieve the end of its implicit, subrational longing.[51]

If, with Norris Clarke, we now turn directly to the Christian revelation, we can see clearly that the intrinsically self-communicative, relational character of being—which in each case is ultimately an expression of its aspiration, whether implicit or explicit, to fulfill itself in the good, and therefore to imitate or effect union with God, the Supreme Good—follows from the fact that every being is fundamentally like Absolute Being itself, like God, the Source of all being. For God has revealed himself to us as a trinity of distinct Persons who communicate themselves to one another in eternal relations of love that subsist in the unity of one divine substance. By creating the world and its creatures, God communicates his own goodness, in a limited way (by way of likeness, not identity), outside himself, such that every finite being, with its inner drive to express itself relationally and to share its goodness, bears the trace of the very Love of which it is a wholly gratuitous expression. Clarke acknowledges repeatedly that the whole direction of his philosophical reflections on the active self-communicability and relationality of being in general, and of the person in particular, is inspired by the Christian revelation of the Holy Trinity.[52]

### The Revelation and Communication of Being as Beautiful

Sometimes the human intellect, through the mediation of the senses, grasps a concrete being spontaneously and intuitively according to its harmonious unity and meaningfulness, giving delight to the will precisely insofar as the being is thus contemplated disinterestedly (rather than as something actually possessed). It is then that we experience being as beautiful, as

49. Clarke, *The One and the Many*, 304.
50. See ibid.; Clarke, *Person and Being*, 24; Aquinas, *Summa Contra Gentiles* III, 16–21.
51. See Clarke, *The One and the Many*, 306; Clarke, *Journey*, 80, 82–87.
52. E.g., see Clarke, *Person and Being*, 11–12, 82–89, 100; Clarke, *Journey*, 81.

the splendor of existence shining through every creaturely form. Each creature radiates the light of its existential intelligibility to the extent that it is actual, reflecting accordingly the Source of its light—namely, the pure, unapproachable light of God, who is the absolute fullness of being, intelligibility, and beauty. Having thus taken his cue from St. Thomas, Clarke suggests that the metaphor of light conveys well how each being is both radiant in itself as a source of light (as an actual existent distinct from all others) and self-revealing (hence related) to intellectual beings through the natural emanation of light from its source. In virtue of that light, we perceive intuitively and enjoy the coalescence of all the transcendental properties of being. Beauty is therefore unique among the transcendentals (if, like Clarke, we consider it as such) because it is the one that encompasses all the others and, consequently, relates simultaneously to both the intellect and the will.[53]

## Wojtyła/John Paul II's Statements on Personal Agency in the Light of Clarke's Thomism

In turning to the work of Norris Clarke to help us enrich the metaphysical underpinnings of Karol Wojtyła/John Paul II's affirmations of personal agency in the most vulnerable human beings, we must state at the outset that the themes we have selected therein are not necessarily absent from Wojtyła/John Paul's work considered in its entirety. Perhaps the most unexpected area of correspondence is where we find both authors discussing St. Thomas's grafting of a modified Platonic (that is, a Neoplatonic and Augustinian) view of participation in the self-diffusive Good into the Aristotelian framework of his philosophy as a whole (the specific point of insertion being an expanded notion of act and potency). For each of our authors, the result is that the act of being (*esse*), in which each creature participates, becomes the locus of its good, or perfection (since only that which actually exists can be good in any way), whereas essence (or nature) determines—imposes limitations on (as potency does to act)—how each creature can realize and express its participation in being and hence in the good (which is convertible with being). This is one of Clarke's signature themes.[54]

Certainly, here and elsewhere, the emphases, purposes, and approaches

53. See Clarke, *The One and the Many*, 298–301.

54. E.g., in Clarke, *Explorations*, see "Limitation of Act," 65–88, and "Participation in St. Thomas," 89–101. See also Clarke, *Journey*, 64–68. The exposure of both Clarke and Wojtyła to authors such as Fabro and de Finance would explain their agreement in the view that St. Thomas's metaphysics incorporates Neoplatonic elements.

of our two authors differ. Wojtyła/John Paul tends to focus on ethical implications. In the example just given, Wojtyła, following Thomas, regards finite beings as exemplifying, in various degrees, the unlimited perfection found in the Exemplar of all being, God. The level of their exemplification determines in each case how they will relate to one another as ends. In that way, Wojtyła establishes the objective basis for our recognizing both a hierarchy of goods and, consequently, a normative ethical order. On that basis, we are able to choose properly our means and ends and to act accordingly, so as to achieve our proper moral and ontological perfection.[55] Clarke, for his part, has tended to stay mostly on the metaphysical and epistemological levels, taking a more sweeping approach to things, as we have shown above. The manner in which he applies Thomas's participation metaphysics to develop his understanding of being as active presence, and hence as intrinsically communicative and relational, is an example of that approach. Still, we can see how both authors sometimes use the same Thomistic principles to develop their respective topics. What is more, there is often a remarkable overlap in Clarke's and Wojtyła/John Paul's work when each takes the human person as his subject, whether from the metaphysical or from the interpersonal perspective.[56] For these reasons, their work is mutually complementary.

We will use Clarke's "creative completion" of Thomas to bring out somewhat latent aspects of Wojtyła/John Paul's thought on the self-communicative and relational power of the most vulnerable human persons, so as to move his anthropology in this area further toward a completion of its own. But we will also see how Clarke's work might benefit from the intuitions of Wojtyła/John Paul about the activity of the vulnerable—intuitions that we have good reason to believe are informed by his well thought-out, Thomistically grounded metaphysics of the person. In a word, we will see that the work of these two authors is reciprocally illuminating.

### Being's Intrinsic Aspiration toward Reciprocal Sharing in Love, Fulfilled in the Human Person

Following St. Thomas, both Clarke and Wojtyła/John Paul agree that *esse,* a being's act of existence, is the root of all the good, or perfection, that the being actualizes through its nature; for a being is good, or perfect, only to the

55. In *PC,* see Wojtyła, "Basis of the Moral Norm," 74–80, and "Perfectionism in Ethics," 46–49. See also *SgC,* 55 for a brief statement of the metaphysical basis of Wojtyła's ethical realism.

56. Both authors are quite familiar with the work of contemporary interpersonal existentialists—philosophers of dialogue—such as Martin Buber, Gabriel Marcel, and Emmanuel Mounier.

extent that it *is*.[57] They also agree on the dynamic character of *esse*, whose vibrancy gives rise to the operations proper to the nature of a given being. It follows that the actualization of a being's natural operations serves to perfect it in the good by fulfilling its inherent potentialities, for this allows being "to be" more fully. At the same time, operation expresses and reveals a being through its nature-specific effects. To that extent at least, each being communicates itself. Summarizing the thought of our two authors so far, we can say that action is the self-manifesting radiation of this-kind-of-being.

But at that point, Wojtyła/John Paul generally develops the theme of being's self-communicability specifically in relation to the person, whereas Clarke develops it first in relation to all being, which will help us in our effort to understand better the personal activity of the most vulnerable human persons.[58] Beings communicate themselves through their activity, not just so each "knows" that the other is there, but because they are dynamically ordered to share their goodness with one another through a mutually enriching exchange—that is, through reciprocal giving and receiving. To give and to receive in some way is woven into the very fabric of being. It is the only path by which a being can reach its proper perfection.

While Wojtyła came to that conclusion with respect to personal being, as we have shown throughout this work, Clarke's development of the theme with respect to being in general helps us see more clearly that it is of the very nature of being itself to "want" to relate to other beings, to give and to receive within the community of existents formed of this relational dynamic.[59] And while a given being can effect this only insofar as its nature will allow,

57. See Clarke, *Person and Being*, 28–30; and Wojtyła, "Basis of the Moral Norm," in *PC*, 74–75.

58. In his last published article, Clarke states that he and others (including Kenneth Schmitz) are carrying further Wojtyła's project of integrating Thomistic metaphysics with personalist phenomenology "by showing how a personalist dimension is actually implicit within the very structure and meaning of being itself in a fully developed Thomistic metaphysics," which uncovers the dyadic, giving-and-receiving structure of real being. Clarke, "The Integration of Personalism and Thomistic Metaphysics in Twenty-First Century Thomism," in *Creative Retrieval*, 227. In turn, this opens the way "to grafting the whole rich contemporary phenomenology of the person as essentially relational and interpersonal onto the more basic metaphysics of being as active presence." From Clarke, "Person, Being, and St. Thomas," in *Explorations*, 219.

59. Again, this is not to say that Wojtyła wholly overlooked the more general idea of being's dynamic inclination toward, and its exchange of goodness with, other beings. In "Perfectionism in Ethics," for example, he touches on it when speaking of the good as the end of being (see *PC*, 49). However, he does not explicitly develop that theme as he might in the context of his statements about the personal activity of the most vulnerable human beings, where it would lend philosophical support. As we will see, Clarke does not seem to have fully mined that possibility either.

its dynamism is informed by a kind of "desire" to give itself to and to receive other beings *personally,* to form a community *of love.* After all, each being has its origin in a community of personal Love and so it inwardly "strives" toward that Love as its goal by some concrete form of imitation.[60] Among the creatures of the visible world, however, only human beings can relate to one another and to Love Itself in knowledge and love. And so the world of finite, material beings reaches its goal in and through human persons. Looking at things Thomistically through Clarke's wide-angle lens, we see a wondrous picture come into view: every human being has cosmic significance as one who can consciously take up the world as a gift received and offer it back with himself to the Creator in gratitude and love.[61]

Reciprocally, the material world directs human beings back to their Source, perhaps without their being aware of it, through their exclusively personal, though never fully realized, capacity to embrace all reality. Clarke explains this mainly in terms of the human intellect and will. The intellect is naturally ordered toward the whole of being as intelligible. For that reason, it can never rest in specific acts of knowledge, nor therefore be satisfied with anything short of "knowing directly the infinite source and fullness of all being, namely, God."[62] Similarly, the will is naturally ordered toward the whole order of the good, such that its specific acts of willing this or that good always leave it empty in some way. It "cannot ultimately be satisfied by anything less than loving union with God as the infinite fullness of all goodness."[63] As infinite intelligibility and infinite goodness, God is co-intended, even if unreflectively, in our every act of knowledge and love.[64]

On the other hand, Clarke recognizes that the actualization of the intellect and the will in precisely this way presupposes, in our personal being, a prior potency for spiritual acts ordered toward the absolute fullness of truth and goodness. But what ultimately explains the reduction of that potency to

60. "The inner measure of a being's perfection necessarily moves outward, so to speak, transcending the being itself: the perfection of a created being always causes that being to tend toward the ultimate end that is God, by virtue of the being's own resemblance to God. The higher this perfection, the more the being tends toward God, for the better it represents God's perfection in the world." Wojtyła, "Basis of the Moral Norm," in *PC,* 77.

61. See Clarke, *Person and Being,* 79–80; Clarke, *Journey,* 82–87. See also Wojtyła, *SgC,* 130–31, on the priesthood of all believers expressed as a *sacrificium laudis* to God on behalf of all creation.

62. Clarke, *Person and Being,* 36.

63. Ibid.

64. See ibid., 106. See also Clarke's essay, "The Turn to the Inner Way in Contemporary Neo-Thomism," in *The Philosophical Approach to God: A Neo-Thomist Perspective* (Winston-Salem, N.C.: Wake Forest University, 1979), 11–32.

act? Clarke's answer is intriguing. He tells us that we are naturally "magnetized" by the Infinite Good,

> which draws us in our very depths, at first spontaneously below the level of consciousness and freedom, but then slowly emerging into consciousness as we grow older—if we let it—by the accumulation of experience and reflection upon it.
>
> This innate, unrestricted drive of the human spirit ... toward the Infinite Good is the great hidden dynamo that energizes our whole lives, driving us and refusing to let us be ultimately contented with any merely finite, especially material, goods, whether we understand consciously what is going on within us or not, whether we can explicitly identify our goal or not.... This radical dynamism rooted in our spiritual nature might be called the *dynamic a priori* of the human spirit as such, and thus of every human person.[65]

Given the narrower scope of the philosophical anthropology that he presented in *Person and Act,* Cardinal Wojtyła was not in a position to take this step as the ultimate explanation of why personal, human *being* unfolds in the dynamic way that it does. However, by following certain leads from Pope John Paul II's theological anthropology, we succeeded in coming to a similar conclusion. It seems, then, that from the beginning of their existence, human beings are open to receiving *every* being in its truth, goodness, and beauty as a partial source of the personal fulfillment that they all seek implicitly (at least initially), so that every being serves as yet another voice urging them from the very center of their existence to press forward toward their greatest possible fulfillment—one that seems ever just beyond their immediate horizon: the glorious fullness of truth, goodness, and beauty, namely, Being Itself. What is more, human beings are intrinsically able, from the first, *to give* their being as good to other beings in an act of ontologically personal sharing inspired (secretly, at first) by love.

But it is precisely here that Norris Clarke concludes to something other than his dynamic ontology would suggest. On the one hand, he affirms clearly that being is intrinsically self-communicative and thus relates—gives itself—to other beings through its operations. Yet, in speaking about *human* self-communicability and the relations to other persons that it implies, he seems to consider only the kind of interpersonal activity that depends on the prior emergence of self-consciousness. According to him, a person must first receive the overtures of other persons from without, calling him out of himself as a *thou* to their *I*'s, before he can initiate relations of his own by

65. Clarke, *Person and Being,* 36–37.

communicating himself in conscious self-giving.[66] Yet, if it is true that "[t]he human person, in fact, comes into existence enveloped in a web of relations of dependence on others even before it can begin to generate its own relations actively,"[67] then it does not seem that Clarke can regard self-communicability and relationality *as such* to be just as primordial a dimension of being as substance itself, even with the understanding that substance has a logical and an ontological priority. As a minimum, however, a human person must be able, from the first, to communicate and thus relate his real, personal presence to other persons, or else his being would not "make a difference": he would be to them as if he were not. If that were so, it would mean that he is in no way "operational," or active, which is impossible. To be wholly in potency is not to be at all. We need, then, to distinguish between (1) self-communicability and relationality as ontologically operative attributes of the personal being; and (2) the fully self-conscious appropriation of those attributes by the human person, a potency that is fully actualized in human nature only after a rather lengthy period of psychosomatic development.

Like Wojtyła, Clarke develops the theme of self-possession, understood as mastery of self (exercised and revealed in the deliberate, self-determining act), together with that of self-consciousness (presence to self, or luminous interiority). That is why he takes the position that human beings must first be inwardly aware of their substantial in-itselfness before they can personally exercise the self-communicative, relational dimension of their being. They must consciously possess their distinct, unified, ontological structure before they can give themselves away in friendship and love as a unique self.[68] Yet, substantiality, or ontological unity, itself implies a more fundamental kind of self-possession, namely, the personal being's ownership of his own spiritual act of existence (received as a gift) and hence of the secondary acts that follow from it. Clarke affirms that "the soul must possess its own spiritual act of existence, transcending the body, which it then 'lends' to the body."[69] In consciousness, we have the experience of appropriating and governing our distinct, ontological identity—of possessing our ontological self-possession, our "metaphysical subjectivity."

66. See ibid., 72–75. As far as it goes, this understanding is identical in content with what we have already seen in some of Wojtyła's writings.

67. Clarke, "Substance-in-Relation," in *Explorations,* 118.

68. See Clarke, *Person and Being,* 57. Conversely, "In giving ourselves we find clear proof that we possess ourselves." *LR,* 98.

69. Clarke, *Person and Being,* 35. See Clarke, "Immediate Creation," in *Creative Retrieval,* 176, 184.

This is a key theme in Cardinal Wojtyła's philosophical anthropology, and Clarke suggests it himself: "Self-possession is the manifestation on the level of conscious experience of ... in-itselfness or substantiality."[70] In fact, that is just another expression of Clarke's summary definition of the meaning of person in St. Thomas: "an actual existent [i.e., with its own act of existence], distinct from all others, possessing an intellectual nature, so that it can be the self-conscious, responsible source of its own actions."[71] He tells us that the first part of the definition "expresses the metaphysical foundation-structure of the person," while the second part "expresses the manifestation of this ontological constitution in the order of [self-conscious] activity."[72] Unlike Clarke, however, Wojtyła/John Paul would eventually reach the conclusion that personal self-giving—self-communication—of some kind is *not* completely delayed until one experiences a mature sense of self with the full emergence of consciousness and rationality. He not only affirms, with Clarke, that personal self-communication is a mode of self-conscious activity that is ultimately rooted in the personal *esse:* he goes further by suggesting that human beings already exercise an incipient mode of personal self-communication right from the start, precisely in virtue of that *esse*. As the owner of his spiritual act of existence, the person is also the owner, or subject, of the self-communicative/relational activity that flows from it naturally, namely, the self-constituting activity by which the development and operation of the psychosomatic structure reveals and communicates a "someone." It is this ontologically personal mode of self-determination that establishes the basis for the conscious and free acts of self-determination that will normally follow sometime later in the person's development.

It would seem, therefore, that Wojtyła/John Paul II's informed intuition about our intrinsic power to communicate ourselves relationally as persons to others from the first moment of our existence is more in keeping with what Clarke's Thomistically based metaphysics would demand, notwithstanding the tensions in this area that we have exposed in Wojtyła's own writings. Recall Wojtyła's very telling remarks: "It is significant that the [newly conceived] child—although deprived for a long time of the personal fullness of activity—nevertheless enters at once into the community as a person, as someone *capable not only of receiving but also of giving....* [R]ight from the

70. Clarke, *Person and Being*, 57.

71. Ibid., 29. Bracketed clarification in original.

72. Ibid., 30. Bracketed interpolation mine.

moment of conception [each child] presents itself as a person and a gift."[73] And as Clarke himself says, "The human person as child first goes out towards the world as poor, as appealingly but insistently needy. The primary response partner is the mother, who meets the growing person's needs ideally with caring love."[74] Here he seems to make our point: the very manifestation of the child as "appealingly but insistently needy" is his personal self-communication—indeed, a very powerful one, capable of drawing the caring love of his mother, to say nothing of other persons as well. The child "goes out" as a self-communicative *person* to invite and to meet that response, which also implies his active disposition to receive and respond to it in some way. He therefore contributes indispensably to the formation of a real communion of persons by his self-communication, which is never anything less than personal. The relations thus formed redound to the good, not only of the child, but also of those who care for him, actualizing new perfections in all the persons so related and thus augmenting their intensity of being.

We can further support Wojtyła/John Paul's statements on the self-communicability of the newly conceived child to his parents and to other persons (and, by extension, on the self-communicability of persons having severe forms of psychosomatic disintegration) by taking as our point of departure what Clarke calls "the dynamic *a priori* of the human spirit," and by considering in that light Wojtyła's idea (outlined briefly above) of exemplarism as the basis for establishing an objective hierarchy of goods. The pull that God, as Supreme Good (or Final Cause), exerts on our being to draw us to himself is existentially reflected in our spirit as an initially hidden love that opens our existence to anticipate, if only unreflectively, the good of everything that is. That is what drives us to move out actively, through the body, to meet the world around us. In thus meeting any finite reality, therefore, we have an anticipatory, perhaps wholly unreflective grasp of its goodness, at least insofar as it enhances our being and brings us closer to complete perfection. On the other hand, while every finite being is good, minimally, as existent or according to its place in the universal scheme of things, it might

73. Wojtyła, "Parenthood," in *PC*, 333. Italics added. The well-documented phenomenon of post-abortion trauma in both mothers and fathers makes it clear that their aborted child(ren) did, indeed, "make a difference"—a distinctively *personal* difference—in their lives. E.g., see Theresa Burke with David C. Reardon, *Forbidden Grief: The Unspoken Pain of Abortion* (Springfield, Ill.: Acorn Books, 2002); Kevin Burke, David Wemhoff, and Marvin Stockwell, eds., *Redeeming a Father's Heart: Men Share Powerful Stories of Abortion Loss and Recovery* (Bloomington, Ind.: AuthorHouse, 2007).

74. Clarke, *Person and Being*, 72–73.

not be objectively good *for us,* in which case we tend to shun it reflexively as somehow detrimental to our being.

Let us be clear that this process is rooted in and initially follows human nature; it is not at first defined intellectually with respect to each being. In time, the intellect will judge definitively whether a being is good or bad for us, based on the objective order of truth.[75] What we are suggesting here is that the human spirit's dynamic *a priori* establishes the ground for and predisposes us toward such judgments, and this is reflected in our personal nature from the start. Accordingly, if we are enriched by some finite good, we continue to press outward, even more fully actualized than before, seeking new encounters with reality for a new exchange of goods that will perfect us further. Throughout that process, we actively discriminate between goods, at first only implicitly and in the broadest way, in that some augment our being more than others because of their place on the scale of being. So thanks to the dynamic *a priori* of our spirit toward the Infinite Good, love's anticipatory grasp of the goodness of being moves us to direct our self-communicating activity toward those beings that have a greater share in the act of existence, since the level of goodness that they have to exchange with us will also be commensurately greater.

This specific, ontologically personal intentionality always marks human activity because, even when we are unaware of it, we always co-intend a fullness of being and goodness—an Exemplar—against which to measure every being we meet. And that is why we tend naturally to communicate ourselves to other persons, even from the earliest stages of our development, or of theirs. In general, we perceive in other persons, at some level, a richness of being and goodness that surpasses that of any other kind of being that we directly perceive. But at the very least, the dynamic *a priori* of the human spirit, the hidden love of the Infinite Good that is ours as the "dynamo" energizing our whole personal existence, directs us implicitly to other persons precisely because their unique richness provides us with goods absolutely essential to the actualization of our inherent potentialities. This would support Wojtyła's statement (echoed in numerous statements of his as John Paul II) that the newly conceived child gives himself specifically to his parents and siblings as a gift. Since his active communication of himself through the natural operations of his psychosomatic structure is informed by the love-dynamic defining the spiritual act of existence of which he is the subject, he shares with

75. Cf. *AP,* 250–51.

his parents and siblings the good of a love that is properly his. And in some way, that same child receives, as *that* good which most fully actualizes his being, the love that his parents and siblings bestow on him in welcoming him unconditionally into the family. The child and his family members are thus mutually enriched as they share their existential goodness with one another through their subtle but profound communion in love. Of course, that same dynamic underlies every such communion that forms between extremely vulnerable persons and those who accept them unconditionally in love.

Given the direction of our reflections at this point, let us consider now the implications of Cardinal Wojtyła's remarks about the self-giving activity of the newly conceived child in the context of what Father Clarke tells us about efficient causality. Clarke explains that a being cannot cause in itself any new, accidental mode of being for which it is in potency (unless perhaps it already has that perfection in some equivalent form that it can draw from and realize in a new way). Still less can a being be the cause of its own existence. It must therefore receive every such perfection from an extrinsic agent, from an efficient cause having the power to produce the effect by which a new being comes to exist either absolutely or in an already existing being—that is, accidentally. Out of the abundance of its own actuality, therefore, one being communicates being to another, in whole or in part. Since a cause cannot be such without actually producing its effect in another, its action—its productive activity—takes place in the effect, not in the cause as such (though that does not preclude change in the cause while causing, the intrinsic change resulting from its own finitude, or imperfection, but not from the nature of efficient causality itself). What is more, the cause acts for as long as it is producing its effect, its bringing-into-being relative to another, such that the act of causing and the effect are always simultaneous. Indeed, they are one and the same ontological event consisting of two different relations: action from the side of the cause and passion on the side of the effect. When its contribution is positive, the efficient cause enriches another being from its own plentitude, without implying any loss to itself (though transfers of energy do occur between *material* causes and their effects).[76]

In view of this understanding, it might surprise us to consider that spouses are not, together, the efficient cause of the absolute coming-to-be of

76. See Clarke, *The One and the Many*, 181–93. See also Clarke, "Causality and Time," in *Creative Retrieval*, 27–38.

their child. Rather, they cooperate with, while being completely subject to, the will of God, who directly causes the child's personal existence at a time soon after the conjugal act has taken place. True, the spouses contribute essentially to the child's natural mode of existence as the joint causes of the body, and God has made his direct action contingent on that contribution. But even so, their causal contribution is a step removed from the moment of the child's actual coming-to-be, whereas efficient causality is, by definition, simultaneous with the production of the effect for as long as it produces that effect. So, the child's existence as such and relative to the spouses is a wholly gratuitous gift from God (hence Eve's words in Genesis 4:1), who creates, or actualizes, the form and preserves it in being.

In keeping with this, Pope John Paul II reminds us that the newborn child, revealing himself visibly as a gift at birth, is already a gift from the very beginning—from conception—in virtue of the gift of personal existence that God has given him as his own to give.[77] Since the child receives his personal existence and its form as his own, and the actual form is the principle of operation, he is in a sense, through God's direct action, a co-cause of parenthood in the spouses and of the responsibilities that it will entail for them.[78] From the first moment of existence, this child's active power of personal being and operation causes the new perfection, the new coming-to-be, of fatherhood and motherhood in the man and the woman respectively. This is particularly evident in the latter case. And it is precisely in virtue of this new coming-to-be in them that the spouses become, simultaneously, the cause of the filial relation in the child. However, the child's self-communication, or self-giving, of his personal being to them cannot reach its term until they accept fully, in all its truth and value, this new life—this personal gift—as well as the task that

77. "The newborn child gives itself to its parents by the very fact of its coming into existence. *Its existence is already a gift, the first gift of the Creator to the creature.*" *LF*, 11.

78. This is not to deny the real sense in which spouses transmit human life and confer parenthood on each other in cooperation with God through the marital act. But one cannot be a parent without one's child. And the child is, from the first and by God's free gift, "his own person," making himself present to his parents *as* a person so that they can *be* parents. At the same time, they *become* parents by accepting and fulfilling the responsibilities that this new little person entails for them. This person is absolutely equal in nature and dignity to each of his parents, who must not, therefore, presume that they are entitled by right to conceive him, for he is the supreme gift of the marital union (see *GS*, 50). It is he, therefore, who has both the right to have been conceived, in love, as the fruit of that union, and the right to be respected as a person from the moment of his conception. See the instruction of the CDF, *Donum Vitae*, II, A, 8 (February 22, 1987), Vatican website. See also *Donum Vitae* II, A, 1 and note 32 of the same document. On the utter uniqueness of the transmission of human life as compared with the transmission of other forms of life in the universe, see *Donum Vitae*, Introduction, 4.

it bestows on them. Only then will their parenthood likewise reach its term—that is, become fully actualized. For the parent-child relation is not mainly biological but spiritual; it is a relation of persons. It therefore requires reciprocity in self-giving and other-receiving.

When spouses have the proper consciousness of and attitude toward their role as parents, the entrance of the child into their marital community strengthens, enriches, and extends their interpersonal life from the very first, as Cardinal Wojtyła reminds us.[79] This is, of course, the basis for the family. The family has a special role in caring for the goods of salvation at the heart of it (beginning with the sacrament of marriage itself), and it is the subject responsible for their realization. While that is true, in the first place, of the parents, the children also

> take part in it from the moment of birth, and especially from the moment of baptism.... We can see the extent to which children are stewards of these manifold goods of salvation, grace, and morality in family life. In going from their wedding toward their family's future, Christian spouses should include in their vision of this future all that children bring to a couple's marital love, fidelity, and honesty, to carrying out their own vocation.[80]

In these ways, Wojtyła indicates just how much children, even from conception and into postnatal infancy, are truly and personally givers, and not just receivers. The self-communication of these children reveals at each stage precisely how they are also to be a "task" for the parents and even for older siblings. It thus contributes essentially to the "law of development" of each member of the family—including the newest members—and of the whole family as a community of persons.[81]

### Summary Reflections

Our findings in this section of the chapter lead us to conclude that the attributes of self-communicability and relationality, as transcendental properties of being as such, are neither potentialities nor options that human beings can exercise only after their structural and rational growth has reached a certain level of maturity. We do not communicate ourselves relationally only *when* we mature: we *must* communicate ourselves relationally *in order to* mature. The person's *ontological* self-possession is the condition of incipient, personal self-giving. In turn, such self-giving, when fully welcomed

79. See "Parenthood," in *PC*, 332–33.
80. "Pastoral Reflections on the Family," in *PC*, 353–54.
81. See "Parenthood," in *PC*, 333–34.

by other persons, is the condition of the emergence in the person of *self-conscious* self-possession. That is, it is the condition of one's giving freely and fully to another the personal gift of self. But even then, we must understand this "fullness" of self-giving in a relative, not an absolute, sense. For one thing, the person as such, as ontologically self-possessed, is incommunicable. What is more, conscious possession of one's own *I* in the order of knowledge and likewise in the order of self-determining action is always more or less partial in this life.[82] So, too, then, is one's self-understanding and, consequently, one's personal self-communication to others. For that reason, we always remain something of a mystery to ourselves and to others.

That is true, above all, because the Efficient Cause of our existence as persons is also its Final Cause. Because our spirit strives, at least implicitly, toward the inexhaustible truth and goodness of our existential Goal, it has a depth that "cannot be plumbed by our explicit consciousness short of the direct vision of God himself, when we shall see ourselves totally as God sees us, i.e., as we really are."[83] Every stage of our existence is informed by the pull of the Final Cause, which is Love itself—the beginning and end of our personal being. We achieve perfection, therefore, not just by actualizing our nature-specific operations, as is the case with nonpersonal beings, but by striving through those operations, whether implicitly or explicitly, to fulfill God's idea of us as *persons,* who, in "obedience" to the dynamism of love that grounds our very existence, come to be as God intends us to be.[84]

Owing to a spiritual mode of existence magnetized by the Infinite Good, we, as human beings, run the whole course of our life passing from being to being in search of the absolute fullness of goodness. Whether or not we are conscious of that, when we encounter another human being, we meet a reality that, while not the limitless Good that we somehow always seek, has nevertheless an inexhaustible capacity to represent and mediate it. For one thing, persons who have reached a sufficient level of maturity can help us in an endless variety of ways to perfect our being—above all, by lovingly communicating themselves to us concretely, yet in surpassing measure. Our own

82. See Clarke, *Person and Being,* 45–46, 60–61.

83. Ibid., 47.

84. In another context, but in a similar vein, Clarke writes that "the perfection of our real being is *represented,* held before us by the divine idea as an ideal goal, a final cause, drawing [us] towards its actual realization through the drawing power of the Good reflected in it. It functions thus as a powerful *motivation* for spiritual growth toward the fulfillment of our true being to-be-realized." From Clarke, "The Problem of the Reality and Multiplicity of Divine Ideas in Christian Neoplatonism," *Creative Retrieval,* 84–85.

love is drawn to that, and so we naturally seek out and communicate ourselves to other human beings, even from the womb. Secondly, such persons possess an inexhaustible capacity to disclose the truth of other beings to us, to contain the world within themselves and to share it with us as only each of them knows it. This presupposes an inexhaustible capacity to receive the world's self-communication, to penetrate the inherent intelligibility of being. The human person is both the one *to whom* the world presents itself, a "dative of disclosure" (of manifestation), and the one *who* presents or manifests the world, a "*nominative* of disclosure," an agent of truth.[85] So, from the moment that God bestows on us the gift of our own personal existence, other human beings mediate our dynamic journey to him, while in some way we mediate theirs through the contributions we make in giving the gift of self, leading them thus to fuller self-knowledge and self-discovery, and in that sense serving as agents of truth ourselves. As we help one another become more fully actualized through the mutual sharing of the good of our personal being and its perfections, we anticipate the goal of our innate quest to be filled to perfection with the fullness of Being and Goodness Itself.

We see in this that God's final causality in human beings directs each of us in essentially the same way to the same predetermined end of loving, interpersonal communion. We follow that direction initially below the level of consciousness, and then through our creative cooperation. In either case, the interpersonal encounter that results always involves a sharing among persons—a giving and receiving—of each one's being as good, so that new perfections for which these persons are in potency come to be in them. Through this diffusion of the good among persons, founded on mutual self-communication in love, we come consciously to possess and thus freely to share ourselves ever more fully. Father Clarke reminds us that "the ultimate mystery of being turns out to be that *to be* is *to be a lover.*"[86] Where finite personal beings are concerned (whether human or angelic), this means: to the extent that we fail to love, we fail to be.

Because we ontologically possess our own spiritual act of existence and the impulse of love that secretly dynamizes it in virtue of its ultimate Goal, we can entrust ourselves in love to other persons right from the beginning of our existence. What is more, because God remains ever the Efficient Cause of our spiritual existence and activity, as well as the ultimate End of these,

85. See Sokolowski, *Phenomenology*, 46, 161.
86. Clarke, *Person and Being*, 97.

he himself is present in our every act of self-giving, simultaneously entrusting us to others, that they might assist us during our hidden journey to him. So, even where the most vulnerable persons are concerned, the act by which they make a gift of themselves to us is always doubly personal and, from God's side at least, always consciously intended as according with his eternal idea of personally subsistent human nature.

When our ontological self-possession and self-determination reach the level of self-consciousness and rational freedom, we enter immediately into our personal history of sanctity or sin, depending on whether we cooperate with or oppose the natural thrust of our spiritual dynamism toward God as our Supreme Good. If we try consciously, in a selfish way, to cut ourselves off from other persons and even from the world at large, then we grate futilely against the very dynamism of our own being, since we are persons who are ordered naturally toward love. In other words, the psychological disposition to share our own good with and to receive the good of this or that particular person or other finite being here and now is subject to change, hence accidental and reversible, whereas the ontological dynamism of self-giving and other-receiving is unchangeable, hence essential and irreversible. It grounds our basic psychological tendency to communicate ourselves relationally to other beings and especially to other persons, but we can willfully oppose it, which is also to oppose ourselves to the pull of the Supreme Good toward which personally subsistent human nature is intrinsically finalized. We can thus deprive ourselves definitively of any possibility of personal fulfillment. As Father Clarke tells us incisively, "There is no viable substitute for communion; this is the law of being itself."[87]

We have already noted the reason for that: every finite being reflects, in some measure, its source in Being Itself, in God, who has revealed himself as a communion of three divine Persons related substantially and eternally in love. As for human beings in particular, God's act of giving us an existence dynamized by love, and our act of receiving it and returning to him in virtue of it, is patterned on the mutually self-giving relation of love between the Father and his eternally generated Son, as well as on the historical mode of that relation in the Incarnation. Among other things, the Incarnation, together with the revelation of the Trinity, teaches us that the Father's love, of which the Son was "sent" as an ambassador, is also essentially that of the Son himself. It is mediated through a human nature whose substantial act

87. Ibid., 82.

of existence is that of an eternal Person. From the moment that the Incarnation was first accomplished, therefore, the divine Son owned personally both the humanity by which he offered himself to us and the Love that radiated through it.

If that is so, then even the most vulnerable human beings can express, through their humanity, the impulse of love that dynamizes and defines their spiritual existence, for they are personally the subject of that existence. On that basis, they can also be ambassadors of Love through grace, whereby human self-communication in love is bound up with and mediates divine Love. What is more, the fact that they can actively receive the personal gift of God's love through grace, as John the Baptist did even prior to his birth, presupposes that they can already actively receive the love that other persons extend toward them or that they themselves first invite through the personal self-communication of their being under the dynamic impulse of love, which urges them to seek interpersonal communion with others as a concrete expression of their hidden desire for interpersonal communion with God. In a word, the most vulnerable human beings can be actively participating members of any true communion of persons and invaluable stewards of grace for the strengthening of that communion. Even if they have not yet reached, or are no longer at, the point of luminous self-presence, their personal being is nevertheless radiant with the resplendent beauty of their spiritual dynamism as it presses ever outward through its form, despite the essential finitude of human nature, to meet the very Source and Goal of that dynamism: the inexhaustible Beauty of Trinitarian Love.

## Helen Keller and the Anthropology of the Vulnerable

By amplifying certain aspects of Karol Wojtyła/Pope John Paul II's anthropology in the broader context of St. Thomas Aquinas's dynamic ontology as developed in the writings of W. Norris Clarke, we have tried to put his statements about personal agency in newly conceived and developing children—and by extension, in the radically infirm and the dying—more firmly and explicitly on solid philosophical ground. Inasmuch as those statements are clearly informed by the light of Christian faith, we sought to complement them with philosophical insights that are likewise inspired by horizons opened to human thought by the Christian revelation. We will now examine the early childhood experiences of Helen Keller to see how our reflections on personal agency in exceedingly vulnerable human beings might find confirmation therein. In turn, Helen's experiences might provide us with further insights about the agency of the vulnerable, and they might even suggest new directions for exploring that topic.[88]

## Helen Keller and Personal Being's Dynamism toward Conscious Self-Possession, Self-Communication, and Relationality

The autobiography of Helen Keller (1880–1968), whom illness deprived of sight and hearing when she was only nineteen months old, illustrates well how the human spirit is dynamically ordered toward communicating itself fully, in knowledge and love, to the world and the people in it. But self-communication of that kind presupposes self-mastery. Helen recounts that prior to the decisive emergence of self-consciousness in her at about age seven, she was like a ship at sea in a dense fog, having no bearing by which to orient herself in life. "'Light! Give me light!' was the wordless cry of my soul."[89]

On the one hand, Helen had developed the somatic skills that allowed her to express outwardly her basic wants and needs, as also her spontaneous, psychically generated feelings, which she communicated ever more frequently in fits of frustration and temper before she reached the personal fullness of her activity. But her "wordless cry" suggests a deep, as yet inexpressible aspiration toward interior illumination, which would allow her to make sense of her experiences and to order her life, in relation to her surroundings, through fully self-determining actions in which her psycho-emotivity would be personally integrated and her inner self freely expressed. Powerfully urged from within to fulfill her rational (or spiritual) nature, she sought her proper end as a person unreflectively, like a ship groping its way to shore in a foggy white darkness.[90] Only in self-consciously possessing and governing herself would she reach the shore toward which her soul directed her, like a ship sailing in the clear light of day.

In view of our earlier anthropological reflections, it seems that Helen Keller's wordless cry for "light" describes an inner sensitivity to the silent but inexorable dynamism of her spirit pressing on toward self-consciousness in and through a body that could not, in some respects, support its effort. In an uncomprehending yet real way, young Helen sought that transparency to

88. Though Helen Keller adopted some lamentable political, social, and religious views later in life, we are interested only in examining how her recollections of her early experiences as a severely disabled child compare with our reflections on the vulnerable and their agency.

89. Helen Keller, *The Story of My Life* (n.p.: Watermill Press, 1993), 21.

90. See ibid.

self, that luminous interiority, that would put her in conscious possession of herself. And her inner drive toward conscious self-possession seems also to have coincided with an inner drive to be freely self-communicative, to relate in knowledge and love to every being and especially to every person she encountered. On the one hand, she had to "own" more fully the riches of her personal existence before she could relate more fully to other beings, hence the cry for "light." On the other hand, she required a fuller relation to other beings before she could be luminous to self and thereby assert full—that is, explicit—ownership over herself. So, included in Helen's wordless cry for the "light" of self-illumination seems to have been both a desire to express that light, her own "I," *beyond* herself—to communicate her deepest interior to other beings through the body that seemed to imprison her—and an intention that something or someone should "give" her the light she needed. Let us consider this further.

In the months following her permanent loss of sight and hearing, Helen "felt the need of some communication with others and began to make crude signs" to make herself understood—nodding, shaking her head, pushing, pulling, and so on.[91] As she got older, she became acutely aware that other people communicated among themselves merely by moving their lips, whereas she, despite her frantic efforts to do likewise, had to use gestures and signs to express herself to others.[92] She even went so far as to try to teach the sign language that she had devised to the family dog.[93] It is important to note that her sign language was not necessarily just spontaneous, imitative, or instinctually associative. It was often self-initiated and creative, including an element of the symbolic and hence the novel. For example, in order to show her friend that she wanted to go egg hunting, Helen would make fists to symbolize the eggs and then put them on the ground in the grass.[94] She achieved considerable success at getting others to understand her by original actions like that.

Helen sought actively not only to make herself understood in the world but also to understand the world. Here, too, she succeeded considerably as she grew, learning "to know many things" by tactile perception and by her awareness of motion.[95] Based on her "observations," she could make simple, accurate deductions about what was going on around her. She could learn and perform household tasks like grinding coffee or folding laundered

91. Ibid., 7.

92. See ibid., 8–9.

93. Ibid., 11.

94. See ibid., 10. See also 7.

95. Ibid., 7.

clothes and putting them away, distinguishing her clothes from those of others. And she could understand when her mother wanted her to go get something, acting accordingly.[96] Helen acknowledged a special debt to her mother's "loving wisdom," which communicated "all that was bright and good in my long night."[97]

In addition, Helen exhibited the natural curiosity of a child. For example, when she would find her father sitting alone with a sheet of (news)paper before his face, she was "greatly puzzled to know what he was doing. I imitated this action, even wearing his spectacles, thinking they might help solve the mystery."[98] Note that Helen did not imitate her father's action merely as an end in itself. Rather, her words betray, retrospectively, an intentional effort to understand its purpose—to reason her way to its meaning.

One can see, then, that Helen's early activity was really quite purposeful. On the one hand, it was marked by an unquenchable desire and a relentless effort to communicate herself fully to the "outer" world. As the condition for that, however, she desired simultaneously, if unreflectively, to receive and to understand fully all that the world and the people around her could communicate to *her*. Before she reached her seventh birthday, she was already remarkably close to fulfilling those hidden aspirations, as she had by that time a well-developed power of intentionality.[99] For example, when once her aunt made her a rag doll to play with, Helen noticed immediately that it had no facial features. Her ability to intend what was absent is evident in her protestations that the doll had no eyes, the lack of which struck her most. She then showed exceptional ingenuity in resolving the problem, pulling two large beads from her aunt's cape and having her sew them on where the eyes should have been. This suggests that Helen had also the ability to intend a part—the eyes—as proper to the doll as a whole.[100] In another instance, she

96. See ibid., 7–9.

97. Ibid., 7.

98. Ibid., 13.

99. "In phenomenology, 'intending' means the conscious relationship we have to an object." That is, intentionality is a "consciousness (or an experience) of" something, whether that "something" is concretely present to us, imaginary, recalled from the past, anticipated, or judged to be the real state of affairs. Sokolowski, *Phenomenology,* 8. In *Person and Act,* Wojtyła regards intentionality as the active directing of cognition to its concrete object in the act of knowledge or self-knowledge. He maintains that this act and its result are registered in consciousness, but he rejects the general phenomenological view that consciousness itself has an intentional character (see *AP,* 303–4n16). Whatever the case might be, our point is that just before her acquisition of formal language, Helen Keller's level of consciousness and cognition was already considerably advanced, given her circumstances.

100. See Keller, *My Life,* 17–18. In other words, it seems that Helen was on the threshold of a *categorical intuition,* an intentional act predicating a certain state of affairs about the object now

locked her newly arrived teacher, Anne Sullivan, in the latter's room and hid the key, which she refused to produce, forcing Miss Sullivan to exit through the window.[101] The fact that Helen retrieved the key months later testifies, first, to her distinctively human memory, to her ability to intend a past event as present here and now (bespeaking a consciousness of time);[102] and, second, to her developed sense of object permanence, to her ability to intend an object as really existing even in its absence.[103] In a word, her acting was distinctly human. It was that of a person.

Nevertheless, during her sixth year, Helen's unfulfilled desire to express herself clearly to others became unbearable, giving rise to frequent, passionate outbursts as she struggled mightily to free herself from the "invisible hands" that seemed to be holding her back.[104] She knew that she was unhappy but not why, because she had not yet become fully self-aware. For the same reason, when her actions—whose consequences she understood well—were followed by a feeling akin to regret, she knew that she had been naughty but not why.[105] Indeed, she was inclined to repeat her naughty behavior when it served her own ends, for the light of self-presence was still too dim for the first glimmers of conscience to affect her behavior appreciably for the better.[106] One might say that she was filled with implicit intentions that she could not yet fill, nor could she ever do so alone, because driving the spiritual dynamism at the core of her being was an abyss of love calling out to love to *fill* it with love. Despite their sincere efforts, Helen's parents were unable to penetrate far enough into their daughter's isolation to help wrest her free of those "invisible hands."

---

presenting itself to one's perception. Human language itself is based on that capacity, which is proper to human rationality. See Sokolowski, *Phenomenology,* 33, 88–93. No wonder, then, that Helen grasped the mystery of formal language at the very time her rationality was approaching this level of achievement.

101. See Keller, *My Life,* 13. Helen had once played the same prank on her mother. See ibid., 12–13.

102. See Sokolowski, *Phenomenology,* 66–70.

103. It is possible that Helen's initial acquisition of formal language, which took place in the period between when she locked her teacher in the room and when she later produced the key, helped cue her memory in this case. But that would still presuppose that her memory was operating at a rather high level prior to her breakthrough with language.

104. Keller, *My Life,* 16.

105. See ibid., 9.

106. This is not to deny that the effects of original sin might have been involved here. But the "voice" of conscience must be developed enough to elicit the personal effort to control those effects (with the help of God's grace), and that presupposes a strong sense of one's own *I* in consciousness.

## The Role of Language and of Love in Helping Helen Keller Fulfill Her Spiritual Dynamism

Clearly, Helen Keller's interaction with the world and with those around her was exceedingly intelligent and dynamic prior to her ability to use words and syntax. But she was still not satisfied. Her inner, unreflective drive to express herself more fully far outstripped her actual power to do so. What is more, her dark, silent prison prevented any outside reality from entering in according to the fullness of her inner capacity to receive it. She unreflectively intended something beyond what her current level of experience and ability could offer. Helen would not understand what that "something" was until her teacher came "to set my spirit free."[107] Anne Sullivan answered the "wordless cry" of Helen's soul for "light," setting her spirit free in two respects: (1) she helped Helen receive the world with self-conscious understanding, and (2) she helped her thereby to communicate with the world in self-conscious love. Miss Sullivan's success was itself the achievement of love, the very light that burst through Helen's darkness.

First, Miss Sullivan succeeded in teaching Helen formal language, in getting her to understand that every object has a name. As soon as she named her first object, Helen's spirit broke free and became self-luminous to a degree that she had not previously experienced.

> Some one was drawing water and my teacher placed my hand under the spout. As the cool stream gushed over one hand she spelled into the other the word *water*, first slowly, then rapidly.... Suddenly I felt a misty consciousness as of something forgotten—a thrill of returning thought; and somehow the mystery of language was revealed to me. I knew that "w-a-t-e-r" meant the wonderful cool something that was flowing over my hand.[108]

Prior to that decisive event, Miss Sullivan's efforts to spell words into Helen's hand seemed to her pupil no more than a game. In consequence of that event, Helen knew herself distinctly as the knower of the object now known by name. "That living word awakened my soul, gave it light, hope, joy, set it free"![109] It is particularly significant that the word "water" turned out to be the key to her spiritual self-awakening, since it was one of the very few words that she had first begun to utter in the months leading up to her illness, and it was the only word for which she continued to make a sound ("wah-wah")

107. Keller, *My Life*, 6.
108. Ibid., 23.
109. Ibid.

right up to the time she learned to spell it.[110] The lifting of the fog that had been clouding her consciousness was, in a sense, the resumption of her original breakthrough with formal language over five years earlier, when an incipiently comprehending use of words first began to mediate both the world to her and her to herself as the condition for the full emergence of her personality.

Helen's autobiography provides further striking evidence that the comprehending experience of objective reality through formal language coincides precisely with the experience of oneself as a subject (that is, with spiritual self-awakening, or self-luminosity)—the condition of psycho-moral personality formation. Just prior to her first real self-experience in the experience of objectifying "water" linguistically, Helen had purposely broken a new doll in a fit of impatience. She initially felt no remorse for her passionate outburst but, on the contrary, a keen sense of delight. Once her soul emerged from darkness into light, however, she experienced real sorrow and regret for the first time on remembering her destructive tantrum.[111] That signaled the real beginning of her psycho-moral development.

From the time Helen learned her first word and something of the world lit up for her as she simultaneously became luminous to herself, each new name she learned "gave birth to a new thought."[112] The miracle of words let the world, with which she had so urgently longed to communicate, enter *her* world more meaningfully than ever before. Consequently, in learning the names and uses of things, she developed a "sense of kinship with the rest of the world,"[113] bespeaking a corresponding sense of her own "I" *with respect to* the world.[114] This would seem to confirm that our power to be luminously self-present is integrally connected with the dynamic power of our personal being to relate, potentially, to *all* being in the order of knowledge through the mediation of formal language. On naming her first object, Helen seems to have understood that connection immediately, if still unreflectively, since from then on she exhibited an insatiable desire to "learn the name of every object that I touched."[115] Through the penetrating power of language, she could get the world to relinquish more of its secrets to her own inner world and thus know herself as the one who unlocks their meaning—that is, as the light that illumines them.

110. See ibid., 5.

111. See ibid., 22–24.

112. Ibid., 23.

113. Ibid., 24.

114. It would not be long before Helen would also understand her "I" as potentially *threatened* by (hence alienated from) the world, as she sat alone outside, up in a tree, during the fury of a sudden thunderstorm. See ibid., 25–27.

115. Ibid., 24.

What is more, since each being communicates itself through its proper operations precisely as *good,* at least insofar as it exists, self-luminous *personal* beings, receiving and knowing it under that aspect, can respond in love by willingly diffusing their *own* goodness to that being (for example, by exercising a providential care over it). Accordingly, as personal being is dynamically ordered to the knowledge of all things insofar as they exist, so, too, is it dynamically ordered to the *love* of all existing things insofar as they are known to be good. Helping her young charge to fulfill the latter dynamism is the second way, intertwined with the first, in which Anne Sullivan brought light and freedom into Helen Keller's life. But this presupposes, before all else, that Miss Sullivan herself was the liberating light—the light of love—that shined on Helen in answer to the wordless cry of her soul.[116] She saw in Helen's helplessness and frustrations one who sought love, one who needed love, and one who was worthy of love. By recognizing Helen's essential goodness and by penetrating the child's darkness with her own goodness, Miss Sullivan freed the child's spirit to pursue the end of its dynamism: to relate to all being in knowledge so as to relate to all being in love.

Though initially resistant, Helen soon welcomed (unreflectively at first) her teacher's offer of love as expressed in the extraordinary patience that Miss Sullivan extended to her and in the "peculiar sympathy" by which she understood Helen's pleasures and desires so as to teach her effectively.[117] Helen's radically improved behavior and her eager willingness to learn bespeak her active receptivity to being—especially to *personal* being—as good. Through Miss Sullivan, the secrets of the natural world revealed themselves to Helen, such that she "learned from life itself" as "the loveliness of things taught me all their use."[118] She came to know and to love the goodness of things, identifying and filling the empty intentions of meaning that she had previously co-intended unreflectively (based on her spirit's dynamism toward universal knowledge and love) in her concrete, limited knowledge of things. Above all, it was the intimate bond, formed of mutual knowledge and love, between Helen Keller and Anne Sullivan that created an opening for the power of truth, goodness, and beauty to pass through the walls of darkness and silence that had so greatly isolated Helen from the world through much of her early childhood. Of Miss Sullivan, she wrote:

116. See ibid., 21.

117. See ibid., 33–34.

118. Ibid., 39 and 34 respectively.

> My teacher is so near to me that I scarcely think of myself apart from her. How much my delight in all beautiful things is innate, and how much is due to her influence, I can never tell. I feel that her being is inseparable from my own, and that the footsteps of my life are in hers. All the best of me belongs to her—there is not a talent, or an aspiration or a joy in me that has not been awakened by her loving touch.[119]

Helen reciprocated that love through a life of gratitude for and devotion to her teacher.

Note that just as prior to her dramatic breakthrough with formal language Helen was capable of rather rich and varied "pre-thematic" knowledge, so, too, was she capable of giving and receiving love before she could do so thematically. One finds a telling example of this in the way she recounts her visit with Dr. Alexander Graham Bell, whom her father was consulting about the possibility of educating her. "Child as I was, I at once felt the tenderness and sympathy which endeared Dr. Bell to so many hearts.... He understood my signs, and I knew it and loved him at once."[120] Interestingly enough, Helen continues as follows: "But I did not dream that that interview would be the door through which I should pass from darkness into light, from isolation to friendship, companionship, knowledge, love."[121] So, on the one hand, Helen *knew* that Dr. Bell understood her signs and she *loved* him for it (and no doubt for his "tenderness and sympathy" as well). On the other hand, she mentions the need to pass into the light of knowledge and love (and so, too, of friendship and companionship). Her own words disclose, retrospectively, an "already" and a "not yet." The final goal of her spirit's dynamism toward the personal fullness of knowledge and love had not yet been reached, but it was nevertheless already anticipated by pre-thematic, partial realizations.

At that stage, Helen's spirit was still confined to the concrete and immediate, where each episode seemed unconnected with another (or perhaps connected by only the most tenuous links). She recounts: "Many incidents of those early days are fixed in my memory, isolated, but clear and distinct, making the sense of that silent, aimless, dayless life all the more intense."[122] Urged on by her spirit's dynamism, she sought unreflectively the meaning of the whole, which would require the release of her spirit's powers to *relate* to the whole in knowledge and love—not as actualized all at once, of course, but as the unifying horizon in which particular acts of knowledge and love take place, and from which they derive their deepest meaning. For that, how-

119. Ibid., 40.
120. Ibid., 19.
121. Ibid.
122. Ibid., 12.

ever, Helen, like any other human being, would have to learn to think abstractly through the medium of formal language, thus freeing her from perceptions bound exclusively to the here and now. We should not be surprised, then, to discover that Helen's first conscious perception of an abstract idea concerned the word "think," and the second concerned the word "love."

She learned that "think" meant the process going on in her head as she pondered the solution to a problem. She thus subsumed into that one, unifying concept all particular instances of thinking. The thinking process itself, in which Helen could now engage through her growing command of formal language, presupposes an abstract knowledge of the intelligible whole as its beginning (or else one would have no reason for seeking solutions in the first place), and it strives, on that basis, toward realizing a particular act of knowledge as its end. In apprehending the meaning of the word "love," moreover, Helen "felt that there were invisible lines stretched between my spirit and the spirits of others."[123] That is a rather apt way of describing the radiative kinship of souls that underlies the silent language of a profound sharing of affection, though it is not clear from the context in which the statement appears that Helen meant it in a strictly interpersonal way. But even if she did not, it seems to express her new understanding of the exchanges of goodness that can take place between herself and other beings. So, with her newly acquired ability to understand the greater meaning behind the things, people, and events that made themselves known to her, Helen was freed to relate to them in knowledge and in love according to the deepest, most personal aspirations of her spirit.

## Concluding Reflections

Our reflections on the early childhood experiences of Helen Keller seem to support the basic anthropological insights about personal agency in the vulnerable that we highlighted in this chapter based on the mutually complementary work of Karol Wojtyła/Pope John Paul II and W. Norris Clarke. We focused mainly on the intrinsic dynamism of Helen's spirit toward communicating herself personally to both the people and the nonpersonal creatures around her, and toward receiving personally their communication to her. Helen's own retrospective reflections on her early life confirm that the hidden impetus underlying her spiritual dynamism was the irrepressible need and desire to relate to the world and, above all, to other people in knowledge and love.

123. Ibid., 31.

We saw that even prior to that special moment when the acquisition of formal language put her in conscious possession of herself at age seven, Helen already perceived that she was somehow different from others, indicating a certain level of self-awareness that was distinctively personal, but that had not yet reached its fullness. She could not, therefore, rest inwardly at that level. We also saw the impressive range of her intentionality during that period of her life. Again, its features were unmistakably personal, though the ends of knowledge and love toward which she strived remained implicit because her limited self-understanding simultaneously placed limits on the meaning that she could derive from her experiences in the world. In turn, those experiences were limited by her loss of the two major sense faculties, for which the power of language to mediate the world to her did not compensate until she grasped its mystery at age seven. Consequently, her interaction with the world could not fully stimulate her intrinsic power of self-consciousness.[124] These obstacles to the full realization of her spiritual dynamism became an increasingly unbearable source of frustration for young Helen. It was the love that reached her in the person of Anne Sullivan that released her spirit. "Thus I came up out of Egypt and stood before Sinai, and a power divine touched my spirit and gave it sight, so that I beheld many wonders. And from the sacred mountain I heard a voice which said, 'Knowledge is love and light and vision.'"[125] In that statement, we might even detect in Helen the hint of a retrospective, though perhaps implicit, awareness that God is ultimately the beginning and end of her personal dynamism.

In Helen Keller's breakthrough experience with formal language, we see the inextricable link, in human beings, between a comprehending knowledge of our outer-world experiences and the comprehending knowledge of our own inner world in self-conscious experience. This would seem to confirm an important aspect of Cardinal Wojtyła's philosophical anthropology. In *Person and Act* he writes that man "never experiences anything external [outside himself] without having at the same time the [inner] experience of himself."[126] By "experience," Wojtyła is referring here to what he regards as strictly *human* experience, as distinguished from purely sensorial or purely emotional experience—the term "purely" meaning unintegrated in and by a personal act. Accordingly, to experience an object *as* an object, conscious-

124. "Hence, the various degrees of knowledge determine the different levels of consciousness." *AP*, 35.

125. Keller, *My Life*, 19.

126. *AP*, 3.

ness must relate it to the *I*, or *self.* This presupposes the simultaneous, if often implicit, experience of the *I* in consciousness—or, more specifically, in what Wojtyła calls "reflexive" consciousness (the "locus" of self-illumination)—as the object of self-knowledge. While Wojtyła does not make the point explicitly, it would seem, in view of Helen Keller's own experience, that the ability to thematize objects and, at least implicitly, oneself through the signifying power of language is indispensable to the process of spiritual self-awakening.

Given the evidence of Helen's "pre-thematic" intentional activity, on the other hand, it would seem necessary to soften Wojtyła's sharp contrast, in *Person and Act,* between experiences generated by self-conscious (or personal) integration, which he regards as strictly human, and the mere consciousness of the unintegrated sensorial or emotional phenomena that happen in us, which he places below the strictly human level of activity. In fact, his integral philosophy of the human person would suggest that where human beings are concerned, there can be no such thing as *purely* sensorial or emotional experience, grounded as each of these is in a unified, personal being, whose consciousness of what happens in himself, even if pre-reflexive or only incipiently reflexive, issues from the rational potentiality and belongs to none other than a human person dynamically ordered toward universal knowledge and love. While the following passage refers to Wojtyła's strict understanding of human experience as self-conscious (hence as "lived through" and ethical), it serves also as an apt way of describing the less explicit (the pre-thematic) levels of human experience.

> Experience is always the first and most basic stage of human cognition, and this experience, in keeping with the dual [body-soul] structure of the cognizing subject, contains not only a sensory but also an intellectual element. For this reason, one could say that human experience is always already a kind of understanding. It is thus also the origin of the whole process of understanding, which develops in ways proper to itself, but always in relation to this first stage, namely, experience.[127]

Helen Keller's early sensorial and emotional experiences clearly included an impressive element of comprehension, paving the way for the more luminous

127. "Self-Determination," in *PC,* 188. In the same volume, pages 113–17 of "The Problem of Experience in Ethics" are similarly applicable. Though presupposing a mature, psycho-moral personality, the following passage from the latter article serves as another apt way of describing the kind of pre-thematic dynamism that we have seen at work in Helen Keller during her early childhood: "[T]here can be no purely sensory experience because we are not 'purely sensory' beings. The sense of knowing contains as an essential and constitutive element a distinctive necessity to tend toward truth" (116). Finally, see *LR,* 23–24, 108.

experiences to follow. It would therefore seem better to understand the quoted passage accordingly.

Given these considerations, we would conclude that while the acquisition of formal language is necessary for the full realization of the human dynamism in self-conscious knowledge and love, it presupposes a foundation intrinsic to the person, namely, the expressive power of the human spirit through the body. Indeed, we have seen convincing evidence that Helen Keller's early efforts to communicate her inner self nonverbally through the body constituted a uniquely personal language in its own right, even though it was not based at that time on an already fully realized capacity for formal language. Her bodily gestures and actions creatively symbolized specific meanings and, precisely for that reason, expressed her person to other persons. So, too, do human beings, as authors of the concrete word, symbolize therein a meaning about themselves or about what they have apprehended in a given reality, that it might be communicated to others as the basis for interpersonal dialogue and mutual understanding. The person's dynamic soul-body constitution is therefore the created template for formal human language and is intrinsically ordered toward it.[128]

In turn, human nature is itself based uniquely on the uncreated Template of the eternal Word, who is the very self-expression of God *within* God, and through whom God expresses himself *beyond* himself—that is, in the created order. Because this Word, who possesses in himself the fullness of the meaning of Being and of beings, has also expressed himself directly and personally in a created human nature, our lifelong quest for meaning, based on our spirit's dynamism toward all being as intelligible and good, has already reached its goal concretely in him. Christ is the meaning of it all—the very embodiment of Truth, Goodness, and Love, and the very Reason for every created good that is. In consequence, our every act of knowledge and of love bears always a relation to him, whether implicitly or explicitly, and our every departure from true knowledge and from true love is always a departure from him. That is why the acts by which we willfully deceive ourselves or others in either order are so heinous.

128. In a word, the human capacity for formal language is innate. It is perhaps worth considering that Genesis 2:18–23 depicts the still solitary Adam as having the ability to name the animals—to understand each one's nature and to "capture," or objectify, it in formal language. Even if his "original knowledge" had been infused, he still expressed that knowledge, and hence his person, linguistically. Prior to that, Adam had expressed himself as a person through the body in the deliberate act of tilling the soil (see Gn 2:15), revealing that he possessed the requisite ontological structure for language.

Through formal language, Helen Keller's inner life and the world around her, as she came to know it, verily blossomed. Each new act of knowledge seemed also to yield for her a new act of love for the goodness of the reality now known, thus fulfilling, in part, her spirit's implicit quest for Meaning. At the same time, we have good reason to suppose that even her earlier, pre-thematic acts of knowledge-tending-toward-love were continuous with that quest. For human nature is dynamized by a proportionate spiritual act of existence, because of which the essence of our *to be* is *to love.* And our *to love* invariably entails the self-communication of our being to another as we personally, if only implicitly, seek and respond to the self-communication of that being, as good, to us. The self-communicative actions of vulnerable persons having little or no self-awareness are therefore informed by the same dynamism that informs the deliberate actions of the fully self-conscious person. And so their actions, too, like the vulnerable themselves, are personal.

# Bibliography

## Works Cited

Abbott, Walter M., SJ, ed. *The Documents of Vatican II*. New York: America Press, 1966.

Ambrose. *Expositio Evangelii Secuundum Lucam, II*. Corpus Christianorum, Series Latina, vol. 14. Turnhout, Belgium: Typographi Brepolis Editores Pontificii, 1957.

Aquinas, Thomas. *Summa Theologica*. Translated by Fathers of the English Dominican Province. Westminster, Md.: Christian Classics, 1981.

Beigel, Gerard P. *Faith and Social Justice in the Teaching of Pope John Paul II*. New York: Peter Lang Publishing, 1997.

Benedict XVI. *Address of His Holiness Benedict XVI to Members of the Pontifical John Paul II Institute for Studies on Marriage and Family on the XXVth Anniversary of Its Foundation* (May 11, 2006). Vatican website.

Billias, Nancy Mardas, Agnes B. Curry, and George F. McLean, eds. *Karol Wojtyła's Philosophical Legacy*. Washington, D.C.: Council for Research in Values and Philosophy, 2008.

Brennan, William. *John Paul II: Confronting the Language Empowering the Culture of Death*. Naples, Fla.: Sapientia Press of Ave Maria University, 2008.

Brown, Raymond E. *The Epistles of John*. Anchor Bible, vol. 30. Garden City, N.Y.: Doubleday, 1982.

Burke, Kevin, David Wemhoff, and Marvin Stockwell, eds. *Redeeming a Father's Heart: Men Share Powerful Stories of Abortion Loss and Recovery*. Bloomington, Ind.: AuthorHouse, 2007.

Burke, Theresa, with David C. Reardon. *Forbidden Grief: The Unspoken Pain of Abortion*. Springfield, Ill.: Acorn Books, 2002.

Buttiglione, Rocco. *Karol Wojtyła: The Thought of the Man Who Became Pope John Paul II*. Grand Rapids, Mich.: William B. Eerdmans, 1997.

Casarella, Peter J. "Solidarity as the Fruit of Communion: *Ecclesia in America*, 'Post-Liberation Theology,' and the Earth." *Communio* 27 (Spring 2000): 98–123.

Clarke, W. Norris, SJ. *The Creative Retrieval of Saint Thomas Aquinas: Essays in Thomistic Philosophy, New and Old.* New York: Fordham University Press, 2009.

———. *Explorations in Metaphysics: Being—God—Person.* Notre Dame: University of Notre Dame Press, 1994.

———. *The One and the Many: A Contemporary Thomistic Metaphysics.* Notre Dame: University of Notre Dame Press, 2001.

———. *Person and Being.* Aquinas Lecture 57. Milwaukee: Marquette University Press, 1993.

———. *The Philosophical Approach to God: A Neo-Thomist Perspective.* Winston-Salem, N.C.: Wake Forest University, 1979.

———. "St. Thomas on the Immediate Creation of the Human Soul by God." Paper given at the International St. Thomas Society session of the APA Convention, Philadelphia, 1997.

———. *The Universe as Journey.* Edited by Gerald McCool. New York: Fordham University Press, 1988.

Congregation for the Doctrine of the Faith. *Donum Vitae* (February 22, 1987). Vatican website.

———. *The Message of Fatima* (June 26, 2000). Vatican website.

De Vos van Steenwijk, Alwine. *Father Joseph Wresinski: Voice of the Poorest.* Translated by Charles Sleeth. Santa Barbara, Calif.: Queenship Publishing, 1996.

Doran, Kevin P. *Solidarity: A Synthesis of Personalism and Communalism in the Thought of Karol Wojtyła/Pope John Paul II.* American University Studies, Series 7: Theology and Religion 190. New York: Peter Lang, 1996.

Dulles, Avery, SJ. *The Splendor of Faith.* New York: Crossroad Publishing, 2003.

Dziwisz, Stanislaw, and Gian Franco Svidercoschi. *A Life with Karol: My Forty-Year Friendship with the Man Who Became Pope.* Translated by Adrian J. Walker. New York: Doubleday, 2008.

Frossard, André, *Portrait of John Paul II.* Translated by Mary Emily Hamilton. San Francisco: Ignatius Press, 1990.

Hallet, Judith Dwan. *Witness to Hope: The Life of Karol Wojtyła-Pope John Paul II.* VHS. W/R Productions, 2001.

The Holy Bible, Revised Standard Version, Catholic Edition. San Francisco: Ignatius Press, 1994.

Jeffreys, Derek. *Defending Human Dignity: John Paul II and Political Realism.* Grand Rapids, Mich.: Brazos Press, 2004.

———. "Euthanasia and John Paul II's 'Silent Language of Profound Sharing of Affection': Why Christians Should Care about Peter Singer." *Christian Bioethics* 7, no. 3 (2001): 359–78.

John Paul II. [See also Wojtyła, Karol.] *Address of His Holiness John Paul II to the 34th General Assembly of the United Nations* (October 2, 1979). Vatican website.

———. *Address of His Holiness John Paul II to the Young People of Gniezno* (June 3, 1979). Vatican website.

———. *Address of John Paul II to Pilgrim Groups and Members of Various Associations* (December 23, 2000). Vatican website.

———. *Address of John Paul II to the Elderly* (November 30, 1986). Vatican website.

———. *Address of the Holy Father to the Congress on Integration of Disabled Children* (December 4, 1999). Vatican website.

———. *Address to the Sick, the Elderly and the Handicapped* (November 23, 1986). Vatican website.

———. "The Canonization of Maximilian Kolbe." *Origins* 12, no. 19 (1982): 289; 291–92.

———. *Centesimus Annus* (May 1, 1991). Vatican website. *AAS* 83, 1991, 793–867.

———. *Christifideles Laici* (December 30, 1988). Vatican website. *AAS* 81, 1989, 393–521.

———. *Crossing the Threshold of Hope*. Translated by Jenny and Martha McPhee. London: Random House, 1994.

———. *Dives in Misericordia* (November 30, 1980). Vatican translation. *Origins* 10, no. 26 (1980): 401–16. *AAS* 72, 1980, 1177–232.

———. *Dominum et Vivificantem* (May 18, 1986). Vatican translation. Boston: Pauline Books and Media, 1986. *AAS* 78, 1986, 809–900.

———. *Ecclesia de Eucharistia* (April 17, 2003). Vatican website. *AAS* 95, 2003, 433–75.

———. *Ecclesia in America* (January 22, 1999). Vatican website. *AAS* 91, 1999, 737–815.

———. *Evangelium Vitae* (March 25, 1995). Vatican translation. *Origins* 24, no. 42 (1995): 689–727. *AAS* 87, 1995, 401–522.

———. *Familiaris Consortio* (November 22, 1981). Vatican website. *AAS* 74, 1982, 81–191.

———. *Fides et Ratio* (September 14, 1998). Vatican translation. *Origins* 28, no. 19 (1998): 317–47. *AAS* 91, 1999, 5–88.

———. *General Audience* (June 10, 1998). Vatican website.

———. *Gift and Mystery: On the Fiftieth Anniversary of My Priestly Ordination*. New York: Doubleday, 1996.

———. *God, Father and Creator: A Catechesis on the Creed*. Vol. 1. Boston: Pauline Books and Media, 1996.

———. "The Handicapped in Modern Society." *Origins* 14, no. 15 (1984): 232–34.

———. *Homily of His Holiness John Paul II: Eucharistic Celebration for the Faithful of the Archdiocese of Newark* (October 5, 1995). Vatican website.

———. *Homily of John Paul II: Jubilee of the Disabled* (December 3, 2000). Vatican website.

———. "The Image of God in People with Mental Illnesses." *Origins* 26, no. 30 (1997): 495–97.

———. *Laborem Exercens* (September 14, 1981). Vatican website. *AAS* 73, 1981, 577–647.

———. *Letter of His Holiness Pope John Paul II to the Elderly* (October 1, 1999). Vatican website.

———. *Letter of the Pope to Children in the Year of the Family* (December 13, 1994). Vatican website.

———. *Letter to Families from Pope John Paul II* (February 2, 1994). Vatican website.

———. *Man and Woman He Created Them: A Theology of the Body*. Translation, introduction, and index by Michael Waldstein. Boston: Pauline Books and Media, 2006.

———. *Memory and Identity: Conversations at the Dawn of a Millennium.* New York: Rizzoli International Publications, 2005.

———. *Message of His Holiness Pope John Paul II for the Celebration of the World Day of Peace* (January 1, 2001). Vatican website.

———. *Message of John Paul II on the Occasion of the Congress of the "Biological and Psychological Foundations of Prenatal Education"* (March 20, 1998). Vatican website.

———. *Message of John Paul II on the Value and Content of Freedom of Conscience and of Religion* (September 1, 1980). Vatican website.

———. *Message of the Holy Father for the World Day of the Sick for the Year 2000: Contemplate the Face of Christ in the Sick* (August 6, 1999). Vatican website.

———. *Mulieris Dignitatem* (August 15, 1988). Vatican translation. Boston: Pauline Books and Media. *AAS* 80, 1988, 1653–729.

———. *Reconciliatio et Paenitentia* (December 2, 1984). Vatican translation. Boston: St. Paul Editions, 1985. *AAS* 77, 1985, 185–275.

———. *Redemptor Hominis* (March 4, 1979). Vatican translation. Boston: St. Paul Editions, 1979. *AAS* 71, 1979, 257–324.

———. *Redemptoris Custos* (August 15, 1989). Vatican website.

———. *Redemptoris Mater* (March 25, 1987). Vatican translation. Boston: Daughters of St. Paul, 1987. *AAS* 79, 1987, 361–433.

———. *Redemptoris Missio* (December 7, 1990). Vatican website. *AAS* 83, 1991, 249–340.

———. *Rise, Let Us Be On Our Way.* Translated by Walter Zięmba. New York: Warner Books, 2004.

———. *Salvifici Doloris* (February 11, 1984). Vatican translation. Boston: Pauline Books and Media, 1984. *AAS* 76, 1984, 201–50.

———. *Sollicitudo Rei Socialis* (December 30, 1987). Vatican website. *AAS* 80, 1988, 513–86.

———. *Veritatis Splendor* (August 6, 1993). Vatican website. *AAS* 85, 1993, 1133–228.

Keller, Helen. *The Story of My Life.* N.p.: Watermill Press, 1993.

Kowalska, Maria Faustina. *Diary: Divine Mercy in My Soul.* 3rd ed. Stockbridge, Mass.: Marians of the Immaculate Conception, 2000.

Kuhse, Helga, and Peter Singer. *Unsanctifying Human Life: Essays on Ethics.* Malden, Mass.: Blackwell Publishers, 2002.

Kupczak, Jarosław, OP. *Destined for Liberty: The Human Person in the Philosophy of Karol Wojtyła/John Paul II.* Washington, D.C.: The Catholic University of America Press, 2000.

Lawrence, Madelaine. [See also Podurgiel, Madelaine.] *In a World of Their Own: Experiencing Unconsciousness.* Westport, Conn.: Praeger Publishers, 1997.

———. "The Unconscious Experience." *American Journal of Critical Care* 4 (1995): 227–32.

Lee, Catherine. "Papal Anniversary: CUA Celebrates Special Bond with John Paul II." *Inside CUA Online,* April 6, 2004.

Leo XIII. *Libertas* (June 20, 1888). Vatican website.

———. *Rerum Novarum* (May 15, 1891). Vatican website.

Leseur, Elisabeth. *The Secret Diary of Elisabeth Leseur: The Woman Whose Goodness Changed Her Husband from Atheist to Priest*. Manchester, N.H.: Sophia Institute Press, 2002.

Levinas, Emmanuel. *Totality and Infinity: An Essay on Exteriority*. Translated by Alphonso Lingis. Pittsburgh: Duquesne University Press, 1969.

Maliński, Mieczysław. *Pope John Paul II: The Life of Karol Wojtyła*. Translated by P. S. Falla. New York: Seabury Press, 1979.

McDermott, John M., SJ, ed. *The Thought of Pope John Paul II: A Collection of Essays and Studies*. Rome: Editrice Pontificia Universitá Gregoriana, 1993.

Nachef, Antoine, BSO. *The Mystery of the Trinity in the Theological Thought of Pope John Paul II*. New York: Peter Lang, 1999.

Paul VI. "Close of the Holy Year." *Origins* 5, no. 30 (1976): 481–82.

———. *Message of His Holiness Pope Paul VI for the Celebration of the Day of Peace* (January 1, 1977). Vatican website.

———. *Populorum Progressio* (March 26, 1967). Vatican website. *AAS* 59, 1967, 257–99.

Perkins, Pheme. "The Johannine Epistles." In *The New Jerome Biblical Commentary*, edited by Raymond E. Brown, Joseph A. Fitzmyer, and Roland E. Murphy. Englewood Cliffs, N.J.: Prentice Hall, 1990.

Podurgiel, Madelaine. [See also Lawrence, Madelaine.] "The Unconscious Experience: A Pilot Study." *Journal of Neuroscience Nursing* 22 (Feb. 1990): 52–53.

Santos, Lucia. *Fatima in Lucia's Own Words: Sister Lucia's Memoirs*. Translated by Dominican Nuns of the Perpetual Rosary. Cambridge, Mass.: Ravengate Press, 1976.

Scheeben, Matthias. *The Mysteries of Christianity*. Translated by Cyril Vollert, SJ. St. Louis: Herder, 1946.

Schmitz, Kenneth L. *At the Center of the Human Drama: The Philosophical Anthropology of Karol Wojtyła/Pope John Paul II*. Washington, D.C.: The Catholic University of America Press, 1993.

———. "The Geography of the Human Person." *Communio* 13 (Spring 1986): 27–48.

Sokolowski, Robert. *Introduction to Phenomenology*. New York: Cambridge University Press, 2000.

Svidercoschi, Gian Franco. *Stories of Karol*. Translated by Peter Heinegg. Liguori, Mo.: Liguori Publications, 2003.

Weigel, George. *The End and the Beginning: Pope John Paul II—The Victory of Freedom, the Last Years, the Legacy*. New York: Doubleday, 2010.

———. *Witness to Hope: The Biography of Pope John Paul II*. New York: Cliff Street Books, 2005.

Williams, George Huntston. *The Mind of John Paul II: Origins of His Thought and Action*. New York: Seabury Press, 1981.

Wojtyła, Karol. [See also John Paul II.] *The Acting Person*. Translated by Andrzej Potocki. Revised by Anna-Teresa Tymieniecka. Boston: D. Reidel Publishing, 1979.

———. *Faith according to St. John of the Cross*. Translated by Jordan Aumann, OP. San Francisco: Ignatius Press, 1985.

———. "The Intentional Act and the Human Act, That Is, Act and Experience." In

*The Crisis of Culture: Steps to Reopen the Phenomenological Investigation of Man*, edited by Anna-Teresa Tymieniecka, 269–80. Analecta Husserliana 5. Boston: D. Reidel Publishing, 1976.

———. *Love and Responsibility*. Translated by H. T. Willetts. New York: Farrar, Straus, Giroux, 1981.

———. *Osoba i czyn*. 3rd ed. Lublin: Scientific Society of the Catholic University of Lublin, 1994.

———. *Persona e atto: Testo polacco a fronte*. Santarcangelo di Romagna: Rusconi Libri, 1999.

———. *Person and Community: Selected Essays*. Translated by Theresa Sandok, OSM. Catholic Thought from Lublin 4. New York: Peter Lang, 1993.

———. "The Radiation of Fatherhood: A Mystery." In *Karol Wojtyła: The Collected Plays and Writings on Theater*. Translated by Boleslaw Taborski. Berkeley: University of California Press, 1987.

———. *Sign of Contradiction*. New York: Seabury Press, 1979.

———. *Sources of Renewal: The Implementation of the Second Vatican Council*. Translated by P. S. Falla. New York: Harper and Row, 1980.

———. "The Transcendence of the Person in Action and Man's Self-Teleology." In *The Teleologies in Husserlian Phenomenology*, edited by Anna-Teresa Tymieniecka, 203–12. Analecta Husserliana 9. Boston: D. Reidel Publishing, 1979.

## Further Reading

Buber, Martin. *I and Thou*. Translated by Walter Kaufmann. New York: Scribner. 1970.

Crosby, John F. "Persona Est Sui Iuris: Reflections on the Foundations of Karol Wojtyła's Philosophy of the Person." In *Karol Wojtyła: Filosofo, Teologo, Poeta*, 25–37. Vatican City State: Libreria Editrice Vaticana, 1984.

———. "The Personalism of John Paul II as the Basis of His Approach to the Teaching of Humanae Vitae." In *Why Humanae Vitae Was Right: A Reader*, edited by Janet E. Smith, 195–226. San Francisco: Ignatius Press, 1993.

Galkowski, Jerzy W. "The Place of Thomism in the Anthropology of K. Wojtyła." *Angelicum* 65 (1988): 181–94.

Grabowski, John S. "Person: Substance and Relation." *Communio* 22 (Spring 1995): 139–63.

John Paul II. *Jesus, Son and Savior: A Catechesis on the Creed*. Vol. 2. Boston: Pauline Books and Media, 1996.

Lawler, Ronald D. *The Christian Personalism of Pope John Paul II*. Chicago: Franciscan Herald Press, 1982.

Marshner, William. "Aquinas on the Evaluation of Human Actions." *Thomist* (July 1995): 347–70.

McCartney, James J. *Unborn Persons: Pope John Paul II and the Abortion Debate*. New York: P. Lang, 1987.

Modras, Ronald. "The Moral Philosophy of Pope John Paul II." *Theological Studies* 41 (1980): 683–97.

Ratzinger, Joseph. "Concerning the Notion of Person in Theology." *Communio* 17 (Fall 1990): 439–54.

Rourke, Thomas R. "The Death Penalty in Light of the Ontology of the Person: The Significance of *Evangelium Vitae*." *Communio* 25 (Fall 1998): 397–413.

Saward, John. *Christ Is the Answer: The Christ-Centered Teaching of Pope John Paul II.* New York: Alba House, 1995.

Schmitz, Kenneth L. "Selves and Persons: A Difference in Loves? *Communio* 18 (Summer 1991): 183–206.

Seifert, Josef. "Karol Cardinal Wojtyła (Pope John Paul II) as Philosopher and the Cracow/Lublin School of Philosophy." *Aletheia* 2 (1981): 131–99.

———. "Truth and Transcendence of the Person in the Philosophical Thought of Karol Wojtyła." In *Karol Wojtyła: Filosofo, Teologo, Poeta*, 93–106. Vatican City State: Libreria Editrice Vaticana, 1984.

Shivanandan, Mary. *Crossing the Threshold of Love: A New Vision of Marriage in the Light of John Paul II's Anthropology.* Washington, D.C.: The Catholic University of America Press, 1999.

Whelton, Beverly J. B. "Human Nature, Substantial Change, and Modern Science: Rethinking When a New Human Life Begins." In *Proceedings of the American Catholic Philosophical Association*, 72:305–13. Washington, D.C.: Office of the National Secretary of the Association, The Catholic University of America, 1999.

———. "Molecular Human Life: An Aristotelian Solution to the Timely Question "When does a new human life begin?" *Cardinal Perspectives: An Interdisciplinary Journal Devoted to Academic Excellence.* Wheeling, W.Va.: Cardinal Perspectives Committee, Wheeling Jesuit University, 2002.

———. "On the Beginning of Human Life." *Linacre Quarterly*, Feb. 1998, 51–65.

Wilder, Alfred, OP. "Community of Persons in the Thought of Karol Wojtyła." *Angelicum* 56 (1979): 211–44.

Wolicka, Elzbieta. "Participation in Community: Wojtyła's Social Anthropology." *Communio* 8 (Summer 1981): 108–18.

Woznicki, Andrew. *A Christian Humanism: Karol Wojtyła's Existential Personalism.* New Britain: Mariel Publications, 1980.

———. *The Dignity of Man as a Person: Essays on the Christian Humanism of His Holiness John Paul II.* San Francisco: Society of Christ Publications, 1987.

# Index

*John Paul II on the Vulnerable* was designed in Meta Serif and Meta Sans and typeset by Kachergis Book Design of Pittsboro, North Carolina. It was printed on 50-pound Natures Book Natural and bound by Thomson-Shore of Dexter, Michigan.